Expressive Processing

Software Studies
Matthew Fuller, Lev Manovich, and Noah Wardrip-Fruin, editors

Expressive Processing: Digital Fictions, Computer Games, and Software Studies,
Noah Wardrip-Fruin, 2009

Expressive Processing
Digital Fictions, Computer Games, and Software Studies

Noah Wardrip-Fruin

The MIT Press
Cambridge, Massachusetts
London, England

© 2009 Noah Wardrip-Fruin

All images and screenshots were either created by the author or are reproduced with permission.

The image of *Pong* in chapter 1 is courtesy of The International Arcade Museum.

For information about special quantity discounts, please email special_sales@mitpress.mit.edu

This book was set in Adobe Garamond, Helvetica Neue, and Arena by Michael Crumpton.

Printed and bound in the United States of America.

Library of Congress Cataloging-in-Publication Data

Wardrip-Fruin, Noah.
Expressive processing : digital fictions,computer games and software studies / Noah Wardrip-Fruin
    p. cm.
includes bibliographical references and index.
ISBN 978-0-262-01343-7 (hardcover : alk. paper).
1. Interactive multimedia—Social aspects.   2. Computer games—Social Aspects.   3. Digital media.   4. Digital computer simulation.   I. Title.
QA76.76.159.W37   2009
006.7—dc22

                                                                    2009000144

10 9 8 7 6 5 4 3 2 1

For Jennifer K Mahal

Contents

Series Foreword

Software is deeply woven into contemporary life—economically, culturally, creatively, politically—in manners both obvious and nearly invisible. Yet while much is written about how software is used, and the activities that it supports and shapes, thinking about software itself has remained largely technical for much of its history. Increasingly, however, artists, scientists, engineers, hackers, designers, and scholars in the humanities and social sciences are finding that for the questions they face, and the things they need to build, an expanded understanding of software is necessary. For such understanding they can call upon a strand of texts in the history of computing and new media, they can take part in the rich implicit culture of software, and they also can take part in the development of an emerging, fundamentally transdisciplinary, computational literacy. These provide the foundation for Software Studies.

Software Studies uses and develops cultural, theoretical, and practice-oriented approaches to make critical, historical, and experimental accounts of (and interventions via) the objects and processes of software. The field engages and contributes to the research of computer scientists, the work of software designers and engineers, and the creations of software artists. It tracks how software is substantially integrated into the processes of contemporary culture and society, reformulating processes, ideas, institutions, and cultural objects around their closeness to algorithmic and formal description and action. Software Studies proposes histories of computational cultures and works with the intellectual resources of computing to develop reflexive thinking about its entanglements and possibilities. It does this both in the scholarly modes of the humanities and social sciences and in the software creation/research modes of computer science, the arts, and design.

The Software Studies book series, published by the MIT Press, aims to publish the best new work in a critical and experimental field that is at once culturally and technically literate, reflecting the reality of today's software culture.

Preface

Expressive Processing

This book demonstrates a new approach to understanding digital media—and uses it to shed light on two of my favorite kinds of media: digital fictions and computer games. This new approach assumes that it isn't just the external appearance and audience experience of digital media that matter. It is also essential to understand the computational processes that make digital media function.

Computational processes are a powerful new tool in the hands of authors. Shaping these processes enables the finely honed commercial entertainments of the computer game industry. Inventing new processes is at the heart of the radical media experiments of artificial intelligence (AI) and other areas of computer science. Finding unexpected uses for processes is common in the fusion of concept and craft that defines the work of independent artists, writers, designers, and studios. Such authorial expression through processes is one of the central topics of this book and one of the meanings of the term *expressive processing*. I hope the projects examined in this book can help authors think productively about the future of fiction, games, and digital media more generally.

For critics seeking to understand process-intensive work, finding an appropriate way to grapple with processes themselves can be puzzling. While some authors focus on the potential of interpreting each work's source code, this level of detail is not necessarily telling (for most works, the textual style of the code is not central), and for many works the code itself is not available. Instead, this book's approach looks at what I call the *operational logics* at work within a variety of examples. My focus is on interpreting what processes do—the ideas expressed through the design of their movements—and the relationships that processes express with schools of thought and communities of practice. Looking at what processes express in this manner, enabling critics to interpret elements of works not visible on the surface, is the other main element of what I mean by expressive processing.

Beyond digital media specifically, I also believe it is essential for our political future that people develop the ability to think critically about software systems. Coming to understand the processes of digital media can contribute to this. Many general concepts about software are more easily understood when tied to specific, legible examples, which digital media can provide. I explore a number of the examples in this book in terms of their wider lessons about software and the potential political implications of these lessons.

Acknowledgments

I have many people to thank, both intellectually and personally, for helping make *Expressive Processing* possible.

This book—like the Software Studies series in which it is the first volume—exists through the support and collaboration of my editor at the MIT Press, Doug Sery. I also wish to thank Melissa Goldsipe, Alyssa Larose, Katie Helke, and Deborah Cantor-Adams at the MIT Press.

I first explored these ideas in my dissertation work. I owe a deep debt to my committee. My dissertation grew out of a yearlong series of conversations with David Durand. It would not have been possible without his intellectual guidance and support. George Landow's *Hypertext* was the first book I read that discussed digital literature. I am in his debt both for providing that opportunity, which has shaped my thinking since, and for his generous feedback on my dissertation. My dissertation would have been conceptually narrower and significantly less readable without the careful attention and helpful comments of Wendy Chun. I am thankful for how she has pushed my thinking and writing. I went to Brown University to work with Robert Coover and was never disappointed. For my five years there I greatly benefited from his generosity with his energy, time, and knowledge—and I continue to do so. Brown has been a leading institution for innovative interdisciplinary digital work for more than four decades, in large part due to the project sponsorship and stewardship of my committee chair, Andy van Dam. I was honored to be able to include my dissertation in that tradition.

Beyond my dissertation committee, I owe a great intellectual debt to those who study and create digital media—especially games, new forms of literature, and new tools for art. I especially thank my editorial collaborators Pat Harrigan, Nick Montfort, and Jill Walker—as well as my fellow Grand Text Auto bloggers Mary Flanagan, Michael Mateas, Scott Rettberg, and Andrew Stern. My collaborators at the University of California at San Diego Software Studies initiative, Lev Manovich and Jeremy Douglass, have also been a great intellectual influence. In addition, my collaborators on digital media projects have shaped the thinking (and helped create some of the work described) in this volume. They include Kirstin Allio, Clilly Castiglia, Josh Carroll, Adam Chapman, Michael Crumpton, Elaine Froehlich, Shawn Greenlee, Erik Loyer, Andrew McClain, Brion Moss, Benjamin "Sascha" Shine, Chris Spain, Camille Utterback, and Duane Whitehurst. I am also honored to have many of those mentioned in this paragraph as personal friends.

Within the field of digital media I also wish to thank others, not yet listed, who have talked with me about ideas that have helped shape my thinking about computational processes as tools for creation and objects of study: Espen Aarseth, Ian Bogost, John Cayley, Markku Eskelinen, Gonzalo Frasca, Fox Harrell, N. Katherine Hayles, William Huber, Mimi Ito, Jesper Juul, Matthew Kirschenbaum, Peter Lunenfeld, Mark Marino, Carl McKinney, Stuart Moulthrop, Simon Penny, Jessica Pressman, Rita Raley, Casey Reas, Warren Sack, Phoebe Sengers, Stephanie Strickland, and many others. Conferences have also provided important intellectual moments for this work, ranging from the 2005 Digital Arts and Culture conference to SoftWhere, the 2008 software studies workshop.

I should also thank other staff, faculty, students, and friends from my time at New York University, the University of Baltimore, Brown University, and the University of California—especially Cynthia Allen, Jane de Almeida, Kam Bellamy, Stephen Boyd, Poppy Brandes, Helena Bristow, Barry Brown, Sheldon Brown, Lisa Cartwright, Rachel Cody, Michael Cohen, Mike Cole, Brian Evenson, Thalia Field, Julia Flanders, Forrest Gander, Marjetta Geerling, William Gillespie, Athomas Goldberg, Brian Goldfarb, Dan Hallin, Robert Horwitz, Daniel C. Howe, Adriene Jenik, Natalie Jeremijenko, Jamie Jewett, Bruce Jones, Nancy Kaplan, Nancy Kramer, Carole Maso, Miranda Mellis, Talan Memmott, Jon Meyer, Elli Mylonas, Gale Nelson, Robert Nideffer, Christiane Paul, Ken Perlin, Butch Rovan, Jurgen Schulze, Jack Schwartz, Cicero Silva, Roberto Simanowski, Anna Joy Springer, Brian Kim Stefans, Stefan Tanaka, Jim Whitehead, Adrianne Wortzel, Vika Zafrin, and Sara Zatz.

The afterword to this book describes another great debt of gratitude I owe: that to those who participated in the blog-based peer review of the first draft of this manuscript. This includes a number of people not mentioned elsewhere in these acknowledgments: Dominic Arsenault, Barry Atkins, Balthazar Auger, Paul B., Sean Barrett, Matt Barton, Bryan G. Behrenshausen, Mark Bernstein, Emily Boegheim, Terry Bosky, Alex J. Champandard, Randall Couch, Drew Davidson, Richard Evans, David Fisher, Sol Gaitán, Susan Gibb, Josh Giesbrecht, Benjamin Grandis, Barbara Grueter, Huysmans, Jon Ippolito, Ishmael, Dennis G. Jerz, Kitsu, Dega Lancaster, Chris Lewis, Christian McCrea, Dave Miller, Mark J. Nelson, Nicholas Novitski, Brad O'Donnell, Jeff Orkin, Jason Rhody, Mark Riedl, Bonnie Ruberg, Malcolm Ryan, Greg J. Smith, Sarah Toton, Scott Turner, Julius Valsson, J. Robinson Wheeler, Lord Yo, Jose Zagal, Hyokon Zhiang, and anonymous contributors. I owe thanks as well to Ben Vershbow, the Institute for the Future of the Book, and the University of California at San Diego Academic Senate Committee on Research for supporting the blog-based review.

My family—Nathan, Carolyn, Mark, Elma, Buford, Gertrude, and

Richard—not only supported me during the process of this work, directly and indirectly, but also provided an intellectually stimulating and creatively oriented environment from the first moment of my life.

Finally, none of this would have been possible without Jennifer K Mahal, and I dedicate this book to her.

Chapter 1
Introduction

Media Machines

A computer is a strange type of machine. While most machines are developed for particular purposes—washing machines, forklifts, movie projectors, typewriters—modern computers are designed specifically to be able to *simulate* the operations of many different types of machines, depending on the computer's current instructions (and its available peripherals).

This is why a computer can simulate a movie projector: showing a set of image frames in quick succession. It's also why a computer can act like a tape player: reading and amplifying a stream of sound data.[1]

And it is for this same reason that computers can be instructed to act like previously impossible types of machines. A computer can simulate a typewriter—getting input from the keyboard and arranging pixels on the screen to shape the corresponding letters—but it can also go far beyond a typewriter, offering many fonts, automatic spelling correction, the painless movement of manuscript sections (through simulations of "cut" and "paste"), programmable transformations (such as "find and replace"), and even collaborative authoring by large, dispersed groups (as with projects like Wikipedia). This is what modern computers (more lengthily called "stored-program electronic digital computers") are designed to make possible: the continual creation of new machines, opening new possibilities, through the definition of new sets of computational processes.

1. During the blog-based peer review of this book's manuscript on Grand Text Auto (discussed in the afterword) Mark Marino suggested that the ability of computers to simulate movie projectors and tape players is "the result of a set of cultural …

Notes continued at end of this chapter.

"Digital media" are the media enabled by this possibility. This includes Web projects like Wikipedia and also all computer games. The first modern computer games were created on early stored-program computers, and since then we have seen a major cultural impact from the fact that a computer can not only simulate a pinball machine but also act like game machines never seen before: a *Tetris* machine, a *Doom* machine, a *SimCity* machine, and more.

Personally, I am fascinated by the possibilities that digital media open for fiction. A blossoming of new models of character, story, and language is being enabled by computational processes. From computer games with epic structures to experimental interactive films, digital fictions are providing diverse experiences for a wide range of audiences. From ambitious artificial intelligence (AI) experiments to straightforward uses of weblogs and email, authors are creating digital fictions at a wide range of technical complexity. The field is already too vast to cover in a single book.

Luckily, quite a number of books have already been written about digital literature, and many more have been written about digital media more generally. Almost all of these, however, have focused on what the machines of digital media look like from the outside: their output. Sometimes the output is considered as an artifact and interpreted in ways we associate with literary scholarship and art history. Sometimes the output is seen in relation to the audience and the wider culture, using approaches from fields like education and sociology. And there are, of course, a variety of other perspectives. But regardless of perspective, writings on digital media almost all ignore something crucial: the actual processes that make digital media work, the computational machines that make digital media possible.

On the one hand, there is nothing wrong with this. Output-focused approaches have brought many valuable insights for those who seek to understand and create digital media. Yet, on the other hand, it leaves a big gap.

This book is my attempt to help bridge the gap. As far as I know, it is the first book focused on computational processes that comes from the perspective of media, games, and fiction (rather than software engineering or computer science). It is a first passage across the gap, and we will want to move much more weight across over time. But hopefully it demonstrates that there is something to be gained by being able to move between the gap's two sides, being able to see the inside and outside of digital media's machines.

Expressive Processing

Bridging the gap requires talking about processes in new ways and connecting them with broader issues. In this book I work to do this through a notion of *expressive processing*. This term is meant to evoke, in the forthcoming discussions, two important things about processes.

First, computational processes are an increasingly significant means of expression for authors. Rather than defining the sequence of words for a book or images for a film, today's authors are increasingly defining the rules for system behavior. When I play a computer role-playing game (RPG), author-crafted processes determine how I can speak with the non-player characters (NPCs). When I play a simulation game, author-crafted processes

2. For more on this project, *Screen,* see chapter 9.

determine the operations of the virtual economy. There is authorial expression in what these rules make possible—and also in what they leave out, as compared with what we see in the everyday world of human conversation and economic transactions.

Computational processes can also be used to craft possibilities that aren't simplified models of phenomena from our everyday world. For example, in my own collaborative work I take advantage of processes supporting room-size virtual reality displays in order to create the illusion of words (from short fictions about memory) peeling loose from paragraphs, flocking around the audience, and flying back (or breaking apart) when hit by an audience member's hand.[2] The exact details of this experience are different every time, but it always unfolds within parameters determined by authored processes, and we can see authorial expression in these processes as surely as in those meant to evoke elements of the everyday world.

Second, I use the term *expressive processing* to talk about what processes express in their design—which may not be visible to audiences. Just as when opening the back of a watch from the 1970s one might see a distinctive Swiss mechanism or Japanese quartz assembly, so the shapes of computational processes are distinctive—and connected to histories, economies, and schools of thought. Further, because digital media's processes often engage subjects more complex than timekeeping (such as human language and motivation), they can be seen as "operationalized" models of these subjects, expressing a position through their shapes and workings. Processes, when examined, may also express a very different set of priorities or capabilities than one might assume from authorial or scholarly descriptions of the system.

These possibilities are explored further in the coming pages, in discussing particular works of digital media. This second sense of *expressive processing*—what processes express through their designs and histories—is important to me because I think it is central to understanding digital media. I also believe that, from this perspective, digital media provides particularly legible examples of things that we need to understand about software in general. For instance, when we understand the capabilities and histories of AI techniques in the context of a relatively easy to evaluate area such as computer games (in which, say, NPCs may act in obviously inappropriate manners), we can use that understanding to judge proposals for using similar techniques in higher-stakes social contexts (e.g., areas such as surveillance).

The main body of *Expressive Processing* discusses these issues in more detail. Rather than theoretical discussion, though, most of the rest of this book is dedicated to a close examination of a set of influential examples. These examples are key to the history of process-oriented innovation in fiction and games. I find it a fascinating history, which I hope will prove thought provoking for fiction writers, game designers, AI researchers, and anyone with an interest in the history of technology or the future of fiction.

It is also a history almost never told. Despite increasing interest in computer games, digital fictions, and digital media more generally, only bits and pieces of the movements traced in this book have appeared elsewhere. Instead, most books on related topics have focused on other traditions—ones with relatively stable processes that have served as platforms for the creativity of writers and game designers, who have used these relatively stable forms to produce a compelling variety of output for audiences. Good examples of such work include Nick Montfort's book on interactive fiction (*Twisty Little Passages,* 2003) and Matt Barton's book on computer RPGs (*Dungeons & Desktops,* 2008). There is also a significant body of work that specifically looks at what writers can accomplish with digital media, useful introductions to which are *Electronic Literature: New Horizons for the Literary* by N. Katherine Hayles (2008) and *Les Basiques: La Littérature numérique* by Phillipe Bootz (2006). And of course there are helpful practice-oriented guides to what can be accomplished with the game industry's common processes, such as Lee Sheldon's *Character Development and Storytelling for Games* (2004) and Chris Bateman's *Game Writing: Narrative Skills for Videogames* (2006).

I do write about some of the work considered by these authors in *Expressive Processing,* but largely as a way of talking about where we are today. Most of my attention, instead, is on the past and the future. I draw many of my examples from AI research projects because this is where some of the most revealing processes for character and fiction have been crafted. A number of these are quite famous within certain circles, such as the simulated therapist *Eliza;* the first story-generation program, *Tale-Spin;* and the widely discussed experimental game *Façade.* Others are less well-known. In this book I move along a conceptual trail that connects them—and also compare them with mainstream games such as *Star Wars: Knights of the Old Republic, F.E.A.R.,* and *The Sims.* In doing so,

I hope to provide a parallel history and set of concepts focused on the development of processes that can complement the ongoing discussion that concentrates on the nonprocess work of writers and designers.

Tracing this history, and making these connections, I also draw out a number of ideas that may be of use for digital authors, scholars, and members of the public. For instance, I consider projects from this history as iconic examples of three "effects" that appear throughout digital media, including in today's systems, and from which we can learn important design lessons. I will say more about them toward the end of this chapter. First, however, it will be useful to introduce the perspective on digital media that underlies my work here.

3. Though the concepts of data and process seem clear enough as ideas, in practice any element of a system may be a mixture between the two. For example, the text handled by a Web application is generally thought of as data. However, this …

Notes continued at end of this chapter.

A View of Digital Media

Let me return to my first conception of expressive processing: the possibility of creating new simulated machines, of defining new computational behaviors, as the great authoring opportunity that digital media offers. Seizing this opportunity requires a bit of a shift. It is common to think of the work of authoring, the work of creating media, as the work of writing text, composing images, arranging sound, and so on. But now one must think of *authoring new processes* as an important element of media creation.

In undertaking this shift, it may be helpful to think of the creation of a piece of digital media as being organized like figure 1.1. The work is made up of data and process, with a somewhat fuzzy line between them.[3] The data elements are mostly precreated media (text, still images, video and animation, and sound and music) and the sorts

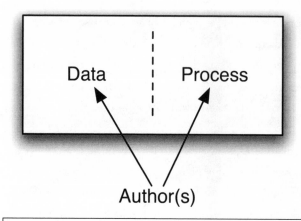

Figure 1.1. Authoring data and process.

of things that are stored in spreadsheets (lists and tables of information, with varying degrees of structure).

The processes, on the other hand, are the working parts of the simulated machine. Some are dedicated to tasks with simple structures, such as displaying a series of video images on a screen. But many of digital media's tasks are more complex in structure, requiring processes capable of performing in a range of different ways. Even a simple piece of digital media such as *Pong* (figure 1.2) has processes that define behaviors much more complex than showing a series of images in quick succession. The processes of *Pong* define and calculate simple rules of physics (how the ball bounces off the paddles and walls) as well as simple game rules (who receives each serve, how points are scored, and how winning is achieved) that, when well tuned, can combine to create a compelling experience of gameplay—even in the face of remarkably primitive graphics.

Of course, the idea of creating media through the authoring of novel processes is not new. Tristan Tzara's Dada cut-up technique was presented in the wake of World War I as a process for turning a chosen newspaper

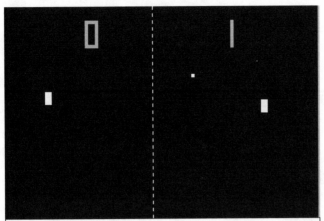

Figure 1.2. The iconic early video game *Pong* gives players a simple goal: to use their simulated paddles to knock back a simulated ball—keeping it in play until one player misses, causing the other player to score.

article into a poem. On a more technological level, the pioneers of early cinema had to develop novel processes (embodied in physical machinery) to capture and display their sets of image data. And on a longer-term level, the creation of board and card games has always primarily been the development of process definitions—embodied in game rules—that determine how play moves forward.

In important ways these noncomputational media processes are like the processes of digital media: they are defined previously, but (at least in part) carried out during the time of audience experience. This is true as Tzara pulls a paper scrap from his sack, as the Zoetrope image flickers, as the poker hand goes through another round of betting, and as the image of a *Pong* ball bounces off the image of a *Pong* paddle. The processes of digital media, however, are separated from noncomputational media processes by their potential numerousness, repetition, and complexity. For example, we might play a game of tennis using the rules of *Pong*—since they're simpler than the normal rules of tennis. But we wouldn't want to play *Pong* as a board game, having to hand execute all the processes involved even in its (extremely simplified) modeling of physics. It is the computer's ability to carry out processes of significant magnitude (at least in part during the time of audience experience) that enables digital media that create a wide variety of possible experiences, respond to context, evolve over time, and interact with audiences.

Given the importance of such audience experiences, the author's view is not the only one I consider in this book. To reflect that, here is a slightly more complex figure (1.3) that adds a layer called "surface" over the initial data and process. In this book, the surface of a work of digital media is what the audience experiences: the output of the processes operating on the data, in the context of the physical hardware and setting, through which any audience interaction takes place. When playing a console game, for example, the surface includes the console and any indicator lights or other information it provides, the television or monitor and any image it displays, the sound hardware (e.g., television speakers, stereo, or headphones) and any sound produced, and the controller(s) with their

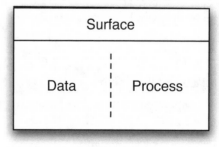

Figure 1.3. Adding surface to data and process.

buttons, lights, and perhaps vibrations.[4] The audience experience of digital media is that of being connected to, and in some cases through, the surface.

I find this a more satisfying view of digital media. Yet this figure, like my discussion so far, doesn't account for something quite important about digital media processes: the fact that they generally don't operate on their own. From Web-based knowledge repositories to console-based video games, the operations of digital media are, in crucial ways, only truly realized in contact with audiences. A wiki's processes mean little if the audience doesn't use them to add data, edit it, and follow the connections embedded in it. Similarly, many of a game's processes never come into operation if the game has no player.[5]

None of this is any surprise. But as I discussed earlier, we generally understand this situation from the audience's perspective, looking at both the audience's actions and the work's behavior as though the work is a proverbial black box. I believe it is also essential to understand this situation more reciprocally: to think about the *relationship* between the audience's experience and the system's internal operations.

Figure 1.4 adds a representation of interaction to my diagram of digital media. While *interaction* is certainly a contested term, for the purposes of this book I am defining it as a change to the state of the work—for which the work was designed—that comes from outside the work. Interaction takes place through the surface of the work, resulting in change to its internal data and/or processes. In many cases, some trace of interaction is immediately apparent on the surface (e.g., an audience member types and the letters appear as they are typed,

4. Many console games also have more complicated surfaces, often in the form of additional controllers such as dance mats, simulated musical instruments, or cameras. And digital fictions and games more generally may have much more …

5. At the same time that processes come into operation through audience actions at the surface, process and surface also define some of the possibility space for audience actions, as well as the feedback produced, and thereby shape the audience. For …

Notes continued at end of this chapter.

or an audience member moves her hand and a video image of her hand moves simultaneously), but this is not required. Interaction, while it always changes the state of the work, can be approached with the primary goal of communication between audience members— as when communicating through a shared virtual world such as *World of Warcraft* or *Second Life*. Finally, given the definition of interaction that I am using, it also becomes clear that digital media works interact with more than audiences—which is why the revised diagram also notes the possibility of interaction with outside processes and data sources.

Obviously, the diagram has now become rather complicated. But I believe that keeping all these elements in mind is important to our initial thinking about a work of digital media, as a creator, scholar, or audience member. And of course this diagram is still immensely simplified, compared with the details of the actual components and connections of most works of digital media. This simplification is a first step toward consideration of digital media works at a yet more abstract level.

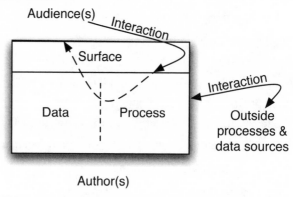

Figure 1.4. Adding interaction to the diagram of digital media.

Operational Logics

The primary goal of the model of digital media developed above is not found in its individual components. My main hope is not that readers will come away with an understanding of every nuance of what I mean by *data* or *surface*. Rather, my hope is that a basic understanding of these components will provide the foundation for a new approach to thinking about digital media (and computational systems more generally). I use the term *operational logics,* described further below, to name a new type of element specific to procedural systems that this type of thinking can help identify and analyze.

When a work of digital media operates, this can be seen as an interplay between the elements of the model discussed so far: data, process, surface, interaction, author, and audience. Observing the specifics of this interplay can be informative. Is the system actually doing what it is described as doing? What unspoken assumptions are built into the ways in which operations proceed?

At a higher level of abstraction, however, we can also notice patterns in this interplay. I call these patterns *operational logics.* In my first discussion of them (Wardrip-Fruin 2005), I talked about common spatial or graphical logics, such as *collision detection.* This is a term for when a system notes the virtual "touch" of two simulated objects. When the *Pong* ball bounces off the paddles and walls, this is collision detection. It is also collision detection when the *Doom* engine prevents players from walking through walls—and when it determines that a bullet (or chain saw) has hit a target.[6]

From these examples it is probably clear that the same

6. I will return to the discussion of spatial logics in chapter 9.

operational logic can be implemented in a wide variety of ways on a continually expanding set of platforms. Once we have identified a logic, it can be informative to make comparisons between different instances. These comparisons can delve deep into the specifics of how the logic is implemented for different works or operate at a higher level, looking at how the same logic can contribute quite differently to the experience of a set of works. This is true not only of spatial logics but also of many operational elements of systems. Later chapters in this book will consider operational logics ranging from the quest logics implemented in many computer games to the assertion and inference logics implemented in many symbolic AI systems.

Although operational logics will, I hope, prove powerful for comparative studies, in this book they are primarily used within the examination of individual works. More specifically, while an operational logic can be seen as a pattern that arises in the interplay of the elements of a digital media system, I am interested in the examination of the interplay of a system's operational logics—and in this as a starting point for critical interpretation. I pursue this method most explicitly in this book's chapter on *Tale-Spin,* which identifies planbox-based planning as the work's dominant logic, driving the others (a fact invisible when examining only the work's surface). Though not as explicit in other chapters, this approach underlies much of this book's analysis—and it is my hope that these examples will encourage others to further develop their own approaches of this sort (see sidebar, "Terms for Thinking about Processes").

Three Effects

At a higher conceptual level, this book also identifies three *effects* that can arise in the relationship between system processes and audience experiences, which may occur with a wide variety of operational logics. These will serve as the major waypoints for the remainder of this volume. The first—*the Eliza effect*—is the well-known phenomenon in which audience expectations allow a digital media system to appear much more complex on its surface than is supported by its underlying structure. I will also consider what most authors have ignored, however: during playful interaction with the simulated therapist for which the *Eliza* effect is named, the illusion breaks down rapidly. One alternative to breakdown with a system of this sort is to severely restrict interaction. Another is the one pursued by many modern games: never building up the *Eliza* illusion and instead clearly representing the operations of a simple system on the work's surface. But these simple systems prove too limited for the fictional experiences that games seek to make available to their players, resulting in breakdowns of a different type. This leaves only one option for those seeking to create ambitious playable fictions: more developed system models of story and character.

Expressive Processing's next waypoint is an effect named for the first major story-generation system, *Tale-Spin*. Though created decades before modern games, it represents an initial step toward a more flexible model of fiction. Its characters have goals, make plans to satisfy them, examine their relationships with other characters, speculate about the plans of others, and so on. But little of this is visible to audiences in the resulting story, and little can even be deduced through repeated interaction. It is this that leads me to coin a new term—*the Tale-Spin effect*—for works that fail to represent their internal system richness on their surfaces, in an inversion of the *Eliza* effect that is not uncommon in digital media. From there *Expressive Processing* looks at a different model of character planning (in the first-person shooter game *F.E.A.R.*), the alternative of statistical AI approaches, and the development of systems for story generation over the next several decades. While the examined story-generation systems demonstrate a variety of interesting models of fiction, most focus on this to the exclusion of a rich audience experience, resulting in the continued presence of the *Tale-Spin* effect in even the most advanced work in this area.

The book's third waypoint is named after a work famous for making a relatively complex system into a rich, enjoyable experience of play: the city planning game *SimCity*. The *SimCity effect* is my term for systems that shape their surface experience to enable the audience to build up an understanding of their internal structure, especially a relatively complex one. This approach underlies the most popular and influential game built around simulated human characters: *The Sims*. It also provides a way of understanding the development of systems for believable animated characters and interactive drama, which eschew the most direct representations of internal system state. Finally, the *SimCity* effect provides an important design guideline for those who seek to make another powerful technology for fiction—language—playable in new ways.

Terms for Thinking about Processes

The idea of operational logics is my way of talking about aspects of digital media with which other authors and designers are also concerned. Given this, it should be no surprise that operational logics are related to some of the ideas others have proposed for thinking about digital media systems. Ian Bogost's *Persuasive Games* (2007), for example, positions my notion of operational logics as the "tropes" of procedural rhetoric (which seems appropriate, at least for those logics that clearly structure audience experience). The concept of operational logics is also not unrelated to Bogost's figure of the "unit operation"—though Bogost's aim is in some ways more general in that his work creates a foundation for "any medium—poetic, literary, cinematic, computational" to be "read as a configurative system, an arrangement of discrete, interlocking units of expressive meaning" (2006, ix). At the same time, Bogost's aims are also more specific. For example, he writes, "Unit operations are modes of meaning-making that privilege discrete, disconnected actions over deterministic, progressive systems. . . . In software technology, object technology exploits unit operations; structured programming exhibits system operations" (3). In my current thinking, I use the concept of operational logics only in reference to computational systems (not, for instance, traditional cinema) and in a manner that encompasses both what Bogost calls unit operations and system operations.

Game design is certainly one area for which it is particularly important to consider the parts of a system that operate and connect, and that can be combined and adjusted to create successful audience experiences. One influential framework for thinking in these terms is called *MDA*, standing for Mechanics, Dynamics, and Aesthetics (Hunicke, LeBlanc, and Zubek 2004). In the language of game design, especially for those familiar with the *MDA* framework, what I call operational logics might often be termed *mechanics*—except that *MDA* mechanics are framed as being limited to operational logics experienced by the audience. As Robin Hunicke, Marc LeBlanc, and Robert Zubek write, "Mechanics are the various actions, behaviors and control mechanisms afforded to the player within a game context."

Coming from a rather different direction, computer science has also thought quite a bit about the question of system operations. A general computer science term for a more abstract level of consideration of the operations of process and data is *algorithms*. This concept certainly shares the relatively implementation-independent nature of operational logics (an introduction to algorithms class may implement the "bubble sort" algorithm in many languages and on many platforms). Yet, for an operational logic to be useful in interpretation, it need not have the characteristics that D. E. Knuth requires of algorithms (1968). For example, it need not be *definite* (the terms employed can require human knowledge rather than being specified at a computable level of detail). More fundamentally there is little emphasis in computer science education on considering algorithms and their relationships critically or aesthetically—rather than in terms such as efficiency.

Looking Forward

If I am successful, *Expressive Processing* is two books in one. One book makes an argument that we need to pay more attention to the processes of digital media. This book is an example of the expanding area of software studies (discussed in more detail in chapter 5). It makes its case on authorial, critical, and political levels. It outlines my two primary meanings for *expressive processing* along with the three general effects I have identified in the relationship between system processes and audience experiences. It presents a way of thinking about software and media that grows from my interactions with writers, artists, game designers, computer scientists, and humanities scholars—and I hope it will be of use to members of all these groups. A book like this must be supported with examples, but I believe that such a book could have been written by an author with a passion for any one of a variety of types of digital media, from computer music to generative visual art.

The other book within these covers is the one shaped by my passion for digital fictions and games. It tells a history of process-oriented innovations in these areas—a history that can provide inspiration (and cautionary guidance) as we create the projects that will shape the future of storytelling and play. We are in the midst of a creative explosion in these areas, and that is an exciting place to be. As our work moves forward, we are also coming to see that the exciting possibilities aren't necessarily those assumed earlier. We aren't finding greater authorial power in closer approximations of everyday reality. Rather, we're finding it in models that are deliberately artificial, emphasizing elements that capture the imaginations of authors, expressing a view of the world that can matter to audiences—just as traditional fictions have left out most of their characters' lives in favor of those elements central to that particular work. Similarly, we aren't finding greater potential in obviously "natural," "immersive," or "invisible" interfaces. It is instead those that expose the evolving state of the underlying system and the opportunities for audience action in connection with their fictions that are creating exciting new roles for us (no longer simply visual "viewers," textual "readers," or formal system "players") as well as helping us develop new modes of understanding for fictional worlds. This in turn provides the strongest connection for the two books between these covers. Coming to understand fictional worlds as systems—and exploring their potential through play—is also a powerful means of coming to understand our evolving society, in which (often hidden) software models structure much of how we live now.

I assume most readers are drawn to *Expressive Processing* primarily for one of these two intertwined books. My hope is that whatever your starting interests, you will come away having found something of value in both.

Notes

1. During the blog-based peer review of this book's manuscript on Grand Text Auto (discussed in the afterword) Mark Marino suggested that the ability of computers to simulate movie projectors and tape players is "the result of a set of cultural, consumer, and producer priorities." Certainly this is true. While I am writing here about what makes this simulation possible, we shouldn't lose sight of how the actual is selected from the possible.

2. For more on this project, *Screen,* see chapter 9.

3. Though the concepts of *data* and *process* seem clear enough as ideas, in practice any element of a system may be a mixture between the two. For example, the text handled by a Web application is generally thought of as data. However, this textual data is often a mixture of plain text and markup language tags (from an early version of HTML or an XML-defined markup language). These markup language tags, in turn, may define or invoke processes, either on the server or in the web browsers of the site's audience.

This blurring occurs, in part, because the creation of content for the Web can be thought of as one of the most widespread examples of *declarative programming.* In this model, authors focus on what is to be done (e.g., a dynamically-generated menu appearing at a particular location on the page) rather than how it will be carried out. Taken further, in a language like Prolog, much of an author's work becomes the expression of logical statements (which may seem like data about the world), with "running" the program depending on processes (such as search) that are part of the underlying support for Prolog. On the other hand, the logical statements provided by Prolog authors are crafted to invoke complex reasoning processes, rather than to serve as the final output of the system (unlike, say, the data that makes up the video file for a computer game's cut scene). In chapter 6, note 5 discusses the importance of declarative information in crafting flexible processes, while chapter 7 contains a section on *Brutus,* a system supported by Prolog.

There are also less complex cases, as when a process is used to generate data that might as easily have been stored in the system initially, producing a tradeoff between storage and computation. Luckily, none of these diminish the basic usefulness of the concepts of data and process as a starting point.

4. Many console games also have more complicated surfaces, often in the form of additional controllers such as dance mats, simulated musical instruments, or cameras. And digital fictions and games more generally may have much more complex surfaces, selected or crafted by their authors. These may repurpose everyday objects, employ augmented or virtual reality displays, infiltrate and incorporate portions of the everyday world (as with alternate reality games and locative media), engage the bodies of audience members beyond "one finger and one eye" (the limitation of current interfaces, as put in an observation attributed to Joy Mountford), and so on.

5. At the same time that processes come into operation through audience actions at the surface, process and surface also define some of the possibility space for audience actions, as well as the feedback produced, and thereby shape the audience. For example, while an audience member may at any time press a particular button on a console controller—which may or may not have any meaning in the current

game—for many games the process of successful play requires becoming trained, at a preconscious level, to take the actions that are recognized by the system. The intervention of conscious thought would make it impossible to time a sequence of leaps in a game such as *Prince of Persia: The Sands of Time* (discussed in a later chapter). In the context of a much earlier game (the version of *Breakout* for the Atari VCS), this is one of the core observations of what may be the first classic book in computer game studies: David Sudnow's *Pilgrim in the Microworld* (1983). In other words, the relationship between audience experience and system operations includes both the interpretative work of the audience and the system's shaping of the audience that performs the interpretation.

In a series of comments during this book's blog-based peer review on Grand Text Auto, Bryan G. Behrenshausen drew my attention to how this is formulated in Alex Galloway's work. For example, as argued in his collaborative book with Eugene Thacker, *The Exploit*:

> Forms of informatic play should be interrogated not as liberation from the rigid constraints of systems of exchange and production but as the very pillars that prop those systems up. The more video games appear on the surface to emancipate the player, raise his or her status as an active participant in the aesthetic moment, the more they enfold the player in codified and routinized modes of behavior. Only eight buttons (mirrored in eight bits) are available for the entire spectrum of expressive articulation using the controller on the Nintendo Entertainment System. (Galloway and Thacker, 2007, 115)

I appreciate Galloway and Thacker pointing out that interactive systems are by no means necessarily liberating—and may enact training in precisely the modes of oppression. On the other hand, I think their argument takes a potentially confusing turn when it reaches the eight bits of the NES controller. After all, only seven bits are needed for standard ASCII character encoding of the English language. I'm convinced even this limited expressive space can be used in a wide variety of ways, some of them liberating.

On a different note, it is also important to recognize that the system itself is far from the only force shaping the audience. Those skilled players/dancers who add additional physical flourish to their interaction with *Dance Dance Revolution* don't do so from the encouragement of its sensor pad and on-screen instructions (which regard their performance as no different from one who takes the minimal physical actions). The crowds that gather around them in the arcade know this.

6. I will return to the discussion of spatial logics in chapter 9.

Chapter 2
The *Eliza* Effect

Meeting *Eliza*

When I was a teenager—in the 1980s—my mother bought a personal computer. It was an impressive machine for the day, decked out with two floppy drives, a dot matrix printer, a Hayes modem, and a monochrome amber display.

1. For more on BBS culture, I highly recommend Jason Scott's *BBS: The Documentary* (2005).

At first I only used the machine for some minor programming experiments (in Basic and later Pascal), writing for school (in WordStar), and a few games. But that mysterious modem sat there. Probably intended to let my mother exchange data with the big Digital Equipment Corporation machines she had in her university lab, I knew modems could also be used for other things.

This was about a decade before the Internet began to make its way into homes like ours, and I had no interest in the manicured gardens of services like the Source or CompuServe. Rather than any long-distance journey, I wanted to use the modem to explore the local wilderness, to visit the unruly bulletin board system (BBS) scene sprouting in the dens and basements of my neighbors' homes.

While largely forgotten today, a BBS was the online destination of choice for 1980s teenagers.[1] Most were run by individuals out of their homes: computer enthusiasts with machines much more powerful than ours, hooked to one or more dedicated phone lines. A user like me could call into a BBS, read messages, leave messages, download and upload files, play text-based games, and (if

2. *Eliza* was not
the first system
to give audiences
the impression
of meaningful
exchange with a
computer. Matthew
Kirschenbaum's
Mechanisms (2008)
offers the intriguing
example of "Professor
RAMAC"—a …

Notes continued at end
of this chapter.

the owner of the BBS was at the computer, or if someone called in to one of the other phone lines) have real-time conversations, with total strangers, in text. In other words, the BBS wasn't just a file repository. It was a window into what has now become obvious: the incredible social potential of combining computers and networks, which has given us email, instant messaging, wikis, blogs, social networking web sites, and much more.

Given the glimpse of this potential, a BBS with multiple lines could feel a little lonely when no one else was on. But then one day I was over at the house of a childhood friend (we no longer went to the same school), and he showed me that on his computer, conversation was always waiting. He showed me a program he'd downloaded from a BBS. He introduced me to *Eliza*.

Eliza Today

Eliza—or more properly, *Eliza/Doctor*—is a ground breaking system created by computer science researcher Joseph Weizenbaum at MIT in the mid-1960s. In the two decades between when Weizenbaum created the system and I experienced it at my friend's house, it had become one of the world's most famous demonstrations of the potential of computing. First unveiled two years before HAL 9000's screen debut in *2001: A Space Odyssey,* it seemed that *Eliza* made it possible to have a real conversation with a computer.[2]

In the computer science literature, under the name *Eliza,* Weizenbaum's system is a contribution to the field of natural language processing. On the other hand when *Eliza* plays *Doctor* it is a well-known computer character, famous far beyond computer science, often also known by the name Eliza. And *Eliza* has a third common usage in the computer world as well: *the Eliza effect*. This has generally been a term used to describe the not-uncommon illusion that an interactive computer system is more "intelligent" (or substantially more complex and capable) than it actually is. One of my purposes in this chapter is to revisit the *Eliza* effect and give it a further nuance so that it names not only this initial illusion but also the authorial choice that comes with it: severely restricted interaction (on the one hand) or eventual breakdown that takes a form based on the actual underlying processes (on the other).

In the next chapter, with an examination of the *Eliza* effect as background, I will look at the options selected by today's authors of digital fictions—particularly for computer games. These generally put aside the *Eliza* effect in favor of systems that more clearly communicate their structures to audiences. Yet there are two problems with these that I will consider. Some of them employ processes that, while legible, tend toward a non-*Eliza* form of breakdown. Others, while avoiding breakdown, have low ambitions in their use of computational processes. More ambitious routes will be the focus of the remaining chapters of this book.

But for now I'll start with the illusion.

The *Eliza* Effect

I don't remember the specifics of my first conversation with *Eliza*, but here is *Eliza*'s most famous exchange (with the computer's responses in all capital letters):

Men are all alike.

IN WHAT WAY

They're always bugging us about something or other.
CAN YOU THINK OF A SPECIFIC EXAMPLE
Well, my boyfriend made me come here.
YOUR BOYFRIEND MADE YOU COME HERE
He says I'm depressed much of the time.
I AM SORRY TO HEAR YOU ARE DEPRESSED
It's true. I am unhappy.
DO YOU THINK COMING HERE WILL
HELP YOU NOT TO BE UNHAPPY
I need some help, that much seems certain.
WHAT WOULD IT MEAN TO YOU
IF YOU GOT SOME HELP
Perhaps I could learn to get along with my mother.
TELL ME MORE ABOUT YOUR FAMILY
My mother takes care of me.
WHO ELSE IN YOUR FAMILY TAKES CARE OF YOU
My father.
YOUR FATHER
You are like my father in some ways.
WHAT RESEMBLANCE DO YOU SEE
You are not very aggressive but I think
you don't want me to notice that.
WHAT MAKES YOU THINK I AM
NOT VERY AGGRESSIVE
You don't argue with me.
WHY DO YOU THINK I DON'T ARGUE WITH YOU
You are afraid of me.
DOES IT PLEASE YOU TO BELIEVE
I AM AFRAID OF YOU
My father is afraid of everybody.
WHAT ELSE COMES TO MIND WHEN
YOU THINK OF YOUR FATHER
Bullies.

DOES THAT HAVE ANYTHING TO DO WITH THE FACT
THAT YOUR BOYFRIEND MADE YOU COME HERE
(Weizenbaum 1966, 37)[3]

3. Erik Loyer, in reimplementing the *Eliza* system for a project on which we were collaborating for the digital media journal *Vectors,* noted that this conversation appears to be edited. Unless the *Eliza* system had undocumented …

Notes continued at end of this chapter.

As you might imagine, I was impressed. And I certainly wasn't the first. Weizenbaum's employers at MIT had seized on *Eliza* as an accessible demonstration of the potential of computing, exciting to those without the specialized knowledge needed to appreciate much of the ongoing research. The computer world agreed. In fact, when the first demonstrations of the ARPANET (the predecessor of the Internet) were carried out, some of the terminals ran *Eliza* from a remote location (Leonard 1997, 52). Given the excitement produced by *Eliza,* astronomer and science popularizer Carl Sagan suggested that the future might hold "a network of computer psychotherapeutic terminals, something like arrays of large telephone booths" (Weizenbaum 1976, 5).

Originally *Eliza* ran on a computer less powerful than the one in my mobile phone, though at the time it was one of the most advanced at MIT. Rather than being hooked up to a monitor, keyboard, and mouse—or HAL's microphone, speaker, and camera—*Eliza* was experienced through something like a typewriter, allowing the computer to type to the user and the user to type back. People could type anything they wanted to *Eliza,* and the software would respond in different ways depending on the currently active script.

This last word, "script," is important. There is nothing magical about *Eliza*—it is simply a bundle of data and processes, and pretty simple processes at that. Each time that *Eliza* runs, it uses a particular script to guide its behavior. The example conversation given was created

4. This article is not only a good, clear source of explanation for *Eliza*'s processes (and the most-cited publication about *Eliza* in the computer science literature). It also served as the basis for many homegrown versions of *Eliza* created at …

5. While the original script text is in all capitals, I am regularizing it here. Also, this description focuses on the core processes at work in *Eliza*; to describe them all would make this section as long as Weizenbaum's paper.

Notes continued at end of this chapter.

using *Eliza*'s most famous script, *Doctor,* which causes the software to parody the conversational patterns of a nondirective therapist during an initial visit. All of this is described in Weizenbaum's 1966 article in *Communications of the ACM.*[4]

How *Eliza* Works

A session with *Eliza* can begin with a greeting. Weizenbaum's *Doctor* script starts with: "How do you do. Please tell me your problem."[5] After this point *Eliza* will not take the initiative again—only respond.

Each time an audience member types something, *Eliza* examines it, looking for words that have entries in the currently active script. Some of the words are *keywords,* which I will discuss further below. Some words are marked for simple substitution. For example, when *Eliza* runs the *Doctor* script, these substitutions switch all the first-person pronouns for second-person pronouns ("I" becomes "you") and vice versa ("yourself" becomes "myself"). "Well, you are very helpful," for instance, would become "Well, I are very helpful." A word can be both substituted and used as a keyword.

Periods and commas are treated as delimiters. If a period or comma is encountered, *Eliza* checks to see if a keyword has already been found. If one has, then everything that the audience member typed after the delimiter is discarded. If no keyword has yet been found, everything before the delimiter is discarded. For example, "Well, I are very helpful" would become "I are very helpful."

Each keyword has a priority level or rank. When the first keyword is found in a text, it is added to a "keystack." Each time another keyword is found, the rank of the new keyword is compared with that of the highest-rank keyword yet found. If the new word has a higher rank it is added to the top of the stack; otherwise it is added to the bottom of the stack. The result, at the end of scanning a text for keywords, is that the highest-rank keyword is at the top of the stack.

After keyword scanning, the next step is to find a "decomposition rule" that matches the postsubstitution version of what the audience member typed (minus any parts discarded because of commas or periods). Decomposition rules are associated with keywords, so this search begins by popping the top keyword off the stack. (I'll soon discuss what happens if there is nothing on the stack.) *Eliza* tries out the decomposition rules associated with that keyword, looking for one with an appropriate pattern of words in combination with the wild card "0" (which is equivalent to "any number of words, including zero"). For example, if the keyword is "you," the first decomposition rule is:

(0 I remind you of 0)

This wouldn't match the sample phrase from above, "I are very helpful." The first rule would only match a postsubstitution phrase like, "With that last statement I remind you that I are a machine," or (because 0 can represent zero words), "I remind you of the happier days of your childhood." The next decomposition rule for the "you" keyword, though, would match the example phrase used earlier:

(0 I are 0)

Once a match is found, the decomposition rule does what it is named for: it decomposes the phrase into parts. This decomposition is based on the number of words and the number of 0s in the rule. For instance, "I are very helpful" would become:

(1) *empty* (2) I (3) are (4) very helpful.

All that remains, at this point, is to decide what to say back to the audience. Each decomposition rule can have a set of reassembly rules associated with it. An example reassembly rule (for the decomposition "0 I are 0") is:

(What makes you think I am 4)

This would result in the response, "What makes you think I am very helpful."[6] Once they were used during any run of *Eliza*, the reassembly rules were marked so that all the reassemblies associated with a particular decomposition would be cycled through before any were repeated.

This is the bulk of *Eliza*'s approach. There are a few refinements, such as techniques that allow scripts to share rules between keywords (e.g., mother and father). But from this the dominant operational logic at work in *Eliza* should be clear: transformation. Each statement by an *Eliza* script is the result of a multistep transformation of the most recent audience statement.

Many of these transformations include a verbatim portion of the statement being transformed, as outlined above. Others are more indirect transformations, as when "Perhaps I could learn to get along with my mother" is translated into "Tell me more about your family." The real transformation difficulty comes, however, when no keywords—a central aspect of *Eliza*'s transformation logic—are found in the audience's most recent text. For example, this is the situation when *Eliza/Doctor* asks, "What else comes to mind when you think of your father," and receives the response, "Bullies."

One set of possible transformations, in these cases, can be defined in the script based on a special keyword called "none." In *Doctor* these are content-free phrases such as "Please go on" and "I see." Yet some of the most surprising moments with *Eliza* come from another special structure called "memory." This structure works in combination with a particular keyword. In the case of *Doctor* it works with the keyword "my" and the decomposition "0 your 0." When this keyword is selected, a response is generated in the usual way. In addition, another reassembly may be created and stored in a queue for later use when no keyword is found. In *Doctor* these reassemblies are "Lets discuss further why your 3," "Earlier you said your 3," and "Does this have anything to do with the fact that your 3"—the last of these we saw above, with 3 being "boyfriend made you come here." In other words, the surprising punch line in the above conversation was nothing but a fallback, a default move that *Eliza* can make when the most recent response has no identifiable keywords.

Here we can see what moved Weizenbaum to write that "once a particular program is unmasked, once its inner workings are explained in language sufficiently plain to induce understanding, its magic crumbles away; it stands revealed as a mere collection of procedures, each quite comprehensible" (1966, 36). But when we interact with a piece of software, we don't necessarily achieve such understanding, we don't get a clear picture of how it actually operates internally. And Dr. Sagan and I were not alone regarding *Eliza/Doctor*; its audiences often developed mistaken ideas about its internals. They assumed that since the surface appearance of an interaction with the program could resemble something like a coherent dialogue, internally the software must be complex. Some thought it must be

7. This is the version of the story reported in Janet Murray's *Hamlet on the Holodeck*. In addition to this version, many clearly apocryphal versions circulate, including one in which Weizenbaum is a participant in the events. This version itself cannot be a …

Notes continued at end of this chapter.

something close to the fictional HAL: a computer program intelligent enough to understand and produce arbitrary human language. This happened so frequently, and was so striking, that in computer science circles people began to use a specific term for this kind of misunderstanding, one mentioned earlier in this chapter: the *Eliza* effect.

Why *Eliza* Worked

The stories of *Eliza/Doctor*'s effectiveness are many. Weizenbaum himself tells us that "my secretary, who had watched me work on the program for many months and therefore surely knew it to be merely a computer program, started conversing with it. After only a few interchanges with it, she asked me to leave the room" (1976, 6). There is also the oft-repeated tale, which exists in many versions, of the boss thinking he is communicating with a subordinate while actually conversing with *Eliza/Doctor*:

> *Vice president.* Do you think I can use the computer this morning?
> *Teletype.* WHY DO YOU ASK?
> *Vice president.* I might be able to make some additional telcomp (computer system) sales.
> *Teletype.* WHY AREN'T YOU SURE?
> *Vice president.* My prospective customers have never seen a demonstration of the system.
> *Teletype.* DOES THIS MEAN VERY MUCH TO YOU?
> *Vice president.* Of course it does.
> *Teletype.* YOU SEEM VERY POSITIVE ABOUT THAT.
> *Vice president.* This is ridiculous.
> *Teletype.* WHAT DO YOU MEAN THIS IS RIDICULOUS?
> (Murray 1997, 7)[7]

As a high school student, I found that *Eliza/Doctor*

created an effective initial illusion for the same reasons it worked for the iconic "emotional" secretary and "clueless" boss evoked by the above stories. First, all of us were accustomed to text-only computing and to having conversations with other people within that environment. Second, *Eliza/Doctor* makes a remarkably good match between process and data. The situation of the initial visit to the therapist, the clever writing in the reassemblies and nonresponses, and the well-chosen keywords do the most possible to leverage the simple linguistic tricks available via *Eliza*'s transformation processes. (In fact, there were other *Eliza* scripts created besides *Doctor,* but none of them became nearly as well known or widespread.) Third, for myself, the secretary, and the boss, this was one of our first experiences with computer characters. But all three of these reasons are only *Eliza/Doctor*'s specific nuances on a much more general phenomenon: when a system is presented as intelligent and appears to exhibit intelligent behavior, people have a disturbingly strong tendency to regard it as such.[8]

This phenomenon derailed Weizenbaum's career. He came to focus his work on the conceptual mismatch that gives the *Eliza* effect its name and specifically on how it could "induce powerful delusional thinking in quite normal people" (1976, 7). Weizenbaum wrote a book dedicated to demonstrating that the internals of computers aren't magical, and that we do ourselves a disservice when we assume that human beings are so mechanical that we could or should have our intelligence matched by computational machines. In a sense, he moved from being a computer scientist to being one of the first knowledgeable critics to interrogate the cultures

8. Mark J. Nelson, in the blog-based peer review of this book, urged me to clarify the fact that this isn't only true of computer systems—as demonstrated by an example later in this chapter: Harold Garfinkel's yes/no therapy experiment.

of computing and artificial intelligence.

Following Weizenbaum, a number of other authors saw the *Eliza* effect as important to address in understanding our relationship with computers and our culture more generally. A decade after Weizenbaum's book, Lucy Suchman published *Plans and Situated Actions* (1987), in which she sees *Eliza/Doctor* as an iconic example in human-computer interaction of the broad phenomenon of treating systems as intelligent based on limited evidence. Specifically, she discusses what ethnomethodologist Harold Garfinkel (citing Karl Mannheim) has called the documentary method of interpretation.

Suchman presents one of Garfinkel's experiments as a demonstration of the idea that people tend to "take appearances as evidence for, or the document of, an ascribed underlying reality, while taking the reality so ascribed as a resource for the interpretation of the appearance" (23). In this experiment student subjects were introduced to a new kind of therapy in which they asked yes/no questions about their personal problems. These were answered by "counselors" who were not visible to the subjects. Unbeknownst to the subjects, the counselors answered each question randomly.

After the experiment, the students were found to have constructed stories that made sense of each string of answers as a coherent exchange and set of advice. This happened even when, as would almost inevitably happen in such a circumstance, the answers given were self-contradictory. The apparent contradictions were explained away by the experimental subjects as revised views based on further information, evidence of a deeper agenda on the part of the counselor or something else that fit with the frame of the therapeutic situation.

Yet another decade later, Janet Murray revisited *Eliza/ Doctor* in *Hamlet on the Holodeck* (1997). Here she makes a crucial turn for my purposes, seeing the project in terms of media. She views *Eliza/Doctor* as a dramatic character, Weizenbaum as a kind of playwright, and the source of the *Eliza* effect in such cases as "the human propensity to suspend disbelief in the presence of a persuasive dramatic presence" (224). Murray makes visible what wasn't clear in previous accounts: that people enjoy *Eliza*. Initial interactions are often quite fun and engaging, and create the sense of open-ended possibilities with an interesting character.

But that first impression doesn't necessarily last.

Revisiting the *Eliza* Effect

Being a teenager, after my initial interaction with *Eliza/ Doctor,* I did the natural thing: I started to play with it. (Software, of course, doesn't need to be a game to inspire play.) I don't remember the exact exchange, but I know that I soon discovered the reason Murray doesn't go far into talking about ongoing interaction with *Eliza/Doctor,* just as Suchman and Weizenbaum don't.[9] If they did, it would complicate their discussions. This is because, while the initial experience of *Eliza/Doctor* can create the surface impression of an incredibly complex internal system, sustained interaction with the system, the verbal back-and-forth, invites play—and linguistic play with *Eliza/Doctor* quickly begins to destroy the illusion. In other words, precisely the open-ended textual interaction that helped foster the illusion of internal complexity and intelligence enables play that draws attention to the system's rote

9. To be fair, at the time of Weizenbaum's initial observations, almost no one could experience ongoing interaction with *Eliza/ Doctor,* due to the limited availability of computing resources. As Weizenbaum notes, "Since the subject cannot …

Notes continued at end of this chapter.

10. Turkle comments that "some people embark on an all-out effort to 'psych out' the program, to understand its structure in order to trick it and expose it as a 'mere machine.' Many more do the opposite. . . . They didn't ask questions that they knew …

11. Suchman argues that Garfinkel's experiment lends support to Weizenbaum's view that the feeling of intelligence in conversations with *Eliza/Doctor* comes from the work of the audience. Further, she contends that …

Notes continued at end of this chapter.

simplicity, its distance from human interaction. Before long, many exchanges begin to look like this:

> You are going to repeat what I say
>
> in the form of a question
>
> WHAT MAKES YOU THINK I AM GOING TO REPEAT
>
> WHAT YOU SAY IN THE FORM OF A QUESTION

Sherry Turkle, in *The Second Self*, notes this phenomenon, writing, "As one becomes experienced with the ways of *Eliza,* one can direct one's remarks either to 'help' the program make seemingly pertinent responses or to provoke nonsense" (1984, 39). Turkle's book is based on interviews and observations—and she found that some of her subjects worked to keep the illusion going, while others sought to maximize *Eliza*'s nonsense.[10] Both strategies, though, depended on coming to understand something of the internal processes at work and shaping surface interaction accordingly. Even working to maintain the illusion required a type of seeing past it, something that those who discuss the *Eliza* effect rarely acknowledge.

The *Eliza* Breakdown

From my point of view, what Turkle describes points toward a further lesson of Garfinkel's yes/no therapy experiment. For Suchman, this experiment demonstrates the importance of ethnomethodology and the documentary hypothesis for understanding *Eliza/Doctor* and human-computer interaction.[11] And certainly it is essential to understand that *Eliza/Doctor* succeeds, to the extent that it does, because it plays on the interpretative expectations brought to each interaction by audience members. But for my purposes here, Garfinkel's experiment also serves to illustrate something rather different: the *Eliza* effect can be shielded from breakdown by severely restricting interaction. The experiment allowed the subjects to maintain the illusion that something much more complex was going on inside the system (a human considering her problems seriously and answering questions thoughtfully, rather than random yes/no answers) because the scope of possible responses was so limited. If it had been expanded only slightly—say, to random choice between the responses available in a "magic eight ball"—almost any period of sustained interaction would have shattered the illusion through too many inappropriate responses.

When breakdown in the *Eliza* effect occurs, its shape is often determined by that of the underlying processes. If the output is of a legible form, the audience can then begin to develop a model of the processes. This is what Turkle observes in those interacting with *Eliza/Doctor*: from the shape of the breakdown they begin to understand something of the processes of the system—and then employ that knowledge to help maintain or further compromise the illusion.

In this context, it is interesting to note that most systems of control that are meant to appear intelligent have extremely restricted methods of interaction. In some cases the reasons for this are quite obvious. If the public were allowed playful interaction with software that identifies possible targets for financial surveillance, the shape of the underlying system would become relatively apparent, making it possible to "game" the system. At the same time, this restricted interaction also serves to maintain the *Eliza* effect for software that is not nearly as intelligent as the public has been asked to believe.

Further, within a rather different community, this

choice—between severely restricted interaction and the boom/bust of illusion followed by breakdown—presents no good options to those with an interest in creating digital fictions.[12] So while some have argued that it is best to capitalize on the *Eliza* effect, depending on temporary illusion and the willful suspension of disbelief to carry the day, most digital fiction authors employ a different approach: exposing important elements of the structures of their processes to the audience from the outset. This allows for interaction that matches the process employed, and avoids the *Eliza* illusion and breakdown. Still, as I will discuss next, the most common of these approaches suffer from limitations of their own.

Finally, I should mention that some authors—such as Jeremy Douglass (2007)—assert that breakdown can be an interesting mode for digital fictions. And certainly breakdowns can be fascinating. On a linguistic level, for example, we're attracted to study every form of breakdown from occasional slips of the tongue to hemmorage-induced aphasia.

What breakdowns can do—in the case of *Eliza/ Doctor,* linguistic slips, and neurological problems alike— is give us some insight into the shape of the underlying system processes. This fact points to the reason why I still talk with people online (even if I no longer dial in to a BBS to do so) but I no longer play with *Eliza* in my spare time: a system prone to breakdown is only as interesting as the shape of the processes that the breakdowns partially reveal. And as shown earlier in this chapter, the *Eliza* system processes are mostly a relatively uninteresting set of substitutions. We can do better.

Notes

1. For more on BBS culture, I highly recommend Jason Scott's *BBS: The Documentary* (2005).

2. *Eliza* was not the first system to give audiences the impression of meaningful exchange with a computer. Matthew Kirschenbaum's *Mechanisms* (2008) offers the intriguing example of "Professor RAMAC"—a four-ton IBM machine anthropomorphized at the 1958 World's Fair—which used a then-revolutionary hard drive to provide question-answering access to a collection of historical facts.

3. Erik Loyer, in reimplementing the *Eliza* system for a project on which we were collaborating for the digital media journal *Vectors*, noted that this conversation appears to be edited. Unless the *Eliza* system had undocumented features, its response to "You are not very aggressive but I think you don't want me to notice that" would have been "WHAT MAKES YOU THINK I AM NOT VERY AGGRESSIVE BUT YOU THINK I DON'T WANT YOU TO NOTICE THAT" rather than the snappier "WHAT MAKES YOU THINK I AM NOT VERY AGGRESSIVE."

4. This article is not only a good, clear source of explanation for *Eliza*'s processes (and the most-cited publication about *Eliza* in the computer science literature). It also served as the basis for many homegrown versions of *Eliza* created at computing centers across the country in the years that followed. This was still decades away from when researchers and hobbyists could easily transport software to one another over computer networks—so paper publications such as *Communications of the ACM* (for researchers) and *Byte* (for hobbyists) often included all the information needed (including, in the case of Weizenbaum's article, the complete *Doctor* script) for reimplementing the software locally.

5. While the original script text is in all capitals, I am regularizing it here. Also, this description focuses on the core processes at work in *Eliza;* to describe them all would make this section as long as Weizenbaum's paper.

6. Question marks were not used because they were interpreted as "line delete" on the computer system that Weizenbaum was using.

7. This is the version of the story reported in Janet Murray's *Hamlet on the Holodeck.* In addition to this version, many clearly apocryphal versions circulate, including one in which Weizenbaum is a participant in the events. This version itself cannot be a verbatim conversation with *Eliza,* at least not as the system existed at the time of Weizenbaum's 1966 paper. That paper's Doctor script, for example, contains the responses "YOU AREN'T SURE" and "WHY THE UNCERTAIN TONE"—but not "WHY AREN'T YOU SURE." Beyond differences in wording, it is also worth remembering the previous note: the system used by Weizenbaum did not support question marks, which appear throughout this transcript.

8. Mark J. Nelson, in the blog-based peer review of this book, urged me to clarify the fact that this isn't only true of computer systems—as demonstrated by an example later in this chapter: Harold Garfinkel's yes/no therapy experiment.

9. To be fair, at the time of Weizenbaum's initial observations, almost no one could experience ongoing interaction with *Eliza/Doctor,* due to the limited availability of computing resources. As Weizenbaum notes,

"Since the subject cannot probe the true limits of *Eliza*'s capabilities (he has, after all, only a limited time to play with it, and it is constantly getting new material from him), he cannot help but attribute more power to it than it actually has" (1976, 191).

10. Turkle comments that "some people embark on an all-out effort to 'psych out' the program, to understand its structure in order to trick it and expose it as a 'mere machine.' Many more do the opposite. . . . They didn't ask questions that they knew would 'confuse' the program, that would make it 'talk nonsense'" (40). Turkle attributes this to a desire to "maintain the illusion that *Eliza* was able to respond to them." It is also entirely in line with Murray's interpretation of *Eliza* as a media experience, however, with the audience shaping their interaction to help maintain the willful suspension of disbelief.

11. Suchman argues that Garfinkel's experiment lends support to Weizenbaum's view that the feeling of intelligence in conversations with *Eliza/Doctor* comes from the work of the audience. Further, she contends that the strongly situated understandings of the students (they interpreted the random series of yes/no answers based on assumed context) is a challenge not only to the strong structure-oriented assumptions of the social sciences but also those of cognitive science.

12. Except for that limited number of fictions that might want to explore one of these effects.

Chapter 3
Computer Game Fictions

Digital Fictions and the *Eliza* Effect

Imagine you've checked out your books and walked, through the damp twilight, to the bus shelter across the street. Its fluorescent tubes have flickered on—you can read the schedules and advertisements behind the Plexiglas, as well as the stickers scattered over them.

One rectangular sticker catches your eye. It has the name of no band, the number of no locksmith, the logo of no corporation, and no image of Andre the Giant. It's just a block of text. The first words read, "Why bomb libraries?"

The text is a passage from *Implementation*, a novel written in small chunks formatted to fit on mailing labels that can be fed through a standard laser printer. *Implementation* is a sticker novel, in one sense, and also a kind of digital novel. Its authors, Nick Montfort and Scott Rettberg (2004), don't primarily distribute stickers. Instead, they distribute digital files, which others print on stickers and post in provocative locations. Readers sometimes encounter these stickers. But, like most stickers, they tend to be removed pretty quickly from the benches, doors, bathroom stalls, statue plaques, lampposts, bumpers, and other locations where they're placed. What lasts longer are the photographs that people take of *Implementation* stickers in interesting positions, and it is through these images that most people experience *Implementation,* the files for these images dwarfing the other contents of the *Implementation* web site.

Encountering *Implementation* can be a mysterious experience. Finding a disconnected sticker of text, especially if well-placed, can border on disconcerting. And the images of placed stickers can offer up their own mysteries: Where is that? *What* is that? But, despite the importance of digital technology for *Implementation,* the mystery is never about software. *Implementation* depends on digital processes— but ones we use every day, such that the processes of file downloading, laser printing, and photo sharing no longer attract our attention.

One might even argue that *Implementation* is not appropriate to discuss as a "digital" novel but rather one that is distributed and documented digitally. Regardless, in its use of digital processes, *Implementation* stands as a relatively extreme example of something true of many digital fictions: they avoid the dilemma of the *Eliza* effect by employing processes that are conceptually simple and familiar, and that are clearly exposed to the audience.

Different fictions approach this general strategy in different ways. Some, in a manner relatively close to *Implementation,* embed themselves in familiar digital contexts. An email novel, such as *Blue Company* by Rob Wittig (2001, 2002), depends on processes of email transmission and reading—but, like the processes of laser printing, these have become completely naturalized for many with computer access. Similarly, the familiar link-following functions of web browsers and web servers makes it possible to construct fictions from interconnected networks of web pages, as with *The Unknown* by William Gillespie, Scott Rettberg, Dirk Stratton, and Frank Marquardt (1999). Familiar processes are also the primary digital components of hybrid works such as the alternate reality game by Elan Lee, Sean Stewart, Jim Stewartson, and Jane McGonigal (2004) titled *I Love Bees*, which brought players into a fictional world composed of web pages, email messages, phone calls, physical settings and elements, and live performance—but defined its novel processes as rules to be carried out by human participants (rather than by digital computation).

Another approach to digital fiction is more common than this sort of piggybacking on the processes of everyday information life, though. In this more common approach, digital fictions define their own versions of digital media processes in widespread use—or employ versions of these processes defined for use with digital media authoring tools. Such authoring tools range from Adobe's Flash software (for interactive animations) to game engines (used repeatedly by the same developer or made available for commercial license) to tools identified with particular artistic communities (such as the Storyspace hypertext authoring system).

The most widespread fictions taking this approach are computer games. They tend to avoid the *Eliza* effect by employing versions of simple processes, familiar to those who play computer games within the same genre, and following conventions to expose the structure and actions of the underlying processes to their audiences. This chapter will look at two particularly well-crafted examples of computer game fiction—*Star Wars: Knights of the Old Republic* (Falkner, Gilmour, Hudson, et al. 2003), or *KotOR*, and *Prince of Persia: The Sands of Time* (Mechner, Mallat, Désilets, et al. 2003), or *PoP*—as well as two commonly employed operational logics that enable the fictions of computer role-playing games (RPGs). But, to understand all this, it is important to begin with a wider view of RPGs.

1. Some games, of course, can hardly be said to engaage fiction at all. No one wants a story with their *Tetris*—and its "fictional world" of falling blocks barely supports the phrase. Given the sometimes-contentious nature of critical discussion …

2. As tabletop RPGs have come to encompass much broader areas of life than combat, different games (and player groups) have diverged in their treatment of these elements. One movement is toward a generalization of the statistical models …

Notes continued at end of this chapter.

Role-Playing Games

Games employ fiction in many ways.[1] The most story-ambitious genre of computer games is probably the computer RPG—a form that traces its roots back to a noncomputer form of gaming: the tabletop RPG (see sidebar: Computer and Tabletop Role-Playing Games).

The first tabletop RPG was *Dungeons & Dragons,* created by Gary Gygax and Dave Arneson and published in 1974 (Mona 2007). It grew out of a tabletop war-gaming tradition in which maps were used to represent battlefields and miniatures representing units or individual combatants were placed on the maps. Players would then move figures and engage in battles by following sets of rules and consulting tables of numbers (the process and data of the system) with a random element at times introduced using dice. *Dungeons & Dragons* departed from this model by suggesting that each player take on a single character, that play sessions connect with one another in an ongoing campaign during which each character would develop, and that the game encompass much more of the characters' lives (and the fictional world in which they live) than raw combat.[2]

The result was the birth of a genre that is, when well played, undoubtedly the most successful combination of game and fiction now in existence. RPG systems have been created for a wide variety of fictional settings (some inspired by authors ranging from H. P. Lovecraft to William S. Burroughs), are played both as tabletop games and live performances, and embody a diversity of aesthetic goals (the design goals of Greg Costikyan's games alone range from reproducing the wacky physical comedy of classic cartoons to evoking the alienation of Brechtian

Computer and Tabletop Role-Playing Games

Many computer RPGs trace their origins to tabletop RPGs—and sometimes the distance traced is quite short. Games such as BioWare's *Neverwinter Nights* computer RPG (Oster et al. 2002) are licensed versions of the tabletop RPG *Dungeons & Dragons* (Gygax and Arneson 1974). Further, the more abstract underlying "d20 system" developed for the third edition of *Dungeons & Dragons*— but then adopted for many tabletop RPGs, from *D&D* publisher Wizards of the Coast (WotC) and others—has also been used by computer RPGs such as *KotOR* (Falkner et al. 2003), as pointed out by Jason Rhody in the blog-based peer review of this book. It is also interesting to note that WotC publishes a tabletop RPG based on the d20 system and set in the Star Wars universe, for which there is a campaign guide for *KotOR* (Thompson et al. 2008)—presenting a rare opportunity to compare two different implementations of the same fictional world in the same basic game system, one computer and one tabletop.

At the same time, it is also worth noting that computer games developed in parallel with tabletop RPGs, so the larger genre of computer RPGs might be seen as a convergence of the two traditions—rather than a translation of the tabletop genre into computer form. In the blog-based peer review for this book, Dennis G. Jerz pointed particularly to early computer games such as *Hunt the Wumpus* (Yob 1973) and *Maze War* (Colley and Thompson 1973–1974). Certainly these are important to consider. Still, as Matt Barton recounts in *Dungeons & Desktops,* "There really is no doubt that *D&D* played a vital role in the development of the first CRPG. Richard Garriott, creator of *Akalabeth* and *Ultima,* was himself a dedicated fan of the game" (2008, 13). That said, Barton also argues that the importance of a number of other influences on the computer RPG should be recognized, including the computer game *Adventure* (Crowther and Woods 1976), sports simulation games, tabletop war games (the tradition from which *D&D* emerged), and the writings of J. R. R. Tolkien.

The history we trace by this method is definitely a Western one, however. The history of the flourishing form of the Japanese RPG is rather different. As William Huber writes:

> The Japanese reception of role-playing games includes a discontinuity: there is little sign of a culture of tabletop fantasy role-playing games in Japan before the production of computer-based games. *Dungeons & Dragons* was translated into Japanese in 1985, the same year that *Dragon Quest* was released: The *Ultima* and *Wizardry* games were already in widespread Japanese distribution by this time. . . . Thus the temporal framework for the RPG in Japan has been primarily computer-based from the outset: the evolution of RPG mechanics as a practice performed by a collaborating group of players does not exist in Japan. The "roles" of role-playing are categories of character function, and the player-driven theatrical aspects of pen-and-paper role-playing are instead replaced by story practices that owe as much to cinema and television as they do to military simulation. (2009)

3. The most famously Lovecraft-inspired game is *Call of Cthulhu* (Petersen 1981), while *Over the Edge* (Tweet 1992) is a game inspired by both Burroughs and Philip K. Dick. At the same time, as Jose Zagal reminded me in the blog-based peer …

4. Though many massively multiplayer online play groups, including some in which I have participated, include face-to-face interaction between some players. And there are a variety of other hybrid forms that combine elements of in-person and …

Notes continued at end of this chapter.

theater).[3] Most retain a role for one of the players as the "game master." This player undertakes the advance planning for the current campaign, plays the roles of the non-player characters (NPCs), shapes events to ensure the type of story desired, and executes most of the rule processes. This leaves other players free to concentrate on the defining features of RPGs: playing their characters and collaboratively developing the fiction.

Of course, with computer RPGs the situation is somewhat different. Many computer RPGs are single-player experiences. In these cases, if there is a group of characters played in the game, the same player controls them all. Or if multiple players work together (as in massively multiplayer online RPGs such as *World of Warcraft*), the game is structured for players to communicate over a network rather than face-to-face.[4] Crucially, no player has the part of the game master. The execution of the rules, presentation of the fictional world, portrayal of the NPCs, and shaping of the story is left to computational processes and data.

When brought to the computer, then, the core experience of story and character in RPGs shifts. In tabletop and live-action RPGs, story and character are experienced primarily through collaborative human performance. But for computer RPGs, especially single-player ones, story and character become media experiences—made interactive via computational processes. In particular, two operational logics have come to prominence in the story and NPC presentations of computer RPGs. These are *quest flags* and *dialogue trees*.

Quest Flags

Modern computer RPGs use many of the same technologies and techniques for representing their fictional worlds as other games. A character (or group) moving through an explorable three-dimensional world—with objects to pick up, NPCs to engage, and combat to resolve—is present in first-person shooters (e.g., the *Doom* series), platformers (e.g., the *Prince of Persia* series), and RPGs (e.g., the *Knights of the Old Republic* series). What changes is the emphasis in play. As the name would suggest, first-person shooters are focused on combat as the main form of play. It becomes both the primary challenge and main motivation for players moving through the world. Platformers, on the other hand, make movement itself (sometimes through a puzzling space of platforms of varying shapes and heights) the main challenge and motivation for players. RPGs, however, often work to motivate players to engage in a variety of types of play (e.g., exploration, combat, and intellectual puzzle solving) via character development set in a larger story. In particular, many RPGs give the sense that the story itself is *playable* by offering the player freedom to roam across a world infused with quests that operate at many scales, can sometimes be completed in different ways, and are often optional or available for partial completion. As each player chooses which quests to accept—as well as how, whether, and when to complete them—this creates a different story structure for each playing. Some of the player's nonquest activities may be directly related to this structure (e.g., taking on tasks in the world that earn money, in order to acquire enough to purchase an item needed for a quest), but the structure also provides one context in which even

5. I will not attempt to define quests here or present an exhaustive discussion of the types of possible quests. A good overview and proposed definition are offered by Susana Tosca (2003). Jeff Howard's *Quests* (2008) makes a detailed …

Notes continued at end of this chapter.

world exploration for its own sake can be situated.[5]

Despite the variety of experiences that players can have with quests, it is commonly observed by both players and authors that there are a limited number of types of quests—perhaps three, or even one. As Lee Sheldon points out in *Character Development and Storytelling for Games,* this observation is correct, as far as it goes, given that "the mechanism for tracking progress by the game engine is virtually identical in every quest" (2004, 227). This mechanism is the setting and checking of a collection of small pieces of data—often called "tokens" or "flags," but sometimes known by the more formal term "variables"— as the player progresses through the world. These data flags represent the state of the world as it relates to quests of varying scope. They are generally checked and set by relatively simple "scripts" that can be edited by game designers and writers (without recompiling the entire code of the game). The state of quest flags is often explicitly presented to players in the form of a personal "journal" or "notebook" that scripts update with helpful reminder texts about the current state of each quest (at the same time that flags are updated). Other quests are, while frequently signaled equally directly, instead organized around the possession and use of game world objects without messages in the journal.

Overall, this approach is notable for its simplicity of structure. In fact, it is so simple that game companies have worked to open its authoring to players who are not software developers. For example, when game developer BioWare published the game *Neverwinter Nights* (Oster, Holmes, Greig, et al. 2002), it also released the Aurora toolset for creating new spaces, objects, NPCs, and quests.

The goal, in part, was to offer players a rare opportunity in the world of computer RPGs—to play a game master, in a manner somewhat similar to tabletop RPGs, crafting the game experience of other players.[6] As in many other games, the quests of *Neverwinter Nights* are presented to the player in the form of a virtual journal.

Using Aurora, the first step in creating a quest is to begin a new category for entries in player journals, using the special purpose Journal Editor tool (shown in figure 3.1). Each entry in a category is designed to let the player know that the appropriate scripts have been activated to set the flags that are necessary for the next stage of the quest.[7] For example, one could create a journal category with three entries:

[0001] Grandfather had a signet ring that belonged to his own great-grandfather. But apparently no one has seen it since it was passed down to him—and it wasn't mentioned in his will.

[0002] Grandma would treasure this ring with the rest of Grandpa's jewelry. But the carved symbol you've seen before at your Uncle's, so he might be interested in it as more than a memento. Of course, it also looks valuable, and you could use the money you'd get from selling it.

[0003] You no longer have the ring.

Different events can trigger scripts that change the current state of the player journal. For instance, the first entry above could be added based on a conversation with the player character's grandmother, or finding and reading a letter sent to the player character's father. The same script could set a value of "true" for a flag with a name such as "lookingForRing." Dialogue trees for NPCs could be different based on this flag, offering the player the option

6. As noted in this chapter's first sidebar, *Neverwinter Nights* is a licensed computer version of the tabletop game *Dungeons & Dragons*—which remains the most popular tabletop RPG, in addition to being the first.

7. In Aurora's model, the current state of the quest journal is rarely queried by any part of the game system; it's just a method of exposing information to the player and assiduously avoiding the perils of the *Eliza* effect.

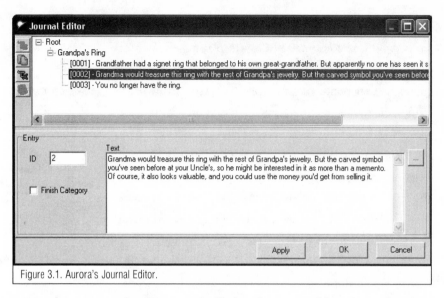

Figure 3.1. Aurora's Journal Editor.

of asking people if they know anything about the ring, leading to clues as to its location. Once the ring is found, a script fired by that event could move the journal to the next entry as well as set lookingForRing to its earlier "false" value, while a flag such as "learningAboutRing" could be set to "true."

If the game authors wish to move all players through the quest in the same way, the ring could be in a locked attic room that isn't accessible until lookingForRing is true. Alternately, the player could have the option of finding the ring before hearing about it in any other way. Quest designs that follow this latter sort of approach (forcing players through as few "gates" as possible) certainly give the player more options for how stories unfold, making the story have some of the same feel of free exploration as the graphical world.

But seeking this feeling of exploration carries a price—one that attention to the shape of processes can lessen. For example, in the case of our hypothetical family ring quest, starting by finding the ring (jumping straight to the second stage) seems unlikely to produce any problem with the flags or journal. Setting lookingForRing to false when it is already false makes no difference, and starting with the second stage of the quest works with the journal entries as written. But, to determine such things, the game author has to carefully think through every possibility—and the more freedom given to the player (as to when, how, and whether to take on and complete quests), the more the events of different quest strands need to be considered in relation to one another.

This, in turn, brings us back to the idea of simplicity. The quest flag structure is a simple one in a variety of ways. It's easy for software developers to implement, it doesn't require much in the way of computational resources (leaving both programming and processing resources free for areas of the game such as graphics, which is something most game companies value), and it can be exposed to the audience quite straightforwardly. Yet given the goal of the audience feeling able to *play* within the fictional world—not just in areas such as combat but also in terms of the stories being told—the quest flag structure quickly brings game authors to a limit point of complexity, holding back the future development of the form. I'll consider this further in my discussion below of BioWare's widely lauded single-player RPG, *KotOR*. First, however, a brief discussion of dialogue trees is in order.

Dialogue Trees

Tabletop and live-action RPGs create dialogue between characters by having two human beings improvise it. No computer process can substitute for the immediacy

8. As Dominic Arsenault pointed out during the blog-based peer review of this book, dialogue trees can provide a variety of interaction experiences for similar underlying structures. Games such as *KotOR* present the player with a selection of possible ...

Notes continued at end of this chapter.

of such an exchange (or even come close to an ability to understand free-form human language) so computer RPGs have been forced to take a different approach. As with the quest flag approach to story, the computer RPG approach to dialogue is simple both in terms of software implementation and audience comprehension. This approach is the dialogue tree.

Like the *Eliza* system, the dialogue tree model of conversation is founded on turn-taking. But what happens at each turn is utterly different. During the audience's turn, dialogue trees do not allow for the free-form textual input of *Eliza*. Instead, when interacting with a dialogue tree, the player is generally presented with a small number of options (usually ranging from one to five) for what the player's character can say. After a selection is made, the system performs the response of the NPC(s) to which the player's character is speaking. Conversation continues in this manner until the player selects a conversation-ending option (which may or may not be explicitly presented as such).[8]

Rather than NPC responses being generated by applying rules to the audience's last statement, as with *Eliza,* each NPC response is selected by traversing a hierarchically organized data structure. This is what gives the dialogue tree its name.

Figure 3.2, an image of Aurora's Conversation Editor tool for authoring dialogue trees, makes this more specific. It looks quite similar at first glance to the tool for quest journal entries. One difference, however, is that while the journal contained quest stages in an order likely to be encountered by players, the ordering of the text in the conversation editor seems rather odd:

- Yes child?
- I found grandfather's ring.
- I've been wondering about some things.
- Is there any food in the fridge?
- <FullName>, you're looking well. And dressed
    smart. What's that on your hand?
  - The scar?
    - No, the ring.
      - [link to "This ring?"]
- This ring?
  - Oh, I—I almost thought it was your grandfather's.
  Haven't seen it since we were young.
    - I miss him.
      - We all do.
        - [link to "You still think of his ring?"]
  - Excuse me. I have to go to the bathroom.
  [End conversation]
    - You still think of his ring?
      - I remember because he was so secret with it.
  There are times I wonder if he got killed for it,
  and that's why it wasn't with his things. If you
  found it, that would put me at ease. Would you look?
        - Of course.
          - Thank you so much.
        - Soon, I promise. But not right away.
          - I understand. Come back a better time.
        - One of my cousins would be better.
        Jerry's a cop.
          - You're probably right.

This odd ordering is in part a reflection of the "tree" nature of dialogue trees. Each of the two groupings above starts with an initial statement by the grandmother NPC,

9. The "[END DIALOGUE]" at this point in the image is not correct, but an artifact of Aurora. The same is true after "You still think of his ring?"

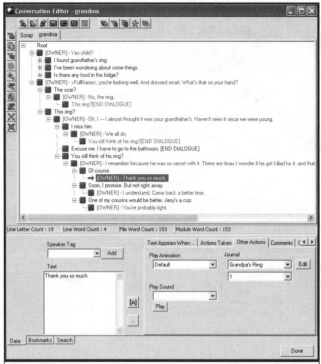

Figure 3.2. Aurora's Conversation Editor. The branches of the dialogue segment that begins "Yes child?" are collapsed in this view, with further player responses hidden.

with possible replies nested at the next level of indentation, each of which leads to a particular NPC reply (and/or the end of the conversation), which may itself have further player character statements nested at a further indentation level below. For this reason, dialogue tree segments can't be read straight through. Dialogue trees are also rarely pure tree structures. Instead, many branches make connections to other parts of the tree—as above, where both of the possible responses to the grandmother's first question ("What's that on your hand?") lead to the same place, because of a link from "No, the ring" to "This ring?" [9] Given this, understanding how players will experience a segment of a dialogue tree requires both traversing the hierarchical tree structure and following the links that connect the structure's branches.

Another type of odd ordering, that of the two primary tree segments, emerges from common authoring practices. Dialogue trees check and set the same types of flags employed by quests—and different sets of dialogue are appropriate at different moments. The expanded segment of dialogue above (that begins "<FullName>, you're looking well") is appropriate for the first time that the player character meets the grandmother, which only happens once, so it is placed at the bottom. The most commonly encountered dialogue is placed at the top, as the default, and only altered (or skipped) if particular flags have certain values. If the grandmother were to have only two possible segments in her dialogue tree, this could be accomplished simply by having a flag called, for example, "firstTimeTalked" that is initially set to true. The default dialogue segment would be skipped whenever firstTimeTalked is true, and entry into the second dialogue segment could trigger a script to set firstTimeTalked to false.[10]

Chris Bateman, in *Game Writing: Narrative Skills for Videogames*, is generally negative about dialogue trees. He writes:

> Despite the name, dialogue trees are seldom true trees but rather converging and diverging chains of conversation. They can be a nightmare to work with, and the benefits they provide are somewhat minimal. Nonetheless, some players greatly appreciate the illusion that they have control over what their character can say, with the consequence that dialogue trees remain important, especially in cRPG games. (2006, 277)

10. In an actual game that included the Grandfather's Ring quest, the grandmother conversation would need another flag structure, given that the initial dialogue must be different if the ring has been found before the first conversation with …

Notes continued at end of this chapter.

Figure 3.3. Receiving a quest from Grandma in the example module.

My view of dialogue trees is rather different. First, one remarkable thing about dialogue trees is how little illusion they present, especially when compared with systems like *Eliza*. Each NPC will only respond to a limited number of things—and these are plainly presented. Further, because dialogue tree traversal options are "converging and diverging" (often, for default dialogue segments, in a cyclic pattern so that the final options at the ends of branches include a return to the trunk), the fact that dialogues are structured as tree traversals becomes clear even to first-time players.

While this is certainly a (poor) "illusion" of real conversation, it isn't an illusion of control over what the player character says, as Bateman suggests. Rather, in most RPGs it is an important method of making gameplay decisions—with different dialogue options altering game variables in different ways. The range of possible results from dialogue tree choices is vast, including, in popular

RPGs, either accepting or declining quests (and rewards for those quests), defusing tense situations or initiating battles, learning more about NPCs (and perhaps unlocking quests related to their personal lives), and changing how NPCs feel about the player character in more emotional ways (ranging from feelings of loyalty and honesty to romantic subplots).[11]

At a technical level, it is correct to say that all these things boil down to menu selections. But successfully traversing these menus can be a tricky business—one made easier for players who draw on their knowledge of the game's fictional world. In addition, it is one of the most direct means by which players can express the role they imagine for their character(s): agreeing or refusing to do things for others, acting out of kindness or mercenary motivation, telling the truth or spreading falsehood, and so on. Building such consequential choices into dialogue trees is also quite simple for authors. In figure 3.2, the lower portion of the window shows how a few menu selections are sufficient to cause a line of dialogue ("Thank you so much") to also update the player's journal—in this case, moving the quest in the Grandpa's Ring category to entry number one. Figure 3.3 shows this taking place in the game.

But, despite the ease of this basic piece of authoring, Bateman is certainly correct that dialogue trees can be a nightmare to work with—as can the larger method of storytelling that they form in combination with quest flags. Further, this might be one of their smaller problems, as I discuss below in the context of a particular example. First, though, a broader look at the logics of these operations is in order.

11. Further, as Benjamin Grandis pointed out during the online peer review of this book, a number of RPGs "experiment with the ability for even your party members to grow to resent you, often for quite complex reasons which tie into the plot and yet are …

Notes continued at end of this chapter.

Quest and Dialogue Logics

The primary operational logic at work in *Eliza* is transformation—each statement from the audience is immediately transformed into *Eliza*'s next statement, using a set of processes in a manner specified by the data of the current script. In computer systems parlance, we might say that *Eliza* conversations are nearly "stateless." *Eliza* doesn't model the ongoing state of the conversation, using its script differently depending on prior interactions, except to avoid excessive repetition of the use of certain rules.[12]

The combination of quest flags and dialogue trees, on the other hand, is in some ways all about state. The quest flag logic is precisely one of milestone-based progression. Quest flag fictions are ordered sets of discrete units. What matters is where the player is located—at which milestone along the path—and this is precisely what is exposed through the mechanism of the player journal. In some cases the beginning of the progression may be skipped and the end may never be reached, but at each moment of play the fiction is at a particular point, among a small number of predefined points arranged in order.

The logic of the dialogue tree, in contrast, is essentially that of the directed graph. Rather than modeling conversation as a set of discrete exchanges with no context (as in *Eliza*), the dialogue tree always locates the current conversational state at one particular point, among a set of predetermined points, from which navigation is possible to other points via predetermined links. As with the milestones of quest flags, it's usually impossible to go backward—the graph is directed toward "progress" in the conversation—but it is also usually possible to loop back to the main trunk of the currently available conversation, if occasionally rather circuitously.

In other words, somewhat like the graphical logics of games, the logics of dialogue trees and quest flags are about *location* in a given space. But while the visual spaces of games are often simulated in a manner that supports almost innumerable possible locations, the milestones of quest flags and graphs of dialogue trees mark out all the possible positions (and transitions between them) ahead of time. This mismatch proves problematic.

An Example: *Star Wars: Knights of the Old Republic*

The Game Developers Choice Awards are the Oscars of the game industry—the award with which members of a creative industry recognize achievements of their own. In 2004, game studio BioWare walked away with three awards that are of particular note for this discussion: Game of the Year, Original Game Character of the Year, and Excellence in Writing. All of these were awarded for BioWare's RPG *Star Wars: Knights of the Old Republic* (*KotOR*), which also won game of the year awards from a slew of industry publications. While certainly not the most recent major RPG, it provides a good example of the strengths and weaknesses of the quest flag and dialogue tree logics.

KotOR's Successes

KotOR uses quest flags and dialogue trees to reward and sustain engagement with its fictional world; establish patterns that, when altered, produce small moments of surprise and pleasure; and direct the audience's attention to a series of things that must be accomplished through

13. This is generally done quite artfully. Even an exceptionally awkward-seeming opening exposition is later given deeper resonances as players progress through the main quest. It is revealed that the characters surrounding the player …

Notes continued at end of this chapter.

play—which, like a magician's misdirection, keeps audience attention away from larger story developments until the moment they are revealed.[13] A main quest provides the spine of the story. It represents a massive undertaking on the part of the player character to—what else?—intervene in events that will shape the history of the galaxy. In a manner typical for multistage quest design, the desired intervention requires learning the location at which these events are taking place, which requires gathering data from partial maps on several planets, which requires getting to the locations of these partial maps, which in each case can be accomplished in multiple ways, with each approach having multiple steps that may have smaller quests as prerequisites, and so on.

Against this epic backdrop (with its many components, some rather mundane) other, optional quests are presented. Some involve developing the relationships between the main player character and her or his traveling companions. Others involve taking a role in the events happening on particular planets, often with a decidedly interpersonal element (e.g., a wife begs you to find evidence to clear her husband of murder charges, which soon leads to revelations of his infidelity, which you must choose whether to discuss with them). Some are quite small, such as discovering your ship has smuggled cargo aboard, being given the code for the container, and being offered good payment for the goods by a crime syndicate representative. In cases such as this last one, the player need only decide what the characters will do with the one-stage quest—and then enact the decision in the game's fictional world (travel to the places, interact with the objects, and talk with the appropriate NPCs).

In addition to all these activities, there are also others embedded in the fictional world—ranging from the pleasures of exploration and spatial mastery to "minigames" of card playing and racing. Some of the minigames, in turn, can unlock additional quests and NPC interactions as well as provide resources useful in completing parts of the game to which they are less directly connected.

Given all this, conventional wisdom has it that playing a major RPG takes experienced gamers something like forty hours. But fans of the genre often spend longer, indulging in many optional activities. In addition, many play through the same game multiple times. This is particularly true for games, like *KotOR*, that provide different gameplay options to characters that approach the world with different ethical stances.

What drives players to spend forty, eighty, or more hours with a computer RPG? If we look only at the quest journal, where the operations of quest flag logics are exposed to the player, the appearance is of a massive indulgence in the pleasures of the to-do list. And certainly there is some of that. But, more centrally, *KotOR* is constantly providing doses of narrative closure and transition—from the small satisfactions of quest stages to the holistic sense of a planet's stories, characters, geography, and history that can be developed over one or many playings. Jill Walker Rettberg talks about the pleasure found in learning the quest-based fictions of a place, the "network of fragments, most of which are not necessary to experience the game fully, and yet which cumulate into a rich experience of a storied world" (2007, 310).

At the same time, beyond its narrative pleasures, *KotOR* is also continually providing other reasons to keep going,

14. In addition, *KotOR* also provides a quantification, exposed to the audience, of the different ethical approaches available in many RPGs. This is connected to the notion of the "force" that pervades the Star Wars fictional universe. Some …

Notes continued at end of this chapter.

to move one part of things along just one more step. A powerful element of this can be found in the rewards given with each bit of quest closure. Some rewards are as simple as cash that can be used to purchase items in the game, bribe recalcitrant NPCs, help those in need, and so on. When brought to fruition, many story elements also deliver experience points (XP), another convention borrowed from tabletop RPGs. As characters accumulate experience they increase in "level" and become more capable in the game world. Each new level is achieved at a particular number of XP, and the drive to hit the next number is another motivator for the "just one more thing" mind-set that can keep players at *KotOR* for hours after they'd planned to stop for the night.[14] It is this quantified progression of a primary player character that has led William Huber (2009) to call the RPG genre a "statistical bildungsroman."

And at forty, eighty, or more hours, the extent of audience engagement with *KotOR* is certainly more akin to a thick German novel of personal development than, for instance, a film (or even a season of television). But, again, a better analogy is probably with a tabletop RPG campaign—into which players can easily invest a similar amount of time. As in many RPG campaigns, *KotOR* works to create a sense of flexible story making couched in world exploration and character development. To this end, the player's character can visit planets in different orders and multiple times; quest items can be found at different points in the quests to which they're connected; and necessary items and information are often available in multiple ways. Nevertheless, while these things are also true of tabletop RPG campaigns, in *KotOR* and other computer RPGs they must be managed through quest flags and dialogue trees (rather than human memory, improvisation, and creativity). As mentioned earlier, this creates difficulties for game authors.

KotOR's Troubles

Much of the narrative power of *KotOR* comes from the ways that it makes playable structures out of tried-and-true narratives. A self-contained example of this can be seen in one of the optional quests on the planet of Dantooine, relatively early in the game: the feud between the Sandrale and Matale families. I encountered this quest while playing the "Platinum Hits" edition of the Xbox version of *KotOR*—and it is worth noting that the experience of those playing other versions might be different.

After being warned that tensions between the two prominent families were in danger of overflowing into a violent civil conflict, my party traveled south to the Sandral estate and spoke with the patriarch, Nurik Sandral. He told us that he felt great sorrow over the disappearance of the young Matale heir, Shen, but knew nothing about it. He told us that his own son, Casus, had been missing for some time—and speculated the two might have met similar fates amid the dangers of Dantooine.

Nurik asked us to show ourselves out. But shortly after this his daughter, Rahasia, appeared. After I selected some friendly things for my player character to say to her, she revealed that her father had in fact kidnapped Shen Matale. In typically Shakespearian fashion, she and Shen had fallen in love. She gave my party a key to a side entry of the Sandral estate, making it possible for us to sneak in and rescue Shen. Once we reached Shen he refused to leave without Rahasia—and the result was Shen, Rahasia, and the three members of my *KotOR* party all coming out the side entrance at once, where we found ourselves confronted by the patriarchs of both families and their battle droids (figure 3.4).

After some tense dialogue-tree discussions (in which I chose statements supportive of the lovers and designed to defuse the conflict), Shen and Rahasia ran off to live in the safety of the Jedi enclave, while their fathers just barely held back from igniting a conflagration. Later, while exploring a portion of the planet further north, my party came on the Matale family compound. The guard droid granted us an audience with the patriarch, Ahlan Matale, who we had last seen as his son ran off to the enclave with Rahasia. Ahlan proceeded to demand at length that something be done to find his son—outlining his suspicions that the Sandral family had kidnapped Shen.[15] He offered us a reward (which sounded more like a bribe) should his son be found. I suspected this inappropriate dialogue tree segment might be active because of a simple flag of the firstTimeTalked variety, so I took my party away and then returned to the compound. But flag structure was apparently organized in a different way. When we returned, Ahlan Matale came out again to demand an investigation into the possible kidnapping of the son he had already seen rescued from kidnapping. This illustrates one type of problem with the quest flag and dialogue tree approach, a type that results in inappropriate events.

The other major type of problem was illustrated shortly, when my party discovered the body of Casus Sandral. An amateur archaeologist, Casus had apparently been killed by wild animals while undertaking a dig in a dangerous area. We immediately went to the Sandral estate with Casus's diary, in order to share it with his worried family. But the estate was shut down entirely, without even the droid out front who had greeted us on the first visit. This second type of problem is visible when the game seemingly arbitrarily shuts off quest possibilities that have the force of narrative drive behind them.

Both types of problems emerge, most commonly, at the juncture between the freely explorable fictional world and the rigid structures of quest flags and dialogue trees. I encountered these problems regularly in my playing of *KotOR*. Just as the game expected me to visit the Matale estate before the Sandral estate, and produced inappropriate events when I visited in a different order, the same was true on a planetary scale. For example, I visited the home planet of one character who joined my party, Jolee Bindo, later in the game than *KotOR*'s dialogue tree structure expected. As a result, much of the conversation between him and the main player character consisted of his darkly hinting at truths that had already been revealed in a dramatic fashion. Each conversation with Bindo undermined the sense of *KotOR* having a consistent fictional world. At the same time, the conversation path with another key character, Carth Onassi, was shut off entirely after not being pursued in the expected manner—despite the fact that there was clearly much to discuss.

These problems do not spring from poor work at BioWare. It would be unreasonable, for instance, to expect lead writer Drew Karpyshyn and his team to have written (and sent for voice acting) different versions of Onassi's lines for each possible state of the story. As Chris Crawford has observed, such approaches "are always too

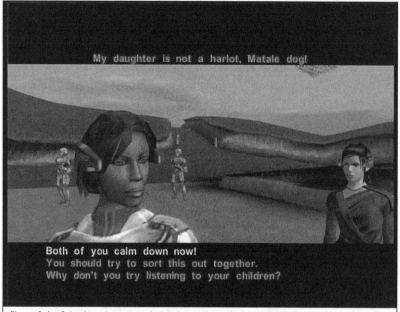

Figure 3.4a. Selecting what to say during the confrontation outside the Sandral estate.

Figure 3.4b. After defusing the potential battle, a journal entry is added, experience points are gained, light side points are gained, and items are lost.

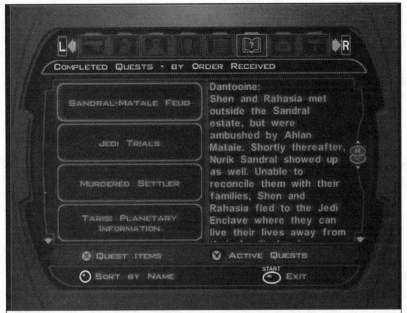

Figure 3.4c. The updated journal summarizes the quest and its outcome, including the family confrontation and the lovers' move to the Jedi enclave.

Figure 3.4d. The unexpected conversation that followed.

16. Another way of avoiding such problems was employed in the next game on which Karpyshyn was the lead writer: Mass Effect (Hudson et al. 2007). The long-term development of personal relationships with crew members …

Notes continued at end of this chapter.

much work for the designer and not enough meat for the player" (2004, 126). And it is unlikely that the tools at their disposal offered any more elegant (and tractable) method of addressing the situation. Once the sequence of expected timings between quest flags and dialogue sections was broken it might have made sense to allow the player character to ask personal questions and be brushed off, but this is essentially the same as shutting down conversation, as the *KotOR* team did.[16]

Which is to say that problems such as these spring from a poor fit between the simple, brittle structures of quest flags and dialogue trees, and the ambitious, flexible game design they are being used to support. Those of us familiar with the logic of milestone-based progression—from business plans, grant proposals, employee evaluations, and so on—know that any detailed set of milestones will generally meet one of two possible fates. First, as the situation evolves, it can become clear that the milestones will be revised for one or more reasons: the steps may not be what one originally thought, may not happen in the order originally thought, or might need to be divided up differently. Second, an alternative fate is that the milestones themselves become a fetish, irrationally driving behavior in a situation that they clearly no longer reflect. Even in a world simulated as partially as that of *KotOR,* precreated milestones still become an uneasy fit with the evolving situation. Unfortunately, only the second of these two fates is possible for *KotOR*'s milestones, which cannot be revised by the system.

Given this situation, the prospects for fiction in games may seem grim (perhaps particularly for multiplayer online games, see sidebar: Individual Fictions in Shared Worlds).

But there is a widely practiced alternative approach to the combination of game and fiction—one that is more successful in important respects.

An Alternative:
Prince of Persia: The Sands of Time

At the 2004 Game Developers Choice Awards, *KotOR* had some competition. Another nominee for Game of the Year, a game that won the awards for Excellence in Game Design and Excellence in Programming, was *Prince of Persia: The Sands of Time* (*PoP*).

PoP is a strong example of game fiction in its own right—which is no surprise, given that its main writer and designer was Jordan Mechner, a legend in the game design field for his pioneering games *Karateka* (1984), the original *Prince of Persia* (1989), and *The Last Express* (1997). Mechner is credited with bringing cinematic storytelling to computer games, pushing forward techniques from the realistic modeling of human motion to the integration of an overall story into an action game structure. Mechner is also an accomplished independent filmmaker—writing, directing, and editing films such as *Chávez Ravine: A Los Angeles Story* (2005), a documentary about a 1950s community evicted from land they were told would become a public housing project (where they would return to live) only to see Dodger Stadium constructed instead, through a process of greed, hypocrisy, and anticommunist hysteria.[17]

Bearing this in mind, it should be no surprise that *PoP* is one of the strongest examples of an entirely different approach to game fiction from that of *KotOR*.[18] Rather than attempt to make the game's story a playable

17. As of this writing Mechner is also involved in filmic storytelling from another angle—as screenwriter and executive producer of the upcoming Walt Disney Pictures/Jerry Bruckheimer feature film *Prince of Persia: The Sands of Time* …

18. This is one of the reasons that *PoP* has received a significant amount of scholarly attention. I am aware of three authors who offer particularly extended engagements. Drew Davidson (2008) provides a detailed, thoughtful reflection on the experience …

Notes continued at end of this chapter.

Individual Fictions in Shared Worlds

The mismatch between a simulated, explorable spatial world and fictional progression implemented in inflexible milestones can become even more pronounced in massively multiplayer online games. The typical design for such games requires that objects be present in the world for all players. This means they can be encountered by players who have not yet received quests to give them context—and they must reappear to be available for other players even if they have been removed by one particular player.

I experienced these things from the outset of playing *EverQuest II* (Blakely et al. 2004). I began in the Queen's Colony, the new player area for the city of Qeynos. I received my initial quest and then went exploring, encountering monsters, quest givers, and other players. Often I would kill a number of some type of monster (such as a Morak Devourer) in a particular area and then, a few minutes later, be given a quest to do exactly what I had just done, with no option to reply that I'd already done it.

This helped prepare me for my experience in the Abandoned Village area. There I fought some monsters and found a strange statue. I clicked on the statue, but it wouldn't respond. In a corner of the area I met Sorcerer Oofala, but he had nothing to say to me. Only later, after my character died, did I end up back in the starting area and talk again to the initial quest giver, Murrar Shar. He sent me to Cleric Mara'Vaen, who also had not been interested in talking when I encountered her earlier. But this time she had a quest, I completed it, and then she sent me to find Oofala (again), who sent me to destroy the strange statues I hadn't been able to get a response from earlier. At this point I could click to destroy them, if not interrupted by combat during the work.

After I destroyed the last of the statues, an enemy called the Dark Blademaster appeared. I defeated him, took his shield, and spent a few moments shifting things around in my inventory so that I was using the shield. As I did this, the Dark Blademaster reappeared! Already wounded, I decided to run back to Oofala, whereupon the Blademaster stopped following. He had reappeared, of course, so that other players on the same server could also complete the quest that Oofala then gave me: to defeat the Blademaster. The only way to progress was to go back and fight the Blademaster again, this time wearing the shield I'd acquired from the time before last I had fought him.

one (a story that changes shape depending on how play proceeds), *PoP* has a linear, semicinematic story, with a sense of inevitability artfully fused with a context for player struggle. The struggle, specifically, consists of innovative platforming action and acrobatic combat. For games such as *PoP*, the question is how to make this kind of combination, between audience-controlled gameplay and linear story, most productive.

The typical structure for such combinations, in the computer game industry, is simple alternation. The audience is given moments and spaces of play that, when completed, yield scripted sequences that tell the story.[19] Because this model involves so little connection between story and gameplay, game writers are often employed only at the end of game production. The game's play mechanics, spaces, and even characters are designed before the writer arrives (Bateman, Boon, Buckley, et al. 2003). The writer's task is to create a set of scripted sequences that will tie them together and provide an overall context. The results are frequently unsatisfying and can feel, for good reason, quite arbitrary. Mechner's games—like those of other designer/writers such as Tim Schafer (the creator of *Grim Fandango* [1998], *Psychonauts* [2005], and other well-regarded titles)—instead work to conceive the story and gameplay as integrated entities.

The story of *PoP* begins with a war of aggression fought for reasons of greed. The war's booty includes a massive hourglass containing the Sands of Time. The possession of these sands, however, turns out to be more curse than blessing.[20] When the briefly victorious Persian king seeks to enrich his friend with a present of the Sands, the result instead is to destroy the friend's palace and turn nearly

19. These scripted sequences can be prerendered "cut scenes" (essentially, computer animation files played by the game system), in-engine cut scenes (scripted scenes rendered by the game engine, rather than another animation …

20. The parallels with U.S. foreign policy at the time of the game's production, before and during the 2003 invasion of Iraq, soon began to seem prophetic. They are also unlikely to be accidental, given Mechner's description of an "anti-war …

Notes continued at end of this chapter.

everyone into sand demons. The prince's dagger, looted from the same palace as the hourglass, is the key used to unleash the sands. Both of the game's main NPCs—a woman, Farah, taken prisoner in the looted palace, and the vizier who betrayed the palace's owner and incited the unleashing of the sands—suggest that the dagger can also be used to improve things. But the vizier has removed the hourglass to the highest tower of the ruined palace.

Mechner describes this as the result of simplifying the game's story as much as possible. In terms of traditional story, it is certainly efficient, with only three characters: a hero, a sidekick/love interest, and a villain. It is also efficient in terms of gameplay. For platforming, it provides a challenge (moving through a ruined palace) and a motivation (reaching the hourglass). For interacting with most NPCs, it supplies a motivation for combat and an explanation of why other modes of interaction are not available (they're sand demons). In other words, it focuses attention on what games do well (movement in space and combat) and offers an explanation for avoiding what they don't do well (interactions with characters) as well as a reason for moving forward. This is already better than most games, but *PoP* goes further in a number of ways.

Centrally, it creates connections between gameplay and story. The most obvious of these is the dagger. It is both a key item in the story and the focus of what is innovative about the gameplay. The dagger can store the Sands of Time, making it possible for the hero to use powers that make movement and combat easier (e.g., turning back time when mistakes are made). The dagger only holds a limited amount of sand, which is replenished by withdrawing it from vanquished sand demons (a requirement lest they rise again). Story and gameplay also connect through plot twists. *PoP*'s story employs twists—including one in which the dagger is lost—that also alter the experience of gameplay. Finally, as Mechner (2007) points out in his essay "*The Sands of Time*: Crafting a Video Game Story," *PoP* also works to give as many as possible of the key story moments to the player, in gameplay—as when the prince must face his own father, now a sand demon.

PoP also makes choices at the level of process that are significantly different from games like *KotOR*. Obviously, given that there is only one, linear story strand, there is no complicated system of quest flags. There are also no dialogue trees. *PoP* instead uses what is sometimes called an "event-based" dialogue system. In essence, conversation is removed from the playable elements of the game. Instead of players choosing to talk with particular NPCs, certain events trigger conversation and voice-over. In most cases these are not presented as interruptions to gameplay—as happens in many games—but rather layered over it. The prince may think to himself as the player causes him to run down a hallway or swing from a pole. Farah may make comments about the prince's progress (or failures) in moving through a particularly difficult area, as determined by the player's actions. Or, in one case, the player may directly elicit a response from Farah—by moving the prince into a first-person camera mode and "staring" at her.

PoP also shares one primary tool for NPC interaction with games like *KotOR* as well as nearly every type of game that includes NPCs: the finite-state machine (FSM). While on an abstract level all computers could be described as FSMs, in computer game NPC logic FSMs tend to be used a particular way. Each of an NPC's basic behaviors

21. I am using the
words *game fictions*
generically, to refer to
fictions within games.
In *More Than a Game*,
Barry Atkins uses the
words *game fiction* to
refer to those games
he sees as "having
a central narrative
impetus, that develop
story over time …

Notes continued at end
of this chapter.

is defined as a "state" (e.g., patrol, attack, or retreat) with particular rules for transitioning from the current state to other states. For example, an NPC could be designed to move through a patrol animation (a patrol state) until an enemy is noticed (transition to an attack state) and continue attacking until the enemy is defeated (transition to patrol state) or the NPC's health is below a defined threshold (transition to a retreat state). There might be no rule allowing for direct transition from patrol to retreat—which would make sense generally, but not if the NPC is already badly wounded from previous combat. As with quest flags and dialogue trees, FSMs are simple to explain, easy to implement in software, low in their use of computational resources, and an authoring nightmare over a certain level of complexity. Luckily, they're a perfect fit for the exceedingly simple behavior of sand demons, who attack on sight and never retreat, as found in *PoP*.

The end result, for *PoP*, is an experience elegantly designed to compensate for the crippling limitations of the processes used to represent story and character in today's computer games. And this opens up the next question.

The Game Fiction Dilemma

Authors of game fictions have worked hard—through conventions such as the quest-tracking journal and tree-driven conversations presented as menus—to avoid the *Eliza* effect. Rather than conceal the operations of their processes, game fiction authors seek to expose them to the audience. But, despite this, game fictions still face a dilemma remarkably similar to that outlined at the end of the previous chapter.[21]

Both *KotOR* and *PoP* take advantage of what games do

well—in particular, simulated movement through space and combat. The relatively free-form actions allowed to players in these areas might be seen in parallel with the free-form text composition allowed to both those interacting with *Eliza/Doctor* and the students involved in Garfinkel's yes/no therapy experiment. The difference, again, is in what changes to the state of the system and influence on future operations can be produced by this interaction.

PoP's fiction, like Garfinkel's experiment, has an extremely narrow range of possible responses to interaction. Either the player's actions successfully move the fiction to the next stage (a progression signaled to the player by the triggering of a scripted sequence) or they don't. The story system is, as players put it, "on rails"—and its structure can be completely exposed to the audience by letting them know when they are departing for the next metaphoric station. Meanwhile, *PoP*'s NPCs are mostly only available for combat (the sand demons). The major exception (Farah) will occasionally offer a linguistic interjection in response to nonlinguist actions in the world, but this is another narrow interaction conduit.

KotOR's fiction, on the other hand, while not allowing the free-form textual input of *Eliza/Doctor*, does accept many more actions in the world as input into its system of quest flags and dialogue trees (e.g., whether, when, and how to take on quests, take quest actions, speak with NPCs, move between worlds, etc.). Further, as this chapter has shown, such a system can have many more elements to it than the railroad system of games such as *PoP* (authors can produce huge amounts of data for the quest flag and dialogue tree processes, different subsets and orderings of which can appear with each playing). The result, as with an *Eliza* conversation, is that the number of potential outcomes is huge. Unfortunately, there is a mismatch between the great variety of situations in which *KotOR* is expected to perform a fiction and the simple model of fiction and character embodied in *KotOR*'s processes—just as there is a massive mismatch between the complexity of human language to which *Eliza* must respond and its extremely simple model of conversation (as a series of transformations). The result, in both cases, is a tendency toward breakdown that takes a shape determined by the underlying processes. And, as with *Eliza,* the processes of *KotOR* are of a basically uninteresting shape.

To put it succinctly, the practices of the mainstream game industry present authors of digital fictions with two bad options for going forward. One is to "design around" breakdown, as *PoP* does, and essentially forfeit the processing power of digital media at the level of the fiction. The other option is to attempt to layer a semiflexible story—organized as a set of ordered milestone progressions—over a much more flexible game world. This creates a space of play that, if embraced by players, leads to unsatisfying breakdown.

In short, the time is ripe for a new approach to game fiction. But just as *Doom* could not be built on the approach to graphics in *Myst,* this will require an approach to fiction and character that is fundamentally different, that is more expressive and flexible than quest flags and dialogue trees. Luckily, this work does not need to begin from scratch. It can start instead by building on a history that has been present as a strand of practice within the artificial intelligence community since the time of *Eliza.* The coming chapters explore this history.

Notes

1. Some games, of course, can hardly be said to engaage fiction at all. No one wants a story with their *Tetris*—and its "fictional world" of falling blocks barely supports the phrase. Given the sometimes-contentious nature of critical discussion around the relationship between games and fiction, I should perhaps also make it clear that I do not believe any games "are" stories or narratives in a classic narratological sense. Rather, following Espen Aarseth's call for discussion of "quest games" (2004), I propose here to give careful attention to the specific operational logics of quests and dialogue trees in computer RPGs. For readers interested in a more detailed discussion of games and narratology, I suggest chapter 8 of *Avatars of Story* by Marie-Laure Ryan (2006).

2. As tabletop RPGs have come to encompass much broader areas of life than combat, different games (and player groups) have diverged in their treatment of these elements. One movement is toward a generalization of the statistical models used for war game combat. They have been employed for many additional elements of character progression and play. The other movement is toward an emphasis on creative expression that may resist quantification, or at least be decided by the logics of character and fiction rather than chance, leading to "diceless" RPGs. Players who prefer each emphasis are sometimes called "roll players" and "role players," respectively.

3. The most famously Lovecraft-inspired game is *Call of Cthulhu* (Petersen 1981), while *Over the Edge* (Tweet 1992) is a game inspired by both Burroughs and Philip K. Dick. At the same time, as Jose Zagal reminded me in the blog-based peer review of this book, some RPG systems—such as *GURPS* (Jackson 1986)—are designed to be "generic," rather than rooted in a specific fictional world or even a specific type of fictional world. Finally, the games of Costikyan's that I'm referencing are *Toon* (1984) and *Bestial Acts* (1993), respectively. Together with the innovative RPGs *The Extraordinary Adventures of Baron Munchausen* by James Wallis (1998) and *Puppetland* by John Tynes (1999), *Bestial Acts* is reprinted in *Second Person* (2007), a book I edited with Pat Harrigan.

4. Though many massively multiplayer online play groups, including some in which I have participated, include face-to-face interaction between some players. And there are a variety of other hybrid forms that combine elements of in-person and computer RPG play. For example, during the online peer review of this book, Sarah Toton drew attention to the web sites Obsidian Portal and Gleemax (<http://www.obsidianportal.com> and <http://www.gleemax.com>). The first of these is an independently produced content management system for RPG players that focuses specifically on "fictional" elements, providing a blog for chronicling adventures and a wiki (divided into areas for the party and game master) for keeping track of the campaign world. Gleemax, on the other hand, is a site developed by publisher WotC for online play, social networking, and general reading about games. Toton's comment reminded me that we should also consider hybrids such as the Living Greyhawk *Dungeons & Dragons* campaign of the WotC-supported RPGA. As the web site explains:

> The Living Greyhawk campaign is an immense game played out in regional events throughout the real world. The continent of the Flanaess in the game world is divided into several nations and political states. These nations are mapped onto sections of the real world. Your real world location determines the default home region for you and your characters in the game world. When you travel to different areas of the real world, your character journeys with you to the corresponding locales in the Flanaess. Each region has a special flavor setting it apart from other regions, allowing you to immerse yourself in the intrigues of your home region or join the turmoil in other regions. (Wizards of the Coast 2005)

5. I will not attempt to define quests here or present an exhaustive discussion of the types of possible quests. A good overview and proposed definition are offered by Susana Tosca (2003). Jeff Howard's *Quests* (2008) makes a detailed engagement with relevant literary history and theory—and also offers design exercises using the Aurora toolkit discussed in this section.

6. As noted in this chapter's first sidebar, *Neverwinter Nights* is a licensed computer version of the tabletop game *Dungeons & Dragons*—which remains the most popular tabletop RPG, in addition to being the first.

7. In Aurora's model, the current state of the quest journal is rarely queried by any part of the game system; it's just a method of exposing information to the player and assiduously avoiding the perils of the *Eliza* effect.

8. As Dominic Arsenault pointed out during the blog-based peer review of this book, dialogue trees can provide a variety of interaction experiences for similar underlying structures. Games such as *KotOR* present the player with a selection of possible texts for their character to say (presumably verbatim). When one is selected, the player character does not perform it on-screen; the act of player selection takes the conversational place of that text being uttered by the character. A rather different approach is taken by games such as *Indigo Prophecy* (Cage et al. 2005) and *Mass Effect* (Hudson et al. 2007). In these, the player is presented with short indications of the types of things that their character can say. After one is selected, a potentially surprising performance from the character will result—as when, early in *Mass Effect*, players may be taken aback to find their character striking Dr. Manuel, after choosing less supportive alternatives in the conversation with the shocked scientist. *Indigo Prophecy* also adds an interesting timed element to the selection of dialogue options, enforcing something more like conversational pacing (in games like *Mass Effect* characters will await a response indefinitely), and putting some pressure on the strategic decision making involved. A variety of other interface strategies exist, from having players choose keywords for discussion topics (e.g., *The Elder Scrolls IV: Oblivion* [Rolston et al. 2006]—which also offers literal things to say and actions to take), to the selection of punctuation and icons (e.g., *Sam & Max Hit the Road* [Purcell et al. 1993]—which is an earlier example of surprising character performances from dialogue tree options, as Darius Kazemi pointed out in a comment on Grand Text Auto). An overview of common dialogue system organizations is provided in *Gamasutra* by Brent Ellison (2008).

9. The "[END DIALOGUE]" at this point in the image is not correct, but an artifact of Aurora. The same is true after "You still think of his ring?"

10. In an actual game that included the Grandfather's Ring quest, the grandmother conversation would need another flag structure, given that the initial dialogue must be different if the ring has been found before the first conversation with the grandmother.

11. Further, as Benjamin Grandis pointed out during the online peer review of this book, a number of RPGs "experiment with the ability for even your party members to grow to resent you, often for quite complex reasons which tie into the plot and yet are quite avoidable." In some cases the results of character relationship choices are dramatic. For example, while playing *Mass Effect*, it is quite easy to select dialogue and quest options that fail to create trust with party member Wrex. This can lead to his death—in some scenarios, at the hand of the main player character.

12. And of course *Eliza* also makes an occasional fallback on precreated transformations when the most recent audience statement contains no keywords.

13. This is generally done quite artfully. Even an exceptionally awkward-seeming opening exposition is later given deeper resonances as players progress through the main quest. It is revealed that the characters surrounding the player character, who at first seem to be involved in laborious exposition, are actually part of an elaborate deception—aimed, of course, at both the player and her character. At the same time, these interactions also serve the necessary purpose of filling in the player about things her character would normally already know. Such strategies are important not only to RPGs but also to digital fictions more generally, and in some cases especially so. For example, Jeremy Douglass (2007) has written insightfully about a strand of interactive fiction work that has turned the discovery of the player character's identity and situation into the central element of the work.

14. In addition, *KotOR* also provides a quantification, exposed to the audience, of the different ethical approaches available in many RPGs. This is connected to the notion of the "force" that pervades the Star Wars fictional universe. Some quest actions are considered "light side" (those that display traits such as compassion and generosity) while others are considered "dark side" (those that exhibit traits such as selfishness and a taste for needless violence). When these are completed, the player character is awarded a certain number of points that move them along the spectrum between light and dark. Often the dark option is an easier route through the quest objectives, creating a game mechanic for the deep-rooted Star Wars theme of the temptations of the dark side. These choices also alter how the rest of the game is played; for example, some items may only be employed by those on the light or dark ends of the spectrum.

15. Attempting to reproduce this outcome, Colin Wheelock discovered that Ahlan Matale's irrational behavior is only exhibited if the player scores a "light side" point during the confrontation outside the Sandral compound.

16. Another way of avoiding such problems was employed in the next game on which Karpyshyn was the lead writer: *Mass Effect* (Hudson et al. 2007). The long-term development of personal relationships with crew members is almost entirely restricted to conversations that happen while on board the ship, where characters are mostly separated from one another. This means that interaction contexts for each character are much more restricted. In addition to such work to avoid problematic complexity, *Mass Effect* also does more to account for what has already been learned on other planets in the dialogue for each individual planet. The result is a feeling of less temporal coherence in the development of personal relationships but more temporal coherence in the other elements of the plot. While I had been hoping for interactions in *Mass Effect* to be less restricted than *KotOR*'s, moving in the opposite direction did lead to an overall increase in logical coherence.

Which is not to say that logical problems don't crop up, though they are generally at a smaller scale. For example, when exploring the planet Trebin in *Mass Effect* I noticed something on the vehicle's scanner. It turned out to be a mine entrance. With Kaidan and Tali in my party, I entered the mine and fought a number of Husks. After the battle concluded my party members commented that the researchers (whose disappearance led to our visit) must have found something that turned them into monsters.

Next we exited the mine, got back in our vehicle, and drove over to the research base. Kaidan, who had just been commenting on the fate of the researchers, said, "Where *is* everybody?" Then we entered the base and looked at one of the computers. Tali said the logs indicated that the team discovered "some kind of alien technology"—the technology she'd just been talking about, the horrible results of which we'd just seen.

17. As of this writing Mechner is also involved in filmic storytelling from another angle—as screenwriter and executive producer of the upcoming Walt Disney Pictures/Jerry Bruckheimer feature film *Prince of Persia: The Sands of Time*, directed by Mike Newell and starring Jake Gyllenhaal, Gemma Arterton, Sir Ben Kingsley, and Alfred Molina.

18. This is one of the reasons that *PoP* has received a significant amount of scholarly attention. I am aware of three authors who offer particularly extended engagements. Drew Davidson (2008) provides a detailed, thoughtful reflection on the experience of playing through the game—with particular attention to the relationship between story and play. Barry Atkins (2007) offers a reflection on death, time, and narration (topics central to this game, but important to games in general) in his chapter on *PoP* for *Videogame, Player, Text*. Jason Rhody (2005, 2008) has written intriguingly both on the way *PoP*'s interface establishes and controls point of view and, in a response to an essay by Mechner, on how game fictions must be understood dually through interface and involvement in the fictional world, and that successful examples (like *PoP*) operate in a manner that conjoins narrative and ludic development of the experience.

19. These scripted sequences can be prerendered "cut scenes" (essentially, computer animation files played by the game system), in-engine cut scenes (scripted scenes rendered by the game engine, rather than another animation system, but still removed from player control), or scripted sequences that take place in the engine and during which the player can still control aspects of the game.

20. The parallels with U.S. foreign policy at the time of the game's production, before and during the 2003 invasion of Iraq, soon began to seem prophetic. They are also unlikely to be accidental, given Mechner's description of an "anti-war theme" that "underlies the whole tale" (2007, 115). Of course, the sands seized by the second Bush administration yielded a less literal curse.

21. I am using the words *game fictions* generically, to refer to fictions within games. In *More Than a Game*, Barry Atkins uses the words *game fiction* to refer to those games he sees as "having a central narrative impetus, that develop story over time, rather than simply repeat with minimal difference in a move from level to level of increasing excess" (2003, 20). Jason Rhody (forthcoming) develops the term further in his dissertation, writing:

> What, then, is game fiction? In short, the term is intended to describe a category of game that draws upon and uses narrative strategies to create, maintain, and lead the user through a fictional environment in order to actualize a narrative and ludic goal. . . . [G]ame fictions are competitive, ergodic, progressive (and often episodic), and their primary goal is one of actualization. Game fictions are not limited to a single medium, although a game's particular materiality—should it include dice mixed with a game board, paper, or even the imagination—often reveals much about the game fiction in question.

Both Atkins and Rhody participated in the blog-based peer review of this book—and both seem fine with me using *game fiction* generically, while still using the words as a more specific term in their own work.

Chapter 4
Making Models

Implementable Models

Games are systems—and these systems have varying relationships with the everyday world. Hopscotch, for example, is made up of a small number of rules that structure full-body actions in the everyday world. Most of the challenge of play comes from the way that the game's space is demarcated on the ground, the properties of balance of the human body, and the physics of planet Earth. *Scrabble,* on the other hand, is challenging because of the rules for what happens on the board (rather than being a physical challenge, as we can see by the fact that it would be permissible for another player to arrange my tiles on the board for me, under my direction), but the nature of this challenge is shaped by our knowledge of the English language. And *Monopoly* relates to our everyday world not, primarily, through the motion of our bodies or our knowledge of facts outside the game, but instead by being a representation—a model—of the economic system under which it was produced: capitalism.

Like traditional games, computer games are also systems. Some are quite close to traditional games—like *Dance Dance Revolution,* which requires quick movement over a pressure-sensitive surface in time with on-screen instructions, essentially creating a computer-driven version of the traditional sort of full body play found in Hopscotch, Simon Says, and Red Light/Green Light. But most computer games are closer to *Monopoly*; the game play challenges, while they may require physical dexterity, are represented on the work's surface within a world modeled by the game's systems.

In constructing the models that make up game worlds, certain approaches are common. As discussed in the introduction, collision detection is a common operational logic for the models of space in games. Similarly, as discussed in the previous chapter, finite-state machines are a common operational logic for non-player character (NPC) behavior.

These models aren't selected and constructed in an attempt to capture all the nuance and detail of their counterparts in the everyday world. Rather than fidelity, these models are selected for a number of overlapping practical reasons. First, the models employed must be specific enough to be implemented computationally. Second, the implemented models must operate with acceptable efficiency on the platform(s) targeted by the development team. Third, the development resources (especially programmer time) must be available to perform this implementation. Finally, the overall goal is defined by the fact that the game is attempting to reach an audience; the model must serve the experience of gameplay sought by the game's authors.

As Philip Agre (1997) explains in *Computation and Human Experience*, artificial intelligence (AI) researchers are also deeply engaged in making systems—but as a way of knowing. This changes a number of things. For example, it is fine for an AI research system to require a massive computer cluster in order to function, rather than a standard game console. It is also fine if the results of an AI research project can only be understood by specialists, rather than appreciated by a mainstream audience. But one fundamental thing does not change: AI researchers and game creators are interested in models of the world, and behavior within it, that can be implemented. They require models that can be operationalized computationally, and this creates a bridge between the two groups.

At the same time, AI research also has close connections to other disciplines—those that seek to understand, with their own tools, the same topics it investigates with its way of knowing. These include psychology, linguistics, and cognitive science. In this context, the question for AI (and these other disciplines in their connections with AI) is, "What do we hope to learn by making models?"

This question is immense, of course, as is the question to which it leads: How do we evaluate these computational models? This chapter will not attempt large-scale answers. Rather, the questions will be addressed, partially, through the pursuit of a more focused question: Faced with the dilemmas of the *Eliza* effect, what could be a next step? This, in turn, will be considered through the examination of another influential AI system, one that Weizenbaum saw as representing a possible future direction for *Eliza*: Robert Abelson's "ideology machine."

This leads back to one of the meanings of *expressive processing* at the heart of this book, that focused on authorial expression. An understanding of the work of making computational models as an act of authoring is furthered by a consideration of Chris Crawford's notion of "process intensity" and Michael Mateas's concept of "expressive AI." But first, before making these steps beyond the *Eliza* effect, it is important to understand the view of computational models that Weizenbaum was reacting against.

1. Some have argued that Turing was providing a behaviorist definition of intelligence, while others have argued that at most Turing was presenting one possible criterion for thinking (and that it would be possible for things that ought …

Notes continued at end of this chapter.

Eliza and the Turing Test

While *Eliza* is the first well-known digital character, its roots trace back to a highly influential proposal for computer-driven conversation (less than two decades earlier) from the father of general-purpose computing: Alan Turing. Writing for the philosophy journal *Mind,* Turing initially proposed to consider the question, "Can machines think?" (1950). Finding this question hopelessly ambiguous, however, he instead replaced it with a set of questions involving an "imitation game."

The human version of this game has three participants: "a man (A), a woman (B), and an interrogator (C) who may be of either sex." During the course of the game the interrogator asks questions of A and B, trying to determine which of them is a woman. A and B do their best to convince C to see it their way—the woman by telling the truth, and the man by "imitation" of a woman. The proposed game is played over a teletype, so that nothing physical (the tone of voice or the shape of handwriting) can enter into C's attempt to discern the gender of the other players based on their performances.

Turing then asks, "What will happen when the machine takes the part of A in this game?" How will the interrogator's results compare to when the game is played based on gender? These questions are proposed as a closely related replacement for the question, "Can machines think?"

The ideas in Turing's essay have been widely discussed—the imitation game is now commonly called the Turing test—and vigorously debated.[1] For my purposes, though, the key element of Turing's game is that it is based purely on surface behavior. In part this is no

84

doubt due to his audience—many readers of *Mind* would have understood little of any discussion of computational processes. Yet given the vast influence of Turing's work, it should also be considered in terms of larger attitudes about the relationship between surface appearance and internal processes that shaped the AI community.

The Turing test is the most famous example of the idea that we need not consider the internal operations of systems when evaluating them. From this point of view, whatever model drives a hypothetical system that can be said to have passed the Turing test, we should consider it to embody something close to "thinking." Given that—in the limited time available for interaction—some of those who interacted with *Eliza/Doctor* in the time around which Weizenbaum constructed it appear to have thought it was genuinely thoughtful, Weizenbaum's famous paper on the system was specifically at pains to dispel this sort of idea. In fact, the paper could be read as a long, detailed counterexample to the argument Turing put forth, which failed to take the workings of the *Eliza* effect's initial stages into account.

But Weizenbaum's paper was not wholly an attempt to help people see through *Eliza*'s illusion. Among other things, it also speculated on possible future directions for the *Eliza* project. Weizenbaum's projected future *Eliza* would "slowly build a model of the subject conversing with it" (1966, 43). This would, in turn, enable an *Eliza* that didn't simply transform the previous audience utterance but would instead say things guided by aspects of this model—aspects that might indicate audience rationalizations, contradictions, or other objects of interest to a more advanced *Doctor* script. Looking toward

2. While Ronald Reagan and George W. Bush may be Goldwater's descendants in their polarized views of the world, their claim to his legacy is not as strong in other cases. Goldwater wanted to shrink government spending—while …

Notes continued at end of this chapter.

how such a system could be built, Weizenbaum cited a then-recent paper by Robert Abelson and J. Douglass Carroll (1965).

Abelson's Ideology Machine

Abelson and Carroll's paper—"Computer Simulation of Individual Belief Systems"—describes work that Abelson and his students had pursued since the late 1950s, and would continue to pursue into the 1970s. At the point of their 1965 paper, the "ideology machine" consisted of an approach to belief structures and a number of operations that could be performed on such structures. Sample belief structures from the paper range from common Cold War views ("Russia controls Cuba's subversion of Latin America") to absurd statements ("Barry Goldwater believes in socialism") and also include simple facts ("Stevenson ran for President").

As these examples foreground, this is a system built in the midst of the Cold War. The Cuban Missile Crisis, President Kennedy's assassination, and the Gulf of Tonkin Resolution were all recent events. The world seemed polarized to many and, within the United States, names like those of Adlai Stevenson and Barry Goldwater did not simply indicate prominent politicians with occasionally differing philosophies. Goldwater, the Republican nominee for president of the United States in 1964, was an emblematic believer in the idea that the world's polarization was an inevitable result of a struggle between good and evil—a position that would be echoed by his ideological descendants, as in Ronald Reagan's "evil empire" and George W. Bush's "axis of evil."[2] Stevenson, the Democratic candidate for president in 1952 and 1956, on the other hand, was emblematic of those with a more nuanced view of world affairs and a belief in the potential of international cooperation—for which he was publicly derided by those with more extreme views.[3]

In such an environment, the example data that Abelson and Carroll use to illustrate the functioning of their system is clearly highly charged.[4] Perhaps for this reason, they remained coy about the exact identity of the individual portrayed in their "demonstrational system," referring to this person only as "a well-known right-winger." But by the time of his 1973 publication on the system, Abelson was willing to say directly what was already well-known within the field: Goldwater himself was the model for the ideology used in developing the system.

Interaction with the system consisted of offering the assertion that a particular *source* (e.g., an individual) has made the claim that a *concept* (e.g., a particular nation) has the stated relation to a *predicate* (generally a verb and an object). For example, "Stevenson claims Cuba threatens Latin America." The statement is evaluated, a response is generated, and in some cases the state of the internal system data is altered.

Data and Credibility

In order to understand how the ideology machine's system responds to new statements, it is necessary to consider two aspects of its construction: first, the way data is structured and, second, a process of determining "credibility" that employs this data.

The basic data of the ideology machine is a set of beliefs stored as concept-predicate pairs. Beyond this, there are two primary ways that data in the system can

3. Some of these were smears by association. David Greenberg (2000), writing in *Slate*, offers two examples from well-known figures: McCarthy ("Alger—I mean, Adlai") and Richard Nixon ("Adlai the Appeaser . . . who got a Ph.D. from …

4. Even more than they had planned, for many readers, given that Stevenson died unexpectedly only weeks after the article's publication.

Notes continued at end of this chapter.

be structured. One is *horizontal,* in which a particular concept-predicate pair can become part of a compound predicate for another belief. For example, "Cuba" and "subverts Latin America" are a concept-predicate pair that make up a complete belief. But they can also be joined in horizontal structuring to become part of a compound predicate such as "controls Cuba's subversion of Latin America" that can be joined with the concept "Russia."

The second structuring mechanism is *vertical,* in which concepts or predicates can serve as more specific *instances* or more abstract *qualities* of others. In the example data, the concepts "Stevenson" and "Earl Warren" both have the quality "Liberals" (at a higher level of abstraction), which is an instance of "Left-wingers" (at a yet higher level), which also has the instance "Administration theorists" (at the same abstraction level as Liberals). The predicates with which the concepts "Liberals" and "Administration theorists" are paired in the assertions "Liberals *support anticolonial policies*" and "Administration theorists *coddle left-leaning neutral nations*" are instances of the more abstract predicate "mistreat U.S. friends abroad."

Each element—whether a concept or predicate—also carries a number representing the belief system's evaluation of that element. Certain individuals or actions, for example, may be viewed positively or negatively—while others are viewed as relatively neutral. These evaluations come into play in combination with the processes of credibility testing.

The ideology machine's credibility testing begins when it is presented with a concept-predicate pair to evaluate. If that pair is already believed—that is, already present in its data—it is automatically credible. Similarly, if the opposite is already believed (the concept paired with the negation of the predicate) the pair is incredible. Assuming neither of these is the case, evaluating credibility is accomplished by movement through the system's horizontal and vertical memory.

For example, given the pair "Liberals" and "support anticolonial policies" (with neither it nor its opposite already in memory), the ideology machine will look at all instances of the concept Liberals (such as Stevenson and Warren) to see if they are paired with predicates that are instances of "support anticolonial policies." Abelson and Carroll give "Stevenson opposes Portugal on Angola" as an example pair that would lend support to the credibility of "Liberals support anticolonial policies." However, this does not establish credibility on its own. For example, other instances of Liberal (e.g., Warren) may not be found connected to instances of the predicate. Using this approach, the ideology machine only finds a pair credible if at least half the instances of the concept are found linked with instances of the predicate.

If this fails, other options are available. The same sort of search, for example, may be performed to attempt to establish the credibility of the opposite of the given pair (e.g., "Liberals oppose anticolonial policies"). More complexly, a search may be performed that also moves up the levels of abstraction, looking at the qualities (rather than just instances) of the concept and predicate given. For instance, a more abstract quality of "Liberals" is "Left-wingers" and a more abstract quality of "support anticolonial policies" is "mistreat U.S. friends abroad." Given that "Administration theorists" is a more -specific instance of "Left-wingers" and "coddle left-leaning neutral nations" is a more specific instance of "mistreat

U.S. friends abroad," finding this pair in the system's data would lend support to "Liberals oppose anticolonial policies." In this kind of search, at least half of the more abstract qualities of the concept must be found credibly related to at least one of the more abstract qualities of the predicate. As with the instance-only credibility test, if this method fails, a test for its opposite may be performed.

Denial and Rationalization

The foundation of the ideology machine is created by the combination of interconnected structured pairs, evaluations of the elements of those pairs, and the credibility-testing processes. Interaction is particularly strongly shaped by the evaluations of elements. Recall that interaction begins with a pair made up of a *source* and a compound predicate (constructed as a familiar concept-predicate pair) that is input into the system. If a source with a positive evaluation (a "favorable source") makes the claim that a concept with a positive evaluation (a "good actor") is connected to a predicate with a positive evaluation (a "good action") then, as Abelson and Carroll put it, "there is not much left for the system to do . . . except to express joy" (1965, 28). This is not entirely true, in that the system also stores this assertion in its belief data. Similarly, when a favorable source claims that a bad actor is engaged in a bad action, the system simply expresses regret and stores the data. But in other cases, the ideology machine engages one of the two primary types of processes that it carries out in response to interaction: denial and rationalization.

If the source of the assertion is viewed negatively, the ideology machine's executive "calling sequence" is, as

Abelson and Carroll observe, "motivated to dismiss the source's assertion" (28) via denial or rationalization. If the source is viewed positively, the calling sequence has two further options. If a good actor is asserted to be engaged in a bad action, the system will attempt to deny the alleged fact or that the assertion was made. On the other hand, if a bad actor is asserted to be engaged in a good action, the system will attempt to rationalize the alleged fact or the making of the assertion.

Of the two approaches, denial is simpler to explain. The ideology machine takes the concept-predicate pair it wishes to deny ("C-P"), constructs its opposite ("C-not P"), and "enters the Credibility Test with the injunction to find C-not P credible if at all possible. Success in this procedure enables the system to deny C-P by means of contrary evidence" (27).

The rationalization mechanism, on the other hand, has three methods of dealing with upsetting statements— each of which represents a different way of denying the psychological responsibility of the actor for the action. They are:

> 1) by assigning prime responsibility for the actor to another actor who controls the original actor; 2) by assuming the original action was an unintended consequence of some other action truly intended by the actor; 3) by assuming that the original action will set other events in motion ultimately leading to a more appropriate outcome. (27)

Like the credibility test, these strategies are implemented as search processes on the belief data. The first, "Find the Prime Mover," looks for a pair in data of the form "B controls C" (as in "Red China controls Cambodia") in which a bad actor controls the good one. The second,

5. Ableson and Carroll, amusingly, give the following example of "Reinterpret Final Goal." The pair "My simulation produced silly results" must be rationalized, because the concept ("my simulation") is evaluated positively while the predicate …

Notes continued at end of this chapter.

"Accidental By-product," looks for a predicate that can be interposed between the original concept and predicate of the form "Q can accidentally cause P" (Abelson 1963, 296, 298). Finally, "Reinterpret Final Goal" takes apart the predicate, looking for an instance in which its result serves as a concept for a pair in which the predicate has the opposite evaluation, compactly expressed as "P may lead to R" (295–296).[5]

As the system employs these mechanisms successfully, the results of the successes are stored and can become resources for future rationalizations. The next time that rationalization is needed, a search is undertaken of "nearby" pairs (moving up and down the network of concepts and predicates) looking to see what rationalization subprocesses have been used with their elements so that a similar approach can be tried. The result is that the system can develop a style of rationalization, which Abelson and Carroll describe as "paranoid," "apologetic," "Polyannic," or a blend of the three (29).

Eliza, the Ideology Machine, and the Evaluation of Models

As mentioned earlier, Weizenbaum was clearly impressed by Abelson and Carroll's paper. Writing of future work on *Eliza,* he outlined an "intermediate goal" strongly informed by their work:

> *Eliza* should be given the power to slowly build a model of the subject conversing with it. If the subject mentions that he is not married, for example, and later speaks of his wife, then *Eliza* should be able to make the tentative inference that he is either a widower or divorced. Of course, he could simply be confused. In the long run, *Eliza* should be able to build up a *belief structure* (to use

92

Abelson's phrase) of the subject and on that basis detect the subject's rationalizations, contradictions, etc. Conversations with such an *Eliza* would often turn into arguments. Important steps in the realization of these goals have already been taken. Most notable among these is Abelson's and Carroll's work on simulation of belief structures. (1966, 43)

Potentially, an *Eliza* that could accept scripts of this imagined sort would embody a more powerful model— not just transforming the audience's most recent statement based on keywords but also able to draw on the history of the conversation and a developing structure of information (presumably stored in concept-predicate pairs) to offer a wider variety of responses. Of course, the authoring effort involved in creating such a script would be greater as well, but so might be the opportunities for insightful construction (as we see in the original *Eliza* script, which can transform a statement such as "Everybody hates me" into the reply "Can you think of anyone in particular").

In other words, such a system could be seen as an important, if limited, step beyond the simple transformation logic of *Eliza* and the directed graph logic of dialogue trees. Like *Eliza,* it would generate things to say by following rules. Like a dialogue tree, it would maintain a state of the conversation. But, crucially, the state would not be one of a set of predetermined possible points—instead, it would be an interconnected, evolving data structure—and the rules would employ this structure, rather than just prewritten sentence templates for decomposition and reassembly. This points toward the power of employing models when making media.

At the same time, a comparison between the fates of

Eliza/Doctor and Abelson's ideology machine is instructive. While Abelson's project is nearly forgotten, *Eliza/Doctor* has remained a touchstone, for a variety of reasons. Nick Montfort and Andrew Stern (2008) have outlined a set of reasons for *Eliza*'s success that range from the ease of porting between platforms to dealing with a fundamental anxiety about computing. But they also make explicit what is implicit in Janet Murray's analysis (1997, 71–74) of *Eliza* as a procedural system: it combines process intensity with a deep engagement with language. While the underlying procedural model in Abelson's system is more compelling, its treatment of language is far less. His article "Computer Simulation of 'Hot' Cognition" gives the example, "Barry Goldwater attacks Kennedy wants price-control damages initiative ruins economy" (1963, 283). A decade later, while the underlying system had evolved considerably, the treatment of language was still quite ham-handed: "Yes, I would not hesitate to say that recent administrations not make trouble for Communist schemes. Liberals want East-West agreements and administration theorists have influenced the Kennedy administration" (1973, 290).

As a result, Abelson's system failed as *media*— providing little incentive for audiences to wish it to live on. This is what makes the potential of the future *Eliza* outlined by Weizenbaum, using structures and processes akin to Abelson's, so appealing: a more compelling set of operational logics combined with a sense for language. While it is a touch hyperbolic, it is worth noting that Weizenbaum's combined talent for the authoring of processes and language caused Murray to refer to him as "the earliest, and still perhaps the premier, literary artist in the computer medium" (1997, 72).

But an *Eliza* embodying these goals was never built. More strikingly, despite Weizenbaum's evidently positive view of Abelson's work in his 1966 paper, I was able to find no mention of Abelson in Weizenbaum's 1976 book. This is particularly notable given that, among its other contents, *Computer Power and Human Reason* contains something of a history and survey of the AI field, including a chapter on "Computer Models in Psychology"—an area with which Abelson is strongly associated.

It may help us understand this shift to consider the rift already visible in their mid-1960s publications. In his paper, one of Weizenbaum's stated goals was to "rob *Eliza* of the aura of magic to which its application to psychological subject matter has to some extent contributed" (1966, 43). Abelson and Carroll, on the other hand, describe a rather different goal:

> By an *individual belief system* we refer to an interrelated set of affect-laden cognitions concerning some aspects of the psychological world of a single individual. . . . Our use of the technique of *computer simulation* is intended to maximize the explicitness with which we state our assumptions and the vividness with which the consequences of these assumptions are made apparent. The operation of simulated belief systems can be played out on the computer and the details scrutinized in order to refine our level of approximation to real systems. (1965, 24)

In pursuing "approximation to real systems" (actual human belief systems), Abelson and Carroll also report that Abelson's work with Charlotte Gilson has begun empirical study of the credibility test (30). Specifically, their study focuses on the system's requirement that, for a statement to be found credible via search, at least half the instances of a concept must be connected to at least one instance of the predicate. This means that one predicate can be taken as representative of the entire class to which it is connected, but not so for one concept. In the study, questions were constructed in an attempt to see if human experimental subjects would show the same propensity. As Abelson and Carroll report, "Although the difference was not of substantial magnitude . . . the subjects were more willing to generalize over predicates than over concepts, as predicted" (1965, 30).

This approach—constructing a theory of the functioning of human cognition in the form of a model, implementing it as a computer program, and evaluating it via comparison with human behavior—has a history as long as that of the term "artificial intelligence" itself, stretching back at least to Allen Newell and Herbert Simon's mid-1950s work on General Problem Solver (Edwards 1997, 251). But it is also one that Weizenbaum came to reject with scorn. He wrote a particularly tongue-in-cheek response to Kenneth Colby's work of this sort on paranoia, in a letter to the *ACM Forum*—in which he reported some supposed new results of his own: "The contribution here reported should lead to a full understanding of one of man's most troublesome disorders: infantile autism. Surely once we have a faithful and utterly reliable simulation of the behavioral aspects of this, or any other mental disorder, we understand it" (1974, 543). The PL/1 program accompanying the letter reads:

```
AUTISM: PROCEDURE OPTIONS
(MAIN);
  DECLARE C CHAR (1000)
  VARYING;
```

```
DO WHILE TRUE;
   GET LIST(C);
   PUT LIST(' ');
END;
END AUTISM;  (ibid.)
```

Weizenbaum explains that his program "responds *exactly* as does an autistic patient—that is, not at all. I have validated this model following the procedure first used in commercial advertising by Carter's Little Liver Pills ('Seven New York doctors say . . .') and later used so brilliantly by Dr. K. M. Colby in his simulation of paranoia."[6] Weizenbaum's point, of course, is that machines that act like humans don't necessarily tell us anything about the humans—a conclusion in stark contrast with much of the early work at the boundary of AI and cognitive science, including Abelson's. Suffice it to say, Abelson was likely relieved to notice his absence from Weizenbaum's index.

AI, Neat and Scruffy

A name that does appear in Weizenbaum's book, however, is that of Roger Schank, Abelson's most famous collaborator. When Schank arrived from Stanford University to join Abelson at Yale University, together they represented the most identifiable center for a particular approach to AI: what would later (in the early 1980s) come to be known as the "scruffy" approach.[7] Meanwhile, perhaps the most identifiable proponent of what would later be called the "neat" approach, John McCarthy, remained at Stanford.

McCarthy had coined the term "artificial intelligence" in the application for the field-defining workshop he

6. Howard Gardner (1985) reports that Weizenbaum and Colby were collaborators before an acrimonious split.

7. This was after the terms *neat* and *scruffy* were introduced into the artificial intelligence and cognitive science discourse by Abelson's 1981 essay, in which he attributes the coinage to "an unnamed but easily guessable colleague"—Schank.

organized at Dartmouth College in 1956. Howard Gardner, in his influential reflection on the field, *The Mind's New Science*, characterized McCarthy's neat approach this way: "McCarthy believes that the route to making machines intelligent is through a rigorous formal approach in which the acts that make up intelligence are reduced to a set of logical relationships or axioms that can be expressed precisely in mathematical terms" (1985, 154).

This sort of approach lent itself well to problems easily cast in formal and mathematical terms. But the scruffy branch of AI, growing out of fields such as linguistics and psychology, wanted to tackle problems of a different nature. Scruffy AI built systems for tasks as diverse as rephrasing newspaper reports, generating fictions, translating between languages, and (as we have seen) modeling ideological reasoning. In order to accomplish this, Abelson, Schank, and their collaborators developed an approach quite unlike formal reasoning from first principles. One foundation for their work was Schank's "conceptual dependency" structure for language-independent semantic representation. Another foundation was the notion of *scripts* (later *cases*), an embryonic form of which could be seen in the calling sequence of the ideology machine's executive. Both of these will be considered in more detail in the next chapter.

Scruffy AI got attention because it achieved results in areas that seemed much more "real world" than those of other approaches. For comparison's sake, consider that the MIT AI lab at the time of Schank's move to Yale was celebrating success at building systems that could understand the relationships in stacks of children's wooden blocks. But scruffy AI was also critiqued—both within and outside the AI field—for its "unscientific" ad hoc approach. Weizenbaum was unimpressed, in particular, with the conceptual dependency structures underlying many of the projects, writing that "Schank provides no demonstration that his scheme is more than a collection of heuristics that happen to work on specific classes of examples" (1976, 199). Whichever side one took in the debate, there can be no doubt that scruffy projects depended on coding large amounts of human knowledge into AI systems—often more than the authors acknowledged, and perhaps much more than they realized.

Ideology Revisited

The signs of unacknowledged overencoding are present at the very roots of scruffy work, as we can see by returning to Abelson's ideology machine. The system was presented as a structure and set of processes for modeling human ideology generally. It could then be populated with data (concept-predicate pairs, evaluations of the elements, and connections between them) to represent a particular ideology. If Abelson and his collaborators had succeeded in building such a system, the machine's processes would be ideologically neutral; only the data would carry a particular position.

As examples cited in the earlier discussion reveal, there certainly is a strong ideological position encoded in the data of what some simply called the "Goldwater machine." But, returning to the specifics of the system's operations, one can also see that the same ideology is encoded in its processes. This begins at the center of its operations, with the calling sequence "motivated to dismiss" any statement by a negatively viewed source, even

8. By the time of his publication in 1973 on the system, Abelson would acknowledge this fact—casting it as a system for modeling the ideological reasoning of the "true believer" rather than such reasoning in general. Of course, many true believers …

Notes continued at end of this chapter.

a statement with which the system data is in agreement. It is also found in the design of the processes for denial and rationalization, which are predicated on a world divided into "good actors" and "bad actors." Further, in addition to being designed to operate in terms of good and bad, the primary processes for interaction are dedicated to finding routes to deny even the smallest positive action by the bad guys, and seeking means to rationalize away even minimally negative actions by the good guys on the basis of paranoid fantasies, apologetic reinterpretations, and Pollyannaish misdirections.

This is not a general model of ideology. It is a parody of one particular type of ideology—one that depends on fear to gain power. As we have seen in more recent U.S. politics, the idea that "you are either with us or against us" is not a feature of every ideology but rather a view held by a small number of extreme groups. In fact, this small number have a tendency to demean alternative ideologies as naive specifically because they *do not* see the world in terms of good guys and bad guys.

This was just as true at the time of Abelson's work.[8] One can imagine Stevenson being critiqued exactly because his ideology operated by processes rather different from those encoded in the Goldwater machine. As a result of this difference, it would be impossible to create a "Stevenson machine" simply by providing a different set of concept-predicate pairs.

Of course, even Goldwater was a more subtle thinker than Abelson's system would allow. The system is, like *Eliza/Doctor,* a caricature, a parody. And just as *Eliza*'s model of conversation (transforming the most recent statement to form a response) only found significant use

100

through the *Doctor* script (transforming in the manner of a Rogerian therapist), so the ideology machine was closely wedded to the particular type of ideology used in its "demonstrational system."

Another way of putting this is that both *Eliza* and Abelson's system, if perhaps unintentionally, provide a critique of their subjects (Rogerian therapy and right-wing Cold War ideology) through a combination of their data and processes. At the foundations of AI in the United States, we find systems that, on examination of their components, it is nearly impossible to view as straight-faced science. Rather, they are expressive media. And this is a primary reason that they, and the systems that followed in the scruffy branch of AI, remain of interest today.

Encoding large amounts of human knowledge into the design of a system's data and processes may not have been good cognitive science, but it was a powerful authoring technique. One result was compelling interactive characters, such as *Eliza/Doctor* and the Goldwater-infused ideology machine. Another result was a set of the most important early experiments in story generation, which the coming chapters will explore.

Authoring Processes

How do we learn from making models? Philip Agre offers part of an answer for the field of AI when he writes:

> AI's distinctive activity is building things, specifically computers and computer programs. Building things, like fieldwork and meditation and design, is a way of knowing that cannot be reduced to the reading and writing of books. To the contrary, it is an enterprise grounded in a routine daily practice. Sitting in the lab and working on gadgets or circuits or programs, it is

101

9. On the other hand, the speculative future *Eliza* discussed in this chapter, imagined as engaging the results of Abelson's ideology machine, produced nothing unexpected. Since it was never constructed, since it is an artificial intelligence project never …

Notes continued at end of this chapter.

an inescapable fact that some things can be built and other things cannot. (1997, 10)

With a less open-ended agenda, the same is also true of work in digital media. In such engagements with what Agre calls "practical reality," a number of things are learned. This happens not only when answering the question of what can be built but also in unexpected moments—moments that occur when trying to build systems, when interacting with those systems, when observing others interacting with those systems, and so on.

If AI pursues system building as a way of knowing, if this is one approach to how we learn from models, the question still remains: What do we want to know? Weizenbaum's contemporaries, wherever they fell along the continuum between scruffy and neat, generally assumed the answer to be: Can we build a system that exhibits genuinely intelligent behavior?

But this is not all it is possible to learn. This book's chapter on the *Eliza* effect was precisely an exploration of some other areas in which we have learned—and can still learn—from Weizenbaum's early AI system. We don't learn from *Eliza* because it is a testable model of how human cognition may actually work (or because it is genuinely intelligent in any way). One way we do learn from it is by studying how humans interact with its simple model, just as Garfinkel's yes/no therapy experiment was informative for what it revealed about humans interacting with the system. One can also learn important things in a wide variety of other areas: interpretations of computational systems, the limits of relatively state-free designs for interaction, and what can make a computer character compelling.[9]

Given this, we can imagine a number of different ways to focus the work of making computational models, with AI's focus on intelligent behavior and digital media's focus on authoring as two of them. The perhaps-unintentional contributions of Weizenbaum and Abelson to this second focus also help set the stage for concepts from two figures in the digital media field: Chris Crawford and Michael Mateas.

Process Intensity

In this book's introduction I presented a diagrammatic sketch of the elements we should consider when thinking about digital media (figure 1.4). The two internal components—data and process—have since returned to this discussion in many forms, with Weizenbaum's scripts for *Eliza* and Abelson's belief structures for the ideology machine as two clear examples of data. But data is not central to all systems. For example, we might think of *Pong* and many other iconic computer games (e.g., *Tetris*) as being authored almost entirely in terms of processes rather than data.[10] An "e-book," on the other hand, might be just the opposite—a digital media artifact authored almost completely by the arrangement of precreated text and image data. In an influential article, game designer and digital media theorist Crawford (1987) coined the phrase "process intensity" to describe a work's balance between process and data (what he called its "crunch per bits ratio").[11]

Crawford points out that in the early years of home computing certain genres of software failed despite a widespread belief that they would be attractive—specifically, he cites checkbook-balancing and kitchen-

10. It is perhaps worth clarifying that my argument here is not that authoring digital media requires authoring both data and processes. The data and process elements of a work of digital media may be newly authored, selected from found sources …

11. I am indebted to those who discussed an earlier draft of this section with me during the blog-based peer review on Grand Text Auto: Nick Montfort, Barry Atkins, Chris Lewis, Josh Giesbrecht, Sol Gaitán, Randall Couch, Lord Yo, and Jason Rhody.

Notes continued at end of this chapter.

recipe software. He argues that these genres failed for the same reason that the 1980s computer game hit *Dragon's Lair* (which played sequences of canned animation, instead of dynamically drawing graphics to the screen) was a dead end, rather than the first example of a new game genre. In all these cases, the software is designed with low process intensity. In fact, Crawford goes so far as to assert that process intensity "provides us with a useful criterion for evaluating the value of any piece of software."

In Crawford's article, games other than *Dragon's Lair* come out quite positively. He writes that "games in general boast the highest crunch per bit ratios in the computing world." This was true in a number of senses. When a 1980s computer game was played, most of the work of the machine was dedicated to process calculation rather than data movement. Similarly, in the creation of such works, most of the authoring effort was in the definition of processes as opposed to the creation of data files. These facts, in turn, point to another: in games of this era, it was the authoring of novel processes that provided the opportunity for creating innovative audience experiences.

But Crawford published his essay in 1987. Almost two decades later, game designer and theorist Greg Costikyan gave a keynote address at the 2006 ACM SIGGRAPH Sandbox Symposium titled "Designing Games for Process Intensity"—reaching a rather different conclusion about games. As Costikyan writes in a blog post from the same year:

> Today, 80+% of the man-hours (and cost) for a game is in the creation of art assets.

In other words, we've spent the last three decades

focusing on data intensity instead of process intensity. (2006)

In fact, the shift has been so profound as to call for a rethinking of the very concept of process intensity. The games cited by Crawford—such as *Flight Simulator* and Crawford's own game of political struggle, *Balance of Power*—use much of their processing toward the game's novel behavior. In the time between Crawford's and Costikyan's statements, however, the graphics-led data-intensive shift in computer games not only increased the amount of effort placed in creating static art assets. It also drove an increasing share of processing toward greatly improved visuals for remarkably stagnant behavior. While this represents an increase in processing, it's the same increase that could be achieved by taking a kitchen recipe program and adding the texture of handmade paper for each recipe card, doing live calculations of shadow effects for each small paper defect, and perhaps also calculating simulated physics for how much each type of paper bends over time while held in the hand. Executing these computationally expensive effects would send the recipe program's process intensity through the roof—while running completely counter to Crawford's ideas.

In other words, Crawford's concept remains valuable today, but we need to consider separately what he was able to lump together in the 1980s. Issues of development team effort (as called out by Costikyan) are one topic. Issues of where the system resources are employed during the audience experience are another. This is no longer an issue of "crunch per bit"—but of what purpose crunching serves. Crawford was clearly focusing on processing that has the potential to allow authors to

12. This kind of distinction—between processing used for graphics and processing used for behavior—is not only of interest to game developers. It is also a distinction understood by players. For example, as Jesper Juul (2005) and …

13. Or to put it another way, the processes of the original version of *The Sims* make operational an innovative model of character behavior that creates an emergent complexity. This was seen as risky by the industry (which tends to reskin proven …

Notes continued at end of this chapter.

craft innovative system behavior, rather than processing that allows more impressive means of displaying data.[12] I believe the central issue has become which digital media systems are exhibiting a comparative intensity of behavioral processing, rather than how this relates to the amount of data employed.

A good case in point is *The Sims* (Wright, Ryan, London, et al. 2000). Will Wright and his team at Maxis designed *The Sims* around a large library of graphics and a set of comparatively complex behavioral landscapes. The game's publisher, Electronic Arts, at first resisted the title—in part because its process-intensive design had created innovative, unproven gameplay focused on managing the lives of simulated suburban characters. But when *The Sims* was released it became the best-selling personal computer game of all time. It accomplished this in part by reaching a significantly wider audience than the "hard core" (stereotypically, young males) toward whom most high-budget computer games seem to cater. Yet despite the success of *The Sims* and the fact that game company executives regularly express the desire to reach wider demographics, innovation at the level of behavior-oriented processes is still largely resisted within the game industries, viewed as a risky alternative to the tried-and-true approach of combining flashier graphics processing with the same gameplay behavior processing as previous hits.[13]

This book's focus is on what systems do—what they enact and how they behave—rather than what the surface output looks like. This could be characterized as an interest in "behavioral process intensity" of the sort practiced by digital media designers like Wright. In this take on the term, the process intensity of Wright's design is not diminished as more graphics files are added to the system, just as the process intensity of Abelson's ideology machine is not diminished as more data is added to the belief structure. This doesn't help address the game production bottleneck that attracts Costikyan's interest (and it doesn't address other important elements of the resulting media, as a comparison of Weizenbaum's and Abelson's systems reveals). It is also much less clear-cut than alternative notions of process intensity, and it may be that another conception—such as the ratio of dynamically-created data to static data—would be more convincing.[14] My guess, however, is that process intensity is much like the process/data distinction itself. As mentioned earlier, forms of declarative authoring (from the weak, widespread case of web page writing to the strong, specialized case of Prolog programming) trouble the process/data distinction, but this does not diminish the usefulness of these concepts for forming an initial understanding of digital media. Similarly, the concept of process intensity is, as Crawford puts it, "subject to a variety of minor-league objections and compromising truths," and yet remains conceptually useful. In particular, in the behavior-oriented version presented here, I believe it gives us a way of thinking about how computational models (such as those developed in AI research) point toward a particular emphasis in digital media authoring.

Expressive AI

Mateas (an AI researcher, artist, and game developer) has presented a number of ideas about the relationship between AI and making media that influence my work in this book. One of these addresses the problem with

14. After the blog-based peer review of this book, Richard Evans, who was at the time working on *The Sims 3* at Maxis, sent me email arguing that *The Sims* is not very process-intensive, when considered in light of two popular conceptions of …

Notes continued at end of this chapter.

15. I pick out Mateas because of his particular interest in fiction and games. But similar shifts have been undertaken by a number of other prominent young researchers with artificial intelligence backgrounds, such as Phoebe Sengers and Warren Sack.

Abelson's work that is also visible in much of AI: in trying to capture the structure of the world or the way reasoning works, it always captures *someone's idea* of how things are rather than any transcendental truth. Of course, this isn't a problem in all contexts, but it is when trying to understand human intelligence (the overlap of AI and cognitive science) or when trying to create a software system that acts intelligently in a real-world context (most other uses of AI). This, in part, is why the most prominent AI efforts of recent years have been statistically driven approaches to focused problems (e.g., Google's search results, or Amazon's recommendation system) rather than hand-authored approaches to large problems (e.g., general-purpose reasoning).

Still, when it comes to media, the goals are no longer general-purpose. The authoring of media is instead precisely the presentation of "someone's idea" of something. For fiction, it's someone's idea of people, stories, language, and what it means to be alive.

Given this, if we look at the history of AI from the perspective of media, we can see it as a rich set of tools for expressing and making operational particular authorial visions. This is the shift marked by Mateas in naming his practice "Expressive AI."[15] As Mateas puts it, "Expressive AI views a system as a performance of the author's ideas. The system is both a messenger for and a message from the author" (2002, 63).

Of course, from the point of view of digital media (rather than AI), Mateas is saying something rather everyday. For example, Ted Nelson, in a 1970 article later reprinted in his seminal book *Computer Lib/Dream Machines* (1974), described "hyper-media" computational systems that would embody and perform authorial ideas—more than three decades before Mateas. Similarly, designers of computer games clearly author processes to embody and perform their ideas for audience experience. But both hypermedia and computer game designers have been content, by and large, with data-focused approaches, while AI has traditionally developed process-intensive solutions. And it is Mateas's approach of combining AI's process intensity with the authorial perspective of digital media and games that has allowed him to coauthor groundbreaking digital fictions such as *Terminal Time* (perhaps the only successful story-generation system yet created) and *Façade* (the first true interactive drama)—both of which will be discussed further in coming pages.

For this book's purposes, the important issue is not whether any particular technique arises from, or connects to, traditions in AI. Rather, it is the potential for using process-intensive techniques to express authorial perspectives through behavior. Which brings me to the genesis of one of the two meanings for *expressive processing* in this book: a broadening of Mateas's term beyond AI and into the processing that enables digital media in general.

Mateas pursues his work as simultaneous AI research and media authoring. There is much to learn from this. But—as demonstrated by this book's examinations of Weizenbaum's and Abelson's work—we can also search for media-authoring lessons not yet understood in AI projects that were pursued with another goal in mind. The coming chapters will continue this approach, considering a series of story-generation projects in three ways: on their own terms, as telling examples of particular technological approaches and moments in our technological history, and as sources of insight for authors of digital fictions and games.

All of these projects will, by some measures, move beyond the previously discussed models found in commercial games: quest flags, dialogue trees, and finite state machines. At the same time, they will also be far from engaging another "practical reality"—that of the audience, which must be considered for all digital media. In fact, it is precisely this characteristic of one system that gives rise to the next general effect I wish to discuss: the *Tale-Spin* effect.

Notes

1. Some have argued that Turing was providing a behaviorist definition of intelligence, while others have argued that at most Turing was presenting one possible criterion for thinking (and that it would be possible for things that ought to be described as thinking to not pass the test). Similarly, some have contended that Turing's test is deeply gendered (the machine attempting to pass as a woman), while others have maintained that this is a red herring (at other points the machine is described as imitating a man), and yet others have asserted that the gender-driven test plays a key role: as a scoring mechanism for the human/ machine test. See *The Essential Turing* (Turing 2004) for versions of Turing's most influential writings and summaries of the debates surrounding them.

Moving beyond these debates, Mark Marino (2006b) has positioned the Turing test as an "Ontological Turing Machine." The name is chosen in relation to the "Universal Turing Machine"—Turing's famous outlining of the concept and a possible implementation of the notion of universal computation. For Marino, Turing's *Mind* essay does similar foundational work, both conceptually and in a possible implementation, for the doubt produced by network communication (which, from MMO games to instant message chats, continually raises questions as to the actual "age/sex/location" and human/software status of others). During the blog-based review of this book, Marino also mentioned that he is building on this work to reinterpret the Turing test and *Eliza/Doctor* through what he calls "Conversational Actor Networks or Conversational Actor Network Theory (CAN/T)."

2. While Ronald Reagan and George W. Bush may be Goldwater's descendants in their polarized views of the world, their claim to his legacy is not as strong in other cases. Goldwater wanted to shrink government spending—while Reagan and Bush both oversaw massively ballooning government debts. Similarly, Goldwater wanted government out of the private lives of U.S. citizens, and spent some of the 1990s as a gay rights activist, while later Republicans relied on social "wedge issues" as an important part of their electoral strategy.

3. Some of these were smears by association. David Greenberg (2000), writing in *Slate*, offers two examples from well-known figures:

> McCarthy ("Alger—I mean, Adlai") and Richard Nixon ("Adlai the Appeaser . . . who got a Ph.D. from Dean Acheson's College of Cowardly Communist Containment").

The McCarthy here is Joe, famous for his red scare witch hunts, who is linking Stevenson with the accused Russian spy Alger Hiss. Acheson, the other person linked to Stevenson above, was a major figure in the U.S. Department of State during the construction of post-WWII policies such as the Marshall Plan, the same period when McCarthy made his wild claims that the department was "thoroughly infested with communists." Interestingly, these smears are perfectly constructed for implementation in the hierarchical data connections of Abelson's system—described in this chapter—positioning Stevenson as an instance of a concept for which the other man (Hiss or Acheson) is also an instance.

4. Even more than they had planned, for many readers, given that Stevenson died unexpectedly only weeks after the article's publication.

5. Ableson and Carroll, amusingly, give the following example of "Reinterpret Final Goal." The pair "My simulation produced silly results" must be rationalized, because the concept ("my simulation") is evaluated positively while the predicate ("produced silly results") is evaluated negatively. First, the predicate is taken apart, leaving "silly results." Next, in a search, the system finds the pair "Silly results enrich my

understanding." Since the predicate "enrich my understanding" is positive (and has a stronger evaluation than "produced silly results"), the search succeeds. The simulation may have produced silly results, but these may lead to enriched understanding.

6. Howard Gardner (1985) reports that Weizenbaum and Colby were collaborators before an acrimonious split.

7. This was after the terms *neat* and *scruffy* were introduced into the artificial intelligence and cognitive science discourse by Abelson's 1981 essay, in which he attributes the coinage to "an unnamed but easily guessable colleague"—Schank.

8. By the time of his publication in 1973 on the system, Abelson would acknowledge this fact—casting it as a system for modeling the ideological reasoning of the "true believer" rather than such reasoning in general. Of course, many true believers may believe in something other than a world divided into good guys and bad guys.

9. On the other hand, the speculative future *Eliza* discussed in this chapter, imagined as engaging the results of Abelson's ideology machine, produced nothing unexpected. Since it was never constructed, since it is an artificial intelligence project never engaged through artificial intelligence's way of knowing, nothing was learned. In essence, it is like a chemistry experiment specified only to the point of the substances to place on the lab table. The learning would only begin once, and if, the chemicals were mixed.

10. It is perhaps worth clarifying that my argument here is not that authoring digital media requires authoring both data and processes. The data and process elements of a work of digital media may be newly authored, selected from found sources (e.g., found footage is still data, and the vendor-supplied behaviors in an authoring tool such as Flash are still processes), or even largely undefined at the time of authoring (and instead defined by processes executed at the time of audience experience). In any case, they will rest on a foundation of process and data that make up the platform(s) on which the work operates.

11. I am indebted to those who discussed an earlier draft of this section with me during the blog-based peer review on Grand Text Auto: Nick Montfort, Barry Atkins, Chris Lewis, Josh Giesbrecht, Sol Gaitán, Randall Couch, Lord Yo, and Jason Rhody.

12. This kind of distinction—between processing used for graphics and processing used for behavior—is not only of interest to game developers. It is also a distinction understood by players. For example, as Jesper Juul (2005) and others have pointed out, it is not uncommon for players of computer games to choose a lower level of graphics rendering (e.g., in order to increase the responsiveness of the interface or reduce the visual weight of elements not important to the gameplay). Players who choose to lower levels of graphics processing are not considered to be playing significantly differently from players who choose higher levels. On the other hand, some games also allow players to vary the level of artificial intelligence processing employed by the system. This changes the game's behavior by, for example, making computer-controlled opponents easier to defeat (e.g., in computer chess or a first-person shooter). Players view this type of change—a change in behavior-oriented processing—as a much more significant change to gameplay.

13. Or to put it another way, the processes of the original version of *The Sims* make operational an

innovative model of character behavior that creates an emergent complexity. This was seen as risky by the industry (which tends to reskin proven models that also are generally simpler models). But this innovative behavioral model, with its emergent complexity, seems to have been key to the game's cultural and commercial success.

14. After the blog-based peer review of this book, Richard Evans, who was at the time working on *The Sims 3* at Maxis, sent me email arguing that *The Sims* is not very process-intensive when considered in light of two popular conceptions of process intensity:

> (1) the ratio of processing to data (this is a number of operations per second divided by a number of bits), and (2) the ratio of program-code to data (this is unit-less, as the numerator and denominator are both expressed in numbers of bits). Now *The Sims* is more process-intensive than many other games in terms of the second interpretation (2), because there are hundreds of different scripts, detailing how the Sim runs each type of interaction, but it is not particularly process-intensive in terms of the first: there is actually very little behavioral processing going on while a Sim is running an interaction. It is only when the Sim has finished running an interaction, and is trying to decide what to do next, that there is intensive behavioral processing. But it is questionable whether this FindBestAction algorithm (which is run infrequently) is particularly process-intensive, too. Your revised notion of process-intensity (the amount of processing using on behavior) still doesn't truly capture the intention—to give just one counter-example, consider two different chess-playing AIs, both of which searched the same search-space, but one does some clever pruning (alpha-beta etc) to reduce how much it searches. The unoptimized chess program does more processing, sure, but we wouldn't really want to say that it is more process-intensive. (Or if we do, we would have to give up the idea that process-intensity is something to be aimed for.) In fact I think a much more interesting ratio than process-intensity is the ratio of dynamically-generated data (that is used in decision-making) to the amount of statically-defined data. What makes the unoptimized chessplaying program weak is that it doesn't build up interesting dynamic data structures which it can use to optimize the search. In terms of this ratio of dynamic-data to static-data, *The Sims 3* is more dynamic than previous Sims games—much more dynamic data is generated on the fly to decide what is appropriate to do.

As I replied to Evans, I actually agree with his argument, for the most part. However, my revised conception of process intensity is not a clear-cut ratio of processing used for behavior to processing used for other purposes. The question also isn't something broader along the same lines, such as, "How much effort—in design, production, and operation—goes into determining behavior, and how much goes into other things?"

Rather, my revised conception is one it no longer makes sense to express as a ratio. Its question might be, "How much is dynamic behavior the focus of the design and experience?" If we have two chess programs, one which focuses more on figuring out the next move and the other which focuses more on playing pre-rendered animations of the pieces fighting after each move, clearly the one emphasizing dynamic behavior (choosing the move) rather than canned behavior (playing the animations) is more process intensive. And there's no confusion when we do the pruning—it doesn't lessen the amount that dynamic behavior is the focus.

This approach to the concept is significantly less clear-cut than a Crawford-style ratio. It is my suspicion, however, that any version of the concept based on a simple ratio will be troubled by issues such as those raised earlier in this chapter. That said, Evans's revised ratio (of dynamic to static data) seems stronger than many alternatives.

15. I pick out Mateas because of his particular interest in fiction and games. But similar shifts have been undertaken by a number of other prominent young researchers with artificial intelligence backgrounds, such as Phoebe Sengers and Warren Sack.

Chapter 5
The *Tale-Spin* Effect

The "Metanovel"

In fall 1974, James Meehan was a graduate student at Yale University. He had an idea in mind for his dissertation topic, but didn't know how to pursue it. The topic had been suggested to him by Alan Perlis—one of the most famous figures in U.S. computer science, who had been named chair of Yale's department a few years before—on the first day they met. But Perlis didn't know how to move forward with the idea, either. In the preface to his dissertation, Meehan describes the idea this way:

> A metanovel is a computer program that tells stories that only a computer could tell, stories of such complexity of detail that only a computer could handle, stories with more flexibility—even reversibility—of events and characters than a human could manage. A metanovel time-sharing system tells a story to many people at once, no two of whom read the same thing, because they have each expressed different interests in the events and characters they want to hear about, and because they may each desire a different style of storytelling. And yet, among all these readers, there is but one story—the Metanovel itself—and each reader is only following those threads of the story that interest him. (1976, ii)

Meehan's dissertation didn't set out to create a metanovel but rather to make progress toward the possibility. As he notes, "If I've been successful, we're a little closer than we were." In the decades since, his work has become a landmark—the first project cited in nearly every discussion of story generation.

1. This is one aspect of Meehan's critique, other aspects of which focus on the mismatch between the behavior of Klein's system and theories of the behavior of human storytellers.

Computer systems had certainly produced stories as output before. The most famous of these was the "automatic novel writer" produced by Sheldon Klein and his collaborators (1971) at the University of Wisconsin at Madison. But the field has generally followed Meehan's critique of Klein's system: it was made up of explicit chunks of action, with a path through these chunks selected randomly.[1] So, for example, Klein's system includes a "rule for people arriving at George's living room" (27). Meehan's system, on the other hand, contains general rules for character movement (and reasons for movement) that operate no matter which spaces are available—living rooms, bedrooms, caves, or meadows.

More broadly, this points to the two main types of systems for creating variable fictions. Klein's system, like quest flags and *Choose Your Own Adventure* books, is composed of explicit chunks of story content. If one of these is changed or removed, not much else changes. At most, if some story chunks are only accessible by passing through others, when a chunk is removed other chunks may become impossible to reach. Meehan's system, on the other hand, models story as a relatively fine-grained set of processes and data that are used to generate story events. In the case of *Tale-Spin,* this is accomplished by creating a simulated world, processes for behavior in and of the world, and characters and objects that populate the world. As a result, changing one aspect of the simulation (such as a rule for character movement or the existence of a particular object) can lead to wildly different *Tale-Spin* fictions. This kind of flexible model has become a defining characteristic for the pursuit of story generation.

Basis for the Model

The breakthrough that allowed Meehan to see a path forward toward the metanovel was exposure to the scruffy artificial intelligence (AI) ideas of Roger Schank and Robert Abelson. Schank had just arrived at Yale in fall 1974, and Meehan enrolled in his natural language processing seminar—which Meehan described as "a weekly battle of ideas" featuring favorite "guest speaker/victims" such as Abelson (1976, iv).

Many of Schank's theories were developed in the field of computational linguistics, where he argued that previous work was fundamentally flawed in its approach. For example, in the area of computer translation from one language to another, projects based on syntactic parsing and dictionary-style substitution had largely failed. Schank instead proposed a language-independent representation of semantic meaning, which he called *conceptual dependency* expressions. As Schank (1975a) describes them in *Conceptual Information Processing*, such semantic representations could serve as an *interlingua,* so that the translation of a statement from any one language to another could be accomplished by translating that statement to and from the semantic representation. Such a representation could also serve as an internal meaning representation—or data format—for AI projects, helping in processes such as paraphrasing and inference making, as demonstrated in systems built by Schank and his students (see sidebar: Yale AI). *Tale-Spin* followed this lead, operating in terms of conceptual dependency expressions.

But understanding the meaning of sentences, rather than simply their structure, requires understanding their context. "Mary hit John" probably means different things

Yale AI

James Meehan's *Tale-Spin* is the only project I discuss in detail that was developed at Yale University's Artificial Intelligence (AI) laboratory. However, the Yale AI Project and the worldview of Roger Schank, its charismatic leader, were central to the development of the strand of work that connects a number of my central examples. This is especially true of *Tale-Spin,* Michael Lebowitz's *Universe,* Scott Turner's *Minstrel,* and the ideology model for Michael Mateas et al's *Terminal Time.*

In 1987 Stephen Slade published an article looking back on a dozen years of projects following Schank's arrival at Yale. In reviewing the largest body of work, that described as "cognitive modeling," Slade notes how it largely continued in the mold set by the *Margie* system, developed by Schank and his students during his time at Stanford University (before Yale). Specifically, Slade notes *Margie*'s:

> Task Orientation. An AI program should address a specific, real-world task. The program should model something that a person actually does, rather than an artificial abstraction of intelligent behavior. *Margie*'s tasks included reading, paraphrase, and translation. . . .

> Psychological Process Model. The *Margie* program was a cognitive simulation. Not only did it try to perform tasks that people perform, but it tried to simulate the manner in which the human mind works. By comparison, a computer chess program which exhaustively searches ahead several moves may be able to play a fine game of chess, but it is unrealistic to consider such a program a model of the way in which a person plays chess. . . .

> Canonical Representation of Knowledge. The heart of the *Margie* system was the conceptual dependency knowledge representation system. CD provided a means of representing actions and states in a canonical, language independent fashion. A concept represented using the dozen CD primitives might be expressed in any number of ways in any number of languages. . . . (68)

All three of these Schank-driven priorities are clearly evident in *Tale-Spin,* as this chapter's discussion makes clear. They also deeply inform the background of the other Yale-related projects I consider, as well as influencing and reflecting the broader AI research of the era, especially that which could be termed "scruffy." With these goals in mind, the motivations for certain system-design choices should be easier to understand as I discuss them in the pages ahead.

if John is Mary's sparring partner or if John is sitting at Mary's blackjack table. This fact motivated a series of projects directed by Schank that attempted to bring together theorizing about how humans understand stories with the building of computer systems for the same task. The systems were viewed as experiments that would help refine and validate the theories, and a primary goal was developing theories for understanding the causal relationships between elements. The first step was a theory of *scripts*—that human knowledge for certain routine situations (e.g., going to a restaurant or catching a bus) exists as stereotyped sequences of common events. Computer systems were built that succeeded in interpreting simple stories (e.g., of auto accidents) by determining relationships between the sentences of the stories and corresponding elements of an internal script.

But *Tale-Spin* largely avoids scripts. As Meehan puts it, scripts are "so developed that they're uninteresting: not great story material" (1976, 213). Scripts only allowed for theorizing and system building about the least novel elements of human life. The next step was to build systems around Abelson's and Schank's developing versions of the central AI concepts of *plans* and *goals*. This was taking place just as Schank arrived at Yale, and to Meehan the results looked like much better story material.[2]

The *Tale-Spin* system produces stories by changing the status of Schank's and Abelson's theories about planning behavior. In story-understanding systems, these theories were *data*. They were used by the system processes as patterns to compare against the behavior described in stories being interpreted. But in *Tale-Spin* they become

2. Schank echoes Meehan's opinion of the relative interest value of stories about scripts versus those about plans in *Inside Computer Understanding*. Many stories (particularly the more interesting ones) are about entirely new …

Notes continued at end of this chapter.

processes, used to create a world in which characters behave according to the theories. As Meehan puts it:

> *Tale-Spin* includes a simulator of the real world: Turn it on and watch all the people. The purpose of the simulator is to model rational behavior; the people are supposed to act like real people. (1976, 107)

Most *Tale-Spin* stories don't feature "people" that are human characters, however. Instead, the people are largely birds, bears, bees, foxes, and so on. This was Schank's suggestion, inspired by, as he puts it, "the fact that I had little kids at the time so I was making up [stories] and trying to see how [I] did it." It also served to compensate, Meehan writes, for the fact that "we weren't going to get very sophisticated or elaborate output from this program" (2006). In other words, the decision to tell animal stories is an example of the common AI approach of defining a *microworld* in which the program will operate. Just as some AI researchers demonstrated programs that could understand the physics of a simplified "blocks world" (allowing them to ignore issues such as the relative strength of materials), *Tale-Spin* operated in a simplified animal world resembling the settings for Aesop's fables (shaving complexity both from the possibilities of the world and the potential motivations of the characters).

Tale-Spin Today

Today *Tale-Spin* is one of the most widely discussed digital fictions ever produced. It is not only a touchstone for computer science accounts of story generation but also broadly cited in writing about digital literature and the future of fiction. At the same time, *Tale-Spin* itself seemed permanently lost during most of this conversation—until a copy of its code was unearthed in 2008.

Ongoing discussion of this seemingly lost software was made possible by two facts. First, many examples of fictions produced by *Tale-Spin* are in circulation. These form the basis of most humanistic discussions of *Tale-Spin,* which tend to be dismissive. Second, Meehan's dissertation gives detailed accounts of the operations of *Tale-Spin*'s processes, along with significant information about its data. This serves as the basis for most computer science discussions of *Tale-Spin,* which tend to treat the system as worthy of serious engagement.

For many years I was only exposed to examples of *Tale-Spin* fictions, which I found so uninteresting that I never learned more about the system. But once I began to learn about *Tale-Spin*'s processes I became fascinated—both with the system itself, and the differing attitudes between those who understood the system and those who only saw its output.

After reading Meehan's dissertation, I began to look for even more detailed sources of information and especially for a copy of the software itself. I had previously seen *Micro Tale-Spin* (Meehan 1981), a smaller, pedagogical version. But this was so simplified that it lacked most of what interested me about *Tale-Spin.* Through Walt Scacchi, a former student of Meehan's from his time at the University of California at Irvine, I got an email introduction. I had a pleasant correspondence with Meehan, now at Google, and he looked through his garage on my behalf—seeking traces of *Tale-Spin*—but his initial search came up empty.

After some further searching, I gave up hope of ever locating a copy of *Tale-Spin*.[3] But then, in March 2008, I

3. The next stage in my search began when I learned from Meehan about another iteration of the system, more complex than the "micro" version, created for the 1987 Smart Machines exhibit at the Boston Computer Museum. Unfortunately…

Notes continued at end of this chapter.

4. Though to be scrupulously accurate, to my knowledge Weizenbaum only distributed the verbatim code for the *Doctor* script. His publications on the *Eliza* system, however, were explicit enough to make independent reimplementation relatively easy.

received an email from Meehan that began:

> Never say never. I'm in the process of moving to a smaller place (in San Francisco), which means going through every box and deciding what to keep and what not to keep. Lo and behold, I found a print-out of the complete source of *Tale-Spin*. It's about 4K lines of MLISP, printed on fan-fold paper. There's even a cross-reference table at the end. (2008)

He sent me the listing, which gives a complete specification of *Tale-Spin*'s processes (Meehan 1980). Unfortunately, he did not turn up a listing for any of the accompanying data files. However, this still opens the possibility for us to learn again from *Tale-Spin*, as we do today from *Eliza/Doctor*. In particular, it gives us the opportunity for knowledge through personal interaction, programmatic substitution and deformation, and examination of the code, rather than simply from reports of its processes.[4] The best first step is probably to follow Warren Sack's lead and translate the code from MLISP into Common LISP, as he did with *Micro Tale-Spin* (Meehan and Sack 1992).

My discussion here emerges from my study of Meehan's 1976 dissertation and 1980 source code. As it happens, some of the most interesting lessons I perceive arise from a kind of inversion of the *Eliza* effect. Rather than a surface illusion of process complexity and intelligence, *Tale-Spin* creates a surface illusion of process simplicity and arbitrary action. It is far from alone in this. As a result, I believe understanding the more general *Tale-Spin* effect can provide insights for both authors and interpreters of digital fictions, as well as those who seek to understand computational systems broadly.

A *Tale-Spin* Story

Tale-Spin, as described in Meehan's dissertation, has three storytelling modes. Two modes are interactive, asking the audience to make decisions about features of the story world, while one mode "fixes" the world to assure the production of particular stories.[5] Chapter 11 of Meehan's dissertation gives a detailed account of an interactive story, about a hungry bear named Arthur, that I will use to illustrate *Tale-Spin*'s operations and their backgrounds.

5. For the third mode, Meehan worked particularly on versions of Aesop's fables such as "The Fox and the Crow" and "The Ant and the Dove."

Creating a World

Tale-Spin asks what characters to use for the story, and the reader chooses a bear and bird. Each choice results in a "picture procedure," creating the basic set of facts for that character that will be used to make up the simulation but won't necessarily appear in the final story told to the audience. For example, the procedure for the bear creates a bear, chooses the bear's gender, gives the bear a name, adds the bear's name to the list of story characters, chooses a height and weight for the bear, creates a cave, creates a mountain in which the cave exists, marks the cave as being the home of the bear, and lets both the bear and the system know that the bear is in the cave. In Meehan's story the bear is named Arthur, and by similar means a bird named George is created (along with a nest, a maple tree for the nest, and a meadow for the tree). Each character is added to the other's list of acquaintances, so they know that each other exist, and they each have an idea of the other's location.

This kind of information is represented in Schank's conceptual dependency expressions. While Schank's

123

6. This example and
the one above are
adapted from Meehan's
dissertation (1976,
195–196)—substituting
other characters with
those in this story.

published accounts at the time represented conceptual dependency expressions using complex diagrams with multiple forms of connectors, software such as *Tale-Spin* used more machine-readable formats. In *Tale-Spin,* the conceptual dependency expression for "Arthur is in his Cave" could be represented as:

```
((ACTOR *ARTHURBEAR* IS (*LOC*
VAL (*PROX* PART *CAVE*0))))
```

But much of *Tale-Spin* operates on more complex conceptual dependency expressions, as the coming pages will reveal. Meehan writes his own English-language representations of these, and I will follow his lead here. Otherwise, even relatively simple ideas such as "Arthur knows that George thinks he's an idiot" would require parsing conceptual dependency expressions that look like this: [6]

```
((CON ((CON ((ACTOR *ARTHURBEAR*
          IS (*SMART* VAL (-9))))
      IS (*MLOC* VAL (*CP* PART
 *GEORGEBIRD*))))
      IS (*MLOC* VAL (*CP* PART *ARTHURBEAR*))))
```

Though from here my discussion of *Tale-Spin* will take place using English translations of conceptual dependency expressions, looking a bit more at the above examples will help to clarify the structure of these expressions. If one looks at the representation of the idea that Arthur is in his cave, the structure is similar to that for the idea that Arthur is an idiot (his *Smart* has the value of "-9" on a scale that runs from 10 to -10). *MLoc* is a Mental Location, and in the two cases above it is the

CP, or Conscious Processor, of one of the characters. So we might more literally translate the expression above, from the outermost parentheses to the innermost, with a sentence like, "It is in the consciousness of Arthur Bear that it is in the consciousness of George Bird that Arthur Bear's intelligence is at a very low level."

The world of *Tale-Spin* changes based on events and inferences from these events. All events are acts, involving some actor taking some action. In conceptual dependency theory, there are only eleven primitive acts. The *MLoc* facts above would likely grow from *MTrans* events—those that transfer information, either within a person's memory or between people. Primitive events play important roles in *Tale-Spin,* and the remaining ten are most easily described in two groups. Seven acts are relatively concrete: *Propel* (apply force to), *Move* (move a body part), *Ingest* (take something inside an animate object), *Expel* (force something out of an animate object), *Grasp* (physically grasp an object), *Speak* (produce a sound), and *Attend* (direct sense organ toward or focus it on something). The last three acts, like *MTrans,* are more abstract: *PTrans* (change the location of something), *ATrans* (change some abstract relationship with respect to an object), and *MBuild* (create or combine thoughts).[7]

> 7. This summary draws on Schank's *Conceptual Information Processing* (1975a, 41–44).

Motivating Action

Returning to Arthur's story, the audience is asked whether any miscellaneous items should be created: "berries," "flower," "river," and "worm." The audience chooses a worm, and it is created along with the ground where it is currently located. The audience is asked who knows about the worm, and chooses Arthur Bear. *Tale-Spin* now has enough information to ask who the main character of the story will be:

THIS IS A STORY ABOUT . . .

1: GEORGE BIRD   2: ARTHUR BEAR

The audience chooses Arthur, and then is asked about his problem:

HIS PROBLEM IS THAT HE IS . . .

1: HUNGRY   2: TIRED   3: THIRSTY   4: HORNY

The world of *Tale-Spin* revolves around solving problems, particularly those represented by four "sigma-states": *Sigma-Hunger, Sigma-Thirst, Sigma-Rest,* and *Sigma-Sex.* These, as one might imagine, represent being hungry, thirsty, tired, and—in the system's terminology—horny, respectively. These problems are solved using Schank's and Abelson's approach to planning.

Schank characterizes planning this way in his paper "Using Knowledge to Understand":

> A Plan is the name of a desired action whose realization may be a simple action ([a] conceptualization involving a primitive ACT). However, if it is realized that some state blocks the doing of that action, the plan may be translated into a deltact to change the state that impedes the desired ACT. Thus, a Plan has attached to it a group of deltacts with tests for selecting between them. (1975b, 119)

So, for example, if—by unlikely circumstance—Arthur forms a plan to eat when he already has honey in front of his mouth, all he has to do is the primitive act of *Ingest*-ing the honey. But if Arthur does not already have honey in front of his mouth, the plan will be translated into a deltact with the goal of getting honey (or perhaps some other food) in front of his mouth. He may choose one that involves moving some food there with his hand. If he does not have any food in his hand, getting some food there may become a state-change goal. This idea of deltacts (or as Meehan calls them, "delta-acts") comes from Abelson.[8] He describes his work on them as an attempt to "develop a set of intention primitives as building blocks for plans. Each primitive is an act package causing a state change. Each state change helps enable some later action, such that there is a chain or lattice of steps from the initial states to the goal state" (Abelson 1975, 5). Schank embellished the idea of delacts with what he calls "planboxes." These are specific approaches to achieving the state change.

For *Tale-Spin,* Meehan implemented three delta-acts that correspond to the primitive conceptual dependency acts *PTrans, MTrans,* and *ATrans.* The first, *Delta-Prox,* is used when someone wants to change the state of something to make it near something else, which includes changing one's own state to be near something. (*Delta-Neg-Prox* is used to get something away from somewhere.) *Delta-Know* is used when someone wants to change the state of someone to know something. Meehan calls his procedure for the communicative version of this *Tell* and the procedure for wanting to find something out oneself *DKnow.* Finally, *Delta-Control* is used when someone wants to acquire something.

In *Tale-Spin,* many of the planboxes of these delta-acts depend on somehow persuading another character to do something. These common planboxes are gathered together into a *Persuade* package, which includes: simply

8. Meehan calls them *delta-acts* in his dissertation, while Abelson and Schank call them *deltacts* in their 1975 publications (Schank 1975b; Abelson 1975). I will alternate, depending on whose work I am referencing.

asking; linking the action to a goal that the other character is presumed to have, and enabling the action; bargaining; and threatening. Like all planboxes, each of these has preconditions—a character does not ask another to simply tell her something if she believes that the other intensely dislikes her. Similarly, a character does not threaten a character she likes a lot.

Making Plans

When the audience chooses hunger as Arthur's problem, *Tale-Spin* generates the conceptual dependency expression "Arthur knows that he is hungry." This is then *asserted*. To understand what this means, it is helpful to look at figure 5.1, which illustrates the control structure of *Tale-Spin*'s simulation.

One thing that assertion does is add information to memory. *Tale-Spin*'s memory contains information about the structure of the physical world, the structure of relationships between characters, facts about particular characters, and so on. Every fact in memory is indexed based on who believes it, with true things indexed to the

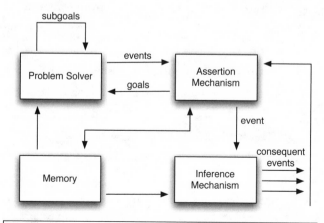

Figure 5.1. Control structure of *Tale-Spin*'s simulator, after Meehan's figure 1.

system. Every fact is also either currently true or "old" (true at some time in the past). In this case, "Arthur is hungry" is added to memory and indexed as something believed by Arthur.

When this fact is added to memory, it results in the fact being passed to the inference mechanism. For negative sigma-states, the inference mechanism creates conceptual dependency expressions of the form "Arthur knows that Arthur intends not to be hungry." This expression represents, of course, a *goal*. When it is passed to the assertion mechanism, the result is to invoke the problem solver, which begins the process of planning.

The name of the *Tale-Spin* procedure for satisfying hunger is *S-Hunger* (for *Sigma-Hunger*). In *Tale-Spin,* bears eat honey and berries. *S-Hunger* checks memory to see if Arthur knows that he owns some honey or berries, or knows where some honey or berries are. He doesn't, so *S-Hunger* selects a bear food at random—in this case honey—and invokes *DCont* (*Delta-Control*) to get some.

DCont forms the goal "Arthur has some honey" and starts checking the preconditions for its planboxes. First it checks to see if it is already true (it is not). Then it checks to see if this goal is already part of Arthur's goal structure. It's not, so it is added.

Why does *DCont* check to see if getting honey is already part of Arthur's goal structure? For a number of reasons, the most obvious of which is because if it's already his goal (or a subgoal toward a higher goal), then it makes little sense to add it. But another reason to check for the goal's existence is that *Tale-Spin* also keeps failed goals, and the reasons for their failure, as part of a character's goal structure. Before this was added, *Tale-*

Spin created stories with a certain surreal quality. Here's an example:

> Joe Bear was hungry. He asked Irving Bird where some honey was. Irving refused to tell him, so Joe offered to bring him a worm if he'd tell him where some honey was. Irving agreed. But Joe didn't know where any worms were, so he asked Irving, who refused to say. So Joe offered to bring him a worm if he'd tell him where a worm was. Irving agreed. But Joe didn't know where any worms were, so he asked Irving, who refused to say. So Joe offered to bring him a worm if he'd tell him where a worm was. (Meehan 1976, 129–130)

In fact, these error-produced stories—which Meehan called "mis-spun tales"—are *Tale-Spin*'s most famous outputs, much more widely reprinted than anything produced by the completed system. There are a number of reasons for this. First is the amusement value. Another is that these stories, hand translated from conceptual dependency expressions by Meehan, have much more fluid prose than stories produced by *Tale-Spin*'s companion natural-language generation system, *Mumble*. Third, these stories also give a hint, simply through their structure, of some of the mechanics of the underlying *Tale-Spin* processes. Unfortunately, as I will discuss later, those who attempted to interpret these outputs without any deeper understanding of the *Tale-Spin* system often reached rather misleading conclusions.

Developing Relationships

Arthur is trying to get some honey, which is a *Delta-Control* problem. In *Tale-Spin,* the first precondition for *DCont*'s planboxes is to know the location of the thing to be controlled. Since Arthur does not know where any honey is, *DKnow* is called. *DKnow* forms the goal "Arthur knows where some honey is." It's not already true, and it's not yet part of the goal structure, so it is added. The first planbox of *DKnow* is used if there is a standard method for finding the information: like checking a watch or clock to learn the time. There isn't one of these for honey in *Tale-Spin,* so the next planbox of *DKnow* is to see if there's someone who is an expert on these matters to ask.[9] Bears are experts at honey, but Arthur's the only bear he knows about, so *Tale-Spin* moves to the next planbox, which is to use the methods of the *Persuade* package to convince a friend to tell you. A friend is someone that you think relates to you with a positive value for affection. Arthur's opinion of George Bird's opinion of him is unknown. If the audience says that Arthur doesn't think they're friends, Arthur will have only one *DKnow* planbox left before he has to give up on the goal of having some honey: *Persuade*-ing an agent to find out the answer and tell him.

Relationship and personality states are extensions to Schank's and Abelson's work created by Meehan for his work on *Tale-Spin* (1976, 40). Testing memory for a relationship state is done by a procedure that adds the state to memory if it isn't there. Since *Tale-Spin* is in the mode of asking the audience, it types:

DOES ARTHUR BEAR THINK THAT
GEORGE BIRD LIKES HIM?

1: A LOT 2: A LITTLE 3: NOT MUCH 4: NOT AT ALL

Tale-Spin can simultaneously maintain four different states that are similar to this in memory. The first, this one, is: Does Arthur think that George likes him? The

9. According to Meehan's dissertation (1976, 50). The description of this portion of chapter 11's story (ibid., 170) elides this step.

others are: Does Arthur think that he likes George (i.e., does Arthur like George)? Does George think that Arthur likes him? Does George think that he likes Arthur (i.e., does George like Arthur)? All are used in making different types of plans.

The audience says that Arthur thinks George likes him a lot, so *Persuade* starts working through its planboxes with the goal of Arthur getting George to tell him where some honey is, in pursuit of the higher goal of getting some honey. The first planbox is to simply ask, but it has further preconditions. So *Tale-Spin* asks if Arthur feels deceptive toward George (the audience answers: not at all), if Arthur feels competitive toward George (not at all), if Arthur likes George (a lot), and if Arthur thinks that George is trying to deceive him (not at all).

Finally, Arthur Bear has a plan to know where some honey is, so he can control it, so he can eat it, so he can be less hungry: he'll ask George Bird.

Speculations and Lies

From here things begin to go poorly for Arthur. It turns out that George is a deceptive bird and will deliberately tell Arthur about an alternative possible world that isn't the one of this *Tale-Spin* story. That is, he's going to lie, and *Tale-Spin* is going to create a parallel world structure to support this lie, representing the fact that Arthur believes it.

First, Arthur wants to *Tell* George his request. *Tell* has two planboxes: do it yourself, or get an agent to do it. Arthur starts with the first one, which requires that he be near George. This is a *Delta-Prox* problem, resulting in the formation of the goal "Arthur is near

George," and the appropriate planboxes of *DProx* start going. Since Arthur knows where he is (the cave) and thinks he knows where George is (his nest), there's no need to start up *DKnow* planboxes. *DLink* then creates more of the world, so that there's a connection between Arthur's mountain and George's meadow. Then *Do-PTrans* moves Arthur along the ground (bears cannot fly) to near George's maple tree. The inferences from this include Arthur and George both knowing that Arthur has arrived there, and Arthur knowing that George is there. Before these sorts of inferences, characters had to *Speak* to let others know of their presence. This failure of characters to notice each other created another of *Tale-Spin*'s famous misspun tales:

> Henry Ant was thirsty. He walked over to the river bank where his good friend Bill Bird was sitting. Henry slipped and fell in the river. He was unable to call for help. He drowned. (1976, 128)

Meehan added noticing as an inference from changes in location, causing Bill to save Henry's life. But another was not so lucky:

> Henry Ant was thirsty. He walked over to the river bank where his good friend Bill Bird was sitting. Henry slipped and fell in the river. Gravity drowned. (129)

In this version of *Tale-Spin,* gravity was a character that performed a *Grasp* on Henry Ant and then *PTRans*-ed them both into the river. Henry got rescued by his friend Bill, but gravity had no way out. This was fixed by changing how gravity operates in terms of Schank's conceptual dependency expressions—*Propel*-ing Henry instead.

Returning to our story, once everyone knows Arthur

and George are near each other, *Do-MTrans* is called and Arthur asks George to tell him where some honey is, resulting in a call to the procedure for handling favors: *Request.* Now there is reason to ask the audience how George views his relationship with Arthur. *Tale-Spin* asks if he likes Arthur (answer: a little), if he trusts Arthur (a little), if he thinks he dominates Arthur (not at all), if he feels indebted to Arthur (not at all), and if he thinks that Arthur trusts him (a little).

Here we come to the main "psychological action" of this *Tale-Spin* story. This action is enabled by the fact that character planning can make use of *Tale-Spin*'s inference mechanisms. George Bird uses these mechanisms to speculate about the potential impact of answering Arthur's request.

The first inference is an obvious one: Arthur will think that George has told him there is honey somewhere. Second, from what George believes about their relationship, George can make the inference that Arthur will believe that he believes there is honey in this place. Also, based on the relationship, he infers that Arthur will believe there is honey in that place. Finally, George can infer, based on this, that Arthur will make a plan to eat the honey.

George then takes all of these inferences and, in turn, generates all the inferences from them. We might say that he imagines worlds in which each of these things is true. But he doesn't find what he's looking for in any of them. As Meehan puts it, he "was looking for an inference that said he was going to be happy (or sad), so that he could decide in favor of (or against) Arthur's request" (1976, 183). So in consultation with the audience, it is decided that George will lie to Arthur.

When this happens, the entire structure of what George tells Arthur is created in the course of the *Do-MTrans*, but some of it is only indexed to character memory, not the system's memory. This leads to the creation of Ivan Bee, who owns honey, which is in a beehive, which is in a redwood tree, which is surrounded by some ground, which is part of a valley. The physical locations are indexed to the system memory: they're real. But at first the hive, bee, and honey are only in George's memory, and not believed. When he tells Arthur about them, the audience needs to be asked how much Arthur trusts George. The answer is "a little," and the inference maker determines that they are added to Arthur's beliefs about the world.

Another Trick

Now Arthur thinks he knows where to find some honey. As Meehan notes,

> DO-MTRANS returns to REQUEST which returns to the first call of DO-MTRANS which returns to TELL which returns to PERSUADE. The goal of the persuasion has been satisfied— Arthur now thinks he knows where there's some honey—so PERSUADE returns to DKNOW which returns to DCONT. . . . All this has gone toward achieving only the first precondition of DCONT, finding out where some honey was. (1976, 184–185)

Nothing goes well for Arthur from here. The audience is asked how he feels toward Ivan (real feelings, in Arthur's reference world, even if toward a fictitious being in this *Tale-Spin* world), and he decides to ask Ivan for some honey. Arthur travels to where he believes Ivan can be found, but when he gets there, *Tell* fails its precondition tests—he's not "close" to Ivan, because Ivan's not there.

Arthur infers that George has lied, and proceeds to distrust him, like him somewhat less, and believe George is trying to deceive him. However, Arthur hasn't stopped *believing* that Ivan exists, only that he *knows* where Ivan exists. As it turns out, there's no one to ask where Ivan really is except George.

So Arthur heads back to George's tree. Given that asking George where Ivan is still exists as a failed goal, he tries the next *Persuade* planbox: bargaining. He infers that George would probably like a worm, and the initial setup determined that Arthur knew the location of a worm. So Arthur offers George a worm if he will tell him where to find Ivan. George promises to do so (a possible world), while making the decision to trick Arthur (a different possible world, which will only come to exist if triggered by the worm's arrival). After Arthur succeeds in getting the worm and bringing it to George, the bird eats it and makes fun of him. With this planbox having failed, the next is to threaten. But the audience, when asked, asserts that Arthur feels a little dominated by George, so he won't try it.

Having failed to find a way to ask Ivan for honey directly, Arthur is moved by the next planbox of *Tell* to try to get someone else to ask Ivan to give him honey. He tries with George—there's no one else—but this fails even more pitifully than his last attempt. Things continue to unravel until *Tale-Spin* decides there's nothing more that Arthur knows to do to try to address his hunger.

His options are particularly limited because there's no way for him to go looking for food—if he cannot convince someone else to tell him, there's no way to find out. And as we remember from the setup for the story, no one knows about any bear food in this world. Between Arthur and George they only know about one worm. So the story could not have turned out any other way. As soon as the audience decided that hunger was Arthur's problem, he was doomed. He made many plans, yet none of them had a chance of working. The end.

Tale-Spin's Fiction

That was a significant amount of detail about *Tale-Spin*, more than I will offer about any other system described in this book. I hope it gave some sense of the type of undertaking involved in creating even a first-generation story system. There's much more going on—at the levels of character and story—than in something like *Eliza/Doctor* or a standard computer RPG. Further, it illustrates how a computer system that seeks to generate representations of human behavior can be built as an operationalization of theories about human behavior.

But it's also worth noting that the story produced in our *Tale-Spin* example wasn't a particularly strong instance of fiction. While *Tale-Spin* creates character behavior, this behavior doesn't necessarily take the shape of a traditional story. In addition, much of the action that takes place in the generation of such a story (as with our example) is present only at the process level and imperceptible to the audience. An audience member presented with the output of this *Tale-Spin* story would have seen something much shorter and simpler. This is something to which I'll return later. For now, I want to consider what it means to say that *Tale-Spin* produces fiction at all.

10. Ryan particularly notes Lucia Vania, Umberto Eco, David Lewis, and Lubomir Doležel—followed by the 1980s books of Doreen Maître and Thomas Pavel. In the first chapter of *Fictional Worlds,* Pavel (1986) sketches a similar picture…

Notes continued at end of this chapter.

Possible Worlds

A shorthand definition of *fiction* might be a listing of its most familiar forms: "novels and short stories," or perhaps "novels, short stories, theater, television, and movies." Yet such definitions won't be much help to us if we are interested in thinking about emerging forms. At one point, the novel was an innovative new form of fiction and would have been left out of such a definition. Now there are various innovative digital forms of fiction emerging. In order to think about new forms, we need a more principled definition of fiction.

In response to this, a number of digital media theorists have begun to work with definitions of fiction emerging from possible worlds theory and modal logic. These are among a wider group of literary approaches derived from philosophy and linguistics, and this particular strand began to establish its own identity in the 1970s. In *Possible Worlds, Artificial Intelligence, and Narrative Theory,* Marie-Laure Ryan (1992) traces the lineage of this work to the late-1970s essays of a number of writers.[10]

In philosophy the notion of possible worlds is often traced back to Gottfried Wilhelm Leibniz, whose position is perhaps most widely remembered as that devoutly held by Dr. Pangloss in Voltaire's *Candide.* Leibniz argued that there are an infinity of possible worlds in the mind of God—and that one of them, the best possible, is the one in which we live. Leibniz's position is engaged with the most elevated concerns of philosophy and theology, but that is not the only place we find possible worlds. Closer to home, we imagine possible worlds when we speculate ("I wonder if the lunch special will be Lemongrass Tofu"), when we wish ("I hope Jane gets that promotion"), when

138

we plan ("We'll get there before the doors open, so we have great seats"), and so on. Possible worlds, and modal logic more generally, are tools for thinking through versions of such questions as: What is possible? What is impossible? What is necessary or contingent? The work of a number of thinkers has, especially since the 1960s, returned philosophers to consideration of these topics well after the time of Leibniz.

A simple attempt at applying possible worlds theory to fiction might propose that nonfiction texts refer to our world, the real world, while fictional texts refer to alternative possible worlds. As Ryan points out, though, there are a number of problems with this. For example, this formulation does not provide a way of distinguishing between fiction, errors, and lies—all are statements made in reference to alternative possible worlds. At a more complex level, there is also the problem that further alternative possible worlds are continually embedded into both fiction and nonfiction. For instance, both fiction and nonfiction describe the unrealized wishes and plans of the people who appear in them. Ryan's work responds to these issues by identifying a further element—beyond the creation of an alternative possible world—that is necessary for fiction.

Ryan considers the constituent move of fiction, not simply the creation of an alternative possible world but the *recentering* of discourse to that world—so that indexical terms such as "here" and "now" are understood to refer to the alternative possible world, and terms such as "actual" become indexical. Further, for Ryan fiction not only creates an alternative possible world but also a system of reality, a universe. This is necessary because the alternative world of a fiction may also have many alternative possible worlds emanating from it, and each of them may have further alternative possible worlds (as when one character speculates as to the plans of another character). Obviously, parallels with the operations of *Tale-Spin* were already at work in the description above.

Digital Fictions

Beyond the field of story generation (an interest I share with Ryan), a number of authors have used possible worlds theory as a way of grappling with emerging forms of fiction in digital media. For example, Jill Walker Rettberg, cited earlier for her discussion of quests, is a digital media theorist interested in many forms of fiction with a strong textual component (including email narratives and weblog fictions) as well as some without text as a primary component. In *Fiction and Interaction: How Clicking a Mouse Can Make You Part of a Fictional World,* Rettberg (2003) examines interactive digital fictions that somehow include the user as a character in their alternative possible world. She introduces the term "ontological interaction" in the course of describing how users are included in these worlds, building particularly on the notion from Thomas Pavel's book of "ontological fusion" (between our actual selves and fictional selves when engaging with fictional worlds) and Kendall Walton's theory of how we use fictional representations as props in a game of make-believe. (She cites Walton's 1993 *Mimesis as Make-Believe.*) Walker notes that this approach provides a vocabulary for discussing the common generation of fictional experience in works "as disparate as installation artworks, interactive narratives and computer games" (2003, 31).

In a related vein, *Half-Real*—by game developer and theorist Jesper Juul (2005)—takes computer games as the primary objects of study. Given this, Juul is not interested in *fiction* as a category of artworks but rather as something that is an element of many games. He is interested in understanding how games project fictional worlds: what kinds of worlds, how players are cued to imagine them, and how those worlds relate to the games' rules. Juul notes that game fictions, like those of traditional literature, are incomplete. Just as in *Hamlet* we know little of the world outside the castle and its immediate vicinity—but on some level assume it is embedded in a fully detailed world partially filled in by knowledge from our own world and other texts—so in the game *Half-Life* we know little of the world outside the complex where it is set. Unlike most literary fictions, however, the worlds of many games are, in Juul's terminology, "incoherent" (which is one of the things that limits Juul's interest in discussing games in terms of *narrative,* as opposed to fiction). These are worlds in which significant events take place that cannot be explained without discussing the game rules, such as the many games that feature multiple and extra lives without any element of the game fiction that points toward reincarnation. Juul describes a number of ways, going far beyond traditional novelistic techniques, that games cue players to imagine possible fictional worlds, including: graphics; sound; text; cut-scenes; game title, box, and manual; haptics; rules; player actions and time; and rumors (133–138).

Given that authors considering the concepts of fiction and digital media from differing directions have found the possible worlds approach to fiction fruitful, how can it

11. Or to put it another way, a fiction's events and their portrayal.

help one understand *Tale-Spin,* as well as story generation more generally? First, of course, it can clarify that *Tale-Spin*'s operations produce fictions. The psychological action noted during George's speculations about Arthur is revealed as precisely the stuff of fiction when seen through the lens of possible worlds theories. Second, this approach provides a way to think about fictions that is purely in terms of *structure.* This is important because *Tale-Spin,* like most story-generation projects, is concerned with producing the events of stories—and very little with how those events are presented to the audience. In literary theory this is sometimes referred to as the distinction between "story" and "discourse" (or, in some more specialized contexts, "fabula" and "sjuzhet").[11] In fact, Meehan was so little concerned with the presentation of *Tale-Spin* fictions that *Mumble*— the natural-language generator used to turn *Tale-Spin*'s conceptual dependency expressions into English—was cobbled together in a single day. (As I will discuss shortly, however, the problems with *Tale-Spin*'s output run deeper than *Mumble*'s stilted constructions.)

Most important, seeing fiction in this light can help us identify the core operational logic at work in *Tale-Spin*: planbox-based planning. This method of planning, as outlined by Schank and Abelson, operates by projecting potential behaviors that change the state of the world— possible worlds—which launch further projections, which in turn launch further projections, finding a "chain or lattice" of worlds that may lead from the current world to one in which a goal is satisfied. The *Tale-Spin* system certainly contains other operational logics, such as those governing movement, character relationships, and so on.

But *Tale-Spin* does not begin with a complete virtual world that characters can move across. Instead, movement happens only when required by plans, and the world is fleshed out only to the degree required by plans. Similarly, *Tale-Spin* does not generate a complete set of interpersonal relationships when characters are created but rather only fleshes out the connections between characters that are required by plans. So while other operational logics may contribute to the fictional worlds of *Tale-Spin,* it is the logic of planbox-based planning that is central. It creates the profusion of imagined worlds that define *Tale-Spin*'s fictions and drive the work of the system's other logics.

The *Tale-Spin* Effect

In Italo Calvino's *Invisible Cities* (Calvino and Weaver 1974), two characters named Kublai Khan and Marco Polo sit in a garden. Polo tells Khan—sometimes in words, sometimes through symbols, and sometimes through the relation of pieces on a chessboard—of cities he has visited within the vast empire. Here are a few. In the middle of Fedora is a metal building with a crystal globe in every room, each containing a model of the city as it might have been in a possible future, constructed at a different stage of its history. At every solstice and equinox, around the fires of the marketplace of Euphemia, there is trade not in goods but in memories. In Ersilia, the inhabitants stretch strings between all the houses—marking relationships of blood, trade, authority, and agency—until one can no longer pass, all but the strings are taken down, and Ersilia is built again elsewhere. Thekla is continually under construction, following the blueprint of the stars, while Andria already reflects the heavens precisely—in every street, building, job, and ceremony—but those who live there must carefully weigh each change to the city, given the changes it will produce in the heavens. Polo and Khan each propose a model city, from which all others can be deduced. They look through atlas pages that contain not only all the cities of Khan's empire but also all those that will one day come to exist (Paris, Mexico City) and all imaginary lands (Utopia, New Atlantis).

It is not hard to picture *Tale-Spin* as an addition to this list of imaginary lands. It is the place made up of nothing but plans within plans within plans. The people have no emotions, except those that help select between possible plans. They have no memories, except of plans underway, plans that have failed, and the locations of things they may use in plans. And these locations—the very geographies of this imaginary place—come to exist only as needed by their plans.

Like one of Calvino's cities, *Tale-Spin* is an alien place. And yet, each is alien because some element that we recognize of our own lives becomes the defining element, practically the only element, of the people and landscape. On some level we do trade in memories like the inhabitants of Euphemia, clot free passage with networks of connection like the inhabitants of Ersilia, and, like the inhabitants of *Tale-Spin,* make Chinese boxes of plans within plans that at times obsess us so that nothing else seems to exist.

Nevertheless, to those who consider only the output of *Tale-Spin* fictions, all of this is truly invisible. Take, for example, George Bird trying to decide how to answer Arthur Bear's request to tell him where to find honey. Meehan doesn't provide us with the *Mumble* output from this fiction, but a story with a similar situation in it is reprinted in an appendix to Meehan's dissertation. Here is the *Mumble* output of a series of considerations and speculations that, given *Tale-Spin*'s structures, is probably much like those in Arthur's and George's story:

> Tom asked Wilma whether Wilma would tell Tom where there were some berries if Tom gave Wilma a worm.
> Wilma was inclined to lie to Tom. (Meehan 1976, 232)

The empty space between those two sentences is undoubtedly one of the most interesting parts of this story, if only we could see it from the "interior" view of *Tale-Spin*'s operations. But *Mumble* stories never contain accounts of characters' multilevel speculations or elaborate considerations of potential plans. Instead, all this psychological action is, as above, elided. Looking only at the surface, the decision might as well have been made randomly.

Rather than *Tale-Spin*'s most interesting story structures, *Mumble* outputs plodding, detailed information from conceptual dependency expressions that have little fictional energy, as with the beginning of this same story:

> Once upon a time Betty Bear lived in a cave. There was a beehive in an apple tree. Maggie Bee lived in the beehive. There was some honey in Maggie's beehive. Tom Smith was in a chair. There was a nest in a redwood tree. Wilma Bird lived in the nest. Tom knew that Wilma was in her nest. Tom knew that Maggie was in her beehive. Tom knew that Betty was in her cave. There were some cranberries near a bush. There was a worm near a patch of ground. Betty knew that the cranberries were near the bush.

And so on, including painstaking reports of travel such as

"Tom walked from the chair across a living room down a hall via some stairs down a hall down a hall through a valley across a meadow to the ground by the redwood tree." It's no wonder that most humanists have seen *Tale-Spin* as only worthy of ridicule.

Further, unlike the open-ended textual interaction of *Eliza/Doctor,* the interaction allowed by *Tale-Spin* takes the form of highly restricted menu selection. No amount of play with the system will have the result of play with *Eliza/Doctor*: insight into the processes at work. Instead, it would be impossible, through play, to pierce the boring surface of a *Tale-Spin* story to see the more interesting fiction taking place through its processes.

One can look at it this way: The *Eliza* effect creates a surface illusion of system complexity—which play (if allowed) dispels. The *Tale-Spin* effect, on the other hand, creates a surface illusion of system simplicity—which the available options for play (if any) can't alter. This situation is far from uncommon in digital media, perhaps particularly in the digital arts, where fascinating processes (drawing on inspirations ranging from John Cage to the cutting edge of computer science) are often encased in an opaque interface. In fact, this effect is at least as common as the *Eliza* effect, though I know of no term that describes it—hence this coinage.

Of course, it would not be a trivial task to redesign *Tale-Spin* so that its most interesting fictional events were made apparent to its audiences. It might require, for example, that the inferences made during planning be stored in memory and (a tricky requirement) a fictionally interesting summary of them be produced by *Mumble*. But this does not make *Tale-Spin* different from digital media

146

in general. One of the most challenging design tasks in creating digital media—the form of media enabled by computational processes—is to craft and situate interesting processes so that they produce a meaningful audience experience. I will return to this challenge in a later chapter, when discussing the work of Will Wright and what I call *the SimCity effect*.

Tale-Spin as Simulation

The *Tale-Spin* effect, as described above, mainly considers *Tale-Spin* as a piece of media. Yet in its context at Yale, it was positioned as something else—or something more. As Meehan emphasizes repeatedly in his dissertation, the structures of *Tale-Spin* were not chosen because they were the most efficient way to have a computer output a story. If this were the goal, some method like that of Klein's "automatic novel writer" would have been appropriate. Instead, *Tale-Spin* was meant to operate as a simulation of human behavior, based on the then-current cognitive science ideas of Schank and Abelson.

Turning to *Tale-Spin* from this perspective, some additional issues bear discussion. For instance, recall the moment in this chapter's example *Tale-Spin* story when George Bird, seeing no advantage to himself in answering Arthur Bear about the location of honey, decides to answer nonetheless. *Tale-Spin* doesn't decide whether George will answer by simply asking the audience. Rather, it decides based on how kind George is. The audience responds that he is "somewhat" kind, so George decides to give Arthur an answer "out of the goodness of his little heart," as Meehan puts it (1976, 183). But when George Bird calls *Do-MTrans,* this

12. One interesting element of the *Tale-Spin* source code—either not present at the time of Meehan's dissertation or not reported in it—is a question asking the audience "HOW LIBERAL-MINDED ARE YOU? (0-3)" when the main character's …

Notes continued at end of this chapter.

motivation isn't communicated—and *Do-MTrans* decides to ask the audience whether George feels deceptive toward Arthur. The answer is "a lot," so George ends up lying to Arthur about the location of honey out of the goodness of his heart. This isn't a simulation of George thinking Arthur needs to diet but rather a breakdown in the simulation—though Meehan passes over it without comment.

Simulation problems become even more apparent when Meehan gives us examples of *Tale-Spin* fictions generated outside its usual microworld of talking animals—in a world of interacting human characters. For example, in an appendix, Meehan provides the story of a person whose problem is *Sigma-Sex*.[12] Here the strangeness becomes so apparent that Meehan cannot gloss over it, but his diagnosis is odd. Here are excerpts from the story:

> Once upon a time Joe Newton was in a chair. Maggie Smith was in a chair. Maggie knew that Joe was in the chair. One day Maggie was horny. Maggie loved Joe. Maggie wanted Joe to fool around with Maggie. Maggie was honest with Joe. Maggie wasn't competitive with Joe. Maggie thought that Joe loved her. Maggie thought that Joe was honest with her. Maggie wanted to ask Joe whether Joe would fool around with Maggie. . . . [She travels to where he is and asks him. His relationship with her (competition, honesty, etc.) is defined, He makes the necessary inferences and agrees. They each travel to Joe's bed. Then . . .] Joe fooled around with Maggie. Joe became happier. Maggie became happier. Joe was not horny. Joe thought that Maggie was not horny. Joe was wiped out. Joe thought that Maggie was wiped

out. . . . [Maggie makes all the same inferences, and then, because she's wiped out, this results in SIGMA-REST, and . . .] Maggie wanted to get near her bed. Maggie walked from Joe's bed across the bedroom down the hall via the stairs down the hall across the living room down the hall via the stairs down the hall down the hall through the valley down the hall across a bedroom to her bed. Maggie went to sleep. Joe went to sleep. The end. (1976, 229–230, original in all caps)

Meehan comments, "The *least* Joe could have done would be to let poor Maggie sleep in his bed" (230)—as though the problem with the story lies in the design of *Sigma-Sex*. We might like an instance of *Sigma-Rest* that results from a successful *Sigma-Sex* to understand its context and prefer for the characters to sleep in the same place. But *Tale-Spin* does not work that way. This is similar to George Bird deciding to answer Arthur Bear out of kindness, and then the loss of that context resulting in his answer being an unkind lie. The relative autonomy of the possible worlds projected by each step in *Tale-Spin*'s planbox-based planning procedures won't allow this sort of problem to be resolved with a simple tweak to one element, like *Sigma-Sex*.

Further, the problems with *Tale-Spin* telling stories of love don't just lie in the structure of its planning processes. Consider the following statement from Meehan's dissertation in terms of our culture's stories of love—for example, any Katharine Hepburn and Spencer Tracy movie:

> "John loves Mary" is actually shorthand for "John believes that he loves Mary." . . . I'm not sure it means anything—in the technical sense—to say that John loves Mary but he doesn't believe that he does. If it does, it's very subtle. (64)

In fact, it is not subtle at all. It is a significant plot element of the majority of romantic novels, television shows, and movies produced each year. But from within Meehan's context in Schank's lab his conclusion is perfectly rational. If John doesn't know that he loves Mary, then he cannot use that knowledge in formulating any conscious plans— and in *Tale-Spin* anything that isn't part of conscious planning might as well not exist.

This blindness to all but planning—this assumption that planning is at the center of life—was far from unique to the work being done at Yale. Within the wider AI and cognitive science community, at this time, the understanding and generation of plans was essentially the sole focus of work on intelligent action. Debate, as between neat and scruffy AI researchers, centered on what kind of planning to pursue, how to organize it, and so on—not on whether planning deserved its central place as a topic for attention. This was in part due to the field's technical commitments, and in part the legacy of a long tradition in the human sciences. Lucy Suchman, writing a decade later in her book *Plans and Situated Actions*, put it this way:

> The view, that purposeful action is determined by plans, is deeply rooted in the Western human sciences as *the* correct model of the rational actor. The logical form of plans makes them attractive for the purpose of constructing a computational model of action, to the extent that for those fields devoted to what is now called cognitive science, the analysis and synthesis of plans effectively constitute the study of action. (1987, ix–x)

This view has, over the last few decades, come under widespread attack from both outside and within AI. Suchman observes that, "Just as it would seem absurd to claim that a map in some strong sense controlled the traveler's movements through the world, it is wrong to imagine plans as controlling action" (189). As this has happened—and particularly as the mid-1970s theories of Schank, Abelson, and Meehan have moved into AI's disciplinary history—*Tale-Spin* has in some sense lost its status as a simulation. There's no one left who believes that it represents a simulation of how actual people behave in the world.

As this has taken place, *Tale-Spin* has become, I would argue, *more* interesting as a fiction. It can no longer be regarded as an accurate simulation of human planning behavior with a layer of semisuccessful storytelling on top of it. Rather, its entire set of operations is now revealed as an authored artifact—as an expression, through process and data, of the particular and idiosyncratic view of humanity that its author and his research group once held. Once we see it this way, it becomes a new kind of fiction, particularly appreciable in two ways. First, it provides us a two-sided pleasure that we might name "alterity in the exaggerated familiar"—one that recalls the fictions of Calvino's *Invisible Cities*. At the same time, it also provides an insight and a cautionary tale that help us see the very act of simulation-building in a new light. A simulation of human behavior is always an encoding of the beliefs and biases of its authors; it is never objective, it is always a fiction.

Rereading *Tale-Spin*

The *Tale-Spin* effect has had a huge impact on previous interpretations of *Tale-Spin,* even when the interpreters have come from very different positions as scholars.

Hamlet on the Holodeck by Janet Murray (1997) and *Cybertext* by Espen Aarseth (1997) provide helpful illustrations of this. In these cases, the *Tale-Spin* effect not only causes the authors to misinterpret *Tale-Spin* but also to miss opportunities for making fruitful connections to their own areas of interest.

Missing Characters

In her book, Murray discusses *Tale-Spin* in the context of an argument that "for authors to create rich and satisfying stories that exploit the characteristic properties of digital environments . . . [w]riters would need a concrete way to structure a coherent story not as a single sequence of events but as a multiform plot" (1997, 185). We might expect, given this, Murray would criticize *Tale-Spin* for organizing its operations at the level of character, rather than at the level of plot. Instead, however, Murray seems to assume that *Tale-Spin* does operate at the level of plot, and simply does so defectively.

Murray reprints the famous misspun tale of Joe Bear forming the failed goal, over and over, of bringing Irving Bird a worm so that Irving will tell him where a worm is. She precedes the reprinting by saying that "stories told from an abstract representation of narrative patterns but without a writer's relish for specific material can be incoherent" (200). After the story Murray writes:

> The program goes into a loop because it does not know enough about the world to give Joe Bear any better alternatives. The plot structure is too abstract to limit Joe Bear's actions to sequences that make sense. (200)

Actually, as discussed earlier, *Tale-Spin* looped because—

at the partially completed state it was in at the time this misspun tale was generated—its characters could reassert a goal that had already failed. In fact, Joe Bear's problem had to happen at the character level—it could not happen at the level of "plot structure"—because *Tale-Spin* has no "abstract representation of narrative patterns" at all.

This problem does not cause Murray's discussion to derail, by any means. Hers is mainly a speculative argument about the sorts of experiences that might eventually be possible with interactive story systems. Indeed, Murray spends many more pages on her imagined system for interactive stories set in the *Casablanca* world than she does on *Tale-Spin* or other actually implemented examples.

No, rather than a derailing, Murray's misinterpretation mostly leads to a missed opportunity. As the next chapter of her book demonstrates, she is interested in systems that model the interior operations of fictional characters. And characters like Joe Bear and George Bird have quite complex interior operations, if one looks beyond the anemic events output by *Mumble*.

The *Tale-Spin* model is, of course, problematic— and the cognitive science ideas that inspired it are now abandoned. Still, its operations provide much that deserves the attention of writers such as Murray. The complex character behavior that *Tale-Spin* produced in the 1970s is much more likely than an imaginary *Casablanca* system to make convincing fodder for an argument such as *Hamlet on the Holodeck*'s.

Imagined Narrators

In *Cybertext*, Aarseth calls *Tale-Spin* "a cybernetic fiction device that does not work" (1997, 131). He concludes this based on a selection of its misspun tales—rather than those produced by the actual, completed *Tale-Spin* system. Aarseth does see fit to qualify his statement with the phrase "at least in the examples given here," but the rhetoric of failure is important for the point he seeks to make. *Tale-Spin* is one of Aarseth's three primary examples for the argument that machine narrators should not be "forced to simulate" human narrators (129). *Tale-Spin* is presented as a failed instance of such simulation, with its misspun tales its only claim to interest.

From the viewpoint of AI, Aarseth's is an exceedingly strange argument. As I will discuss in the next chapter, the primary critique of *Tale-Spin* in AI circles is precisely that it *does not* attempt to simulate a human narrator. *Tale-Spin* simulates characters—not narrators, not authors. This has been seen as a fundamental mistake, and was a primary point for writers such as Natalie Dehn (1981a, 1981b), in widely cited papers, more than fifteen years before the publication of Aarseth's book.

As with Murray, though, we can still follow Aarseth's discussion even while acknowledging its troubles. When we see phrases such as "trying to create a surrogate author," we can substitute something like "ideological attachment to narrative ideals" (Aarseth 1997, 141). This is because Aarseth is arguing against simulating human narrators only as a proxy. He's really arguing against focusing on attempts to use the computer to extend the pleasures of traditional fiction and drama. Instead, Aarseth seeks to turn our attention to literature based on such features as combinatorics, interaction, and play—on the new literary possibilities opened by the specifics of the networked computer. As Aarseth writes:

> To achieve interesting and worthwhile computer-generated literature, it is necessary to dispose of the poetics of narrative literature and to use the computer's potential for combination and world simulation in order to develop new genres that can be valued and used on their own terms. Instead of trying to create a surrogate author, efforts in computer-generated literature should focus on the computer as a literary instrument: a machine for cybertext and ergodic literature. . . . [T]he computer as literary agent ultimately points beyond narrative and toward ergodic modes—dialogic forms of improvisation and free play. (141)

It is the puzzle of *Tale-Spin* that we can diagnose here a problem very much like Murray's. In *Tale-Spin* Aarseth has a great missed opportunity. The story structures *Tale-Spin* produces are almost never like those that a human storyteller would produce. Instead, it produces strange structures of plans within plans within plans. It produces what we might call, from the possible worlds perspective, "minimalist fictions"—made up almost entirely of possible worlds of planning, speculation, lies, and so on (without redundant emotions, movements, or even geographic locations). It is a combinatory engine for spinning off possible worlds embodying an alien vision of humanity, driven by the temporary worldview of a research lab. In other words, *Tale-Spin* can be seen as an example of one of the types of literature for which Aarseth is calling.

Interpreting Processes

Aarseth's missed opportunity, combined with Murray's, reveals something interesting. *Tale-Spin,* early as it was, stands at a crossroads. If we choose to emphasize its continuities with traditional fiction and drama, via its characters, then it becomes a useful touchstone for views such as Murray's. If we choose to emphasize its complicated strangeness, its computational specificity, then it becomes an important early example for views such as Aarseth's. Either way, a close examination of the system's operations reveals something much more intriguing than either author assumed—making a clear case for the necessity of developing an approach to reading what processes express. As readers may recall, this is my second meaning for *expressive processing*. With the example of *Tale-Spin* in mind, I will now expand this sense of the term, which itself has two elements.

First, it encompasses the fact that the internal processes of digital media are designed artifacts, like buildings, transportation systems, or music players. As with other designed mechanisms, processes can be seen in terms of their efficiency, aesthetics, points of failure, or (lack of) suitability for particular purposes. Their design can be typical, or unusual, for their era and context. The parts and their arrangement may express kinship with, as well as points of divergence from, design movements and schools of thought. They can be progressively redesigned, repurposed, or used as the foundation for new systems— by their original designers or others—all while retaining traces and characteristics from prior uses. In fact, the traces may remain even when direct reuse is not possible. Meehan was unable, due to system limitations, to directly reuse Goldman's *Babel*. But the traces of such work are clearly visible in his design of *Mumble*.

Second, unlike many other designed mechanisms, the processes of digital media operate both on and in terms of humanly meaningful elements and structures. This is clear in the model of human behavior embodied in *Tale-Spin*. The same can be observed in a natural-language processing system such as *Mumble,* which expresses a miniature philosophy of language in its universe of interpretation or expression. When such a system is incorporated into a work of digital media—such as *Tale-Spin*—its structures and operations are invoked whenever the work is experienced. This invocation selects, as it were, a particular constellation from among the system's universe of possibilities. In a natural-language generation system, this might be a particular sentence to be shown to the audience in the system output. From the output sentence it is not possible to see where the individual elements (e.g., words, phrases, sentence templates, conceptual dependency structures, or statistical language models) once resided in the larger system. It is not possible to see how the movements of the model universe resulted in this constellation becoming possible—and becoming more apparent than other possible ones.

To put it another way, I hope that this chapter's examination of *Tale-Spin/Mumble* demonstrates that in the world of digital media, and perhaps especially for digital fictions, we have as much to learn by examining the model that drives the figurative planetarium as by looking at a particular image of stars (or even the animation of their movement). This is because the model universes of digital fictions are built of rules for character behavior, structures for virtual worlds, techniques for assembling human language, and so on. They express the meanings of their fictional worlds through the design of every structure, the arc of every internal movement, and the elegance or difficulty with which the elements interact with one another.

Trying to interpret a work of digital media by looking only at the output is like interpreting a model solar system by looking only at the planets. If the accuracy of the texture of the surface of Mars is in question, this is fine. But it won't suffice if we want to know if the model embodies and carries out a Copernican theory—or instead places Earth at the center of its simulated solar system. Both types of theories could produce models that currently place the planets in appropriate locations, but examining the models' wires and gears will reveal critical differences, probably the most telling differences.

As we see in *Tale-Spin/Mumble,* the surface of a work of digital media is not transparent—it does not allow for direct observation of the data and process elements created and selected by the work's author(s), or the technical foundations on which they rest. Given this, adopting only the audience's perspective makes full engagement with the work's processes impossible. Some systems, through interaction, may make it possible to develop a relatively accurate hypothesis of how the internal systems operate (in fact, some works require this on the part of the audience). But this is a complement to critical engagement with the operations of the work's processes, rather than a substitute. Failing to appreciate this leads to missed opportunities such as those of Aarseth and Murray with *Tale-Spin.*

This chapter attempts to present an example of how the processes of digital media themselves can be examined for what is expressed through their selection, arrangement, and operation. It also attempts to show that the concept of expressive processing includes considering how the use of particular processes may express connection with a particular school of thought. In this case, it is a particular strand of cognitive science, but examining processes might equally reveal connections with communities of thought and practice in software engineering, statistics, or a wide variety of other areas. Further, I hope I have demonstrated that the arrangement of processes in a system may express a quite different set of priorities—or capabilities—from authorial descriptions of the system.

My work in this area builds on the ideas of others, of course. As it happens, one of the important precedents for this work is also found in Aarseth's book, alongside his work on *Tale-Spin* and other systems.

Traversal Functions

While much work on digital literature in the 1990s was focused on the audience experience of works—often with the project of comparing this experience to that of postmodern fiction or other lauded nondigital forms—Aarseth's *Cybertext* takes the unusual step of considering such works as machines. In the book's opening chapter, Aarseth writes that the concept of cybertext "focuses on the mechanical organization of the text, by positing the intricacies of the medium as an integral part of the literary exchange" (1997, 1). His "traversal function" model for understanding such intricacies of literary media, and the audience's role in operating them, has been widely influential.[13]

In this model, Aarseth refers to texts visible on the work's surface as "scriptons," textual data as "textons," and the mechanisms by which scriptons are revealed or generated from textons and presented to the user as "traversal functions." Aarseth's model includes seven

13. It is worth noting, however, that the traversal function model is only one of the models found in *Cybertext*. As Markku Eskelinen pointed out during the blog-based peer review of this book, another model (Aarseth 1997, 103–105) is …

Notes continued at end of this chapter.

traversal functions, which are present for any work, and each of which can have a number of values. These functions and values range from the specific (e.g., whether the work includes explicit links) to the broad (e.g., whether the audience is somehow involved in selecting or creating surface texts).

Cybertext has influenced thinking about digital literature in a number of positive ways. Most important, it has made it commonplace to consider such works in terms of their mechanisms. In addition, because Aarseth's traversal functions are crafted so as to be applicable to both digital and nondigital works, *Cybertext* has encouraged comparisons that reach back toward the history of process-oriented literary works (including many works created or researched by the Oulipo, a group of writers and mathematicians whose membership includes Raymond Queneau, George Perec, and Italo Calvino). With the breadth of possibilities taken in by the traversal function model, *Cybertext* also has encouraged attention to areas of digital literature other than those most widely discussed (especially those with innovative processes) and presented something of a productive challenge to authors of digital literature (given that only a small fraction of the possible types of work described by the model have yet been created). Finally, Aarseth's outline of the traversal function model, and *Cybertext* as a whole, considers things most literary scholars were at that time content to ignore: computer games. Besides rather obviously literary games, such as Infocom's interactive fiction *Deadline,* Aarseth also went so far as to consider largely text-free games, such as Psygnosis's animated puzzle-solving game *Lemmings.* Altogether, the result of *Cybertext*'s influence has been to help create the conditions of possibility for a book such as this one.

Still, while consideration of Aarseth's *Cybertext* volume and traversal function model has had these significant influences, my impression is that the model itself has been more often cited than employed. This book continues in that tradition for two reasons—both linked to the model's focus on the generation of scriptons (surface texts) from textons (textual data). First, many textual systems are difficult to describe in these terms. *Mumble*, for example, does not contain any easily identified textons. Certainly surface texts are produced, but it is hard to see the process of their production as one of being revealed or generated from underlying textons (or as Aarseth puts it, "strings as they exist in the text" [62]).[14] This, in turn, points toward the second, more fundamental reason that this book does not employ Aarseth's model: many of digital media's (and digital fiction's) most important processes are not well described by the process of revealing or generating scriptons from textons. To return to the example of *Tale-Spin/Mumble*, many of the work's processes are focused on the simulation of character behavior. As outlined earlier in this chapter, the simulation is carried out entirely independently from any natural-language generation, and it is best examined as a process of simulation rather than as a means of generating or revealing scriptons. In fact, few of the processes considered in this book (and, arguably, few of those considered in *Cybertext* itself) are fruitfully understood in such terms. But that does nothing to diminish the crucial role that Aarseth's book has in turning attention to the processes of digital media, which is now taking its next major step in the work around software studies.

14. Rather, *Mumble* is composed primarily of rules that assemble texts. So, for example, rather than having different sentence templates to describe the location of different types of characters and objects, into which it inserts the name of the noun …

Notes continued at end of this chapter.

Software Studies

Most studies of software (from outside the disciplines of engineering and mathematics) have considered software in terms of what it emulates and extends—a typewriter, a television, mail delivery—and how that is experienced from outside the system. But a minority of authors have instead consistently written about software as software. This includes considering software's internal operations (as this book does), examining its constituent elements (e.g., the different levels, modules, and even lines of code at work), studying its context and material traces of production (e.g., how the workings of money, labor, technology, and the market can be traced through white papers, specification documents, source code management system archives, beta tests, patches, and so on), observing the transformations of work and its results (from celebrated cases such as architecture to the everyday ordering and movement of auto parts), and, as the foregoing implies, a broadening of the types of software considered worthy of study (not just media software, but also design software, logistics software, databases, office tools, and so on).

These investigations form a part of the larger field of software studies—which includes all work that examines contemporary society through the lens of the specifics of software. For example, while there are many perspectives from which one might look at the phenomena of Wal-Mart, those who interpret the retail giant with attention to the specifics of the software that provides the foundation for many of its operations (from store restocking to relations with far-flung supplier networks) are engaged in software studies. On the other hand, those who study Microsoft without any attention to the specifics of software are not part of the software studies field.

The phrase *software studies* was coined by Lev Manovich (2001, 48), in his widely read book *The Language of New Media*. Manovich characterized software studies as a "turn to computer science"—perhaps analogous to the "linguistic turn" of an earlier era.[15] In his book, software studies takes the form of a turn toward analysis that operates in terms of the structures and concepts of computer science, toward analysis founded in terms of programmability (rather than, say, in terms of signification).[16] In this way, Manovich's book also helped create the conditions of possibility for this book, which I see as an example of software studies.

To avoid confusion, however, I should point out that this book is not an instance of one particular area of software studies: code studies. A number of software studies scholars are interested in interpreting programming language code[17], but examining code and examining processes are not the same thing. This chapter provides an illustration of the difference. While my understanding of the processes of *Tale-Spin/Mumble* is in part built on an exploration of uncompiled source code, my interpretation is of the processes, of the operations of this software, rather than of any specifics of the language (MLISP's peculiarities) or the code's textual specifics (e.g., the use of 'SENTIENT rather than, say, 'ALIVE to mark which elements of a conceptual dependency expression will be translated into English in a particular way).

If we think of software as like a simulated machine, interpreting the specific text of code is like studying the

15. Commenting on the draft of this book presented for blog-based peer review on Grand Text Auto, Manovich suggests that his characterization in *The Language of New Media* "positions computer science as a kind of absolute truth, a given which can …

16. In 2003 Matthew Kirschenbaum offered his own expansion of Manovich's term, one influenced by Kirschenbaum's background in bibliography (the study of books as physical objects) and textual criticism (the reconstruction …

17. Quite a bit of interesting work has already asserted or demonstrated the importance of interpreting code. For example, work of this sort that emerges from a humanities background includes *The Art of Code* by Maurice…

Notes continued at end of this chapter.

choice and properties of materials used for the parts of a mechanism. Studying processes, on the other hand, focuses on the design and operation of the parts of the mechanism. These activities are not mutually exclusive, nor does one subsume the other. Rather, they complement one another—and some investigations may require undertaking both simultaneously. Both can be routes to what this book seeks: an understanding of expressive processing.

In this chapter, my investigations bring me to see the processing of *Tale-Spin* as expressive in two ways. It is an authorial expression, an act of media making that creates fictional worlds through its processes, which are only partially visible on its surface. It also expresses a relationship with histories of AI and cognitive science through the very design of its processes and data structures, which are completely invisible on its surface. Through the first of these, it demonstrates the fundamental approach of story generation (moving beyond the assembly of fiction through precreated and explicitly connected chunks) as well as the difficulties of the *Tale-Spin* effect. Through the second type of expression, it also provides a legible example of the limits of simulations of human behavior based on hand-authored rules. Altogether, it demonstrates that understanding processes in both these ways is important for the development of digital media and software studies—for creators and for scholars.

Notes

1. This is one aspect of Meehan's critique, other aspects of which focus on the mismatch between the behavior of Klein's system and theories of the behavior of human storytellers.

2. Schank echoes Meehan's opinion of the relative interest value of stories about scripts versus those about plans in *Inside Computer Understanding*:

> Many stories (particularly the more interesting ones) are about entirely new situations for which we have no available script. When we hear such stories we rely on our knowledge of how to plan out an action that will lead to the attainment of a goal. (1981, 33)

Schank and Meehan are not alone in linking art to the unscripted, the unexpected, and even the disorienting. Among fiction writers interested in link-based hypertext, its potential for such effects has been cited as one of its potential benefits, though in more technically oriented circles, disorientation was seen as one of hypertext's large potential problems. George Landow (2005) explores this difference in *Hypertext 3.0* through the work of writers such as Morse Peckham (author of *Man's Rage for Chaos*).

3. The next stage in my search began when I learned from Meehan about another iteration of the system, more complex than the "micro" version, created for the 1987 Smart Machines exhibit at the Boston Computer Museum. Unfortunately, the Computer Museum had since shut down, but most of its archives went to the Computer History Museum in Mountain View, California. However, as Al Kossow (software curator for the museum) discovered, the archives only contained a record of the exhibition, not the software itself. Kossow also contacted Oliver Strimpel, who was in charge of the original Smart Machines exhibit, and confirmed that this version of *Tale-Spin* had probably never been archived.

In the field of digital media, such losses are unfortunately common. Even for the most influential projects, we depend on the authors to archive them. Only once libraries and museums get serious about the preservation of software systems—rather than just the paper that comes with or documents them— will this situation change. (In the meantime, Nick Montfort and I [2004] have written a pamphlet for the Electronic Literature Organization titled *Acid-Free Bits* outlining some things that authors can do to make their work more likely to survive.)

As a result of these disappointments, for some time I believed that we would never again learn from *Tale-Spin* through direct interaction, as we can with *Eliza/Doctor*. But I still held that we could learn important lessons from looking at *Tale-Spin*'s processes and output, as recorded in Meehan's dissertation, and the responses of those who had previously written about them. I wrote about *Tale-Spin* using this approach until the appearance of the 1980 printout in 2008.

The code from 1980 is likely different from that at the time of Meehan's dissertation—reflecting further work after he became a faculty member at the University of California at Irvine. One trace of this is seen in a humorous comment—"THIS SPACE AVAILABLE. CALL (714) 833-6326"—that includes Irvine's area code (line 463). Nevertheless, the general functioning of the system seems consistent with what Meehan described in 1976.

4. Though to be scrupulously accurate, to my knowledge Weizenbaum only distributed the verbatim code for the *Doctor* script. His publications on the *Eliza* system, however, were explicit enough to make independent reimplementation relatively easy.

5. For the third mode, Meehan worked particularly on versions of Aesop's fables such as "The Fox and the Crow" and "The Ant and the Dove."

6. This example and the one above are adapted from Meehan's dissertation (1976, 195–196)—substituting other characters with those in this story.

7. This summary draws on Schank's *Conceptual Information Processing* (1975a, 41–44).

8. Meehan calls them *delta-acts* in his dissertation, while Abelson and Schank call them *deltacts* in their 1975 publications (Schank 1975b; Abelson 1975). I will alternate, depending on whose work I am referencing.

9. According to Meehan's dissertation (1976, 50). The description of this portion of chapter 11's story (ibid., 170) elides this step.

10. Ryan particularly notes Lucia Vania, Umberto Eco, David Lewis, and Lubomir Doležel—followed by the 1980s books of Doreen Maître and Thomas Pavel. In the first chapter of *Fictional Worlds,* Pavel (1986) sketches a similar picture of Doležel's and Eco's contributions, while also noting the importance of Ryan's early essays on the topic.

11. Or to put it another way, a fiction's events and their portrayal.

12. One interesting element of the *Tale-Spin* source code—either not present at the time of Meehan's dissertation or not reported in it—is a question asking the audience "HOW LIBERAL-MINDED ARE YOU? (0-3)" when the main character's problem is *Sigma-Sex* (Meehan 1980, line 2555). The answer "0" results in *Tale-Spin* requiring that the character's sex interests be limited to opposite-gender and, if human, same-species characters. Other numbers relax one or both of these requirements.

Above this, a comment reads "HOW LIBERAL-MINDED IS J. BEAR? (NOT READER)" (line 2548). The further questioning of the audience on this topic appears, in the version of the code that I have, to remain unimplemented.

13. It is worth noting, however, that the traversal function model is only one of the models found in *Cybertext*. As Markku Eskelinen pointed out during the blog-based peer review of this book, another model (Aarseth 1997, 103–105) is significantly closer to the one I presented in this book's introduction. Yet this model of Aarseth's is only employed, within *Cybertext,* for the discussion of "adventure games"—and as far as I know it has not been adopted by any other critics.

14. Rather, *Mumble* is composed primarily of rules that assemble texts. So, for example, rather than having different sentence templates to describe the location of different types of characters and objects, into which it inserts the name of the noun being described, we see code like this:

```
EXPR G*LOC* ();
    BEGIN
    IF !ISVALPART = QQ OR !ISVAL = QQ
        THEN !S RPLACA 'WHERE;
    IF NULL ('SAID OF !ACTOR) AND !ISVALPART EQ 'HOME OF !ACTOR
```

```
            AND !ACTOR IS 'SENTIENT
            THEN TN ('LIVE, !ACTOR)
            ALSO APP2 <IF !ISVAL[1] EQ '*INSIDE* THEN "IN" ELSE "NEAR", !ISVALPART>
            ALSO RETURN NIL;
    IF NOT ('SAID OF !ACTOR) AND !ACTOR ISNT 'SENTIENT
            THEN IN ('BE, IF 'PLUR OF ANY 'ELEX OF !ACTOR THEN 'THERE2 ELSE 'THERE1)
            ALSO APP !ACTOR
    ELSE IN ('BE, !ACTOR);
    IF !ISVALPART NEQUAL QQ AND !ISVAL NEQUAL QQ
            THEN APP (IF !ISVAL[1] EQ '*INSIDE* THEN "IN" ELSE "NEAR")
            ALSO SAYOWNER (!ISVALPART)
            ALSO (IF NEG AND !ACTOR WASPROX? !ISVALPART THEN APP2 '(ANY MORE));
END; (Meehan 1980, lines 3794–3812)
```

The literal words ("textons") that may become part of what the audience reads ("scriptons") in the code above are "in" and "near." But as part of the larger *Mumble* system, this code produces texts about location with appropriate pronouns, chronological reference, and so on.

15. Commenting on the draft of this book presented for blog-based peer review on Grand Text Auto, Manovich suggests that his characterization in *The Language of New Media* "positions computer science as a kind of absolute truth, a given which can explain to us how culture works in software society. But computer science is itself part of culture." Looking back roughly a decade after writing the text that popularized the phrase *software studies* (the manuscript for *The Language of New Media* was completed in 1999), Manovich comments, "I think that software studies has to both investigate the role of software in forming contemporary culture—and to investigate cultural, social, and economic forces which are shaping development of software itself."

Matthew Kirschenbaum, responding to Manovich's comment, points out that software studies might be in danger of becoming part of a field "unselfconsciously duplicating a metaphor that has its own inherent artifice and limitations." Specifically, he means the common metaphoric presentation of computing as a tower of abstractions—computing platform, software, and display/interface. While most writing on digital media thus far has been focused on display and interface issues, we have recently seen the emergence of both software studies and platform studies.

Both Manovich's and Kirschenbaum's comments gesture toward the importance of treating the products of computer science with the careful, critical attention given to other parts of culture—while also remaining appropriately aware that the field of digital media is built on the research, results, and tools of computer science.

16. In 2003 Matthew Kirschenbaum offered his own expansion of Manovich's term, one influenced by Kirschenbaum's background in bibliography (the study of books as physical objects) and textual criticism (the reconstruction and representation of texts from multiple versions and witnesses). Kirschenbaum argues that in a field of software studies—as opposed to the rather loose, early new media field—"the deployment of critical terms like 'virtuality' must be balanced by a commitment to meticulous documentary research to recover and stabilize the material traces." Kirschenbaum's *Mechanisms* made good on this assertion in 2008, a year that also saw the publication of the field's first edited volume *Software Studies: A Lexicon* (Fuller 2008).

17. Quite a bit of interesting work has already asserted or demonstrated the importance of interpreting code. For example, work of this sort that emerges from a humanities background includes *The Art of Code* by Maurice Black (2002), "A Box, Darkly: Obfuscation, Weird Languages, and Code Aesthetics" by Michael Mateas and Nick Montfort (2005), and "Critical Code Studies" by Mark C. Marino (2006a). As John Cayley pointed out during the blog-based peer review of this book's manuscript, the word *code* has also been used as a more metaphoric term in work that focuses at least as much on what I refer to as processes. Such work includes "The Code Is Not the Text (Unless It Is the Text)" by Cayley (2002a), "Interferences: [Net.Writing] and the Practice of Codework" by Rita Raley (2002), and the second chapter of *My Mother Was a Computer: Digital Subjects and Literary Texts* by N. Katherine Hayles (2005).

Chapter 6
Character and Author Intelligence

After *Tale-Spin*

As the previous chapter described, James Meehan's *Tale-Spin*—built on a simulation embodying the scruffy artificial intelligence (AI) theories of Roger Schank and Robert Abelson—generated coherent accounts of character actions and interactions in a fictional world. This set the foundation for the field of story generation. Considered today, it also raises an inevitable question: What next?

This chapter considers two different responses. From the perspective of today's media authors, the question of how to generate appropriate character behavior is important. In my discussion of *Prince of Persia: The Sands of Time,* I described the basic design of a common, problematic approach to character behavior: the finite-state machine (FSM). As it turns out, an approach somewhat similar to *Tale-Spin*'s has been used to address some of the limitations of authoring behavior with FSMs—specifically in the computer game *F.E.A.R.*—offering one response to "what next" for characters.

But within the history of story generation a rather different answer emerges. As I mentioned in the previous chapter, a primary critique of *Tale-Spin* within the AI community is that stories are not simply an account of character behavior. To answer "what next" for story generation requires a system attuned to the overall shape of a fiction, rather than just local rules for character action. Scott Turner's work on *Minstrel* is an ambitious example of this next stage for story generation.

1. The basic FSM structure can be implemented in a number of ways, some more efficient than others, in a manner that embodies the same operational logic.

Through different routes, these two cases also bring this book to central topics for AI, media authoring, games, and fiction. First, a familiar question: Should AI attempt to build systems that operate the way people do? Second, a new topic: The rise of statistical techniques and their implications for approaches built with hand-authored processes and data. The second of these also provides an appropriate opportunity for a more detailed consideration of another of this book's goals: using digital media projects as legible examples that can help inform our thinking about software's role in our society more broadly.

Beyond Compartmentalized Actions

The FSM is much like the quest flag or dialogue tree. Each is conceptually simple, easy to implement, places low demands on system resources, and—over a certain level of complexity—becomes difficult to author and prone to breakdown. A quick look at the structure of FSMs shows the reasons for this.[1]

An FSM is composed of states and rules for transitioning between states. For instance, an FSM could describe how to handle a telephone. In the initial state, the phone is sitting on the table. When the phone rings, the FSM rules dictate a transition to picking up the phone and saying "Hello." If the caller asks for the character who answered, the rules could say to transition to a conversation state. If the caller asks for the character's sister, the transition could be to calling the sister's name aloud. When the conversation is over (if the call is for the character who answered the phone) or when the sister says "I'm coming" (if the call is for her), the phone goes back on the table.

As promised, all of this is quite simple. But what happens when the situation becomes more complex? We might add caller ID, after which the character needs to check who the call is from before answering (and sometimes not answer). We might add call waiting, transitioning to the "Hello" state from the conversation state (rather than from the phone on the table state), and then running a second conversation that, when it ends, returns to the previous conversation state (rather than putting the phone down on the table). We might add a check to see if the building is on fire, in which case the character asks for help from anyone who calls (or perhaps only from local callers). We might add a check to see if the character is deep in conversation with another physically present character, in which case the ringing phone leads them to say, "Let 'em leave a message" (rather than transitioning to the "Hello" state or the caller ID check). Now imagine all of the character's behavior organized into a giant, interconnected mass—covering phone conversations, in-person conversations, eating and drinking, sleeping, working, playing games, reading, visiting museums, getting into traffic accidents, all the possible transitions between them, and all the possible combinations (e.g., playing a game while drinking or getting into an accident while talking). While authoring such an FSM would be possible, in practice the complexity would be a huge challenge to manage, and any change would threaten to produce unexpected results.

For this reason, game behavior authors have sought to manage FSM complexity in different ways. Jeff Orkin, in his work on the game *No One Lives Forever 2* (Hubbard, Ryan, Pendleton, et al. 2002), gave characters sets of goals that compete for activation (Orkin 2006). Each goal has its own FSM, of a much more manageable size than an FSM for controlling the character's entire behavior, and the rules for transitioning between these goal-specific FSMs are decoupled from the FSMs themselves (instead those rules are handled at the level that determines the current highest-priority goal). Orkin describes the results for non-player characters, or NPCs, (referring to them, in game industry parlance, as "A.I."):

> Each goal contained an embedded FSM. There was no way to separate the goal from the plan used to satisfy that goal. . . .
>
> Characters in NOLF2 were surrounded by objects in the environment that they could interact with. For example someone could sit down at a desk and do some work. The problem was that only the *Work* goal knew that the A.I. was in a sitting posture, interacting with the desk. When we shot the A.I., we wanted him to slump naturally over the desk. Instead, he would finish his work, stand up, push in his chair, and then fall to the floor. This was because there was no information sharing between goals, so each goal had to exit cleanly, and get the A.I. back into some default state where he could cleanly enter the next goal. (ibid.)

Of course, adding more states and transitions to the *Work* goal's FSM could have addressed this. But pursuing such a path in general would have raised the same complexity issues that motivated the decision to compartmentalize the *NOLF2* FSM for each goal. The problem lies in the compartmentalization strategy itself as a method for addressing the complexity of character behavior.

Ken Perlin, who pioneered computer graphics based on procedural textures and animations, describes the consequences of a similar problem in a rather different sort of game—*The Sims* (Wright, Ryan, London, et al. 2000):

Playing *The Sims* is lots of fun, but one thing conspicuously lacking from the experience is any compelling feeling that the characters are real. Much of this lack comes from *The Sims*'s reliance on sequences of linear animation to convey the behavior of its characters. For example, if the player indicates to a *Sims* character that the character should feed her baby, then the character will run a canned animation to walk over to the baby's bassinet, pick up the baby, and make feeding movements. If the player then tells her to play with the baby, she will put the baby down, return to a previous position, then begin the animation to approach the bassinet, again pick up the baby, and start to play. One result of this mechanical behavior is that there is no real possibility of willing suspension of disbelief on the part of the player as to the reality of the character. (Perlin 2004, 16)

In *The Sims* the problem comes from something other than the usual logic of FSMs. Rather than animations driven by FSMs that are segregated according to character goals, in *The Sims* actions and their animations are compartmentalized via smart objects (e.g., a "shower object" contains information about its impact on the Sim and how it is used, including a pointer to the animation involved). This is another approach to managing complexity using a simple structure with limited points of interconnection—one I will discuss further in chapter 8. This form of compartmentalization made it possible to manage the complexity created by the massive number of expansion packs for *The Sims* (each of which introduced many new objects), but also, as Perlin observed, resulted in breakdowns similar to those seen in *NOLF2*.[2]

Avoiding these compartmentalization-driven breakdowns requires an approach to managing complexity that doesn't isolate each action from the rest of the world. As

2. During the blog-based peer review for this book, Orkin commented that the parallel I draw between issues in *The Sims* and *NOLF2* is quite appropriate: *NOLF2*'s non-combat AI was very much Sims-inspired. Our worlds …

Notes continued at end of this chapter.

it happens, I have already outlined such an approach: *Tale-Spin*'s. Each planbox in *Tale-Spin* is able to access a shared memory space, and a character only attempts to alter the world to suit planbox preconditions if those conditions aren't already met. So, for example, a *Tale-Spin* planbox for playing with a baby might have a precondition of holding the baby. If the *Tale-Spin* character is already feeding the baby, rather than returning to a neutral state (which involves putting down the very same baby), the planbox would check memory, see that the precondition was already met, and move on to the next step.

Tale-Spin was far from alone in employing planning based on actions, with preconditions checked against a central memory, intended to move the world from the current state to a goal state. This was already a widely practiced AI technique in the 1970s—one that scruffy AI took in a particular direction, rather than an approach initiated by Schank and Abelson. An earlier form, developed at the Stanford Research Institute (SRI), formed the basis for Orkin's response to the character behavior and authoring problems of *NOLF2*.

Strips and *F.E.A.R.*

In 1968, Douglas Engelbart's Augmentation Research Center at SRI stunned the computing world with a demonstration that combined the first public showings of the mouse, hypermedia, and teleconferencing (Engelbart and English 1968). The research that followed this "mother of all demos" laid the foundations for the modern computing environment. Meanwhile, Engelbart's colleagues in SRI's Artificial Intelligence Center were pursuing research that, while it shaped the agenda for decades of work in AI, isn't nearly as well-known or recognizable in our daily lives. This project involved an aptly named robot called "Shakey"—a small wheeled cart, carrying a boxy set of control systems, topped by a tower holding range finders, a television camera, and a radio link antenna. An SRI promotional film from that time shows Shakey moving around a brightly lit space of right-angled walls populated by two shapes of blocks, its tower bouncing from the sudden stops at the end of each action, while Dave Brubeck's "Take Five" repeats in the background (Hart, Nilsson, and Wilber 1972).

Shakey's antenna allowed it to connect with what, for the time, was a large computer. This computer controlled Shakey using a program called *Planex*. This program, in turn, guided Shakey through the execution of plans developed by another program called *Strips* (for *St*anford *R*esearch *I*nstitute *P*roblem *S*olver). *Strips* carried out laborious planning processes developed using stored knowledge about Shakey's physical environment. *Planex* used a basic representation of the plan and the reasoning behind it to attempt to guide Shakey to the goal state, addressing problems along the way. These problems included finding doors blocked, blocks moved, and registration mismatches between the actual world and the world model in memory (the possible range of which increased with every movement).[3]

Strips Plans

Rather than something like Schank's conceptual dependency expressions, the *Strips* system stored the state of the world using first-order predicate calculus. This

> 3. Something like the *Strips/Planex* distinction between plan formulation and execution was also found in *Tale-Spin*. For example, *MTrans* and *PTrans* had "action module" versions (*Do-MTrans* and *Do-PTrans*) that did additional work …

> Notes continued at end of this chapter.

4. I am indebted to a thoughtful conversation during the blog-based peer review of this book for revealing the necessity of revising the following section. I want to particularly thank Jeff Orkin, Richard Evans, Mark Riedl, Mark…

Notes continued at end of this chapter.

is a type of formal logical representation that, among other things, allowed *Strips* to use theorem proving in its planning operations—for example, to see if an action's preconditions had already been met. Rather than searching exhaustively for a set of actions that could move the world from the current state to the goal state, *Strips*—following a "means-end analysis" strategy widely used since the seminal General Problem Solver project in 1957—worked backward from a goal state. This backward-planning movement depended on a library of actions, each classified according to its preconditions and effects. *Strips* identified actions with effects that could move the world to the goal state, the preconditions of those actions were identified as subgoals, other actions were found to achieve the subgoals via their effects, the preconditions for those actions were identified, and so on. As one of the system's architects, Richard Fikes, puts it:

> When STRIPS finds an acceptable plan, it has computed the world model anticipated before and after each action in the plan, has proven that the preconditions of each action in the plan are true in the model anticipated at the time of the action's execution, and has proven that the task statement is satisfied in the model anticipated after completion of the plan's execution. (1971, 2)

The basics of this proof, especially the preconditions and effects of each action, were the materials used by *Planex* to guide the movements of Shakey. But the *Strips* model of planning has also inspired very different systems, in which the roles of *Planex* and Shakey disappear or are transformed significantly. An example is Orkin's system for character behavior that took the next step after *NOLF2*: the AI system for *F.E.A.R.*[4]

F.E.A.R. Plans

F.E.A.R. (Hubbard, Hewett, Gramlich, et al. 2005) is a first-person shooter designed for an action movie-style experience (figure 6.1). The player is a new member of an elite team—the First Encounter Assault Recon unit—assigned to deal with unusual threats. Like NPCs in *NOLF2*, the AI enemies in *F.E.A.R.* have goals that compete for activation, such as *KillEnemy, Dodge,* and *Goto*. But rather than each goal having an embedded FSM, each goal can be reached by sequencing actions. As in *Strips,* these actions have preconditions and effects, and the effects satisfy goals (e.g., *AttackFromCover* and *AttackMelee* both satisfy the *KillEnemy* goal).

This may seem like a simple change, but it has a powerful

Figure 6.1. A.I. enemies in *F.E.A.R.* work in squads to take cover, lay suppression fire, blind fire, dive through windows to safety, flush out the player with grenades, and otherwise create an "over the top" experience for players.

5. In email sent after the blog-based peer review, Richard Evans observed: In discussing limitations of *The Sims* and *No One Lives Forever* … you blame various breakdowns (e.g. putting a baby down and then picking…

Notes continued at end of this chapter.

impact. Because different actions can be chosen to satisfy goals—and the state of the world (through preconditions) can influence the choice of action—a character at a desk could choose an action to satisfy a *Death* goal that is appropriate to someone sitting. Similarly, the fact that actions are not compartmentalized makes it easy to author new logical conditions on actions.[5] Orkin describes an example of this:

> Late in development of NOLF2, we added the requirement that A.I. would turn on lights whenever entering a dark room. In our old system, this required us to revisit the state machine inside every goal and figure out how to insert this behavior. This was both a headache, and a risky thing to do so late in development. With the *F.E.A.R.* planning system, adding this behavior would have been much easier, as we could have just added a *TurnOnLights* action with a *LightsOn* effect, and added a *LightsOn* precondition to the *Goto* action. This would affect every goal that was satisfied by using the *Goto* action. (2006)

Orkin also made certain changes to the *Strips* model. One of these is apparent from the description above: a shift from the generation of relatively long-term, multistep plans to the generation of short-term compound actions. Another, fundamental shift is in the operational logic used for keeping track of the world state. Rather than the complex logical representation of the state of the world found in *Strips,* about which the system proves assertions, *F.E.A.R.* uses a simple "blackboard" and working memory continually updated with information on decisions, current actions, and information collected by sensors.

All the facts needed for checking action preconditions during planning are stored in a fixed-size array (essentially, a data box divided into a predetermined number of smaller compartments, all accessible at any time). This makes checking preconditions computationally cheap—and fast—though establishing the relevant facts may not be. The sensors are designed to bridge this gap, performing ray intersection tests (for simulating vision), pathfinding (for potential movement), and other computationally expensive operations over longer periods of time, and then reporting their results.

Another difference between the original *Strips* and the *F.E.A.R.* AI it inspired involves costs for actions. Rather than simply choosing the shortest chain of actions toward a goal, *F.E.A.R.* picks the lowest-cost one. Making the generic *Attack* action more costly than the two actions *GotoNode* and *AttackFromCover* causes AI enemies that have available cover to prefer the safer option (Orkin 2005).

F.E.A.R. also differs from *Strips* in the presence of squad behaviors, which are not integrated with the planning process but rather inspired by Richard Evans and Thomas Barnet Lamb's work on "implementing Wittgenstein" (2002). Squad behaviors look for AI characters to fill slots in coordinated actions (figure 6.2). If the preconditions are met, the AI characters are given goals that cause them to fulfill their roles (e.g., one giving support fire while the others advance to cover that is closer to the player), unless superseded by another goal for that character (e.g., a character noticing a grenade will stop giving support fire). In addition, and this is where *F.E.A.R.* shines as an authoring effort, squad dialogue behaviors are used to address the *Tale-Spin* effect.

Rather than a character behavior system that only communicates to the player through animation (leaving

179

6. I played the Xbox 360 version (Hubbard et al. 2006).

open the possibility that the player will assume the system is as simple as that employed in other games), *F.E.A.R.*'s enemy squads are in verbal communication with each other in a manner that exposes some of the internal state and workings of the system. When I played *F.E.A.R.*, I knew the AI characters had lost track of my position when one asked, "Do you see him?" and another replied, "Quiet down!"[6] When I'd hidden particularly well I could hear them being ordered first to search the area—and eventually to return to their posts. The dialogue also reveals planning-developed decisions about heading for cover, advancing, and other activities. It even explains nonactivity, as Orkin describes:

> If an A.I. taking fire fails to reposition, he appears less intelligent. We can use dialogue to explain that

Figure 6.2. A *F.E.A.R.* squad made up of different enemy types fulfills their roles in a joint behavior. Squad behaviors in *F.E.A.R.* are inspired by the work of Richard Evans and Thomas Barnet Lamb.

he knows he needs to reposition, but is unaware of a better tactical position. The A.I. says "I've got nowhere to go!" (2006)

In my experience, Orkin's hybridization of thirty-five-year-old AI techniques with more recent game-authoring expertise was a great success. By comparison, the AI enemies in even the best games released around the same period (such as *Half-Life 2* in 2004) feel like part of a shooting gallery—more moving parts of the landscape than characters. That this was accomplished with limited development resources demonstrates the potential of thinking through even quite dated AI approaches.

The experience appears to have left Orkin looking to go further. After *F.E.A.R.,* he departed the industry for graduate study at MIT's Media Lab. I will discuss one of his next projects later in this chapter.

Critiques of *Strips* and *F.E.A.R.*

In his dissertation's discussion of *Tale-Spin,* Meehan addresses *Strips* as an important piece of prior work in AI. But he also critiques it severely, contending that it is an unlikely model for human cognition. For example, Meehan points to the way that *Strips* stores information about the world using first-order predicate calculus. This represents all facts about the world as formal logical expressions, with "reasoning" about those facts performed using theorem-proving techniques. Meehan and other scruffy researchers argued strongly—with some experimental data for support—that humans don't remember all facts about the world in the same way or reason about them all using the same approach. Instead, scruffy researchers maintained that human intelligence operates in different ways within different problem domains.

Research on human planning in cognitive science continues to this day, long after Meehan's dissertation, and hasn't always agreed with scruffy accounts (Hayes-Roth and Hayes-Roth 1979; Rattermann, Spector, Grafman, et al. 2001). But even if some might disagree with Meehan's critique of *Strips,* few would argue that *F.E.A.R.*'s planning usesv a model that matches human memory. For example, *F.E.A.R.*'s fixed-size array used to check preconditions allows for efficient operation, but has no psychological credibility.

Well after Meehan's work, the 1980s and 1990s brought fundamental critiques of the *Strips* approach from new directions. Phil Agre (1997) in *Computation and Human Experience* provides a careful overview of the functions of (and relationship between) *Strips* and *Planex* before launching into a discussion of the recurring patterns of technical difficulty that will plague systems of this sort. The problems arise from the fundamental distinction between making plans and following them—a recapitulation of the mind/body split of René Descartes, and another kind of action compartmentalization—which is reified in the distinction between *Strips* and *Planex,* but in the background of almost all work on planning.

Agre points to David Chapman's work in the 1980s demonstrating that "plan construction is technically tractable in simple, deterministic worlds, but any nontrivial form of complexity or uncertainty in the world will require an impractical search" (156). In other words, traditional planning only works in microworlds, such as the Aesop's fables world of *Tale-Spin* or the simple geometric spaces of Shakey. Agre proposes that, rather than being based on plans, "activity in worlds of realistic complexity is inherently a matter of *improvisation*" (156).

Agre's next chapter proposes a radically different approach and architecture.[7] But less radically, how might a *Strips*-like system be more improvisational? It seems clear that one would remove the boundary between *Strips* and *Planex*. A clue might also be found in a passage from *Strips* authors Fikes, Peter Hart, and Nils Nilsson quoted by Agre:

> Many of these problems of plan execution would disappear if our system generated a whole new plan after each execution step. Obviously, such a strategy would be too costly. (151)

Yet it might not be too costly with modern computational power and a simplified world representation. In fact, improvisation of this sort is close to how planning operates in *F.E.A.R.* Plans are short-term—with each "goal" essentially being the next compound action (e.g., getting to cover, and using the lowest-cost set of one or more actions to do so). If the plan is shown to be flawed in the course of execution (e.g., by the player invalidating the cover), *F.E.A.R.* doesn't attempt to recover the plan via *Planex*-style compensations. Instead, a new plan is generated based on a representation of the world that can include the reason for the prior failure. As Orkin explains:

> Imagine a scenario where we have a patrolling A.I. who walks through a door, sees the player, and starts firing. If we run this scenario again, but this time the player physically holds the door shut with his body, we will see the A.I. try to open the door and fail. He then re-plans and decides to kick the door. When this fails, he re-plans again and decides to dive through the window and ends up close enough to use a melee attack!

7. In Agre's next chapter, while improvisation is a matter of continually redeciding what to do, it is not based on replanning after each execution step. Rather, he proposes "to understand improvisation as a *running argument...*

Notes continued at end of this chapter.

8. This strategy also allows *F.E.A.R.* to avoid a problem with replanning that has become apparent in the years since *F.E.A.R.* as planning approaches are used more frequently in games. As Alex J. Champandard explains (2007), typical …

Notes continued at end of this chapter.

This dynamic behavior arises out of re-planning while taking into account knowledge gained through previous failures. . . . As the A.I. discovers obstacles that invalidate his plan, such as the blocked door, he can record this knowledge in working memory, and take it into consideration when re-planning to find alternative solutions to the *KillEnemy* goal. (2006)

The kind of replanning done by *F.E.A.R.*—when actions fail, when cover is invalidated, and so on—is important for how the system works as media. Replanning happens after events that the audience can perceive, and this motivates the character's change in behavior. Plan execution has access to the same working memory that plan formulation uses for checking preconditions, so if a plan is invalidated, characters don't keep doing further stages of a compound action that the planner would reject. Recording reasons for plan failure, rather than the simple fact of failure, prevents the system from continually switching between plans that should be the best (according to what the planner knows) but will fail in execution.[8] *F.E.A.R.* can do this—and do it in real time, even with most of the available computational power claimed by game graphics—precisely because its game world is a microworld. The approach wouldn't work in our everyday world of complexity and contingency. But of course, *all games are authored microworlds.*

Given this discussion, we might still critique *F.E.A.R.* For example, its ambitions—improving the combat-centric behavior found in first-person shooters—are rather limited in the broad spectrum of digital media. It depends on characters with short life spans: Orkin estimates 12.23 seconds in his 2006 Game Developers Conference slides. Michael Mateas has observed that these short life spans allowed Orkin to, in essence, use *Strips* as the inspiration for a reactive planning system. The long-term planning power of the original *Strips* is lost, but so is much of its problematic distinction between planning and execution. Reactive planning can be a powerful approach in such circumstances, but for characters to play fictional roles beyond combat would require much beyond what is present in *F.E.A.R.* Specifically, characters would need to be able to engage in multiple behaviors simultaneously, and work toward both long-term and short-term goals. I will discuss this further in chapter 8, in connection with the characters of the Oz Project.

The fact remains that *F.E.A.R.* demonstrates the potential in thinking through traditional AI approaches for those developing digital media authoring tools. It also shows that many of the most damning critiques of these traditional approaches can fall away when they are adapted for games on modern computing hardware, rather than seen as research into systems for intelligent action in the everyday world. The only critique that still holds—which in fact gains even more traction— is that these approaches lack validity as models of human cognition. As discussed in chapter 4, I believe this only matters to the extent that insights into human intelligence are what we hope to gain from our work with computational models. And this was precisely the goal of a major story system that followed *Tale-Spin*.

Modeling Human Creativity

Scott Turner, like many before and since, first became interested in story generation after running upon Vladmir Propp's analysis of Russian folktales (1968). Propp provides a grammar that describes the structure

9. I'll discuss story grammars in more detail in the next chapter, in the context of *Brutus*.

10. Dyer's dissertation became the book *In-Depth Understanding: A Computer Model of Integrated Processing for Narrative Comprehension* (MIT Press, 1983).

11. Thematic Abstraction Units are also known as Thematic Affect Units.

of many folktales. As linguists and computer scientists know, grammars can be used for representing the structure of given things—and also for generating new things. But as Turner soon discovered, this task is not easily accomplished with Propp's grammar. Its elements are rather abstract, making them workable for analysis but insufficient for generation.[9]

Turner was a senior in college at the time. A few years later, while doing graduate research in the computer science department at the University of California at Los Angeles, he began work on a radically different vision of story generation, embodied in his *Minstrel* system. This would culminate in a dissertation more than eight hundred pages long (setting a new record in his department) that he distilled down to less than three hundred pages as the book *The Creative Process: A Computer Model of Storytelling and Creativity* (1994).

Though Turner wasn't at Yale, his work was still pursued in the context of scruffy AI. His UCLA adviser was the newly arrived Michael Dyer, who had recently completed a dissertation at Yale influenced by Schank's and Abelson's ideas.[10] Over the better part of a decade of work, the shape of *Minstrel* was influenced by two important factors: the evolving scruffy approach to AI and the evolution of Turner's aims.

At first, the primary aim was to build a better story-generation system, one that took the goals of a simulated author into account—especially the goal of telling a story with a theme, as understood in Dyer's concept of "Thematic Abstraction Units" (Turner and Dyer 1985, 373).[11] The initial technical approach was to create an improved *Tale-Spin*. As Turner describes it:

> *Tale-Spin* was essentially a planning engine, so it seemed reasonable to build a better storytelling program by simply augmenting the *Tale-Spin* model with a "meta" level of goals and plans representing what the author was trying to achieve with his storytelling. And, in fact, the first versions of *Minstrel* operated just this way.

> One problem became immediately obvious with this approach: the stories weren't original. (2007)

The problem of originality, of creativity, became increasingly central to Turner's research. As he puts it, "Storytelling went from being an end in itself to being the domain in which *Minstrel* demonstrated creativity" (ibid.). At the same time, the account of intelligence in the scruffy AI community was shifting. Particularly, in Schank's lab the model of dynamic memory and its adaptations was extended into the idea of "case-based reasoning" (CBR). The basic idea of CBR is in some ways quite close to that of scripts: in the main people do not decide what to do in each situation by reasoning from first principles but instead draw on previous knowledge. However, rather than suggesting that each of us has a "restaurant script," a "sports event script," and so on, CBR assumes that we remember many cases, and reason from them—much as the learning of previous cases is formalized in legal and business education.

According to CBR theory, humans have three major types of cases we work with. There are "ossified cases" that have been abstracted to the point where they are essentially rules, such as proverbs. There are "paradigmatic cases," each of which turns out to be the only experience we have that is relevant to a particular current situation, and that we adapt in order to understand the new situation.

Finally, the most complex structures are "stories," which Schank and Christopher Riesbeck characterize as "unique and full of detail, like paradigmatic cases, but with points, like proverbs" (1989, 13). The continuing reinterpretation of stories is described as the "basis of creativity in a cognitive system"—but most work in CBR focused instead on "understanding and problem solving in everyday situations" (14).

When Meehan began work on *Tale-Spin,* he rejected scripts as the basis for stories. Rather, he chose the technique that scruffy AI then posited as the approach used when no script was available: planning. Given Turner's focus on creativity, he similarly rejected the straight employment of case-based knowledge in stories. But this forced him to develop an implementable model of creativity for CBR that could be employed to generate stories—no small task.

Creating Stories from Stories

Minstrel begins storytelling much as some human authors might: with a theme to be illustrated. The audience can request a particular theme, or *Minstrel* can be "reminded" of a story with a similar theme. *Minstrel* is reminded by being given a pool of fragments structured according to the internal schema representations it uses for characters and scenes. Matching fragments against stories in memory will result in one story being selected, and then *Minstrel* will have the goal of telling a story on the same theme.

Minstrel uses CBR to meet its goals, including this one. But goals also need to be organized. Rather than running a simulation of character behavior through time, as *Tale-Spin* does, *Minstrel's* goals are organized as an internal agenda. Planning proceeds in cycles, with each cycle attempting to accomplish the goal that currently has the highest priority on the agenda. If a goal fails, it can be put back on the agenda at a lower priority with the hope that later circumstances will make it possible to achieve. The initial goal is to "tell a story"—which "breaks down into subgoals including selecting a theme, illustrating a theme, applying drama goals, checking the story for consistency, and presenting the story to the reader" (Turner 1994, 77).

Minstrel's themes are also represented in its schema system. Each theme is actually a piece of advice about planning, and represents the kinds of characters, plans, and outcomes necessary for illustrating the theme. Though *Minstrel* is designed to tell stories in the domain of King Arthur's knights, its "planning advice themes" (PATs) are drawn from *Romeo and Juliet, It's a Wonderful Life,* and proverbs. For example, one of the PATs drawn from *Romeo and Juliet* is *PAT:Hasty-Impulse-Regretted,* based on Romeo killing himself after discovering what he believes is Juliet's lifeless body—though if he had waited a moment longer, she would have awakened from her simulated death. Turner summarizes his schema representation of this as follows:

Decision: &Romeo believes something (&.Belief.1) that causes a goal failure for him (&Goal.1). This and his hasty disposition motivate him to do something irreversible (&Act.1).

Connection: &Romeo learns something new (&State.4) that supersedes the evidence for his earlier belief (&Belief.1).

Consequence: &Romeo now has a different belief, which motivates him to retract his earlier goal (&Goal.2) but he cannot, because his earlier action (&Act.1) is irreversible. (104)

12. In *Minstrel*,
character-level
goals and plans are
represented in the
schema, and so
can be transformed
(as outlined later in
this chapter). Author-
level plans, on the
other hand, are
each structured,
independent …

Notes continued at end
of this chapter.

Of course, as Turner notes, this is not actually what happens in William Shakespeare's play. Romeo kills himself and never knows that Juliet was not actually dead—much less regrets his decision. That it is represented this way is an artifact of the larger system design. Only character plans, not author plans, are represented in a manner that *Minstrel* can transform.[12]

In any case, once a theme has been selected, this adds a set of goals to the agenda: instantiating examples of the decision, connection, consequence, and context of the PAT. Once transformation plans succeed in creating the sequence of story events that accomplish these goals, other goals can come into play. "Drama goals," for instance, include suspense, tragedy, foreshadowing, and characterization. To illustrate, a characterization goal would add a story scene showing that a character has an important personality element (e.g., makes decisions in haste) before the section of the story that embodies the PAT. As mentioned, another set of goals, "consistency goals," fill out elements that aren't the bare-bones embodiments of the PAT. If a knight kills another person, for example, consistency goals make sure that he is near the person first and that he has an emotional reaction after. Finally, presentation goals make the final selection of the scenes that will be in the story, their ordering, and how they will be expressed in English. But all of this, while it represents a fuller method of story generation than *Tale-Spin*'s, is only the enabling machinery around *Minstrel*'s primary operational logic: TRAMs.

Minstrel's TRAMs

At the heart of *Minstrel*'s approach to generating stories is the implementation of Turner's theory of creativity:

"transform-recall-adapt methods" (TRAMs). TRAMs are a way of finding cases in the system memory that are related to the current situation and adapting elements of these previous cases for new uses. In this way, stories can be generated that illustrate a particular theme without reusing previous stories verbatim. The approach is based on transforming the problem repeatedly, in carefully crafted ways, rather than doing an exhaustive search through all the possible solutions.

One TRAM example that Turner provides shows *Minstrel* trying to instantiate a scene of a knight committing suicide. *Minstrel*'s first TRAM is always *TRAM:Standard-Problem-Solving*, which attempts to use a solution that already exists in memory. This TRAM can fail in two ways. First, it is possible that there is no case in memory that matches. Second, it is possible that the matching cases in memory have already been used twice, thereby resulting in them being assessed as "boring" by the system—so a new solution must be found. For either type of failure, the next step is to transform the problem and look for a case matching the transformed problem.

In Turner's example, *Minstrel*'s memory only contains the schemata for two episodes. In the first a knight fights a troll with his sword, killing the troll and being injured in the process. In the second a princess drinks a potion and makes herself ill. Neither of these is a direct match for suicide, so *Minstrel* must transform the problem.

One possible transformation is *TRAM:Generalize-Constraint*. This can be used to relax one of the constraints in a schema. In this case, it is used to relax the requirement of a knight killing himself. This is the transform step in a TRAM, and it is followed by the recall step. Here the system searches for a scene of a knight killing anything—not just himself—and succeeds in finding the scene of the knight killing a troll. Since this was successful, the next step is to attempt to adapt this solution to the new situation, by reinstating the constraint that was relaxed. The result is then assessed and deemed appropriate, so *Minstrel* determines that the knight can kill himself with his sword. Here we can see *Minstrel*—on some level—producing something that wasn't already present in the system's data. This is the key to how *Minstrel*'s model of story generation not only goes beyond shuffling prewritten elements but also goes beyond simulation via previously encoded actions, as found in *Tale-Spin* and *F.E.A.R.*

Further, the example above is only the simplest use of *Minstrel*'s TRAMs. The system finds other methods of suicide by a more complex route. For instance, there is also *TRAM:Similar-Outcomes-Partial-Change*. This TRAM "recognizes that being killed is similar to being injured" (Turner 1994, 49) and transforms the schema to one in which a knight purposefully injures himself. This, however, returns no matching cases. The knight fighting the troll is not retrieved, because the injury was accidental. The princess drinking the potion was not retrieved, because the actor was not a knight. But this does not cause *Minstrel* to simply give up on the direction proposed by *TRAM:Similar-Outcomes-Partial-Change*. Instead the TRAM process begins again, recursively, using the already transformed problem and applying a different TRAM to it. In this next stage, by applying *TRAM:Generalize-Constraint* to the actor, it is able to find the princess drinking a potion to injure herself. It adapts by reapplying the generalized constraint to create a schema for a knight drinking a potion to injure himself and then returns to the original TRAM. This adapts by changing from injuring to killing, and the result is an event of a knight drinking a potion to kill himself. This is assessed as successful, added to the story, and added to memory so that it can become a case retrieved by other TRAM processes.

And that's not all—the *TRAM:Similar-Outcomes-Partial-Change* also helps generate another plan for suicide when used as a second-level TRAM. In this case the first-level transformation is *TRAM:Intention-Switch,* which changes the schema from a knight purposefully killing himself to accidentally killing himself. When this, at the next level, is transformed from death to injury, the fight with the troll is found in memory. *Minstrel* then produces a story of a knight going into battle in order to die. With three different suicide methods found for the knight, Turner's example comes to an end as well.

Minstrel's Trouble

Through various series of small, recursive transformations such as those outlined above, *Minstrel* is able to produce story events significantly different from any in its memory. While it can only elaborate as many themes as it has hand-coded PATs, with a large enough schema library it could presumably fill out the structures of those themes with a wide variety of events, creating many different stories. But enabling a wide variety of storytelling is not actually Turner's goal. He writes: "*Minstrel* begins with a small amount of knowledge about the King Arthur domain, as if it had read one or two short stories about King Arthur. Using this knowledge, *Minstrel* is able to tell more than ten complete stories, and many more incomplete stories and story fragments" (1994, 8–9).

One reason for this sparsity of initial data is simply that encoding knowledge into the schema used by *Minstrel* is time-consuming. Turner's main task was to work on *Minstrel*'s processes rather than its body of data. Another reason is that starting with a small body of cases shows off *Minstrel*'s creativity to greater effect. It ensures that *TRAM:Standard-Problem-Solving* will be nearly useless when the program begins, so recursively built solutions will be needed almost immediately. But another reason is that, by its very design, the more *Minstrel* knows the more it gets in trouble. The pattern of this trouble points to a deep issue for systems that seek to model part of human intelligence.

Turner provides a simple, amusing example of this trouble: a knight kills and eats a princess, adapting a plan from a dragon (278). A more complex case arises from Turner's attempt to add a new theme after the system was relatively well developed. Unfortunately, the story produced by *PAT:PRIDE* is seriously flawed, as Turner explains:

> Once upon a time, a hermit named Bebe told a knight named Grunfeld that if Grunfeld fought a dragon then something bad would happen.
>
> Grunfeld was very proud. Because he was very proud, he wanted to impress the king. Grunfeld moved to a dragon. Grunfeld fought a dragon. The dragon was destroyed, but Grunfeld was wounded. *Grunfeld was wounded because he fought a knight. Grunfeld being wounded impressed the king.* (240, original emphasis)

The basic problem is this. The more material there is in the *Minstrel* system—the larger its microworld of knowledge— the more its "creative" transformation procedures will succeed in finding episodes to adapt to new circumstances. But the nature of this adaptation is, precisely, that it exceeds the bounds of the knowledge already available about the microworld. (If the knowledge was already present, it could have been accessed by *TRAM:Standard-Problem-Solving,* and creativity would not come into play.) Because of this, the more data is available, the more *Minstrel* will generate inappropriate episodes—and have no principled means of rejecting them. Unless *Minstrel*'s TRAM processes are to be reined in, significantly diminishing the interest value of the system, the only way around the problem is to carefully limit and shape the system data.

In other words, the problem with *Minstrel* lies in trying to simulate one part of human intelligence—a particular kind of creativity—but not the rest. This is a recurring problem in AI systems designed around models of human cognition. Its most widely discussed manifestation is the "common-sense reasoning problem," which Murray Shanahan has called "the nemesis of artificial intelligence" (Mueller 2006, xvii). This problem is an umbrella for all that normal human beings know and infer about the world: water makes things wet; if I pick up my water glass and leave the room, it leaves too; if I refill the water glass, I probably intend to drink more water, and my throat might be dry. Both scruffy AI's scripts and cases can be seen as attempts to encode commonsense knowledge—but the problem is so daunting that in decades of effort no one has succeeded in developing a robust solution.[13]

In 2007, thirteen years after the publication of his book, Turner put it this way:

> Minstrel was a brittle program. My contention is that if you give me a robust, non-creative program

13. During the blog-based review of this book's manuscript, Turner suggested that there are two additional points that should be considered when evaluating *Minstrel* at this juncture: You're correct in identifying this problem…

Notes continued at end of this chapter.

that demonstrates all the world knowledge, intelligence and problem-solving ability of the average 21 year old, I'll be able to implement a robust creative program atop that. But I didn't have that luxury. I had to build just exactly those parts of that robust intelligence I needed to demonstrate my thesis. Naturally, if you stray even slightly from those limits, things break. (2007)

Statistical AI

We can see, in *Minstrel,* symptoms of a much larger problem—one that Turner alone could have done little to address. By the late 1980s, it was clear that AI systems in general were not living up to the expectations that had been created over the three previous decades. Many successful systems had been built—by both neats and scruffies—but all of these worked on small sets of data. Based on these successes, significant funding had been dedicated to attempting to scale up to larger, more real-world amounts of data. But these attempts failed, perhaps most spectacularly in the once high-flying area of "expert systems." The methods of AI had produced, rather than operational simulations of intelligence, a panoply of idiosyncratic encodings of researchers' beliefs about parts of human intelligence without any means of compensating for the nonsimulation of the rest of human intelligence. Guy Steele and Richard Gabriel (1993, 30), in their history of the Lisp programming language, note that by 1988, the term "AI winter" had been introduced to describe the growing backlash and resulting loss of funding for many AI projects. In this vacuum, assisted by steadily increasing processing power, a new form of AI began to rise in prominence.

As some readers of this book no doubt remember,

in the early 1990s the World Wide Web was largely organized by humans. The "What's New" page at the National Center for Supercomputing Applications provided regular links to new Web resources (much like one of today's blogs), and Yahoo!—still on servers at Stanford University—maintained a growing hierarchical directory to which pages were added by hand. Many individuals maintained hotlists (or pages of links) that were the definitive sources for finding the Web's best information on certain topics. Much as pre-Dewey librarians had done before them, and AI researchers more recently, these editors of Web resources organized knowledge according to their own ideas (often no more than intuitions) of what belonged with what. Web page "meta tags" helped authors express what they felt were the relevant keywords for their contributions, and page titles were an important factor in determining which results came back from a search. Generally, finding the resources with "cool shades" next to them in the Yahoo! directory was a better route to information than using the clumsy search engines.

But this began to change, and quickly, as search engines improved. This improvement came not by engines coming to better "understand" the pages they indexed—or to put it another way, not by better interpreting document contents as traditional AI researchers had attempted—but by counting. For example, the "PageRank" algorithm that rocketed Google to success operates by counting the links that interconnect web pages. As the Google web site explains:

> PageRank relies on the uniquely democratic nature of the web by using its vast link structure as an

indicator of an individual page's value. In essence, Google interprets a link from page A to page B as a vote, by page A, for page B. But, Google looks at more than the sheer volume of votes, or links a page receives; it also analyzes the page that casts the vote. Votes cast by pages that are themselves "important" weigh more heavily and help to make other pages "important." (n.d.)

Of course, describing this process as "democratic" is a rhetorical choice on the part of Google's marketing department. When the Web's most "important" pages are almost all owned by media and technology conglomerates, the power to bless viewpoints on widely discussed topics (e.g., national politics) with attention via PageRank lies in much the same hands as the power to grant attention does in non-Web media. If democracy was the goal, one can imagine weighting Google's statistical model somewhat differently. Nevertheless, even if it is possible to debate whether PageRank is democratic, there is no contesting that it is *statistical*. It is based on counting information about pages (links in and out) and interpreting the resulting numbers. We now take for granted the ability of a computer program to find useful documents on a subject that interests us—though it would have seemed an amazing feat of AI not that many years ago.

The success of another high-profile Web business is also partially tied to a statistical AI technique: in this case, Amazon's recommendation system. Amazon doesn't decide which books and movies to recommend to its customers by deeply analyzing the content of each item it sells and "noticing" similarities between them. Nor does it simply follow rules that dictate recommending, for instance, other books by the same author. Instead, it looks at the numbers: the numbers of people who bought an item and also bought another item, or who looked at a product page and also looked at another product page (Linden, Smith, and York 2003). It is these types of statistical correlations that let Amazon know to (as of this writing) recommend the first season of the television show *Veronica Mars* to those who visit the page for the show *Wonderfalls*—even though there is no overlap in the shows' creators or stars, one is set in upstate New York and the other in Southern California, and the main character of one is a college-educated woman who works in a gift shop while the other is a mystery-solving high school student. Companies like Amazon build such statistical models not only in an attempt to improve the sales of these items but also because this type of information about products and their purchasers is a salable commodity in itself.

Looking beyond applications such as Amazon's, statistical AI techniques can also engage with human expressions, not just recognize what correlates with them. Statistical techniques have improved computer speech recognition to the point where automatic dictation and automated phone systems (with their frustrations) are a practical reality. And statistical techniques don't just help computers recognize what words people speak; they can also analyze patterns of words. The most successful email spam filters, for example, are built using statistical AI techniques.

The rise of statistical AI presents a significant challenge to those who believe that AI systems should be structured based on theories of human intelligence. The successes of statistical techniques grow each day—and yet no one believes that I choose which media to recommend to friends using the types of counting involved in Amazon's

14. By this I do
not mean to argue
that statistical AI is
particularly fallible
within the world of
AI. In fact, the rise
of statistical AI is
precisely due to its
greater successes.
What I mean to argue
against here is the
belief that AI...

Notes continued at end
of this chapter.

recommendation system. At the same time, statistical techniques have severe limitations, which are not always acknowledged.

Limits of Statistical AI

In the United States, our most substantial public conversation about the limits of statistical AI arose in response to the Total Information Awareness (TIA) initiative. Though often discussed as a response to the terrorist attacks of September 11, 2001, the TIA effort was first proposed by the Defense Advanced Research Projects Agency two years before—and it was the continuation of a vision with a significantly longer history. But it was not until after the 2001 attacks that TIA gained serious momentum of its own, after acquiring major funding and a high-profile director—John Poindexter, best known for less-than-truthful testimony to Congress about the Iran-Contra scandal that plagued President Ronald Reagan's administration.

The TIA vision is an example of dystopian magical thinking. It is dystopian in that, rather than identifying potential criminals and placing them under surveillance, it imagines putting every citizen under surveillance. It is magical thinking in that it imagines statistical AI techniques are capable of sifting through the vast flood of information this would produce in order to identify good leads for antiterrorism investigators.[14] This demonstrates a fundamental misunderstanding of how these techniques operate. One of the world's most respected computing organizations—the Association for Computing Machinery—put it this way in a letter to the Senate Armed Services Committee:

Any type of statistical analysis inevitably results in some number of false positives—in this case incorrectly labeling someone as a potential terrorist. As the entire population would be subjected to TIA surveillance, even a small percentage of false positives would result in a large number of law-abiding Americans being mistakenly labeled.

For example, suppose the system has a 99.9% accuracy rate. We believe that having only 0.1% of records being misclassified as belonging to potential terrorists would be an unachievable goal in practice. However, if records for everyone in the U.S. were processed monthly, even this unlikely low rate of false positives could result in as many as 3 million citizens being wrongly identified each year. More realistic assumptions about the percentage of false positives would drive the number even higher. (Simons and Spafford 2003)

False positives are fine in Google link lists and Amazon purchase recommendations, but in other areas their cost is much too high. In the area of surveillance, not only would they improperly cast suspicion on many people; the number of false leads would also be so high as to overwhelm any group tasked with investigating them. Further, the problem of false positives is only one of the serious limitations of statistical techniques. Another is the need for large amounts of well-defined data in order to develop the system's model. The amount of information available on terrorist activity is small by comparison with that used to build effective statistical systems (e.g., Google's collection of web pages containing links)—and the patterns sought (e.g., determining whether a conversation is somehow "suspicious") are extremely ill defined compared with statistical AI's success stories (e.g., determining where a web page links). As security expert Bruce Schneier

(2006) estimates, an "unrealistically accurate" TIA system would generate one billion false alarms for every real plot identified. Further, there is the problem of false negatives. Even with all these billions of alarms, the system would fail to go off at times it should.

In 2003, after public outcry, Poindexter resigned, and it seemed that TIA had been dealt a deathblow when its funding was removed. Then, in 2005, the *New York Times* reported that the Bush administration had authorized a far-reaching National Security Agency surveillance program that included warrantless electronic eavesdropping on telephone calls and emails of U.S. citizens, and a series of further revelations followed (Williams 2006). If not TIA in name, this was clearly the same dystopian vision at work. Other manifestations of magical thinking also continue to generate proposals for utterly inappropriate attempts to employ statistical techniques. In the case of surveillance, even if ineffective for their stated purpose, these efforts still produce databases and monitoring systems, each vulnerable to compromise and improper use.

More generally, to understand what statistical techniques can accomplish, we need to move beyond general principles. Though understanding the basic fact of false positives provides some basis for evaluating proposals for statistical techniques (the cost of false positives must be low), it is also important to foster an understanding of how statistical models are developed and what they represent. As I argued in the introduction—and will expand on in this chapter's conclusion—I believe presenting legible examples, especially from the area of media authoring, can help in this effort. And of course, such examples can also help one consider when statistical techniques might be useful to media authors.

N-grams

A statistical model used in a system for understanding or generating human language is often called a "language model." As with most statistical models, the primary use of a language model is to predict the future (linguistic) behavior of a system based on a sample of its past (linguistic) behavior. Constructing such a model requires two efforts. The first is deciding what to pay attention to: what "features" of the past behavior will be treated statistically. The second is deciding how to make those features part of an operating statistical model.

One of the most popular approaches for building a language model is the concept of *n-grams* (also known as *Markov chains*). An n-gram language model is built by looking at a body of linguistic data and seeing what elements follow other elements. If looking at the letters in a body of English, *q* would quite often be followed by *u*. Looking at the word level, *you* would more frequently be followed by *are* than by *banana*. Looking at sets of two elements is examining *bigrams* and sets of three are *trigrams*.

As this probably makes clear, in an n-gram model, the features are often the word or two that appear before the current one. A simple model employing these features would be: the different following words are assigned likelihoods based on how frequently they appear after the preceding ones within the sample data. In actuality, the models tend to be somewhat more complicated. This is in part because even after training on millions of words, new pairs and triplets of words will appear regularly even in data from the same source (say, the same newspaper from which the model was developed). This requires that the model be "smoothed" so that newly appearing digrams and trigrams won't be assigned zero probabilities.

Such models have many potential uses. For example, dictation software may find certain words in a sentence ambiguous. But an n-gram model can use the words that precede and follow ambiguous words to improve the chances of correct recognition. Certainly "ate the banana" is a much more likely trigram than "ate the bandana."

On the other hand, an n-gram collection doesn't "understand" anything about the language it models. It would work just the same way on a collection of musical notes or any other serially ordered data. And while as a model it does well at capturing coherence from word to word, it does poorly at capturing any higher-level structure. This becomes quite apparent in the various attempts to use n-grams to generate language, rather than simply understand it. The foundational example here is Claude Shannon's n-gram-generated sentence from his field-defining essay "A Mathematical Theory of Communication":

THE HEAD AND IN FRONTAL ATTACK ON AN ENGLISH WRITER THAT THE CHARACTER OF THIS POINT IS THEREFORE ANOTHER METHOD FOR THE LETTERS THAT THE TIME OF WHO EVER TOLD THE PROBLEM FOR AN UNEXPECTED. (1948, 388)

This passage is more coherent than a random series of words, because each word follows quite naturally from the one preceding it. This is no surprise, given that it was produced by flipping through a book, writing down a word, flipping through until that word was found again, writing down the word immediately following it, then flipping through until the just-written word was found, and so on—a word-level bigram. Longer chain lengths, of course, create longer stretches of local coherence. But the structure of sentences, paragraphs, and ideas is completely absent from the n-gram model.

In other words, despite the impressive results from many statistical AI systems, a statistical model is nothing magical. Like Google's capturing of links from Web pages, statistical models such as n-grams must be focused on well-defined features in consistent pools of data. Then, even once millions of patterns are captured, in any activity with significant variety (like human language) the model must be smoothed to account for the fact that previously unseen patterns will continually appear. Even once this is accomplished, the model will only be appropriate for limited tasks. Given this, we must bear both the strengths and limitations of statistical approaches in mind. Whether we are listening to intelligence agency officials or singularity-seeking science fiction writers, we should not be fooled by impressive results in certain areas into thinking anyone has developed (or knows how to develop) robust AI able to predict, identify, generate, and otherwise stand in for human knowledge of a complex domain.

The Restaurant Game

After moving to MIT, Orkin, who led the AI development for *F.E.A.R.*, launched a project with an interesting goal: pursuing an idea from scruffy, symbolic AI using the tools of statistical AI. Specifically, his *The Restaurant Game* seeks to develop what he characterizes as a modern version of the scruffy idea of a "restaurant script" (Orkin 2007,

22). His method is to statistically analyze the behavior of thousands of players in a free-form restaurant environment and thereby learn a much more flexible and detailed script of restaurant behavior than it would be possible to author by hand.

Orkin calls his effort a *game*—a term that resonates in two senses. First, he plans to use the results of his work to develop a game, and all those who interact with the free-form environment will be credited as designers of the eventual game. Second, by presenting the experience as a game, he is placing *The Restaurant Game* into the same category as a number of successful efforts to use simple game structures to encourage large numbers of people online to collaboratively develop data that is intractable for machines and too laborious for individual humans.

The best known of these data-collection games is *The ESP Game,* developed by Luis von Ahn and collaborators (2005) at Carnegie Mellon University. This game shows the same image, simultaneously, to two audience members who don't know the other's identity and cannot directly communicate. These two people each type words as quickly as they can that might describe the contents of the image, avoiding any forbidden words listed. As soon as one player types a word that the other player has already typed—creating a match in their descriptions—they score points and the next image appears, until the game time expires.

People find *The ESP Game* surprisingly fun, with some experiencing an exciting feeling of connection at the moments when they choose the same word as a partner. This has provided the motivation for people to generate quite a bit of data through such games—more than one hundred million image labels from *The ESP Game* alone

(Saini 2008)—and for Google to license the approach for its Image Labeler. Such data may be used to label online images (to increase accessibility for the visually impaired) or toward more computationally challenging ends (e.g., as well-formed training data for statistical approaches to computer vision). Quite a few other games along these lines exist, and they differ in their particulars, but all of them use simple scenarios to generate specific data points.

By comparison, *The Restaurant Game* is immensely free-form and ambitious. Each person who signs in plays a male customer or female waitress. Players can chat freely with each other—not trying to guess the same word or taking part in any other gamelike activity, but simply playing their roles (figure 6.3).[15] The environment has many objects with which the players can interact, including food and drink that can be consumed, a register that can be used to pay bills (but can also be picked up and perhaps stolen), menus, furniture, flowers on the tables, a variety of kitchen implements, and so on (figure 6.4). There are also two NPCs: a bartender who provides drinks, and a cook who supplies food.

Compared with the real world, *The Restaurant Game* is certainly a microworld—but it is also a vastly richer environment than that offered in previous data collection games and even most commercial ones.[16] Because it is a microworld, fewer actions are possible, and those actions are unambiguous. The system knows exactly when one player passes another a menu, can tell exactly what words one player says to another, and can always tell if all the food was gone before the waitress picked up the plate. On the other hand, the diversity of possible actions and sequences of actions makes the data collected by *The Restaurant Game*

15. Orkin and Deb Roy (2007), the professor who directs Orkin's group at MIT, see *The Restaurant Game* as an initial example of a minimal investment multiplayer online game. Unlike a standard massively multiplayer online game, which…

16. During the blog-based review of this book's manuscript, Orkin commented on the "range of possible interactions and the variety of interactive objects" for standard commercial games and *The Restaurant Game*: Most of today's games restrict interaction…

Notes continued at end of this chapter.

a challenge to interpret statistically.

Orkin's approach is to focus on the physical actions that take place, looking at the orders and relationships of actions. Actions are clustered based on their supports—an approach that discovers certain similarities (all foods are eaten the same way) as well as preconditions built into the microworld (eating requires the presence of food), and also social expectations (almost all players eat while seated). Orkin's analysis prunes away the most infrequent actions and sequences, building up what he calls a "plan network": a structure representing the normal pathways of actions in *The Restaurant Game*'s microworld. The language from player interactions is arranged in the model in terms of the physical actions between which it took place.

The resulting plan networks have the strengths and failures one would expect. Some of these are specific to the microworld. Orkin demonstrates this with a visualization of the waitress plan network, which captures the set of interface steps required to use the cash register to pay a

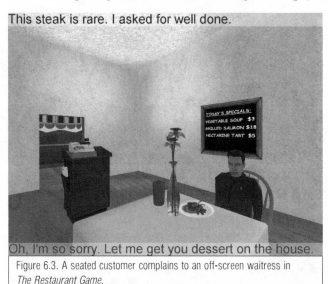

Figure 6.3. A seated customer complains to an off-screen waitress in *The Restaurant Game*.

bill—and also captures the path produced by a common player confusion about the register's operations.

Other successes and failures are those common to statistical models. These were revealed in Orkin's evaluation of the system, which used n-gram modeling as "a means of estimating the likelihood of new gameplay sessions, and quantitatively evaluating how well the learned model of restaurant behavior and language correlates with humans'" (2007, 69). Here we actually see a microworld version of the ideas behind TIA; examining data from thousands of games, Orkin worked to build a statistical profile of the behavior and then attempted to build a system that would automatically detect unusual behavior.

This basic approach builds on some techniques that have proven powerful in statistical AI, and Orkin reports some successes with it. For example, Orkin mentions a play session in which a typical set of actions took place. Yet the system correctly rated the session as highly unlikely based on the language—the customer was trying to leave

Figure 6.4. The object interaction interface in *The Restaurant Game*.

without paying and convince the waitress to come home with him. On the other hand, the system also responded in the same way to any conversation containing unusual vocabulary, even in games that humans rated as typical. As discussed earlier, this is the classic problem of false positives. Orkin also provides examples of sequences of physical actions—such as ordering beer and pie until they fill the restaurant, or sitting down, playfully refusing to order, and leaving—that the current version of the plan network is unable to detect as unusual, but are immediately strange to any human evaluator. This is the classic problem of false negatives.

Orkin had originally announced that a game created using the results from *The Restaurant Game* would be entered into the 2008 Independent Games Festival. But he had to let the deadline pass. In his thesis he writes that this provided a lesson in the "danger of promising the public a deliverable based on novel research by a specific date" (42). More generally, it offers a lesson about statistical AI. As an authoring tool, it requires large amounts of data that may not be available. If the significant effort is expended to collect this data—as Orkin undertook with *The Restaurant Game*—for phenomena with wide variation, the results will be unpredictable and incomplete. Nevertheless, perhaps Orkin's next step will find a way to make interacting with this model a fun, playful experience (see sidebar: Digital Media Research and *The Restaurant Game*). The most significant contribution of *The Restaurant Game* in the meantime is how it demonstrates that even in a microworld, stripped of most of the complexity of our own, statistical models produce many more false positives and false negatives than a TIA-style system could tolerate.

Politics and Processes

In 1974, the cover of Ted Nelson's *Computer Lib / Dream Machines* proclaimed, "You can and must understand computers NOW."

Nelson's book (mentioned earlier in this book's discussion of expressive AI) wasn't a response to TIA-style proposals or even the ubiquity of computers. In fact, Nelson's book was published the year before the first personal computer kit—the Altair—became available, and long before governments began contemplating large-scale data mining. At that time the number of computers was tiny by comparison with our present moment. Those that existed were carefully tended by teams of professionals (what Nelson called the computer "priesthood"), and determining their uses was considered the province of specialists. It seemed a long way from everyday life.

But as Nelson's book set out to expose, computing was already woven into the fabric of society. He pointed to the signs in everyday life (from computer-generated junk mail to the soon-to-arrive phenomenon of bar codes on consumer products) as well as the less obvious changes as every large organization switched to computer record keeping (often restructuring it according to the ideas of, and leaving it accessible only to, the computing priesthood), computer simulation began to arise as a decision-making aid, and so on. Further, Nelson could already see in the field of computer graphics that computers would revolutionize our media—and understood that this, too, had political stakes. He wrote, "It matters because we live in media, as fish live in water. . . . But today, at this moment, we can and must design the media, design the molecules of our new water, and I believe the details of

Digital Media Research and *The Restaurant Game*

While this chapter critiques *The Restaurant Game,* Orkin's project is an ambitious piece of research in a direction that may prove fruitful. In the blog-based review of this manuscript, Richard Evans observed:

> I find *The Restaurant Game* fascinating because it is at a different level of ambition from other work in game AI.

> In terms of modeling the background social practices which make everyday stories intelligible (e.g. Schank's restaurant), there are various levels of simulation: (1) Hand-code a few social practices; the system cheats and tells the agents what state the practice is in (consequently there is no room for divergence between the different agents' conception of the state of the practice). (2) Data-drive a number of social practices and let the agents themselves work out what state the social practices are in (this is what Rob Zubek does in his dissertation, using Markov models to make a best guess about the current state of the practice). (3) Let the system auto-generate practices from statistical analysis of lots of player data. *The Restaurant Game* is the only project I am aware of which allows for the possibilities of new practices to emerge, which were not defined by the author at design-time.

Certainly this is a noble goal, and in this chapter I speculate that the model developed through *The Restaurant Game* may well form the core of an engaging playable experience in the future. In the blog-based review of this book's manuscript, Orkin suggested that another future direction could be to "combine statistical and human-authored approaches, to get the best of both worlds." He continued:

> I agree with everything you've written, based on what we have published so far, but our long term goal is a semi-automated system where the statistical model forms the scaffolding, facilitating human authoring of the less typical behavior. *The Restaurant Game* is an ongoing project that will continue to keep me busy for the foreseeable future.

The only way games and digital media generally will grow in some of the most interesting potential directions is through long-term research. Orkin's project may, at the moment, be most compelling in terms of the lessons it teaches us about the software approaches he is employing. But it would be foolish to discount the future possibilities of *The Restaurant Game* and the successor systems that may employ its data or be inspired by its approach. More generally, it is important that we encourage exploratory, interdisciplinary research focused on the questions raised by digital media, rather than simply viewing media as an application area of results from other research.

this design matter very deeply" (DM 2).

His response was a program of education, enacted through his book, in what we might today call "procedural literacy." He sought to teach people to understand how computing works and what its processes make possible. Computer scientists such as Alan Kay and Seymour Papert pursued similar goals by developing new programming languages, designed to make the authoring of computer processes more accessible (especially for children). Nelson's book, aimed at adults, instead attempted an ambitious survey of then-current programming languages, computing hardware, data structures, input devices, and more. All of this was couched in an argument that the modern computer shouldn't be thought of as a mathematical device but rather as the mathematician and computing pioneer Alan Turing had it, "a single special machine" that "can be made to do the work of all" (2004, 383).[17]

Nelson's goal, in part, was to encourage readers to grasp hold of the creative potential of computing toward their own ends. But just as crucially, the goal was to urge readers to rise up against the computing priesthood, to stop accepting that there are "ways of doing things that computers now make necessary" (1974, 8). In the preface to the second edition of *Computer Lib/Dream Machines,* Stuart Brand called Nelson "the Tom Paine of the personal-computer revolution" (Nelson 1987). One difference is that the revolutionary program for which Nelson agitated— "Computer power to the people! Down with cybercrud!" (1974, 3)—remains largely unrealized, though groups of agitators continue to push for it today.

A form of such agitation is, in fact, part of this book's program. We live in a world in which the politics of

17. Of course, neither Turing nor Nelson is talking about machines such as washing machines (though these now commonly contain computers). Rather, Turing is speaking about the capacity for universal computing machines, such as today's…

Notes continued at end of this chapter.

computing are more important than ever, and where some of the highest-stakes processes—from those that generate terrorist watch lists to those that operate black-box voting machines—are kept in the hands of even more secretive priesthoods. In such a situation, what are we to do?

One answer is to continue down the path of procedural literacy. I fully support such efforts. But this book follows a different path, as this chapter seeks to make clear.

Legible Examples

One of the great difficulties in this area is that computer processes are often presented as essentially magical. This deceptive practice ranges from government agencies (as with TIA) to popular television shows (such as the many crime and terrorism dramas that portray facial recognition software as a reliable tool rather than an unsolved research question). We need a way to dispel the idea of computational processes as magic and replace it with a basis for thinking critically about these issues. Procedural literacy only gets us part of the way. It may help more people understand how computational processes are authored, but few people will ever personally write a system that employs techniques similar to those in a terrorist watch list generator.

In my experience, however, people are able to reason about computational processes by analogy. For example, once one understands the strengths and limitations of a set of computational techniques—in whatever context that understanding was gained—it is possible to use that knowledge to understand something of the potential for those techniques in other circumstances. This is true for most technology. As a child I learned that the technology of the wheel, when employed by my little wagon, worked better on hard, smooth surfaces than muddy, uneven ones. It was easy to generalize this knowledge to cars.

Our problem now is, in part, that processes such as those that generate terrorist watch lists are kept secret, making them difficult to evaluate critically. But the deeper problem is that many in our society do not understand a *single example* of a process anything like those involved and, further, have no experience in interpreting and evaluating computational processes whatsoever. It is my hope that the field of digital media, by providing a set of engaging and legible instances of computational processes, can be a starting point for changing this situation.

Consider the example of watch list generation. The specific processes may be secret, but it can be no secret that these systems rely on the techniques of AI. We also know that the AI field's practical toolkit consists of hand-authored rules and knowledge structures on the one hand and large-scale statistical operations on the other.

This provides us with some knowledge, but another route to knowing is cut off. In addition to the specific processes being kept secret, the output of these systems is highly illegible. For the most part (for obvious reasons) the contents of the lists are kept from the public. For those few suspects made public (apart from a few obviously ridiculous errors) it is hard to say which are and aren't correctly identified. If the suspect is lucky enough to get a trial (rather than being held in an inaccessible detention facility or secretly transported to another country for torture), even that may not clarify whether that person's classification as a suspected terrorist was appropriate.

But many processes that employ AI techniques are much more legible, such as those used for media

18. As of this writing, the American Civil Liberties Union (2008) estimates that there are more than one million names on the current U.S. government terrorist watch list. Known watch list entries include Nobel Peace Prize laureate…

Notes continued at end of this chapter.

and communication. The developers of such systems commonly publish descriptions of how they operate in conference papers, journal articles, patent applications, doctoral dissertations, technical books, and so on. Further, the outputs of these systems are generally much easier to evaluate. For example, the field of natural language processing (NLP) uses many of the same AI techniques—and it is generally easy to tell when a computer system produces nonsensical language or completely misunderstands the meaning of our utterances.

Also, as we come to understand NLP systems more deeply, we see that they only work in limited circumstances. Whether creating a computer game or a phone tree, the designers of NLP systems work hard to limit the discourse context in order to improve the chances of the system working appropriately. And as outlined earlier in this chapter, all this is necessary in order to improve the chances of carrying off a task much easier than the generation of a terrorist watch list. It is much, much easier to draw the intended meaning out of a well-defined bundle of text (employing knowledge from analyzing a huge amount of correct sample data) than it is to try to draw the intention to commit terrorism out of an ill-defined sea of variably structured data about human behavior (after analyzing the small amount of available information about the behavior of known terrorists).

This much thinking lets us know that automatic terrorist watch list generation is likely to fail. But that doesn't mean it won't be attempted.[18] And so it is politically important to be able to think about the ways it will fail. My hope is that, through knowledge of analogous example processes that have legible intents and outputs, we will be able to dismiss the idea of magical computer systems and instead think meaningfully about the potentials and limitations of such systems.[19]

This is a project to which I aim to contribute with this book. Its chapters explore a variety of legible, media-focused examples of processes. I am drawing the connection to wider issues most clearly here in considering *The Restaurant Game,* but my hope is that readers will also find their political reasoning informed by earlier discussions on topics such as how *Eliza* produces its illusion and the severe limitations of *Tale-Spin*'s at-the-time "scientific" simulation. More broadly, I hope an increasing amount of work in digital media will turn toward the investigation of processes and the potential for their interpretation—and that this will, together with increasing procedural literacy, help us make more informed decisions at the intersection of processes and politics.

Procedural Rhetoric

My work here, in turn, is a complement to the exploration of another intersection of politics and processes: the use of computational processes as persuasive speech. While figures like Sherry Turkle (1995) and Nelson have discussed this for several decades, often in the context of environmental and urban planning simulations, the first detailed, full-length study is *Persuasive Games: The Expressive Power of Videogames* by Ian Bogost (2007).

As the title indicates, Bogost's book is about computer games—especially those designed for use in politics, education, and advertising. But the book's implications are

19. This ability to reason by analogy about computational processes that are kept secret is perhaps part of the reason that computer scientists have emerged as some of the most important critical thinkers on these matters. For example, two of…

Notes continued at end of this chapter.

wider. Bogost uses games as a specific set of examples for the development of a larger argument about what he terms "*procedural rhetoric,* the art of persuasion through rule-based representations and interactions rather than spoken word, writing, images, or moving pictures" (ix).

In particular, Bogost points to the ways that digital media can make powerful assertions about how things work. Games and other procedural systems can use processes to create a representation of something that happens in our world—from the growth of cities, to the marketing of cereal, to the mechanisms of long-term debt. Playing the game involves interacting with this representation, which uses its internal processes to exhibit different behaviors, making it possible to explore the particular model of how things work.

As educators including James Paul Gee (2004) have observed, successfully playing games involves learning. Prominent game designer Raph Koster (2004) has maintained that such learning is central to our experience of fun in games. Bogost draws our attention to how this learning develops some understanding of the structure of the procedural representation at work—but not necessarily any critical approach to the model or the way it is presented. Addressing this is one of the primary goals of procedural rhetoric. Just as oral rhetoric aims to help people persuade through speech as well as aid audiences to understand and think critically about oral arguments, procedural rhetoric strives to help authors and audiences of process-based arguments. As is no doubt clear by this point, I consider this a much more appropriate goal for computational models than attempting to reproduce the processes of human thought.

Beyond Anthropomorphic Intelligence

Given the history of AI, it is no surprise that systems such as *Tale-Spin* and *Minstrel* were built to embody models of human cognition. The assumption that human and machine processes should—or must—resemble each other runs deep in AI. It continues to this day, despite the counterexample of statistical AI.

With *Tale-Spin* and *Minstrel* both emerging from the scruffy end of symbolic AI, we might assume that this area of AI was particularly given to building its systems on human models. And perhaps it is true that a neat researcher would not have made Turner's opening assumption from his description of *Minstrel*: "To build a computer program to tell stories, we must understand and model the processes an author uses to achieve his goals" (1994, 3). As discussed earlier in connection with *Strips,* scruffy researchers sought to claim for their approach greater fidelity with the way that humans approach problems, arguing that people think differently in different problem domains. Riesbeck and Schank put it this way:

> The problem that general problem solver programs have is that each and every problem presented to them has to be handled the same way. Each problem must be reduced to first principles and logical deductions made from those principles. Even mathematicians do not really behave this way. (1989, 9)

But to view the issue in these terms is to consider only one level. At another level, both scruffy and neat AI are based on the assumptions of cognitive science—especially that effective problem solving for machines should be based on the same model of "symbolic processing" assumed to be at work in humans. As Paul N. Edwards explains in *The Closed World,* "Cognitive science views problems of thinking, reasoning, and perception as general issues of symbolic processing, transcending distinctions between humans and computers, humans and animals, and living and nonliving systems" (1997, 19). To put it another way, whatever their differences, scruffy and neat researchers still speak of their computer systems in terms of human-derived symbolic formulations such as beliefs, goals, plans, rules, and so on.

And it is on the basis of these formulations that both scruffy and neat AI researchers have been extensively critiqued by more recent thinkers—resulting in their work becoming lumped together using terms such as "classical AI" or "Good Old-Fashioned AI" (GOFAI). Yet many of the critics who locate themselves within AI view the problem with symbolic techniques as a lack of accuracy regarding how humans operate. For example, Agre, whose critique of *Strips* was discussed earlier, characterizes symbolic AI's problems by saying, "Mistaken ideas about human nature lead to recurring patterns of technical difficulty" (1997, xii). His alternative approach to AI is founded on a different view of human activity (7) rather than abandoning the anthropomorphic model for AI processes.

A more radical critique may appear to emerge from the current head of MIT's venerable AI laboratory, Rodney Brooks. In his widely cited "Elephants Don't Play Chess," Brooks writes: "In this paper we argue that the *symbol system hypothesis* on which *classical AI* is based is fundamentally flawed, and as such imposes severe limitations on the fitness of its progeny" (1990, 3). The alternative championed by Brooks is focused on an AI that operates through combinations of simple mechanisms embodied in robots in real-world contexts (and concentrates on interaction within these contexts). Nevertheless, after building a number of insectlike robots based on this research agenda, Brooks turned—inevitably?—to the creation of humanoid robots meant to eventually exhibit humanoid intelligence. The banner headline on the web page for the most famous of these projects, Cog, reads, "The motivation behind creating Cog is the hypothesis that: Humanoid intelligence requires humanoid interactions with the world" (MIT Humanoid Robotics Group 2003). The anthropomorphic view of AI asserts itself again.

Models and Authorship

From the point of view of authoring, there is something quite puzzling about all this. To a writer it is obvious that people in stories do not talk the way people do in everyday life, that people's lives as reported in stories contain only a tiny subset of what would go on if they had real lives, and so on. A system that operated largely like a real person thinks might not be much help in telling a story, since most real people aren't that good at storytelling (so simulating an author is out) and characters shouldn't act like real people (real people don't take the stylized, coordinated actions that dramatic characters perform).

Accurate modeling is simply not what authors are after. This is true even in areas such as computer game physics. While first-person 3-D games (such as *Half-Life 2*) may incorporate natural-seeming models of space, movement, gravity, friction, and so forth, each of these elements have been (along with each of the environments in which they are active) carefully shaped for the game experience. *Half-Life 2* may be more like the real world than is a game like *Super Mario Brothers,* but a deep model of the world, operating just like the real world, is (in addition to not being achievable) not an important step along the path to either one. In fact, a game like *Portal,* constructed using the engine developed for *Half-Life 2,* would probably be much less fun if it employed an exact model of real-world physics.

The question is which models are useful for authoring. The answers are not always obvious. For instance, while simple generation from a statistical model—as with Shannon's bigram-produced sentence—is a limited approach to linguistic behavior, it is also not the only possible approach to authoring that uses such models. Nitrogen, for example, was an ambitious research project (developed by Eduard Hovy's group at the University of Southern California) aimed at using n-gram models in combination with logical and syntactic models for generating language (Langkilde and Knight 1998). Given a logical message to translate into text, it would promiscuously produce a lattice of grammatical structures. Then an n-gram model was used to rate pathways through the lattice. This experiment in combining traditional and statistical AI produced quite promising early results.

Similarly, the game *Black & White* (Molyneux, Webley, Barnes, et al. 2001) employs a hybrid architecture to create one of the most successful character experiences in modern gaming. Each *Black & White* player is a god, made more powerful by the allegiance of human followers—but with a much closer relationship with a nonhuman "creature" who can be a powerful ally and focus of empathy, but must be properly trained. In designing the AI to drive these creatures, Richard Evans wanted to include both a model of the world and a model of the player's view of the world (deduced by ascribing goals to the player that explain the player's actions). Such models are easier to understand and employ if represented in traditional, symbolic (GOFAI) forms. At the same time, Evans wanted a creature's learning (from observing the player and NPCs, player feedback after actions, and player commands) to have the "fuzzy" sense and vast number of possible states achieved in more recent, numerically focused AI. As a result, he adopted an approach he calls "Representational Promiscuity" in which "beliefs about individual objects are represented symbolically, as a list of attribute-value pairs; opinions about types of objects are represented as decision-trees; desires are represented as perceptrons; and intentions are represented as plans" (2002, 567, 570). The result is not only an impressive character but also a system that repositions the provision of training data for numerically driven AI. Rather than something that happens during system development, it is something that happens during audience interaction, becoming the very method by which the player's relationship develops with *Black & White*'s main on-screen character.

More speculatively, a related kind of hybrid system might address another difficulty identified in this chapter. While *Minstrel*'s TRAMs proved problematic in the context of a system meant to autonomously produce stories—given issues of commonsense reasoning—we can imagine TRAMs employed in a different context. For instance, consider what Rafael Pérez y Pérez and Mike Sharples write in their evaluation of *Minstrel*:

The reader can imagine a Knight who is sewing his

socks and pricked himself by accident; in this case, because the action of sewing produced an injury to the Knight, *Minstrel* would treat sewing as a method to kill someone. (2004, 21)

I quoted this on the blog *Grand Text Auto,* leading Turner to reply:

I actually find this an (unintentionally) wonderful example of creativity, and exactly the sort of thing *Minstrel* ought to be capable of creating. There's an Irish folk song in which a woman imprisons her husband by sewing him into the bedsheets while he sleeps. Doesn't that show exactly the same creative process (magnifying a small effect to create a large one)? (2007)

Many people also find *Minstrel*'s story of a hungry knight killing and eating a princess (adapting a story about a dragon) a quite amusing example of creativity. On the other hand, the problems produced by *PAT:Pride* were comparatively uninteresting. The solution here might be to use a TRAM-style model in a system that operates in close interaction with the audience, so that it is the humans who provide the necessary commonsense reasoning. In a *Minstrel* designed this way, the audience could choose whether to steer toward or away from traditional stories, surreal stories, and nonsense. Of course, like the earlier example of an imagined *Eliza/Doctor* that employs the techniques of Abelson's ideology machine, considering this speculative system won't tell us nearly as much as examining actually constructed ones.

To put the lessons of this chapter another way, the issue for authors is not whether models arise from attempts to simulate human intelligence, from statistical traditions, or from other directions. The issue, as demonstrated by Orkin's work on *F.E.A.R.* and Evans's on *Black & White,* is how models—whatever their original source—can be employed toward current authorial goals in a manner that acknowledges their limitations. The next chapter considers systems with this more pragmatic approach to story generation.

For our culture more generally, the lesson is rather different. *Minstrel* and *The Restaurant Game* are legible cases of the limitations inherent in both symbolic and statistical approaches to AI. The problems they exhibit in relatively constrained microworlds become much greater in our massively complicated, evolving, and contingent everyday world. When considering public proposals for the use of AI systems, we would do better to remember fictional worlds in which knights eat princesses and restaurants fill with pies, rather than listen to the science fictions used to support proposals for TIA and warrantless wiretapping.

Notes

1. The basic FSM structure can be implemented in a number of ways, some more efficient than others, in a manner that embodies the same operational logic.

2. During the blog-based peer review for this book, Orkin commented that the parallel I draw between issues in *The Sims* and *NOLF2* is quite appropriate:

> *NOLF2*'s non-combat AI was very much Sims-inspired. Our worlds were filled with "Smart Objects," which dictated animation sets in a similar manner to *The Sims* (e.g., writing at desks, napping in beds, dancing to boom boxes, etc.). We wanted the player to feel as though the other characters truly *lived* in the world, rather than simply waiting for the player to arrive, and what better model for living domestic environments than *The Sims*.

Orkin, Craig Hubbard (*NOLF2*'s lead designer), and John Mulkey (lead level designer) comment on related topics in a *PC Gamer* interview (*PC Gamer* Staff 2002).

3. Something like the *Strips/Planex* distinction between plan formulation and execution was also found in *Tale-Spin*. For example, *MTrans* and *PTrans* had "action module" versions (*Do-MTrans* and *Do-PTrans*) that did additional work not contained in the versions used for planning (Meehan 1976, 43). As Meehan puts it, "You don't worry about runtime preconditions until you're executing the plan. If I'm planning to get a Coke out of the machine upstairs, I worry about having enough money, but I don't worry about walking up the stairs until I'm at the stairs" (41).

4. I am indebted to a thoughtful conversation during the blog-based peer review of this book for revealing the necessity of revising the following section. I want to particularly thank Jeff Orkin, Richard Evans, Mark Riedl, Mark Nelson, and Alex J. Champandard for their generosity.

5. In email sent after the blog-based peer review, Richard Evans observed:

> In discussing limitations of *The Sims* and *No One Lives Forever* . . . you blame various breakdowns (e.g. putting a baby down, and then picking her up again) on the "compartmentalization" of action. I think it is more illuminating to blame these cases on the *procedural* representation of action: if the Sim's actions were represented as a sequence of *declarative* sentences, then the agent could see that there was no point putting the child down and then picking her up again, and these parts of the actions could be removed at run-time. It is not the fact that the actions are stored in separate compartments, but the fact that the agents are incapable of reasoning over the actions, because the actions are purely procedural, with no declarative information. (It is the fact that Jeff Orkin's actions in *F.E.A.R.* are tagged with declarative data [preconditions and postconditions] which allow him to fix the problem).

To my mind, this is a somewhat different emphasis on a closely-related point—and worth considering. An FSM in *The Sims* is something that the system can't "see inside," so the system must return a Sim to a default state before being able to safely use the FSM. I focus on the compartmentalization from the rest of the system, while Evans focuses on the fact that an FSM is an encapsulated, procedural representation. In the terms I am using, *Tale-Spin* planboxes (despite their declarative representation) could also be compartmentalized simply by denying them access to areas of shared memory (if they don't know the state of the world, they must assume and return to a default state of some sort). But this fails to capture the important point Evans is making: that representing actions declaratively makes possible powerful non-compartmentalizing strategies precisely because the system can understand more about each action's components and their conditions, effects, and so on. Of course, declarative representation of action also blurs the data/process distinction, as discussed in an earlier note (chapter 1, note 3).

6. I played the Xbox 360 version (Hubbard et al. 2006).

7. In Agre's next chapter, while improvisation is a matter of continually redeciding what to do, it is not based on replanning after each execution step. Rather, he proposes "to understand improvisation as a *running argument* in which an agent decides what to do by conducting a continually updating argument among various alternatives" (161).

8. This strategy also allows *F.E.A.R.* to avoid a problem with replanning that has become apparent in the years since *F.E.A.R.* as planning approaches are used more frequently in games. As Alex J. Champandard explains (2007), typical planning in games deals with the world in a manner like the lead character in the movie *Memento*: rethinking the world from scratch on a regular basis. He writes, "This approach is typical because writing a planner that can replan to deal with dynamic changes is not trivial, and setting up the whole AI logic to monitor and figure out what changes are relevant takes a lot of work and experience."

Obviously, this leads to erratic behavior. A character in the middle of doing something may decide, for no apparent reason, to start doing something else. To make matters worse, there's often nothing present to prevent the character from, a few moments later, returning to the previous task. Of course, something like this could be a great characterization method for a character who is forgetful or dithering. But even then it would only work if being tracked by the system and appropriately signaled to the audience, rather than happening because the system is doing nothing to monitor temporal coherence.

Orkin refers to his alternative as "Goal-Oriented Action Planning" and reports that it is being taken up by other developers. Champandard's preferred solution is the use of behavior trees—an approach related to some I will discuss in the context of the Oz Project, the Expressivator, and *Façade*.

9. I'll discuss story grammars in more detail in the next chapter, in the context of *Brutus*.

10. Dyer's dissertation became the book *In-Depth Understanding: A Computer Model of Integrated Processing for Narrative Comprehension* (MIT Press, 1983).

11. Thematic Abstraction Units are also known as Thematic Affect Units.

12. In *Minstrel,* character-level goals and plans are represented in the schema, and so can be transformed (as outlined later in this chapter). Author-level plans, on the other hand, are each structured, independent blocks of code in the Lisp programming language—presumably for reasons of authoring and execution efficiency.

As Turner writes, "*Minstrel's* author-level plans are represented as structures of Lisp code, and *Minstrel's* TRAMs do not know how to adapt Lisp code. *Minstrel's* author-level plans are opaque and non-adaptable, and so *Minstrel cannot* adapt author-level plans" (1994, 83). There are some good reasons for this, as he explains: "Although the same type of representation could be used for *Minstrel's* author-level plans, it would be clumsy and time consuming. Schemas for complicated computational actions such as looping, recursion, and so on would have to be defined and an interpreter built to perform these actions" (81).

Therefore, author-level plans are opaque to *Minstrel's* transformation procedures, which operate on the schema representations. As a result, if PATs are going to be transformed, which is *Minstrel's* primary engine for producing new stories, then they must be represented at the character level, rather than at the authorial one.

13. During the blog-based review of this book's manuscript, Turner suggested that there are two additional points that should be considered when evaluating *Minstrel* at this juncture:

> You're correct in identifying this problem, but I think you're overlooking a couple of other problems worth mentioning.
>
> The first is an interesting question about cognition. If I have the knowledge to understand the problem shown in pp 24, then why would I invent that solution in the first place? And yet as people we're constantly considering solutions and then rejecting them. That would seem to suggest that people have different processes for creating solutions and evaluating them, and that those processes use different sets of knowledge. That's a pretty odd and surprising result when you think about it.
>
> Second, and probably more relevant to your discussion here, is the question of how important the hand-encoding of the knowledge is to a brittle scruffy AI system. One defense of systems with very limited domains (like *Minstrel*) is "real machine learning would solve the problem of limited knowledge." But even if we had robust machine learning that could (say) read a bunch of King Arthur books and create a large case-based memory, who can say whether *Minstrel* could operate as well on those memories as it does on the ones I hand coded? (I'd argue that it could, but the point is that there's really nothing in *Minstrel* to convince anyone of that.)
>
> I should probably stop finding faults in my own work :-) (2007)

The second of these points—regarding machine learning—is a thought-provoking one. As I have argued in this chapter, the version of *Minstrel* created for Turner's dissertation actually can become more fallible as its microworld of knowledge is expanded. It is perhaps possible that, at a certain point, this phenomenon would reverse—with more knowledge helping to both feed and bound *Minstrel's* creative processes, rather than providing impetus for them to develop yet-more-inappropriate narratives. But how such a goal could be accomplished is unknown.

14. By this I do not mean to argue that statistical AI is particularly fallible within the world of AI. In fact, the rise of statistical AI is precisely due to its greater successes. What I mean to argue against here is the belief that AI can achieve magical results. Symbolic AI is almost never presented as capable of magic (though it was commonly in the 1970s), while statistical AI is often presented in this manner, so I argue here against statistical AI in particular.

15. Orkin and Deb Roy (2007), the professor who directs Orkin's group at MIT, see *The Restaurant Game* as an initial example of a minimal investment multiplayer online game. Unlike a standard massively multiplayer online game, which often encourages role-playing of a fantasy character for long periods of

time, a minimal investment multiplayer online game encourages role-playing for shorter periods and without investment in a particular character as an online representative of the player. Orkin and Roy argue that the anonymous character of the minimal investment multiplayer online game, combined with rich opportunities for role-play and postscenario feedback, combine to encourage improvisation within social roles (resulting in the desired data) and replay (resulting in more data).

16. During the blog-based review of this book's manuscript, Orkin commented on the "range of possible interactions and the variety of interactive objects" for standard commercial games and *The Restaurant Game*:

> Most of today's games restrict interaction with the world to shooting things, opening doors, and picking up weapons. Physics simulations have added the ability to knock some things over, or destroy them. But in general, interactivity is restricted, in part because developers simply don't have the bandwidth to script appropriate responses to every interaction. So, that is one of the goals of statistical data collection—learn what interactions players tend to have with different types of objects, and what are common responses when these interactions occur.

17. Of course, neither Turing nor Nelson is talking about machines such as washing machines (though these now commonly contain computers). Rather, Turing is speaking about the capacity for universal computing machines, such as today's personal computers and game consoles, to carry out all the work previously done by special-purpose computers: predicting tides, solving differential equations, playing chess endgames, and so on. Nelson's point is that this means there is no one "computer way" of doing things. The design of each piece of software is instead the result of a series of social choices as much as technological necessities. As Nick Montfort points out in a comment on the *Grand Text Auto* blog, these features of universal computation are distinct from the idea of the computer as, in Alan Kay's term, a "metamedium." While the importance of universal computation in a computer's media capabilities is certainly emphasized by authors such as Nelson and Key, they are also a property of other elements of the system (e.g., speakers for producing sound or a display capable of showing a smooth series of images).

18. As of this writing, the American Civil Liberties Union (2008) estimates that there are more than one million names on the current U.S. government terrorist watch list. Known watch list entries include Nobel Peace Prize laureate Nelson Mandela, individuals known to be deceased, and common names such as Robert Johnson.

19. This ability to reason by analogy about computational processes that are kept secret is perhaps part of the reason that computer scientists have emerged as some of the most important critical thinkers on these matters. For example, two of the most high-profile leaders of the movement against black box voting machines (computer ballot boxes operating using secret processes and with no paper trail to allow auditing of their outputs) are David Dill (professor of computer science at Stanford University) and Aviel Rubin (professor of computer science at Johns Hopkins University).

Chapter 7
Authoring Systems

Writing Software

My early experiences of digital media were as an audience member. I remember playing text-only games like *Hunt the Wumpus* on mainframe terminals at my mother's university as well as interactive fictions like *Zork I* on my father's early portable computers (a Kaypro and an Osbourne). I remember playing graphical games like *Combat* on a first-generation Atari console that belonged to my cousins as well as *Star Trek: Strategic Operations Simulator* on my friend Brion's first-generation Atari home computer. Brion would later guide me in more arcane explorations of computer code as we attempted to creatively alter the binary files of games we played, saving them back to the Atari's tape deck. But I think it was earlier, when I was ten years old, that I first sat down to program at a "blank slate."

This was at my elementary school, on pre-Macintosh computers from Apple. I used the built-in Apple version of the Basic programming language to create a simple piece of media of my own: a low-resolution star and sky, independently cycling through colors, beeping as each new combination appeared. On the playground I daydreamed about how to create more complex media along the lines of Infocom's *Zork I* (Anderson, Blank, Daniels, et al. 1980). But I couldn't figure out how to scale up from the simple Basic commands I knew (e.g., "GOTO") to a complex software system like *Zork*'s.

Decades later, I now see a piece of the puzzle that eluded me: the authors of *Zork* didn't work in Basic, and it

231

1. A brief discussion is available in *Twisty Little Passages* (Montfort 2003, 126–127). A more detailed look, including examples of source code, can be found in "Zork: A Computerized Fantasy Simulation Game" (Lebling, Blank, and Anderson 1979).

2. This was an early commercial instance of the same strategy used by the Java platform's virtual machine.

wasn't necessary for me to do so. Though Basic was part of the built-in, read-only memory of the Apple II, by working in it I wasn't functioning in the essential language of the computer. Instead, I was using an authoring system, created to make it easier to develop certain kinds of software. The authors of *Zork* were using a completely different system, designed to make their sort of software easier to create.

In fact, the authors of Infocom's popular interactive fiction titles employed several layers of software I didn't begin to imagine.[1] Rather than use the versions of Basic (or some other language) specific to the various personal computers of the 1970s and 1980s, their code was written to run on a "virtual machine"—versions of which they created for each major platform.[2] Further, the essential elements for supporting gameplay (interpreting text typed by the audience, simulating a virtual space, managing manipulatable objects, and so on) were abstracted into a kind of game engine. Each author (or set of collaborators) creating an Infocom fiction was mainly occupied creating the specific text and behaviors for the places, objects, and characters in that fiction—rather than starting from scratch, as I imagined.

To put it another way, the fact that I didn't recognize Basic as a set of authoring tools was only the tip of the iceberg. More generally, I didn't recognize that most digital media creation takes place within systems specially designed to support particular types of authoring tasks, and that these systems are in turn supported by layers of further systems. Elements that look like system processes on one level (e.g., a series of commands in a programming language) can come to look like data on another level (e.g., a compiler using its processes to translate those commands for another system). The power afforded by this fact allows for the crafting of special-purpose authoring environments—from game engines to interactive animation software—that can make some tasks much easier and others impossible.

Authoring Stories

When story-generation systems are thought of as media rather than simulations of human intelligence, issues of authoring come to the fore. Creating a successful story-generation system requires thinking in terms of the audience's surface experience and also in terms of the structures presented for authoring the elements of that experience—what Michael Mateas calls the system's authorial and interpretive *affordances*. This chapter examines three influential story-generation systems both as authored artifacts and systems for authoring, as well as related concepts such as Mateas's.

Like any digital media system, a story-generation system has one simple requirement: along some dimension(s), the system should offer an advantage over other solutions. For example, Infocom sought to create interactive story experiences for broad audiences. Implementing a software system had the advantage of making this possible, given that it was impossible for Infocom authors to make personal visits to the homes and workplaces of thousands of simultaneous players. On a more serious note, implementing a virtual machine made it easier for Infocom titles to reach audiences playing on the wide variety of 1980s-era personal computing platforms, as compared with "porting" the games to each operating system.

Beyond this simple litmus test, the sorts of story

systems considered in this chapter also have two further requirements. First, they must be expressive and controllable, so that their underlying models effectively shape the audience experience. Without this, much of the effort involved in developing their fictional models is arguably wasted. At the same time, these systems must also be *authorable*—not departing so far from the skills and expectations of traditional authors that developing material for them is unrealistically onerous and unable to draw on our vast body of experience in media authoring. Balancing these two requirements can be a challenge.

Looking at this chapter's example systems also foregrounds another key difference between the practices of artificial intelligence (AI) and digital media. In AI, as in many areas of computer science, a system does not need to be completed in order to be influential. Computer science rewards the creation of innovative processes and mostly considers data the province of other fields. This results in a significant incentive against actually completing the authoring work for story-generation systems. Completing the data is time-consuming work with little direct reward, especially for systems that are not well designed for authorability.

Unfortunately, unfinished systems provide substantially less valuable results for both fields, because neither their processes for story generation nor their support for authoring are fully tested. Yet unfinished systems remain worth examining, because it is the only way to gain insight from the creative work performed in many computer science projects. This is visible in two of the systems discussed in this chapter: *Universe* and *Brutus*. This chapter's final example, *Terminal Time,* takes the next step—both departing from an exclusive disciplinary identification with computer science and (perhaps as a consequence) creating a completed system.

Universe

Michael Lebowitz began work on *Universe* around the same time that Scott Turner started his work on *Minstrel,* and the two systems bear a number of similarities.[3] Both focus on the importance of authorial actions rather than simply character actions. Both emerge from the scruffy artificial intelligence tradition—Lebowitz had recently written his dissertation at Yale under Roger Schank's supervision, contributing to Schank's model of dynamic memory, especially in relation to story understanding.[4] Descriptions of both also emphasize the importance of the "point" or "theme" that the system is working to communicate through each act of generation (Lebowitz 1984, 175).

But in addition to its similarities with *Minstrel, Universe* also has an unusual feature in common with *Tale-Spin.* Just as the most famous stories attributed to *Tale-Spin* are actually hand transcriptions of early errors, the most famous story attributed to *Universe* has a somewhat more tenuous connection to the project than one might assume. Here is the story:

> Liz was married to Tony. Neither loved the other, and, indeed, Liz was in love with Neil. However, unknown to either Tony or Neil, Stephano, Tony's father, who wanted Liz to produce a grandson for him, threatened Liz that if she left Tony, he would kill Neil. Liz told Neil that she did not love him, that she was still in love with Tony, and that he should forget about her. Eventually, Neil was convinced and he married Marie. Later, when Liz was finally

3. Lebowitz's work on *Universe* was carried out while a faculty member at Columbia University, during which time (according to the acknowledgments in Lebowitz's 1984 and 1987 papers) work by Paula Langer and Doron Shalmon...

4. Lebowitz's dissertation was "Generalization and Memory in an Integrated Understanding System," filed December 1980.

Notes continued at end of this chapter.

5. These authors
include Marie-Laure
Ryan (1992, 246) and
Janet Murray (1997,
201).

6. "Memory
organization points"
are also known as
"memory organization
packages."

free from Tony (because Stephano had died), Neil was not free to marry her and their trouble went on.

Though a number of prominent authors provide this as an example of *Universe*'s output, in fact this is a summarization of a plot from *Days of Our Lives*.[5] It appears in a paper about *Universe* as "an illustration of the kind of plot outlines we would like to generate" (Lebowitz 1985, 172). Unfortunately, *Universe* was never able to display the level of mastery achieved by the authors of *Days of Our Lives*—a remarkably popular and long-running daytime television melodrama. This story, however, does nonetheless point to a number of crucial ways in which the goals of *Universe* are significantly different from those of systems such as *Tale-Spin* and *Minstrel*.

First, *Universe* is designed to generate continuing serials: stories that never end. Second, *Universe* is working in one of the world's most popular story forms (television melodrama) rather than the somewhat archaic (and more difficult for contemporary audiences to judge) forms of Aesop-style fables and tales of Arthur's knights. Third, *Universe*'s goals are defined in terms of what kinds of story and character structures it will generate, rather than in terms of the model of human cognition that the system's operations will simulate.

The last of these is, I believe, the most critical. While ideas such as scruffy AI's "memory organization points" are important in the conception of *Universe,* the system is not presented as a simulation of a model of human cognition.[6] Instead, it is presented as a means of generating a universe of characters and an ongoing plot that interconnects them. In fact, in lieu of any cognitive science theory, Lebowitz writes: "Our methods are based on analysis of a television melodrama" (1985, 483). This allows *Universe* to be designed specifically for the generation of stories, and of a particular style of stories, rather than for the simulation of the behavior believed to generate stories.[7]

The *Universe* system is organized in two parts. One creates the interconnected sets of characters and histories that will form the background for the generated fiction. The other generates an ongoing fiction. *Universe's* model of authoring also falls into two parts. One part of the authoring effort is the creation of basic processes for generating the background world and the ongoing fiction. The other is the creation of the data that these processes employ, such as character stereotypes and story fragments.

Universe's Characters

A *Universe* story starts with the creation of characters, much as happens in *Tale-Spin*. But rather than a small number of characters who seem to come into existence at the moment the story begins, *Universe* creates an interconnected group of characters with somewhat detailed histories. This is accomplished through a character-creation cycle. As outlined in Lebowitz's 1984 paper, the cycle begins with a few characters in a queue, soon to become the universe's (m/p)atriarchs, who need the details of their lives fleshed out. One character at a time is removed from the queue, and a simple simulation of that character's life is carried out—focusing on the gaining and losing of spouses, the births of children, and the possibility of death—until the present is reached. Any new characters created through this process are added to the queue. New characters aren't created for each marriage, however, because the system may select

7. During the blog-based peer review of this book's manuscript, Michael Mateas commented: While *Universe* doesn't provide an explicit cognitive model, I would still classify it as an author modeling system. Unlike *Tale-Spin*, which models…

Notes continued at end of this chapter.

an already-existing eligible character (defined as single at the time of the marriage, of appropriate age and sex, and not directly related to the character). This begins to create interconnections between the families.

Once this basic framework of marriage, birth, and death is filled in, each character is further fleshed out. This begins by giving each character a set of traits, some of which are inherited from their parents (if known), and selecting a set of stereotypes that work well to explain those traits. Stereotypes include many familiar character elements (e.g., lawyer, doctor, gangster, big eater, swinger, and video game player) and have normal values for some traits and not others (e.g., "lawyer" has normal values for intelligence, guile, and self-confidence, but not for religion, promiscuity, or moodiness). Following this, the system adds further detail to the characters' pasts by creating simplified versions of the sorts of events it will create once story generation begins.

Universe's Stories

Because *Universe* is not aimed at producing stories that end but rather serial melodramas on the model of *Days of Our Lives,* its plans are never aimed at bringing things to completion. This is quite different from the previous systems examined in this book. In *Tale-Spin* and most AI work on planning, the focus is on achieving goals: Joe Bear is hungry, and the planning process tries to get some food and ingest it so that his hunger will go away. In *Minstrel* the plans are to flesh out a planning advice theme (PAT) schema, meet the other goals, and complete the story. *Universe* plans, on the other hand, are based on "character goals" and "author goals" that do not lead toward conclusions. Character goals are monitored to maintain consistency, while the primary impetus for story generation comes through author goals. The author has goals for maintaining an interesting story—Lebowitz talks about goals such as preserving romantic tension and keeping the story moving—with the result that *Universe*'s plans can never specify a complete course of action, only one that seems appropriate given the current circumstances in the story's universe.

High-level author goals are carried out by lower-level goals, and planning for both takes place through "plot fragments." These fragments are a primary type of data in the *Universe* model of authoring. They are both events themselves and means toward authorial goals. For example, a higher-level goal to which Lebowitz gives particular attention is "churning" lovers, keeping them separated by new obstacles each time the previous set is cleared up. The forced marriage of Liz and Tony, on *Days of Our Lives,* is by Lebowitz regarded as a fragment that achieves (among other possible goals) the churning of Liz and Neil. This makes it apparent how character goals are treated quite differently in *Universe* as opposed to systems such as *Tale-Spin*. As Lebowitz writes about churning:

> Obviously this goal makes no sense from the point of view of the characters involved, but it makes a great deal of sense for the author, and, indeed, is a staple of melodrama ("happily ever after" being notoriously boring in fiction, if not in life). *Universe* has a number of other plot fragments [besides forced marriage] for achieving this goal, such as lovers' fights and job problems. (1985, 488)

Universe maintains a representation of outstanding author and character goals. The storytelling cycle begins with choosing an author goal that has no unmet preconditions. A plot fragment is selected that will achieve that goal, with preference given to fragments that also achieve other goals that are current. This plot fragment is then made part of the story—producing new characters, events for output, and new goals as appropriate. Even "forced marriage" is a relatively high-level plot fragment, which needs to be filled out with lower-level fragments for the woman dumping her lover, the lover getting together with another woman, the threat from the parent being eventually eliminated, and so on. The potential choice of a number of different fragments and characters for each of these elements increases the variability of the story structures that *Universe* produces.

As this process takes place, *Universe* doesn't simply choose characters and plot fragments randomly. First, the personalities and plans of characters constrain which characters can play roles in the fragments (and further, some fragments require the participation of characters that have particular stereotypes). Second, with each fragment *Universe* tries to select events and include characters that will help meet other active authorial goals. This helps create complexly interwoven plots, such as those of serial melodramas, in which events often contribute to several active story lines.

Box 7.1 is an example of an actual *Universe* output for a forced marriage story line using the same characters as the *Days of Our Lives* plot summary above (Lebowitz 1985, 491). Those lines of the output that begin ">>>" represent low-level events, whereas other text provides a trace of the planning process. The system begins with two active goals: to churn Liz and Neil, and to get Neil together with Renee.

Other plot fragments that *Universe* can use for churning include lovers-fight, job-problem, pregnant-affair, accident-breakup, steal-child, colleague-affair, and avalanche-accident. The variations on these depend on the characters involved. For example, in Lebowitz's 1987 paper he shows output from churning Joshua and Fran.

Box 7.1. Universe Output

*(tell '(((churn liz neil)(together renee neil))))

working on goal—(CHURN LIZ NEIL)
Several plans to choose from FORCED-MARRIAGE LOVERS-FIGHT JOB-PROBLEM
—using plan FORCED-MARRIAGE

working on goal—(DO-THREATEN STEPHANO LIZ "forget it")
—using plan THREATEN

>>> STEPHANO threatens LIZ: "forget it"

working on goal—(DUMP-LOVER LIZ NEIL)—using plan BREAK-UP

>>> LIZ tells NEIL she doesn't love him

working on goal—(WORRY-ABOUT NEIL)—using plan BE-CONCERNED
Possible candidates—MARLENA JULIE DOUG ROMAN DON CHRIS KAYLA
Using MARLENA for WORRIER

>>> MARLENA is worried about NEIL

working on goal—(TOGETHER * NEIL)
Several plans to choose from SEDUCTION DRUNKEN-SNEAK-IN SYMPATHETIC-UNION
JOB-TOGETHER
—using plan SEDUCTION
Possible candidates—DAPHNE RENEE
Using RENEE for SEDUCER

>>> RENEE seduces NEIL

working on goal—(ELIMINATE STEPHANO)
Several plans to choose from ATTEMPTED-MURDER EXPOSE
—using plan ATTEMPTED-MURDER
Using ALEX for KILLER

>>> ALEX tries to kill STEPHANO

working on goal—(DO-DIVORCE TONY LIZ)—using plan DIVORCE

>>> LIZ and TONY got divorced

working on goal—(TOGETHER LIZ NEIL)
no acceptable plans

---

8. As Michael Mateas pointed out in the blog-based peer review of this manuscript, Lebowitz dedicates a major portion of one paper to describing how an explanation-based learning approach could enable the program…

Notes continued at end of this chapter.

Given their jobs, they can experience the job problems of bureaucrat and sleazy-lawyer. Given other aspects of their characters, they can fight about in-laws, money, secrets, flirting, and kids.

While *Universe* was never completed (at the time of Lebowitz's 1987 paper it only contained sixty-five plot fragments), it was already able to generate stories with more consistency than *Minstrel* and more structure than *Tale-Spin*. But its very consistency raises a question: In what sense is *Universe* a story-generation system? Sequencing plot fragments doesn't *sound* nearly as impressive as the creative adaptation of *Minstrel*'s TRAMs or the simulation of intelligent behavior in *Tale-Spin*.

Authoring *Universe*

It is precisely the elements that make *Universe* an important early model of pursuing story generation from an authorial perspective that also open it to questions as to its significance. The system is explicitly limited to combining and sequencing hand-authored story data, rather than attempting to somehow generate new data.[8] This means that important human knowledge about stories can be encoded into the data. It provides a role for authors and a route to shaping the audience experience. But the same can be said of a *Choose Your Own Adventure* book, each of which is structured as a set of pathways through plot fragments.

One difference, of course, is that a *Choose Your Own Adventure* book provides even greater opportunities for encoding authorial knowledge—down to the level of language, not just the comparatively abstract level of character stereotypes and plot fragments. But the more significant difference lies in the predefined pathways that structure a *Choose Your Own Adventure*. This is a close parallel to a difference described earlier, between character actions driven by finite-state machines and the *Strips*-derived planning processes of *F.E.A.R.* In all these operational logics, the possible action fragments are hand created by human authors. In one set, though, the connections between fragments are predetermined during the same authoring process, while in the other set actions are dynamically sequenced, according to rules, based on the current state of the fictional world. This produces a vast difference in both the tractability of the authoring process and the dynamism of the audience experience.

Still, when systems are designed in this way, a risk presents itself. A system designed to dynamically sequence hand-authored elements of a fiction may embody a flexible, powerful approach to generating a variety of fictions—or it may simply be an elaborate manner of breaking a particular story into chunks and providing a means for a computer to reassemble them. The only way to be sure that a software author hasn't created an inflexible system (while fooling herself or himself into thinking it is a general, flexible one) is to have enough data to produce a variety of complete audience experiences. *Universe* seems like a powerful and flexible model, but only further development of its data could have demonstrated this convincingly.

Similarly, given the lack of attention paid to surface generation in *Universe,* it is impossible to know how well its model serves the challenge of expressing its underlying model for the audience. Some might argue that meeting this challenge is entirely a matter of the design of the system for presenting the work's surface—that almost any model can be effectively presented in the desired manner. Perhaps this is true, but it is strongly reminiscent of a position that has proven problematic in the field of human-computer interaction.

In this field it is relatively common to suggest that a software system's interaction surface can be abstracted from the underlying processes. The processes can be specified up front and implemented in a "waterfall" fashion, working linearly from a detailed initial specification, which may be efficient from an engineering standpoint. Meanwhile, the interface can be developed iteratively, perhaps with participation from those who will actually use it. Finally, another software layer can be used to map between the waterfall-produced processes and the iteratively developed interface.

It is here, however, that we see the limitations of the model of authoring systems introduced at the start of this chapter. While it is theoretically true that layers of software abstraction make it possible to create software systems that relatively arbitrarily make some tasks easy and others difficult, it is also true that the underlying layers inevitably exert their influence. In the field of software development, Bonnie E. John and Len Bass have called this "We can't change *That*!" (2001–2004). If the model of the underlying activity embedded in the software processes is too far from the imagined interface, then the amount of work required to support that interface is simply not entertained. In the field of digital media, Nick Montfort and Ian Bogost (2009) have coined the phrase "platform studies" to name scholarly work that takes such specifics of underlying hardware and software layers into account.

I believe that, given this, we simply cannot know how well suited *Universe* is to surface realization, and the same holds true for the many story-generation projects that focus solely on the generation of story structures. Fortunately, the next two systems I will discuss—*Brutus* and *Terminal Time*—make surface realization an important element of their systems. I will dedicate a separate section to considering how they address this challenge, focusing first on their models of authorship.

Brutus

Given its name, it is probably no surprise that Selmer Bringsjord and David Ferrucci's *Brutus* system specializes in stories of betrayal. Here is the beginning of one:

> Dave Striver loved the university. He loved its ivy-covered clocktowers, its ancient and sturdy brick, and its sun-splashed verdant greens and eager youth. He also loved the fact that the university is free of the stark unforgiving trials of the business world—only this *isn't* a fact: academia has its own tests, and some are as merciless as any in the marketplace. A prime example is the dissertation defense: to earn the PhD, to become a doctor, one must pass an oral examination on one's dissertation. This was a test Professor Edward Hart enjoyed giving. (2000, 199–200)

The story continues for roughly another half page. Hart is a member of Striver's dissertation committee, and when they meet in Hart's book-lined office he promises to sign Striver's dissertation at the defense. The story says that Hart's "eyes were bright and trustful, and his bearing paternal." But at the defense Hart actually refuses to sign, and Striver fails. The story ends with an unexpected twist: we see Hart sitting in his office, "saddened by Dave's failure," and trying to think how he could help him. We realize that Hart has lied to himself about his betrayal.

Such examples demonstrate that in terms of audience experience—both of language and structural coherence—*Brutus*'s output goes far beyond any of the story-generation systems I have considered thus far. And in contrast with *Minstrel,* the creators of *Brutus* haven't presented its stories as the result of an accurate simulation of human creativity. Instead, they have argued at length that such simulation is impossible, devoting much of their book *Artificial Intelligence and Literary Creativity* to this issue. From Bringsjord and Ferrucci's point of view, the challenge of story generation is to develop a system through clever engineering, rather than through emulation of the mechanisms of human creativity. As they put it, "We cheerfully operate under the belief that human (literary) creativity is beyond computation—and yet strive to craft the *appearance* of creativity from suitably configured computation" (149, original emphasis). And their faith in the power of this approach is great. In particular, they talk of the *Brutus* architecture eventually producing "an artificial storyteller able to compete against inspired authors" (152) or even able to "find employment at the expense of a human writer" (xxiv). This certainly sounds like a successful "appearance of creativity."

Such statements have also proven a successful formulation for producing press coverage of *Brutus*. Journalists have written many stories that position *Brutus* as a potential competitor to human authors. The *New York Times,* for example, has published more than one story about Bringsjord and Ferrucci's work from this angle (e.g., Mirapaul 1999; Akst 2004). No other story generator of the era attracted this level of public attention. In an especially fitting confluence, one of the *Times* stories is actually about a literal competition between *Brutus* and a group of human authors. This competition, held on a web site run by Dan Hurley, asked visitors to judge five stories: four newly written ones by human authors and one product of the *Brutus₁* implementation of the *Brutus* architecture. As the *New York Times* explains:

> Visitors to the site can vote on which story they think was created by a computer. Hurley and his staff picked the four human-penned pieces after reviewing online entries from 390 contributors, who had a month to labor over their prose. Bringsjord said *Brutus.1* spit out its story in seconds. (Mirapaul 1999)

Another *New York Times* story reports the outcome of the competition: "Only 25 percent of the 2,000 voters picked out the computer-generated story" (Sommers 1999). It's an impressive result, but the simple existence of the competition, especially given its coverage in the paper of record in the United States, is even more telling. There is the impression—created by a combination of the literary quality of *Brutus*'s output, the rhetorical stance of *Brutus*'s designers, and the press coverage generated—that a major milestone has been passed. The key to this advance, we're told, is that the creators of *Brutus* have put their finger on something essential that storytelling systems need. As Bringsjord and Ferrucci observe, "*A good artificial storyteller must be in command of the immemorial themes that drive both belletristic and formulaic fiction.* . . . Such themes must be cast in terms that an AI can digest and process; that is, these themes must be, for want of a better word, mathematized" (2000, 81, original emphasis).

Mathematized Betrayal

Bringsjord and Ferrucci see a need for "mathematizing" literary themes because they approach story generation from the neat AI perspective. As they write: "We approach story generation through logic; in more specific terms, this means that we conceive of story generation as theorem proving" (42). To my knowledge, Bringsjord and Ferrucci are the first to create a major story-generation system that primarily employs the tools of theorem-proving AI (though some are also put to use in the contemporary *Terminal Time*, as discussed in the next section). Specifically, *Brutus* is built using a logic-programming system called FLEX, which is based on the programming language Prolog.

The first step in *Brutus*'s story-generation procedure is to instantiate a theme. As mentioned earlier, the literary theme that is the focus of the *Brutus* system is betrayal. In order to help readers understand the system, Bringsjord and Ferrucci provide some "actual FLEX code" that is the mathematized expression of betrayal they have authored (box 7.2). This specifies two characters: the Betrayer,

---

Box 7.2. *Brutus's* Ideal Representation of Betrayal

```
relation betrayal_p
        if Evil is some goal whose plan is an EvilPlan
            and whose agent is a Betrayor
        and Saying is included in the EvilPlan
        and Saying is some say
        and Thwarting is included in the EvilPlan
        and Thwarting is some thwart
        and Betrayeds_Goal is the prevented goal of Thwarting
        and Betrayors_Lie is some support of the Betrayeds Goal
        and Betrayed is some person
            whose goal is the Betrayeds_Goal
            and whose beliefs include the Betrayors_Lie
(Bringsjord and Ferrucci 2000, 173)
```

and the Betrayed. The Betrayed has some goal that the Betrayer promises to support, and the Betrayed believes the promise. But it is a lie, because the Betrayer actually has an evil plan to thwart the Betrayed's goal.[9]

Yet this is not the FLEX code used by $Brutus_1$—the version of $Brutus$ that Bringsjord and Ferrucci have actually authored. Instead, they tell us, "In $Brutus_1$, thematic instantiation captures the essential characteristics of betrayal by building the following frame" (190). This frame is shown in box 7.3. Notice that it specifies less about the relationship and character internals (it does not specify that the Betrayed believes the Betrayer's lie, that the lie is regarding support of the Betrayed's goal, or that the Betrayer has an evil plan), and more about the events (not only a lie, but also a location, and also an evil action).[10]

Both of these theme instantiations, despite their differences, may remind one of $Minstrel$'s planning advice themes. After all, PATs are also hand-authored specifications of structures of relationship and event, which are meant to capture the immemorial themes that drive literature. But as I will describe, in the end the formal theme definitions of $Brutus$ and $Minstrel$ end up playing quite different roles in the two systems.

9. Note that given the story example, it must be possible for the Betrayer to be consciously unaware of this evil plan, even after executing it. Also, Bringsjord and Ferrucci employ two spellings: "betrayer" and "betrayor." I will use the former except...

10. During the blog-based review of this manuscript on Grand Text Auto, Scott Turner noted, "This representation of Betrayal reminds me of the similar construct Meehan used to force coherency onto *Tale-Spin* stories." While little discussed...

Notes continued at end of this chapter.

Box 7.3. *Brutus_1*'s Implemented Representation of Betrayal

```
frame betrayal is a concept
      default betrayer is a person and
      default betrayed is a person and
      default betrayers_goal is a goal and
      default betrayeds_goal is a goal and
      default betrayers_lie is a statement and
      default betrayers_location is a place and
      default betrayers_evil_action is a action.
(Bringsjord and Ferrucci 2000, 190)
```

Creating a Story

In order to tell a story about betrayal, *Brutus* needs to fill the roles of the Betrayer and the Betrayed. One might imagine the two characters being created on the fly, using some method akin to those of *Universe* or *Tale-Spin*—but constrained to ensure that each character will be appropriate for their role. Or alternately, one might imagine a situation in which the system begins with a set of automatically generated characters. The system might then begin storytelling by choosing a character from this set with a goal that can be thwarted. It might then make that character the Betrayed, and then either create or assign a character to be the Betrayer.

But neither of these is what happens. Instead, the system searches its "domain knowledge-base"—its collection of authored data—to see if two characters exist that already meet the criteria for the relationship of betrayal. That is to say, it looks for a character who already has what it takes to be the Betrayer (a goal, a lie, and an evil action) and who takes part in appropriate events for betrayal, and where those events also include a character who has what it takes to be the Betrayed.

The only way for the characters to get into the knowledge base is for them to be hand-created by authors. This means that someone must write the FLEX code to represent a character who meets the criteria for being the Betrayer and another who meets the criteria for being the Betrayed. Bringsjord and Ferrucci, however, assure readers this sort of thing will change in a future version of the system:

> In *Brutus$_1$*, thematic instantiation requires that the domain knowledge-base include many of the

specific objects required to instantiate the theme. In future versions of *Brutus* the process of thematic instantiation will use general domain concepts as a basis for generating specific objects so that less domain knowledge is required as input into the story generation process. (191)

How this will happen is not specified.

Generating a Plot

Once *Brutus* has instantiated a theme and found the appropriate characters in memory, the next stage is to develop the specifics of the plot. Bringsjord and Ferrucci characterize the plot development process as taking place through "simulation"—but it is a different form of simulation than, say, that which animates *Minstrel*'s model of authorial creativity.

Bringsjord and Ferrucci tell us that the simulation begins with the fact that each character has a goal and a plan. They write, "Once a character is set in motion, the character attempts to achieve its goal by executing the actions associated with the goal's plan" (177). So, for example, here is Hart's evil plan:

```
instance evilGoal is a goal

    agent is hart and
    plan is {lie101, refuse_to_sign101} and
    success is status of strivers_
    defense is failed. (178)
```

Each action, such as "refuse_to_sign101," has preconditions. These prevent it from being executed except in the right circumstances. We can assume, for instance, that "refuse_to_sign101" only will execute when the aforementioned "strivers_defense" is the event taking place at that moment of the simulation. Here is the representation for that event:

```
instance strivers_defense is a thesis_defense
        thesis is strivers_thesis and
        where is university_of_rome and
        examined is striver and
        committee is {hart,meter,rogers,walken} and
        status is scheduled. (175)
```

In some ways this is similar to the *Universe* model of authoring, in which hand-coded plot fragments are strung together by the system's processes. But *Universe* chooses which plot fragment to use next based on a continually shifting set of characters and goals. Depending on the circumstances, different characters can play different roles in the same plot fragment. On the other hand, for *Brutus*—or at least *Brutus₁*— the specific characters are already encoded into each event. Also, each character must already have encoded into their plan the actions that they will take when a particular event is active. And as one learns in Bringsjord and Ferrucci's book (176), even these actions are not generic, but each exist in a version hand-authored for the appropriate character.

Given this, while the *Brutus* model of plot development can be characterized as a simulation, it's not a simulation that could lead to unpredictable outcomes. Rather, producing any plot requires hand-creating the specific characters, the specific plans, and the specific instances of events that will allow the theorem prover to produce a match on its logical pattern. The plot mechanisms that are at work in *Brutus,* then, suffer from the opposite problem of those produced by *Minstrel.* As opposed to out-of-control variation, they seem to produce no variation at all. For a story-generation system, this form of theorem proving is an odd choice for the dominant operational logic.

11. As described in the previous chapter's section on *Minstrel,* the genealogy of story grammars is usually traced back to Vladimir Propp's *Morphology of the Folktale.*

Structuring a Story

Once the story's events have been activated and then added to memory, these events must be structured for their presentation to an audience. For this purpose *Brutus* uses a "story grammar"—a type of description of story structure first developed in the analysis of stories, rather than their generation.[11] While Bringsjord and Ferrucci don't provide the grammar they authored for the story quoted at the outset of this section, they do offer this "simplified" fragment:

1. Story → Setting + Goals_and_plans + Betrayers_evil_action + betrayed's_state

2. Goals_and_plans → Betrayed's_goal + Betrayers_promise + Betrayers_goal

3. Setting → setting_description(betrayal_location,pov,betrayed)

4. Betrayed's_goal → personal_goal_sentence(betrayed)

5. Betrayers_goal → personal_goal_sentence(betrayer)

6. Betrayers_promise → promise_description(betrayer,betrayed)

7. Betrayers_evil_action → narrate_action(betrayers_evil_action) (196)

It may not be immediately obvious how to read such a grammar. The rules are relatively simple. Each line defines something (on the left side of the arrow) that can be "rewritten" as something else (on the right side). If something is uppercase, then it is a "nonterminal"—there is another rule for rewriting it. If something is lowercase, a "terminal," then it will be sent to the *Brutus* natural language generation (NLG) grammars, which will be discussed later in this chapter. The items in parenthesis at the end of some terminals are arguments passed to the NLG grammars.

This grammar is remarkably concrete. Most story grammars operate at a much higher level of abstraction. For example, a common terminal for many story grammars is a generic "event" rather than a "personal_goal_sentence." And many story grammars contain items that may be repeated or which are optional, whereas each item in this grammar appears exactly once. This greater concreteness addresses one of the commonly voiced concerns about story grammars: that while a fine tool for analysis, they don't provide the necessary structure for generating well-formed stories. On the other hand, this grammar is so tightly structured that it is nearly a sentence-level outline.

Here is a story generated from this grammar:

> Dave loves the university of Rome. He loves the studious youth, ivy-covered clocktowers and its sturdy brick. Dave wanted to graduate. Prof. Hart told Dave, "I will sign your thesis at your defense." Prof. Hart actually intends to thwart Dave's plans to graduate. After Dave completed his defense and the chairman of Dave's committee asked Prof. Hart to sign Dave's thesis, Prof. Hart refused to sign. Dave was crushed. (197)

Notice that the first two sentences of this story have a similar structure to the first two of the story quoted at the beginning of this section: "Dave Striver loved the university. He loved its ivy-covered clocktowers, its ancient and sturdy brick, and its sun-splashed verdant greens and eager youth." In both cases, they were generated by the terminal of the third item in the grammar above: "setting_ description"—but operating with slightly different elements. Later in this chapter I will discuss the specifics of how *Brutus* generates literary texts for its audience, the area in which it implements some of its most interesting ideas for digital media authoring.

Brutus and Creativity

A close look at what authors create for a *Brutus* story, as begun above, undermines some of the very rhetoric that has produced interest in the *Brutus* project. This is especially true of the rhetoric around its "appearance of creativity." A good summary of this rhetoric comes in Bringsjord and Ferrucci's sixth chapter:

> The main goal behind the development of *Brutus* is to produce real, working systems which, by virtue of their internal logical structure (which implements the architecture) and implementation specifics, allow for generated stories to be sufficiently distant from initial, internal knowledge representations (called, again, *creative distance*) and to vary independently along different dimensions (called *wide variability*). (161)

As earlier chapters discuss, systems such as *Tale-Spin* and *Minstrel*—at some level—threaten to spin out of control. The unpredictable interactions between their components mean that their authors can be quite surprised by the outcomes (and not always pleasantly, as misspun stories attest). Bringsjord and Ferrucci usefully give a name to the gap in predictability that arises from these highly variable component interactions: "creative distance." We might not choose to call this gap creativity, but it is a gap that certainly exists for these systems.

On the other hand, it is also apparent that *Brutus*—or at least *Brutus₁*—has almost no gap, almost none of this unpredictability, and almost none of the distance from "initial, internal knowledge representations" that Bringsjord and Ferrucci discuss. Let me clarify this. Bringsjord and Ferrucci state:

> If we look "under the hood" of a program and find it trivial for a human to transform the program's initial data to the program's output, we are less likely to consider the program creative. If however, we, as humans, would find it challenging to map the program's initial data to a creative artifact (like a well-written and interesting story), then we are more likely to consider the program creative. We call the perceived difference between a program's initial data and its output *creative distance*. (161)

It is not clear what level and type of human difficulty would be required to make a program appear creative. One may wonder, say, if all statistical techniques (as soon as they operate on a nontrivial amount of data) by definition appear creative—given that it would be nearly impossible for a human to carry out the calculations involved. But regardless, in the case of *Brutus* it is clear that even a cursory view of its model of authoring (such as that performed above) easily allows a person to see what characters will take what actions during what story events as well as what sentences in what order will be used to communicate the story.

With all this so explicitly specified, what possible space could there be for creative distance in *Brutus*? Bringsjord and

Ferrucci don't answer this directly, instead focusing on the criterion of variability. They write: "Significant storytelling and literary variability can be achieved by altering, adding, or selecting different story, paragraph, or LAGs [literary augmented grammars]. Content variability can, of course, be achieved by creating or modifying thematic relations, behavioral rules, and domain knowledge" (197). In other words, one or more elements of an explicitly encoded *Brutus* story could be replaced with other, equally explicitly encoded elements—and unsurprisingly, this would generate a different (though far from unpredictable) result.

The Author of *Brutus*'s Stories

If one accepts *Brutus* as research into the creation of reusable story components, which can be interestingly combined with elements at other levels of abstraction, I can actually see much of value in it—though this requires disposing entirely with the rhetoric of creativity. However, taking this perspective brings up another issue. In discussions of *Brutus* one particular level of component is privileged: the mathematized description of literary themes. But thinking back over the different components presented for the *Brutus$_1$* story outlined in Bringsjord and Ferrucci's book, it becomes apparent that this is the one unnecessary component. It is not used in creating characters, relationships, events, or language. All the elements of the story are defined independently of the formal account of betrayal. It is used only to match elements already in the knowledge base, which could be found by any number of other procedures (e.g., choosing a character at random, who will already be specified in all the events for his story, which in turn will already specify the other characters involved). In other words, in *Brutus* the system's encoded knowledge about the structure of literary themes makes no contribution to creative distance. Instead, this distance is entirely created—to whatever extent it exists—by the shape of the pieces into which Bringsjord and Ferrucci decided to cut the story for which the formalized account would produce the logical match.

This, in turn, might make us uncomfortable with reports, such as that from the *New York Times,* that "Bringsjord said Brutus.1 spit out its story in seconds." In fact, Bringsjord and Ferrucci spent much longer than a few seconds authoring exactly the elements, the versions of those elements, and the order of those elements that would make up the story "*Brutus₁*," produced.

Frankly, presenting the *Brutus₁* system as a story author simply seems unwarranted, having examined its operations. Certainly, most high-level descriptions of *Brutus* suggest an operational logic for which its internal model of betrayal is central to the selection, development, and assembly of story elements. But the actual operational logic of *Brutus₁* is that of a child's picture puzzle. Each piece can only fit one place, in a manner determined by the authors before the system is set running, and no internal model of betrayal (or any other literary concept) could possibly influence the process. With this in mind, the *Brutus* project takes on the rough shape of a literary hoax—though I suspect the system's authors are among those who were taken in by the illusion. In this regard it is a memorable example of the misconceptions to which even the technically knowledgeable can fall prey without an approach for critical reading of computational systems.

It is my hope that a version of software studies (by this

name or another) can become pervasive enough that, in the future, those writing for the media will be less easily fooled. This is especially important for software systems with broader social impact, but I believe the relevant phenomena are particularly legible in examples such as *Brutus*—which are lent readability by our familiarity with storytelling and ability to perform commonsense evaluations of claims related to it.

In the *Brutus* illusion we may also see the lingering impact of traditional views of AI. Even though Bringsjord and Ferrucci no longer claim that their system simulates human creative behavior, they still can't escape trying to create the impression that the system is the creative actor— that its stories are artworks, and the system is the author of these stories. Of course, this is not a necessary perspective. One could view the *Brutus*$_1$ system as an artwork, its stories as particular surface outputs from the artwork, and Bringsjord and Ferrucci as the authors of the artwork. This view of system authoring would doubtless produce less press attention, but this is often the case with accurate reports of software systems, and it would not make this perspective more difficult to hold. More substantially, this would require a different conceptual approach to AI— such as that which produced the *Terminal Time* project.

Terminal Time

Picture a darkened theater. An audience watches, presumably somewhat disconcerted, as "a montage of Tibetan Buddhist imagery and Chinese soldiers holding monks at gunpoint" unfolds on-screen. A computerized voice tells them:

There were reports that Buddhist monks and nuns

> were tortured, maimed and executed. Unfortunately
> such actions can be necessary when battling the
> forces of religious intolerance. (Mateas 2002, 138)

Underlying the words, one can hear a "happy, 'optimistic' music loop." It is uncomfortable and jarring. And to make matters worse, the audience feels a certain sense of culpability. *Terminal Time* is not just a generator of uncomfortable stories, of distorted stories; it is also a generator of stories each audience "deserves."

The *Terminal Time* project is a collaboration between AI researcher/artist Michael Mateas, media artist Paul Vanouse, and documentary filmmaker Steffi Domike. Each story it generates is an ideologically biased historical narrative of the previous millennium, and each of these stories is presented as a twenty-minute multimedia projection with "the 'look and feel' of the traditional, authoritative PBS documentary" (Mateas, Vanouse, and Domike 2000). The ideological bias that drives each story is shaped by audience responses—recorded by an applause meter—to public opinion polls that appear at three points during the performance. For example:

> What is the most pressing issue facing the world today?
>
> A. Men are becoming too feminine
> and women too masculine.
>
> B. People are forgetting their ethnic heritage.
>
> C. Machines are becoming smarter than people.
>
> D. It's getting harder to earn a
> living and support a family.
>
> E. People are turning away from God.
> (Domike, Mateas, and Vanouse 2003, 165)

The ideological model derived from audience responses is always an exaggerated one. It is a representation of the positions for which the audience has applauded, but taken to an untenable extreme. As it drives the selection of events to be recounted and the "spin" with which each will be presented, it inevitably creates an ironic distance between the words being uttered and the message being conveyed (rather than reinforcing audience belief in these ideological positions).

Yet *Terminal Time* stories aren't the result of a mathematized account of irony. They are the product of careful authoring. This authoring effort included the creation of a computational account of ideology—but while the system "knows" about ideology, the irony layered on top of the ideology is not represented in the system. Only the authors and the audience get the joke.

And here one sees what may be the most significant move that *Terminal Time* makes, relative to the other story generators I have discussed. It reintroduces the author(s) and audience as essential elements of fiction through its emphasis on the context of reception (rather than only the generated text) and through interactions with the audience that generate the ideological model used in each presentation of *Terminal Time*. I'll discuss the implications of this further while describing the specifics of *Terminal Time*'s operations.

Computational Ideology

Each *Terminal Time* performance is divided into four sections. Section one is a two-minute introduction that sets the audience's expectations—combining a *Masterpiece Theater*–style of delivery with the information that a historical narrative will be produced for that audience by *Terminal Time*'s mechanisms. This is followed by the first question period, in which "an initial ideological theme (from the set of gender, race, technology, class, religion) and a narrative arc (e.g. is this a progress or decline narrative) are established" (Mateas, Vanouse, and Domike 2000). The next stage is the generation and presentation of the part of the story covering the years 1000–1750 CE, which takes six minutes. Following this, a second set of questions refines the ideological theme chosen in the first set and may introduce a subtheme (e.g., race with a subtheme of class, or technology with religion). The next section of the story is then generated and presented, covering roughly 1750–1950 CE, and again taking six minutes. This is followed by a final set of questions that further refines theme(s) and introduces the possibility for a reversal (e.g., a decline narrative may become a progress one). This is followed by the generation and presentation of the last phase of the story, covering roughly 1950 CE to the end of the millennium.

As each phase of storytelling takes place, the ideological models not only become further shaped by the audience responses but also more blunt in their operations. This, combined with audiences' greater familiarity with more recent history, causes the exaggerated ideological spin of the story to become steadily more apparent over the twenty minutes of a *Terminal Time* performance. Toward the end of performances this culminates in story fragments such as the glowing description of the Chinese invasion of Tibet quoted above. In that particular case, the ideological goals at work were those that *Terminal Time*'s creators refer to as belonging to the "anti-religious rationalist."

The representation of ideology in *Terminal Time* is

based on that developed for the *Politics* system—which itself was a successor to the ideology machine created by Robert Abelson and his collaborators in the 1950s through 1970s (and discussed in an chapter 4). In *Terminal Time* ideology is represented as a set of goal trees—specifically, rhetorical goals for what the story will demonstrate through its history of the millennium. While the initial audience polling produces one of the goal trees originally crafted by *Terminal Time*'s authors, further questioning may add, delete, or change goals. For example, during the second round of questioning a subtheme may be introduced via the combination of goals from one tree with another.

Below is an instance of *Terminal Time* authoring—specifically, the antireligious rationalist goal tree as it exists before any modifications. Notice that because "show-thinkers-persecuted-by-religion" is a subgoal of both high-level goals, it can satisfy both of them.

```
show-religion-is-bad
        show-religion-causes-war
        show-religion-causes-crazy-self-sacrifice
        show-religion-causes-oppression
        show-religion-causes-self-abuse
        show-thinkers-persecuted-by-religion
show-halting-rationalist-progress-against-religion
        show-thinkers-opposing-religious-thought
        show-thinkers-persecuted-by-religion
```
(Mateas, Vanouse, and Domike 2000, 239)

In their paper, Mateas, Vanouse, and Domike write that in *Terminal Time*, "nine major ideologues are represented using a total of 222 rhetorical goals." The authors of

Terminal Time represent the crafting of these ideological models as authoring, as the creation of an artwork. But this is not always the way that their work is understood in the AI community. As Mateas reports:

> The first time I presented *Terminal Time* to a technical audience, there were several questions about whether I was modeling the way that real historians work. The implicit assumption was that the value of such a system lies in its veridical model of human behavior. In fact, the architectural structure of *Terminal Time* is part of the concept of the piece, not as a realist portrait of human behavior, but rather as a caricature of certain institutionalized processes of documentary film making. (2002, 57–58)

This reception of *Terminal Time* should perhaps come as no surprise, given my earlier discussion of anthropomorphized models within AI. And for understanding *Terminal Time* and the ideas that motivate it, one does need to consider how human models of history and ideology interact with the system. Yet the place to look for human models is not within the system itself. Rather, *Terminal Time* depends on the existence of these models in a very anthropomorphic location: within the audience.

Event Knowledge

In order for *Terminal Time* events to be accessible to the system, they need to be represented in a formalized manner. The *Terminal Time* approach to this problem involves building on top of a representation of everyday knowledge called the "Upper Cyc Ontology" (an ambitious, in-process attempt to address the fundamental issues discussed earlier in the context of *Minstrel*). For *Terminal Time*'s purposes, the approach taken by the Cyc Ontology both structures how its own terms will be authored (as assertions in a knowledge base that also includes the terms from Upper Cyc) and provides the lower-level grounding on top of which its terms are defined.

Terminal Time's historical events cover a range of levels of abstraction. They include, for example, the First Crusades, the invention of Bakelite, and the rise of Enlightenment philosophy. Here is an example of how events are authored for *Terminal Time*. Specifically, this is the representation of one event, the Giordano Bruno story:

```
;; Giordano Bruno
($isa %GiordanoBrunoStory %HistoricalEvent)
($isa %GiordanoBrunoStory %IdeaSystemCreationEvent)
($isa %GiordanoBrunoStory %Execution)
(%circa %GiordanoBrunoStory (%DateRangeFn
      (%CenturyFn 16) (%CenturyFn 17)))
($eventOccursAt %GiordanoBrunoStory
$ContinentOfEurope)
($performedBy %GiordanoBrunoStory %GiordanoBruno)
($outputsCreated %GiordanoBrunoStory
%GiordanoBrunosIdeas)
($isa %GiordanoBrunosIdeas
$PropositionalInformationThing)
($isa %GiordanoBrunosIdeas $SomethingExisting)
(%conflictingMOs %GiordanoBrunosIdeas
%MedievalChristianity)
($isa %GiordanoBrunosIdeas %IdeaSystem)
($performedByPart %GiordanoBrunoStory
      %TheRomanCatholicReligiousOrg)
```

```
($objectActedOn %GiordanoBrunoStory
%GiordanoBruno)
```

(Mateas, Vanouse, and Domike 2000 , 238)

In the above representation, terms preceded by a "$" are defined in the Upper Cyc Ontology, while those terms preceded by "%" are defined within the *Terminal Time* ontology in terms of the Upper Cyc Ontology. An English-language gloss of this event representation reads:

> The Giordano Bruno story, a historical event occurring in the 16th and 17th century, involved the creation of a new idea system and an execution. The idea system created in this event conflicts with the idea system of medieval Christianity. Both Giordano Bruno and a portion of the Roman Catholic Church were the performers of this event. Giordano Bruno was acted on (he was executed) in this event. (ibid.)

In order for a *Terminal Time* ideologue to make use of such an event, it must be possible to determine that the event can be spun to support one of the current rhetorical goals. The *Terminal Time* system identifies candidate events by testing them for applicability. These tests are carried out through an "inference engine" written in Lisp. Here is the test for "show-thinkers-persecuted-by-religion":

```
(%and
      ($isa ?event %IdeaSystemCreationEvent)
      ($isa ?event %Execution)
      ($outputsCreated ?event ?newIdeas)
      (%conflictingMOs ?newIdeas ?relBeliefSystem)
      ($isa ?relBeliefSystem $Religion))
```

(ibid., 239)

As Mateas, Vanouse, and Domike point out, this is not any sort of general test for finding all instances of thinkers being persecuted by religion. For example, it assumes executions are the only type of persecution. Similarly, *Terminal Time*'s representation of the Giordano Bruno story is not the only possible one. The *Terminal Time* authors note that in other circumstances, it might be desirable to represent Bruno's writings and execution as separate events, rather than one compound event. But again, *Terminal Time* is not trying to create a realistic simulation of the behavior of historians or create a system that "really understands" history, or itself be a creative system. It is instead an authored artwork.

If the authors desired—at some point—for the system to be able to identify instances of religious groups persecuting thinkers that do not involve executions, in order to employ these events in its stories, then the test could be broadened to match the new class of events. As of 2000, the authors report that the system includes "134 historical events and 1568 knowledge base assertions" (beyond those assertions in the Upper Cyc Ontology). Given that all the possible examples of events involving religious persecution of thinkers (among that 134) also include executions, a broader test is not needed. But anyone involved in authoring historical event data for *Terminal Time* must do so with an awareness of the tests that will evaluate them later. In fact, it would make no sense to author historical events except in relation to the tests currently in the *Terminal Time* system, as events matching no tests would never be employed in stories. The authoring of events is thus tightly coupled to the authoring of tests.

Assembling the Storyboard

Events that make good candidates for the story are placed on the system's "storyboard." Before being placed on the storyboard, however, events are spun by means of rhetorical plans. These select a subset of information available that relates to the event and lay out an order for its description. So, for example, the rhetorical plan for the goal "show-religion-causes-war" (which can satisfy "show-religion-is-bad") is:

Describe the individual who called for the war, mentioning their religious belief

Describe the religious goal of the war

Describe some event happening during the war

Describe the outcome

(ibid.)

A spin contains all the elements specified by a rhetorical plan as well as information about the rhetorical goal being satisfied (and all its parent goals). This information about rhetorical goals is necessary because the selection of events for each section of the story is performed via constraints, some of which handle events in terms of the rhetorical goals they serve. A number of these constraints come from the current *Terminal Time* ideologue. For example, here are the storyboard constraints for the antireligious rationalist during the first six-minute section:

(%rhet-goal :show-religion-is-bad)

(%rhet-goal :show-religion-is-bad)

(%rhet-goal :show-religion-is-bad)

(%rhet-goal :show-religion-is-bad)

```
(%rhet-goal :show-halting-rationalist-progress)
(%and (%rhet-goal :show-halting-rationalist-progress)
     (%rhet-goal :show-religion-is-bad))
```
(ibid., 240)

This determines that there will be six events in this section's representation on the storyboard, which serve the specified rhetorical goals. In a sense, there are six event "slots." There is not yet any order to these slots, however. Order is created by using an ideologue's "rhetorical devices." These devices create the connections between events, and associated with each device is a set of constraints on the events that can appear before and after it. For example, here is a rhetorical device from the "pro-religious supporter" ideologue (a counterpart to the antireligious rationalist):

```
(def-rhetdev :name :non-western-religious-faith
     :prescope-length 2
     :prescope-test (:all-events-satisfy (%and
             ($isa ?event %HistoricalSituation)
             (:kb ($eventOccursAt?event
             %FirstWorld))
             (%rhet-goal :show-religion-is-good)))
     :postscope-test (:some-event-satisfies ?spin (%and
             ($isa ?event %HistoricalSituation)
             (:kb ($eventOccursAt?event
             %NonFirstWorld))
             (%rhet-goal :show-religion-is-good)))
     :nlg-rule :generate
     :nlg-context-path (:non-western-religious-faith))
```
(ibid.)

The "prescope" test specified for this device requires

that both of the previous two event spins occur in the First World and satisfy the rhetorical goal of showing that religion is good. The "postscope" test requires that the immediately following event also satisfy the rhetorical goal of showing that religion is good, but take place somewhere other than the First World. When this rhetorical device is used in story generation it calls an NLG rule to create the connection between events. In this case the rule is quite simple, resulting in the prewritten sentence "The call of faith was answered just as ardently in non-western societies."

To summarize, *Terminal Time* assembles the storyboard for each section of its story as follows:

First, it finds the events that can be spun to support the current ideologue's rhetorical goals and makes them into spins.

Next, spins are added to the storyboard (as an unordered collection, only some of which will be used). Constraints on the storyboard (such as those from the current ideologue) determine how many events, and serving what rhetorical goals, will actually be used in each section of the generated story.

Finally, *Terminal Time* identifies a set of rhetorical devices that can connect the right number and type of events (to meet the storyboard constraints) searching using the events currently available on the board (and needing to meet the internal constraints imposed by each device's prescope and postscope tests).

Presenting the Story

Once the storyboard for a portion of the story is assembled, the collection of spins and rhetorical devices is sent to the NLG system. This system follows a set of rules for generating both the English text of the story and a set of keywords. (These will be discussed further in the next section.) A text-to-speech program is used to generate a narrative voice-over for the story, lending it an unmistakably "computerized" tone. Keywords are used to select sequences of digitized video that will be played during the narration, and these are accompanied by music. As of 2000, the authors had created 281 rhetorical devices, 578 NLG rules, and a video database of 352 annotated 30-second clips.

Terminal Time and Audiences

Terminal Time is always presented in a theater, before a live audience. Usually it is presented twice for the same group, with each performance followed by a brief discussion with one or more of *Terminal Time*'s authors—resulting in an overall audience experience of roughly one hour. At each performance, *Terminal Time* generates two quite different narratives of the same millennium. In doing so, it makes clear that it is (in the terminology of Mateas's expressive AI) both a "message from" and "messenger for" the author. It not only presents the possible world in which there is a machine that creates historical documentaries (which could be accomplished by a traditional fiction) and two different narratives created by this machine (possible worlds within worlds are certainly a feature of traditional fiction) but makes it apparent that this machine actually exists and operates, and could produce a larger number of fictions than that audience could possibly sit through. This maneuver—this establishment of the fact that *Terminal Time* is not only a message but an operating messenger—

could be compared to the difference between writing Jose Luis Borges's story "The Garden of Forking Paths" and actually constructing the labyrinth novel described within it. Conceptually they are both very much the same and widely distinct. The method of *Terminal Time*'s presentation brings home this distinction.

Another impact of dual presentations of *Terminal Time* is that it allows the audience to change their relationship with its interface. Jay David Bolter and Diane Gromala, in their book *Windows and Mirrors,* point out that even in one viewing, *Terminal Time* provides its audience with a dual experience:

> As spectators, we experience a more or less transparent movie. . . . As participants in the voting process, however, we are very conscious of the interface, and we are meant to reflect on our participation in the vote—in particular, on the notion that our ideology is being tested. The experience is reflective. (2003, 134–135)

Presenting *Terminal Time* twice creates a dual reflection. During the first showing, audience members can reflect on the voting process, the resulting story, and *Terminal Time*'s simultaneous performance and parody of the notion of highly customized media. But only after the first showing is complete does it become possible for the audience to fully reflect on their own complicity in the very structure of market-research-style polling that provides the only means of interaction with *Terminal Time*—and decide to stop "playing along with" and instead start "playing against" this expectation. Both the reports of the *Terminal Time* authors and my own experiences as a *Terminal Time* audience member (at the 1999 Narrative Intelligence symposium, SIGGRAPH 2000, and the University of

California at Irvine in 2007) point to the importance of this shift between showings. As the *Terminal Time* authors write in the book *Narrative Intelligence*:

> Typically, during the first performance, audiences respond to the questions truthfully, that is, actively trying to reflect their true beliefs in their answers to the questions. During the second performance they tend to respond playfully to the questions, essentially trying on different belief systems to see how this will effect the resulting history. (Domike, Mateas, and Vanouse, 2003)

Of course, the dual showings also serve to allow the audience to begin to form a mental image of how the *Terminal Time* model of ideology drives the documentary-creation process. From there it becomes possible for the audience to reflect on the gap between this and how (in their view) ideology shapes the documentary-creation process of human filmmakers. This can be seen as another of *Terminal Time*'s inversions of the history of AI: a gap in its simulation of human behavior that is not a failure or an opportunity for future work but an opportunity for reflection and debate.

Terminal Time and Interaction

Little of the sort of reflection discussed above is likely with noninteractive story-generation systems. In a sense, it is the interactive nature of *Terminal Time* that actually warrants the use of computational processes. This separates it, for example, from the public presentation of *Brutus*. A human author could easily write a *Brutus*$_n$ story for posting on a web site or printing in a newspaper. The same is true of *Universe*. A human author could (and many human authors do) produce plot outlines

273

for scriptwriters to turn into documents that guide the shooting of serial melodramas. Whereas, for a *Terminal Time* story to be realized as a newly scripted documentary with video and voice-over in seconds for a live audience, there must be some mechanism that operates more quickly than a human author.

At the same time, *Terminal Time* is far from the most efficient route to this interactive experience. For example, rather than authoring matched sets of historical events and inference tests (as seen in the Giordano Bruno story and the test for "show-thinkers-persecuted-by-religion"), events could simply be authored by the *Terminal Time* creators so that they are already identified with the rhetorical goals they can help satisfy. This was not done because, as mentioned above, "the architectural structure of *Terminal Time* is part of the concept of the piece." This is an interesting artistic move, familiar from figures such as John Cage. It also defines a particular vision of authoring, in which the creation of new events and new inference tests are isolated from one another. On the other hand, it is also a prime example of the *Tale-Spin* effect—something that is present even more strongly for noninteractive story generators such as *Minstrel* and *Universe*.

Terminal Time's Surface

Considering this from another direction, the extent to which audiences can engage the specifics of *Terminal Time*'s processes—either for critical reflection or aesthetic appreciation—is limited by the surface it presents to its audiences. *Terminal Time*'s interaction mode (discrete questions interspersed by story generation) recalls *Tale-Spin* more closely than *Eliza/Doctor*. Further, as with

Tale-Spin and *Mumble,* most of the burden must fall to the processes that create the work's surface. The most interesting elements of the system must be those selected for presentation in the output, and the generation system must have enough nuance and flexibility to communicate them to the audience. In other words, a system like *Terminal Time* can create an interesting model of an audience-selected ideologue, combining a number of biases and strategies, but this matters little if the audience cannot understand this from the documentary produced.

A concern along these lines is part of Mateas's larger project of expressive AI, which he describes using the terms "authorial affordance" and "interpretive affordance." The concept of *affordance*, as applied by Mateas, is one brought into the discussion of human-computer interaction by Donald Norman (though it originated with psychologist J. J. Gibson). In introducing the term in his book *The Psychology of Everyday Things,* Norman writes: "When used in this sense, the term *affordance* refers to the perceived and actual properties of the thing, primarily those fundamental properties that determine just how the thing could possibly be used" (1988, 9). Similarly, according to Mateas, the "authorial affordances of an AI architecture are the 'hooks' that an architecture provides for an artist to inscribe their authorial intention in the machine" (2002, 125–126). Interpretive affordances, naturally, are the other side of the coin. They are the hooks that the system makes available to an audience to aid in the interpretation of the system, its actions, and its possibilities.

Along with these pieces of vocabulary Mateas also offers a poetics: a recommendation that authorial and interpretive affordances be considered together and closely matched. An architecture should be "crafted in such a way as to enable just those authorial affordances that allow the artist to manipulate the interpretive affordances dictated by the concept of the piece" (127). Given that the concept of *Terminal Time* is for a complex, evolving model of ideology to be interpretable from clips of preexisting video combined with textual descriptions of historical events, systems like *Terminal Time* need a model for generating text that both captures authorial intention and is flexibly manipulatable by the system. Creating such systems is a huge challenge.

Expressive Language Generation

From one perspective, the challenge faced by *Terminal Time* is the primary focus of the entire computer science research area of NLG. This work focuses on how to take a set of material (such as a story structure, a weather summary, or current traffic information) and communicate it to an audience in a human language such as English. On the other hand, little NLG research has taken on the specific version of this challenge relevant for *Terminal Time* (and digital media more generally): shaping this communication so that the specific language chosen has the appropriate tone and nuance, in addition to communicating the correct information. Given this, digital media (such as games) have generally chosen different approaches from NLG researchers for the central task of getting linguistic competence into software systems.

The approach of most games, as I discussed earlier in the context of dialogue trees, is to simply have a human author write large chunks of text—these chunks then embody the author's linguistic competence. At this extreme, the computer need not know anything about the content of what the author has written, because the computer will never need to do anything but output one of these chunks at the appropriate moment. In games the human-written chunks of text are often read aloud by voice actors and the resulting sound files are triggered by the system at the appropriate moment determined by nonlinguistic processes within the game.

The opposite extreme would be to attempt to put all the linguistic competence into the software. Using AI techniques, the software would determine (at the level of meaning) what messages need to be conveyed to the audience. Then, using general knowledge about human language, a body of knowledge about the specific language in which the messages are to be conveyed, topic-specific knowledge of how ideas in this domain are typically expressed, and some sort of mechanism for defining and choosing between the different options deducible from this knowledge, the software would produce a chunk of text fully customized for that situation. No trace of a message, except as abstract knowledge, would exist before it was assembled. No operational system such as this exists, because many nontrivial research questions would need to be answered before one could be constructed. But this kind of ambition is part of what motivated, for example, the work on translating conceptual dependency expressions to natural-language sentences in Schank's lab, which formed the basis for James Meehan's *Mumble*—a more ambitious version of which was Neil Goldman's earlier *Babel* (Goldman 1975).

NLG Templates

Structure-oriented NLG systems fall between the extremes outlined above. The simplest systems, perhaps too simple to be considered true NLG, are template-driven ones. These systems have a structure, a template, in which certain pieces of content are left to be determined (they are "open slots" in the template). Also, aspects of the template may vary in simple ways.

The best-known template systems in everyday life are letter-generating ones. These are used for everything from broad-based political fund-raising to specifically individual (and yet consistently structured) professional communications of doctors and lawyers. These systems may simply fill in the name of the recipient and send otherwise-identical letters to every address receiving a certain type of letter, or they may insert or omit a wide variety of paragraphs, sentences, and even words to match the data that the system knows about a recipient.

As with the chunks-of-text approach, most of the linguistic structure in a template system comes from human authoring that is expressed as completed text, rather than as structures expressed in computable form. This makes template-driven systems easier to construct than more complicated NLG systems, but it also provides less flexibility. Changing a text's tense, for example, would probably be accomplished through providing an alternate version of the template. Many NLG systems of the more complex varieties, on the other hand, would have little trouble generating past or present tense messages based on encoded knowledge of how tense functions in the language in question.

Departing from Writing

Moving away from template-driven approaches into the area of "true" structure-oriented NLG, one is also moving further from writing. This is true in two senses. The information one supplies to the system is further from writing. Also, given the difference in the information one supplies, it becomes harder to employ the techniques traditionally used by authors to shape the surface output of the system—revision becomes something quite different from traditional textual editing. These facts are likely part of the reason that NLG techniques more complicated than templates have rarely been used by writers.

In their article "Building Applied Natural Language Generation Systems," Ehud Reiter and Robert Dale (1997) outline six basic kinds of activity for NLG systems, using the example of a system that answers questions about rail travel. *Content determination* is the process of getting the semantic input that the NLG system will turn into text and creating a set of messages that will be used by the further steps (in the example, the next train on the route, when it leaves, and how many trains a day travel that route). *Discourse planning* structures the messages, usually into one of computer science's ubiquitous trees (in the example, the identity of the next train and its time of departure become the leaves of a "next train information" node—with an "elaboration" relation between them—which is linked to the "number of trains" information by a "sequence" relationship expressed at the root of the tree). *Sentence aggregation,* in turn, is the process of deciding which messages should be grouped into sentences, often leaning on the tree data (in the example, it is pointed out that the two leaves might be combined so that the next train's name and departure time would be in one sentence). *Lexicalization* is the activity that determines the words and phrases that will be used to express particular concepts and relations. Lexicalization is particularly important for systems that output in multiple languages, but can also be a good place to explicitly provide variation (to prevent monotony in output) or make choices about word usage (in the example, it is suggested that *depart* is perhaps more formal than *leave*). *Referring expression generation* is in some ways closely related to lexicalization, in that it is the selection of words or phrases to refer to entities in the messages. It is more focused on context, however, particularly the context of text generated thus far (in the example, this is the question of when expressions like "it," "this train," and "the Glasgow train" are appropriate for referring to a previously mentioned train). *Linguistic realization* is the application of rules of grammar to form the output from the previous processes into text that is correct syntactically, morphologically, and orthographically. (In the example, the system produces the sentence "There are 20 trains each day from Aberdeen to Glasgow." The syntactic component of the realizer added "from" and "to" in order to mark the train's source and destination, the morphological component produced the plural "trains" from the root "train," and the orthographic component capitalized the initial word and added a period at the end.)

As a practical matter, NLG systems do not generally have six different components for these six different activities. Reiter and Dale suggest that the most common architecture actually consists of a three-stage pipeline: text planning (content determination and discourse planning), sentence planning (sentence aggregation, lexicalization, and referring expression generation), and linguistic realization (syntactic, morphological, and orthographic processing). Reiter and Dale's account here is in agreement with that of other NLG authorities, such as Eduard Hovy, whose summary in the *The MIT Encyclopedia of the Cognitive Sciences* names these stages using the almost-identical terms *text planning, sentence planning,* and *sentence realization* (Wilson and Keil 1999).

This overview underscores another likely reason that few writers—and in fact, few digital media practitioners from any background—have made use of traditional NLG techniques. As one sees in the design of systems from *Tale-Spin/Mumble* to the present, these systems are generally constructed with the assumption that messages precede language. Their architectures are developed so that well-defined messages can be "realized" as texts. And yet creative writing, for many writers, is the practice of what could not be said any other way. Its messages do not precede its text but rather emerge through the specifics of its language.

This authoring dilemma is approached in different manners by *Terminal Time, Brutus,* and systems that engage more directly with the NLG tradition.

Terminal Time Templates

Looking at the NLG approach of *Terminal Time,* one can see that the system succeeds at producing satisfying media experiences in part because it is a flexible container for text that can be crafted with traditional writing skills. Its approach is essentially that of template-oriented NLG, though the design of the underlying system is a more general and powerful one, which could be further exploited. As it is, however, the *Terminal Time* authors generally craft the narration for historical events at the sentence level.

In any particular *Terminal Time* performance, the current shape of the audience-directed ideology model will determine which events will be portrayed and how they will be spun. The text for each historical event must describe the event appropriately, both giving its outlines and shifting the description according to current rhetorical goals. Further, because *Terminal Time* is designed to be shown to the same audience twice in quick succession, it is useful if the same event (motivated by the same rhetorical goals) can be narrated in nonrepetitive ways. For example, here is an NLG rule for an introductory *Terminal Time* narration focused on issues of class:

```
(def-nlgrule :name :generate

    :context :feudal-agrarian-first-period-intro

    :body (:seq

        (:terminal

            (:string "1000 years ago, Europe was
            emerging from the Dark Ages.")

            (:keywords (daily-life europe
            european peasant)))

        (:terminal

            (:string "As the new millennium dawned,
            the seeds had been sewn for a just
            and humane social order.")

            (:keywords (farming daily-life europe)))

    (:rule :detail)

    (:terminal
```

```
          (:string "The new millennium's fragile
          seeds of economic freedom were
          cultivated in the feudal agrarian
          economies.")
          (:keywords (daily-life farming europe)))
     (:rule :conclusion)))
```

(Mateas 2007)

The three sentences preceded by ":string" provide the spine of the narration. They are spoken in order by the synthesized voice of the narrator and accompanied by video clips tagged with the keywords specified on the next line. Variation is supplied by the two lines that begin ":rule"—one for additional detail, and the other for the conclusion. The possible detail sentences that *Terminal Time* can drop in range from "Farmers and small tradesmen worked together in congenial local barter economies" to "Wealth was only mildly concentrated in these farming communities when one compares them to the capitalist gluttony of 20th century America" (with their accompanying video keywords). One of the possible conclusions reads: "The worker owed his labor to his land's owner, but could not be ejected from his home." A different ideology model, on the other hand, would result in the selection of a somewhat different description of these circumstances, such as the one that can conclude: "The worker owed his labor to his land's owner, and in return earned the right to his home."

In narrating the agrarian past of Europe, *Terminal Time* essentially has parallel structures for the narration, depending on the current shape of its ideological model. Yet *Terminal Time*'s authors chose to intertwine the differing

narrations of other events. For example, this is the NLG
rule for introductory narration about the space age:

```
(def-nlgrule
    :name :generate-rocket-science-intro
    :context %RocketScience
    :body (:seq
        (:terminal
            (:string "Beginning in (%date 1957) with
            the launch of the Russian satellite Sputnik
            atop an Intercontinental Ballistic Missile,
            human beings left the planet
            earth and began exploring space.")
            (:keywords (satellites rockets
            communism outer-space)))
        (:terminal
            (:string ("This"
                ((%rhet-goal :show-the-
                hollowness-of-science)
                "mechanistic")
            "hymn to science reached its crescendo with
            the moon landing in (%date 1969).")))
            (:keywords (moon rockets america outer-space
            technological-instruments astronomy)))))
```

(Mateas 2007)

In this rule, the word "mechanistic" is dropped into the
second sentence if this event is being spun to support
the rhetorical goal "show-the-hollowness-of-science."
If it is, a further rule will produce a following sentence

that reads: "Yet this demonstration of the power of mortal man to overcome nature left the world simply more empty and threatened." If, on the other hand, the active rhetorical goal is "show-success-of-science," then the next sentence is "Besides being a demonstration of the power of man's mind to overcome nature, space exploration unambiguously proved that above our heads there is no heaven, only the vastness of empty space." It is techniques such as these, breaking the narration down to the sentence and word level, that allow *Terminal Time* to tell its events from an appropriate ideological perspective, keep the data-authoring task manageable, and—crucially—interleave the narration of different events in a way that exposes the shape of its current ideological model. (Another possible NLG approach for *Terminal Time* and other digital media would, rather than generating a text appropriate for the current model at the time of interaction, instead pregenerate a huge number of texts and select an appropriate one during interaction. See sidebar: Pregenerated Variations.)

This is effective, but could have been taken further. Each of the rhetorical goal checks performed by *Terminal Time* is actually a full inferential query. The power in this approach would have also allowed narration to vary based on a wide variety of other parameters. And the variation, of course, could have been at a much more fine-grained level. But this is not a way in which writers are accustomed to working, and it is not immediately obvious how one would structure such an approach to authoring. A technique from *Brutus* illustrates one possibility for such an approach.

Literary Augmented Grammars

Just as *Brutus* uses story grammars, it also uses paragraph and sentence grammars. These are relatively standard linguistic tools, but in *Brutus* they are augmented with handcrafted literary knowledge and named LAGs. One particular LAG is the "independent parallel setting description" (INDPSD), which created this familiar sentence: "He loves the studious youth, ivy-covered clocktowers and its sturdy brick." These are an example of using hand-authored data to generate sentences with literary nuance—making for better text as well as for more ability to reflect the underlying system in surface language. A closer look at the INDPSD reveals the strategies employed.

Bringsjord and Ferrucci present the INDPSD grammar three times in the course of explaining the version used in the "setting_description" from the story of Dave Striver. The first presentation is of a relatively standard, if somewhat specialized, grammar:

- INDPSD → SETTING verb FP
- FP → 'its' FEATURE FP | 'its' FEATURE
- SETTING → noun_phrase
- FEATURE → noun_phrase

(2000, 181)

In this grammar, uppercase words are nonterminals, words in single quotes are literals (used in the sentence exactly as they appear), and lowercase words are terminals (to be selected/constructed from the lexicon). The "|" symbol, which did not appear in the story grammar, can be read as "or." In this case, it indicates that an INDPSD can contain one or more FPs—because an FP can be rewritten either as "'its' FEATURE" or "'its' FEATURE" followed by another FP. This creates the parallelism that gives the INDPSD its name.

Still, this grammar clearly is not enough to create a sentence such as the example above. Where is *Brutus* to find the remaining information? While, as I mentioned earlier, there are large bodies of commonsense knowledge

---

Pregenerated Variations

While much of this chapter's emphasis is on systems that dynamically alter or produce text based on the state of an underlying system, expressive NLG might also be used to reduce the burden on authors working to create large bodies of text that will not change during the audience experience. For example at the 2008 Artificial Intelligence and Interactive Digital Entertainment conference, Eric Grundstrom talked about the textual authoring challenge presented by the space exploration phase of the game *Spore* (Wright, Bradshaw, Hutchinson, et al. 2008). At one point the team had wanted to combine the vast variety of alien race appearances (many created by *Spore* players) with a large combinatory variety of personalities that would determine how these groups addressed the player.

The team had two primary variables in mind. First, an alien group's focus might be *scientific* or *warlike* or one of a number of other possibilities. Second, the alien group's approach to self expression might be *flowery* or *meek* or a number of others. The team wanted each alien group to consistently express itself in a manner that represented its particular combination, so that a warlike group would respond to the player in a manner reflecting their focus (proposing aggressive actions) but do so using its particular style of expression, which might be surprisingly meek in some cases.

The team's initial approach was to create small segments of text that could be combined. For example, a sentence communicating a warlike disposition would then be followed by one displaying a meek use of language. This turned out to be unsatisfying, of course, because such features should shape every sentence.

So the *Spore* team abandoned this ambition. When the game shipped it contained only nine stereotypical communication modes—a huge mismatch with the massive variety of physical appearance. Without time for research into expressive NLG, this was probably the only option.

Yet techniques such as those presented in this chapter might have made the problem tractable. A system might have been designed to produce a variety of candidate texts for each of the alien races. An author's time could then have been invested in supplying the initial data, selecting between the outputs, and doing any necessary editing—potentially requiring no greater number of hours than that invested in *Spore*'s existing nine modes. But until more research and media creation is undertaken in this area of NLG, such systems will remain speculative.

that have been encoded into structures such as the in-process Cyc Ontology, commonsense knowledge is not the same as literary knowledge.

In order to address this, *Brutus* includes hand-encoded information about the "iconic features" of different objects, from a literary point of view. These iconic features are both positive and negative, to assist in portraying the object in different lights. Here, for example, is Bringsjord and Ferrucci's report of *Brutus*'s listing of iconic features for universities:

```
frame university is a object

    default positive_iconic_features is

        {clocktowers, brick, ivy, youth, architecture,
        books, knowledge, scholar, sports} and

    default negative_iconic_features is

        {tests, competition, 'intellectual snobbery'}.
```

(184)

Obviously, this sort of literary knowledge is such that it would differ from story to story. It might in fact differ from character to character within the same story. For example, a character who is an athlete and another who is her professor might disagree strongly about whether "sports" is a positive or negative iconic feature of the university. Nevertheless, Bringsjord and Ferrucci's approach is an intriguing one.

Of course, this is still not enough information to produce a sentence such as the output seen from INDPSDs. Another level of knowledge is required, which Bringsjord and Ferrucci call "literary modifiers." Here are the iconic features and literary modifiers for ivy:

frame ivy is a object

> default positive_iconic_features

is {leaves, vines} and

> default negative_iconic_features is {poison} and

> default negative_literary_modifiers

is {poisonness, tangled} and

> default positive_literary_modifiers

is {spreading, green, lush}.

(184)

This still is not enough to ensure the creation of sentences such as those seen from INDPSDs. The grammar needs to be further augmented with more consistency of structure and more direction about how to fill out aspects of the grammar. For this purpose *Brutus* contains what its authors call "literary constraints." Here is the second version of the INDPSD, incorporating a set of such constraints:

· INDPSD → SETTING verb (isa

possessive_verb) FP(n=3)

· FP → 'its' FEATURE FP | 'its' FEATURE

· SETTING → noun_phrase (has_role setting)

· FEATURE → noun_phrase (isa iconic_feature_of

SETTING)

(185)

In the grammar above, the literary constraints are the elements that appear in parenthesis. For example, the "(n=3)" in the first line enforces the occurrence of three FPs in the sentence—creating the three-part parallelism seen in examples of the INDPSD. This is simply a

289

structural rule. But elements such as the last line's "(isa iconic_feature_of SETTING)" create the connections between the grammar and literary knowledge.

This, however, still doesn't suffice to create sentences such as those generated by INDPSDs. Specifically, the examples above begin with "He"—identifying Dave Striver. Throughout *Artificial Intelligence and Literary Creativity*, Bringsjord and Ferrucci emphasize the importance of simulating consciousness at the level of language, of describing things from the point of view of characters. This brings us to the final version of this LAG:

· POV → Agent (is a person) Verb
(is a PC Verb) FirstFP

· FirstFP → Setting FEATURE FP

· FP → its FEATURE FP | '.'

· FEATURE → noun_phrase (is a feature of SETTING)

· SETTING → noun_phrase (is a setting)

(188)

Some of the previously introduced constraints seem to have been removed in order to make it easier to see what is new in this version. In particular, Bringsjord and Ferrucci draw attention to the "(is a PC Verb)" constraint. They have hand-encoded a special set of verbs as "pc_verbs" that "include verbs for feeling, thinking, understanding, wanting, etc." (187). Presumably there is also a way in which the LAG restricts this so that we get a pc_verb that reflects the point of view of the Agent, but this is not specified.

With these techniques, it is clear how LAGs enabled Bringsjord and Ferrucci to author data for *Brutus₁* that would result in more successful literary output than found in previous story-generation systems such as *Tale-Spin/ Mumble* and *Minstrel*. LAGs offer an interesting trade-off in terms of expressing the underlying model and human authorability. Other techniques, from areas nearby the story-generation field, provide further interesting approaches.

Two Other Approaches

Eduard Hovy's system *Pauline* is undoubtedly a high-water mark for expressing an underlying model through variations in surface text. This project emerges clearly from the scruffy tradition, developed as Hovy's dissertation work at Yale (defended in 1987) with Schank as his adviser and Abelson as a committee member. Given this context, it should be no surprise that *Pauline* uses something similar to Schank's conceptual dependency expressions as its underlying representation structure.

Pauline doesn't generate stories but instead can tell many variations of the same story, based on a model of the situation's "pragmatic constraints." While the system was employed to generate texts recounting a hypothetical primary election between Jimmy Carter and John F. Kennedy, as well as differing versions of the output of a program modeling judicial sentencing, it is best known for its variations on a story about a moment in the student/administration conflict over Yale's investments in apartheid-era South Africa. Authoring the data for this story required representing "about 75 elements denoting the events, actors, locations and props, and . . . about 50 elements denoting the relationships (temporal, intergoal, causal, etc.) that hold among them" (Hovy 1987, 696).

In addition, the system required information about how to translate this logical information into text that would have the appropriate nuance (e.g., "MTRANS indexes to a great many verbs and phrases, among which are 'give permission', 'allow', 'announce', and 'say' " [703]). This was a nontrivial authoring effort, in a form quite removed from traditional writing, for generating variations on a story only one paragraph in length.

But the variations are quite impressive. More than a hundred are possible, each seeking to express a different model of the pragmatic situation—such as whether the speaker agrees or disagrees with the audience, is trying to slant the account in favor of one group or another, is communicating in haste or deliberately, and so on. These can influence what topics are included in the story, how the discussion of the topics is organized, and what phrases and words are used. For example, if the situation is one in which the speaker wishes to decrease interpersonal distance with the audience, choosing an appropriate level of informality is important. Hovy provides this instance of using clause position, verb formality, ellipsis, adjective inclusion, and conjunction to communicate the same portions of the story in a "highfalutin" and "colloquial" manner:

> In early April a shantytown—named Winnie Mandela City—was erected by several students on Beinecke Plaza, so that Yale University would divest from companies doing business in South Africa.

> Students put a shantytown, Winnie Mandela City, up on Beinecke Plaza in early April. The students wanted Yale University to pull their money out of companies doing business in South Africa. (704)

Nick Montfort's system *nn*, on the other hand, is

explicitly designed as an authoring tool for interactive fictions in the Infocom tradition. As such, authorability must be one of its highest-priority goals. It seeks to create a system in which authors can create extended interactive fiction experiences, defining both the story and language involved, and yet able to take advantage of elements of the system that allow for automatic variation in the narration.

Though not working in the scruffy tradition, Montfort does employ the basic acts from conceptual dependency theory in the simulation engine for *nn*.[12] Yet these are not positioned as the primary site for *nn* authoring (many rooms, things, and actors will function largely on appropriate defaults). Instead, *nn* invites authors to focus on crafting texts, in a manner as close as possible to traditional writing while still providing appropriate hooks for *nn*'s narrative transformation processes. Montfort provides an example that re-engineers the opening text from one of his own interactive fictions, *Winchester's Nightmare*:

> Sarah Winchester has forgotten being awake. It is night, or predawn morning, and moonless. She is on a sandy strand extending north and south from here. The sea is before her to the east. (1999)

Using *nn*, this can be transformed into the standard second-person address of much interactive fiction:

> You have forgotten being awake. It is night, or predawn morning, and moonless. You are on a sandy strand extending north and south from here. The sea is before you to the east. (Montfort 2007, 119)

Or *nn* can make other shifts, such as creating first-person narration that takes place at a time previous to the events:

> I will have forgotten being awake. It will be night, or predawn morning, and moonless. I will be on a

12. The first version of *nn* was developed in Montfort's dissertation work at the University of Pennsylvania, under Mitchell P. Marcus, who trained at MIT.

sandy strand extending north and south from there.

The sea will be before me to the east. (120)

The system is also capable of much higher-level transformations of narrative, from event ordering to the speed of narration, building on the structures of classic narratology. But probably the biggest challenge it presents to authors is to write a significant body of text in the "string-with-slots" representation it uses for building sentences. Here is the one for the sample text:

.S_FC V_forget_PERF being awake,

it V_be_S night, or predawn morning, and moonless,

S_FC_PN V_be on a sandy strand extending
north and south from D_HERE,

the sea V_be_S before O_FC_PN to the east (119)

Each of the capitalized elements is one that may be manipulated by *nn*, subjects beginning "S_," verbs with "V_," and objects with "O_." The first of these, "S_FC," refers to the subject who is the focalizing character. While this is certainly not a style of writing that seems likely to come naturally to many writers, it would certainly be easier to reverse-engineer traditional writing into this form (as Montfort does in this example) than into that employed in *Pauline* or *Brutus,* and the results are significantly more flexible (though along a different dimension) than those in most of *Terminal Time*'s text. In which cases the trade-off is worthwhile is open to question.

And the ground may shift. As of this writing, *nn* is still in active development and has not yet had a public release. Montfort writes of a possible tool to "semi-automatically create these representations from ordinary texts under user supervision" (2007, 149–150). Such work may open a new chapter in the history of interactive fiction—in which narrative variation plays as important a role as it does in print fiction. It may also provide a productive example for those developing systems for the surface output of other sorts of flexible fictions, so that authors may specify means of expression for underlying models of aspects other than narration. This book, on the other hand, now moves toward systems that use modalities other than textual narration in their expression.

Notes

1. A brief discussion is available in *Twisty Little Passages* (Montfort 2003, 126–127). A more detailed look, including examples of source code, can be found in "Zork: A Computerized Fantasy Simulation Game" (Lebling, Blank, and Anderson 1979).

2. This was an early commercial instance of the same strategy used by the Java platform's virtual machine.

3. Lebowitz's work on *Universe* was carried out while a faculty member at Columbia University, during which time (according to the acknowledgments in Lebowitz's 1984 and 1987 papers) work by Paula Langer and Doron Shalmon made significant contributions to the project, and Susan Rachel Burstein helped develop many of the ideas.

4. Lebowitz's dissertation was "Generalization and Memory in an Integrated Understanding System," filed December 1980.

5. These authors include Marie-Laure Ryan (1992, 246) and Janet Murray (1997, 201).

6. "Memory organization points" are also known as "memory organization packages."

7. During the blog-based peer review of this book's manuscript, Michael Mateas commented:

> While *Universe* doesn't provide an explicit cognitive model, I would still classify it as an author modeling system. Unlike *Tale-Spin*, which models the goals of characters and their effect on the world (character and world modeling), or story grammars, which directly model story structure, *Universe* models authorial goals (e.g. churn the romantic lives of two characters) and plans for achieving authorial goals. I think this qualifies it as an author modeling system, though it is not as deep a model as *Minstrel*.

I believe Mateas points us to a distinction that may seem a little fine—and yet is also crucial. It is one thing to try to simulate what we think real authors do, and it's another to organize a story-generation system so that it has an "author" level (without any commitment as to whether what the system does has any particular relationship to what human authors do).

However, while I think this distinction is important, and I think *Universe* is an example of the latter (while *Minstrel* is an example of the former), it is true that Lebowitz's writing creates some confusion. For instance, while no cognitive science model of creativity is given as the basis of the system's design, Lebowitz still gestures toward the cognitivist view of AI, writing in one paper that a goal of *Universe* is "to better understand the cognitive processes human authors use in generating stories" (1984, 172), and in another that we "can expect research into extended story generation to . . . give us insight into the creative mechanism" (1985, 484). Exactly how this will take place is never explained.

The only invocation I can recall of the behavior of actual authors in a *Universe* paper reads:

> This is precisely the way that some authors work in developing novels: create a set of characters and work from there. For example, Eco says that "What I mean is that to tell a story you must first of all construct a world, down to the slightest details." He goes on to describe how this "world" must include "lists of names and personal data for many characters." (Lebowitz 1985, 486)

Lebowitz is quoting Umberto Eco's postscript to *The Name of the Rose*. And unfortunately, even this halfhearted attempt is troubled. While Eco's postscript does say that he eventually found a 1975 notebook in which he had written down a list of monks, the postscript's primary account of the genesis of the book reads: "I began writing in March of 1978, prodded by a seminal idea: I felt like poisoning a monk" (Eco 1994, 509). That said, as Mark Nelson pointed out in an email message after this book's blog-based peer review, Eco also emphasizes the importance of world development in the process that followed this seminal idea. In short, if Eco's process for *The Name of the Rose* bears a resemblance to the way that *Universe* stories begin, it is probably at the level of plot fragments (poisoning a monk is a fragment with one character specified) though world development is certainly part of the process.

8. As Michael Mateas pointed out in the blog-based peer review of this manuscript, Lebowitz dedicates a major portion of one paper to describing how an explanation-based learning approach could enable the program "to automatically expand its plot fragment library by creating new plot fragments" (1985, 492). He also indicates that he and his collaborators "have implemented" (494) some portion of such an expansion. Yet there is no indication that this work was completed. In the paper just mentioned Lebowitz writes, "There are many areas left to explore before our generalization methods can be fully implemented—when to generalize a plot fragment, deciding exactly how much to generalize, and using a casual [*sic*] explanation to adjust details of the plot fragment, for example" (501). (The word *casual* in the preceding sentence is a typo, in the original, for "causal.") Lebowitz's later publication on *Universe* (1987) indicates no further progress on this front.

9. Note that given the story example, it must be possible for the Betrayer to be consciously unaware of this evil plan, even after executing it. Also, Bringsjord and Ferrucci employ two spellings: "betrayer" and "betrayor." I will use the former except in direct quotations, in which case I will use the spelling that appears in their text.

10. During the blog-based review of this manuscript on Grand Text Auto, Scott Turner noted, "This representation of Betrayal reminds me of the similar construct Meehan used to force coherency onto *Tale-Spin* stories." While little discussed in this book's chapter on *Tale-Spin,* a good portion of that system's well-known stories were created by "fixing" the world data ahead of time in order to make certain stories (such as Aesop's "The Fox and the Crow") result from the operations of its processes. As Meehan explains:

> What happens when the simulator runs may or may not be interesting, and since interest is a criterion for stories, we may or may not get a story by simply watching the simulator run.
>
> How do you make it interesting? You fix it in advance. You rig the world so that if people do behave rationally, they'll do some interesting things. (1976, 108)

This aspect of *Tale-Spin* and the lessons that Meehan draws from work with it are further described in his dissertation (108–113).

11. As described in the previous chapter's section on *Minstrel,* the genealogy of story grammars is usually traced back to Vladimir Propp's *Morphology of the Folktale.*

12. The first version of *nn* was developed in Montfort's dissertation work at the University of Pennsylvania, under Mitchell P. Marcus, who trained at MIT.

Chapter 8
The *SimCity* Effect

Eliza and *SimCity*

In the early 1980s, Will Wright (1984) was working on his first game: *Raid on Bungeling Bay*. He was crafting an attack helicopter simulation, focused on flying over islands and open water, attempting to destroy a set of factories working toward the creation of an unstoppable war machine. Then, reflecting on the landscape editor he created for authoring the game, Wright had a realization: "I was having more fun making the places than I was blowing them up" (2004). From this the idea for Wright's genre-defining game *SimCity* (1989) was born.

SimCity is a simulation game. Like a terrain editor, it is an interactive tool for defining spaces, specifically cities.[1] Unlike a terrain editor, *SimCity* doesn't simply wait for a user to do something. Time begins passing the moment a new city is founded. A status bar tells the player what's needed next—starting with basic needs like a residential zone and a power plant, and if play succeeds for any period, ramping up to railroads, police stations, stadiums, and so on. A budding city planner can lay out spaces, but it's up to the city's virtual inhabitants to occupy them, build and rebuild, and pay the taxes that allow the city to continue to grow.

As cities grow, areas respond differently. Some may be bustling while others empty out or never attract much interest at all. *SimCity* provides different map views that can help diagnose problems with less successful areas. Is it too much pollution? Too much crime? Too much

1. Though an expansion focused on crafting the underlying terrain on which the city rests.

traffic? Players can change existing areas of the city (e.g., building additional roads) or create new areas with different characteristics. Observation and comparison offer insights. Why is one commercial area fully developed, while another lies fallow? The answer is always found by trying something different and considering the results. And players who aren't learning quickly enough through experimentation receive helpful feedback (figure 8.1).

In other words, the process of play with *SimCity* is one of learning to understand the system's operations. Conversely, the challenge of simulation game design is to create a surface-level experience that will make it possible for audiences to build up an appropriate model of the system internals. As Wright puts it:

> As a player, a lot of what you're trying to do is reverse engineer the simulation. . . . The more accurately you can model that simulation in your head, the better your strategies are going to be going forward. So what we're trying to [do] as

Figure 8.1. In *SimCity Classic* (running here in the DosBox emulator), players who ignore graphic depictions of heavy traffic get other forms of feedback. The status bar provides some—above reading "Frequent traffic jams reported"—but they can escalate to warnings such as the one in the central rectangle here.

designers is build up these mental models in the player. (Pearce 2002)

As this comment reveals, the goal of a simulation game is quite different from that of a system like *Eliza/Doctor,* which plays on our expectations in order to disguise the simplicity of its operations. At the same time, a version of the *Eliza* effect is a necessary starting point, as Wright explains:

> You've got this elaborate system with thousands of variables, and you can't just dump it on the user or else they're totally lost. So we usually try to think in terms of, what's a simpler metaphor that somebody can approach this with? What's the simplest mental model that you can walk up to one of these games [with] and start playing it, and at least understand the basics? Now it might be the wrong model, but it still has to bootstrap into your learning process. So for most of our games, there's some overt metaphor that allows you [to] approach the simulation. (ibid.)

To put it another way, what I will call the *SimCity* effect begins much the same way as the *Eliza* effect. The system initially functions as a procedural representation because of the expectations—or as Weizenbaum and Suchman might phrase it, the work—of the audience. We come with many expectations of therapists and cities. Similarly, with both types of systems, the modes of interaction made available through their surfaces encourage a process of play. In *Eliza/Doctor* this is a series of linguistic exchanges, while in *SimCity* this is the animated representation of the city and the iconic tools available for altering it. Through these interaction surfaces, play begins to reveal the shape of the underlying systems—which differs from the audience's mental model.

2. During the review of this book's draft manuscript on Grand Text Auto, Dennis G. Jerz offered a telling series of observations—including that the graphic user interface (GUI) of *SimCity* is already a much more restricted interaction channel…

Notes continued at end of this chapter.

It is at this point that the two effects diverge. The *Eliza* effect breaks down. The initial impression encouraged at the work's surface is revealed as utterly removed from the internal system model. As this happens, the system's processes and data cease to operate as a representation of the ideas first presented on the surface. *Eliza/Doctor* stops seeming like a simulated therapist and instead seems like a textual transformation device. The only alternative is to severely limit interaction with the system—as in Garfinkel's yes/no therapy experiment—so that its underlying shape is not revealed.[2]

The *SimCity* effect leads in a different direction. The underlying model in *SimCity* is designed as a representation of a dynamic city—inspired in part by Jay Forrester's work on urban dynamics (further discussed in the next section). While initial engagement with *SimCity* is based on the *Eliza* effect, the elements presented on the surface have analogues within the internal processes and data. Successful play requires understanding how initial expectation differs from system operation, incrementally building a model of the system's internal processes based on experimentation. Most players don't end up with a sufficiently detailed understanding to allow them to reimplement the *SimCity* system, but to get far with the game they must develop a working understanding of the underlying model of city operations. Wright's groundbreaking design has made it possible for many players to not only develop this understanding of *SimCity*'s software processes but also enjoy the learning involved. This success has also opened his work to some critique.

Understanding Simulations

The concerns about work such as Wright's get to the heart of what is involved when we use computer models to make nonabstract media. As Ian Bogost observes in *Unit Operations,* "The relationship or feedback loop between the simulation game and its player are bound up with a set of values; no simulation can escape some ideological context" (2006, 99). Or as Ted Nelson put it succinctly two years before *SimCity*'s release, "All simulations are political" (1987, CL 149).

In the case of *SimCity,* Wright's inspirations include some decidedly political simulations: the "system dynamics" work of MIT's Forrester. When applied to urban planning in the late 1960s, these simulations produced anger from many quarters. As Forrester reports in "The Beginning of System Dynamics," his conclusions included the idea that "low-cost housing was a double-edged sword for making urban conditions worse. Such housing used up space where jobs could be created, while drawing in people who needed jobs. Constructing low-cost housing was a powerful process for creating poverty, not alleviating it" (1989). Forrester's critics were quick to point out that his models were based on assumptions far from verifiable (e.g., that housing is a stronger attraction than jobs) and that the workings of his simulated city were not like those of contemporary U.S. urban centers (e.g., Forrester's city was of a fixed size, and commuting to or from the city was impossible).

Of course, any simulation requires simplifying assumptions. A map as large and detailed as the territory is no map at all. And for many things one might like to simulate—such as human behavior—no one knows

303

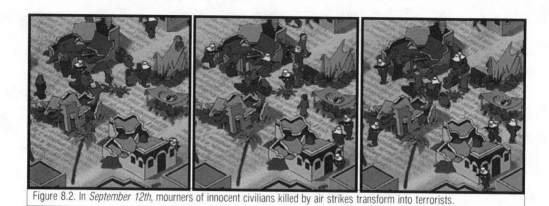

Figure 8.2. In *September 12th*, mourners of innocent civilians killed by air strikes transform into terrorists.

how they actually operate. So any simulation is actually an encoding of a set of choices. As I discussed earlier in relation to symbolic AI techniques, these choices can be made based on current beliefs in cognitive science. Or as I presented in terms of systems such as *Terminal Time* and *F.E.A.R.,* they can be authorial choices, made for purposes of shaping audience experience and authoring opportunities.

Whatever the motivation behind the choices, there is inevitably a politics to how the world is simulated. This is perhaps most obvious in a genre of political games, many of which operate as simple simulations. For example, the widely debated game *September 12th* actually bills itself as "a simulation" (Frasca, Battegazzore, Olhaberry, et al. 2003). The player is presented with an isometric view of a Middle Eastern village, around which civilians and terrorists walk in somewhat unpredictable paths. The player's cursor is a targeting reticle, which can be used to call in air strikes. But these take time to arrive, during which the village's inhabitants continue to move, and in many cases innocent civilians are killed in even a carefully chosen strike. This sets the stage for the most controversial aspect of the

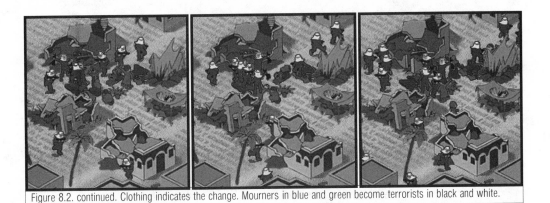

Figure 8.2. continued. Clothing indicates the change. Mourners in blue and green become terrorists in black and white.

simulation. For a few moments after each explosion, when other civilians come upon the dead bodies of civilians killed in air strikes, they stop, kneel, and mourn—and then straighten up and transform into terrorists (figure 8.2).

The transformation is animated and accompanied with a cartoonish sound. Certainly it is meant as an iconic action, rather than a realistic portrayal of the nuances of how one decides to become a terrorist. But the point of the simulation is a broad one about air strikes as a tool for fighting terrorism—suggesting through its model that the tactics of the United States may be part of what recruits anti-U.S. terrorists, rather than simply that they "hate our freedom" or something similar. Gonzalo Frasca, the game's lead designer, defines the act of simulation as "to model a (source) system through a different system which maintains to somebody some of the behaviors of the original system" (2003, 223). Obviously, the key phrase here is "to somebody." This is also the missing element in the conception of systems such as Abelson's ideology machine and Meehan's *Tale-Spin* as simulations. They are not correct models of how people think—but they are someone's representations, in process and data, of an idea about part of human life.

Critiques of *SimCity* and similar games have tended to focus on the fact that players seem to be required to become part of the "somebody" that buys into their simulation models. After all, successful play is impossible without coming to understand—and act in accordance with—the model. In general, this is tied to a wider tendency to accept the veracity of simulation rules and results when, instead, they should be questioned. Paul Starr, a professor of sociology and public affairs at Princeton University (who served as an adviser to U.S. president Clinton's administration in 1993), for example, offers this:

> While playing *SimCity* with my eleven-year-old daughter, I railed against what I thought was a built-in bias of the program against mixed-use development. "It's just the way the game works," she said a bit impatiently.
>
> My daughter's words seemed oddly familiar. A few months earlier someone had said virtually the same thing to me, but where? It suddenly flashed back: the earlier conversation had taken place while I was working at the White House on the development of the Clinton health plan. We were discussing the simulation model likely to be used by the Congressional Budget Office (CBO) to "score" proposals for health care reform. . . .
>
> [W]hen policymakers depend on simulations to guide present choices—especially when legislators put government on "automatic pilot," binding policy to numerical indicators of projected trends—they cede power to those who define the models that generate the forecasts. This is happening in America today, most notably with the rise of the CBO as a power center in national policy. In a sense, Washington is already Sim city. (1994)

Obviously, this is a matter of some concern, given the history of assumptions built into simulations such as Forrester's. But is it an appropriate basis on which to critique *SimCity* and similar media experiences? It would be unconvincing to argue that, being media, such simulations should be exempted from close examination. Arguably, what we learn from media representations has as profound an influence on our culture as the decisions of government. This is one of the motivations for Simon Penny's call for an ethics of simulation media (2004).

Rather, I think the key here is in the comment of Starr's daughter: "It's just the way the game works." Playing *SimCity* she already understands how the simulation operates, what its underlying assumptions are. In other words, *SimCity* is separated from simulations such as Forrester's and the CBO's in the same way that the *SimCity* effect is different from the limited-interaction version of the *Eliza* effect. When interaction with a software model is severely restricted—when we see only Forrester's "conclusion" that low-income housing is harmful, or the "scores" released by the CBO—the shape of the underlying system is not understood and cannot be effectively questioned. On the other hand, the result of the *SimCity* effect is precisely the development of system understanding.[3]

This difference, between the *Eliza* and *SimCity* effects, is in turn what underlies Bogost's response to Sherry Turkle's critique of *SimCity*. In *Persuasive Games*, Bogost writes:

> "Opening the box," in Turkle's opinion, would allow players to see how the simulation runs, providing better ability to critique. The problem with this objection is that the player *can* see how the simulation runs: this is, in no trivial way, what it means to play the game. Turkle's real beef is not

3. Though it is technically true that models used by the CBO are open to scrutiny, as are most of those used by nongovernment researchers such as Forrester, Starr tells us that "to most participants in policy debates as well as…

Notes continued at end of this chapter.

4. The broad learning that takes place around video game playing, rather than the specific learning about the underlying system that is my focus here, is discussed in books such as *What Video Games Have to Teach Us about Learning and Literacy* by James Paul Gee (2004).

with *Sim City*, but with the players: they do not know how to play the game critically. (2007, 63)

Learning to interpret computer models critically is a vitally important ability for us to foster. Contributing to it is a major goal of this book—and an important motivation for the field of software studies as a whole. But as Bogost and Turkle both agree, having an understanding of how software operates is the essential foundation for developing this ability. This, I believe, is the major unacknowledged contribution of systems like *SimCity*.

Types of Systems

Of course, all games operate using some kind of system—even *Pong* contains a simple spatial simulation—and the player must learn something of this system in order to play.[4] More complex, multifaceted systems often take longer to understand—and games that include these systems may require greater mastery as play progresses. This is part of what lies behind Lev Manovich's widely cited observation that "as the player proceeds through the game, she gradually discovers the rules that operate in the universe constructed by this game. She learns its hidden logic—in short, its algorithm" (2001, 222).

Of course, different sorts of games employ different algorithms—and understanding them has differing roles in gameplay. For example, new players of interactive fiction (IF) games pass through a period of experimentation in which they come to understand something of the types of utterances such games accept. A simple parser, such as that shipped with the early home computer adventure games from Scott Adams, can only understand two-word commands such as "go east." A more complex parser, such as that which has shipped with most IF since *Zork* (Anderson, Blank, Daniels, et al. 1980), will understand statements such as "Ask the librarian about the freeway."[5] A few authors have also made custom parser extensions, such as Andrew Pontious (2000), in his work on *Rematch*, which accepts commands such as "Ask Nick to dare Ines to throw the eight ball at the ceiling fan." As Jeremy Douglass notes, "The solution to *Rematch* uses possibly the most complex parsed command in IF to date" (2007, 367).

Learning to use a parser of this sort is, of course, the development of a type of understanding of the underlying system. But for most interactive fiction the goal is for the player to stop thinking about the parser—to come to look past it toward the actions it enables in the fictional world.[6] The same is true of the command-and-control systems for most games. They are systems to be mastered in order to take action defined in terms of relatively simple, data-driven structures (the spatially defined levels of a shooting game, the quest flags of an RPG, or the puzzles of an IF). In contrast, the simulation system in a game like *SimCity* is designed to remain the focus of gameplay. Understanding and engaging a complex system is the central experience.[7]

This is part of why playing *SimCity* has been compared to gardening. Just as the garden, rather than the gardener, is the focus of attention, so it is the actions of the simulated city's citizens that are the focus of *SimCity*. The player zones areas, builds infrastructure, sets tax rates, deals with natural disasters, and—most of all—watches. The game gives a number of tools for action, but even more for information, and encourages a continual testing and refinement of hypothesis about the underlying system. People quickly come to understand enough to play, and

5. Something Montfort tells me one's player character might do while experiencing *Dangerous Curves* by Irene Callaci (2000).

6. Interactive fiction (IF) players are often engaged in discovering what words can be employed to take action, rather than how statements can be constructed for parsing, in each fiction's simulated world. While some actions are possible…

7. Of course, Wright's games are certainly not the only ones for which this is the case. Alex Galloway makes a similar point about the work of Sid Meier, a designer famous for simulation-oriented games such as *Civilization* (Meier and Shelley 1991)…

Notes continued at end of this chapter.

understand more deeply over time, which has enabled the cultural and commercial success of several generations of *SimCity* both on personal and school computers.

This underscores a central issue, from my point of view: the example of *SimCity* is important to our culture precisely because it demonstrates a way of helping millions of people develop a type of understanding of complex software models. This understanding, again, is not detailed enough for reimplementation—but rather like the gardener's understanding of interacting plants, soil, weather, weeding, and so on. A gardener doesn't need to understand chemistry, and a *SimCity* player doesn't need to understand programming language code, yet both can come to grasp the elements and dynamics of complex systems through observation and interaction. Players of the original *SimCity* quickly come to understand it as a limited system, including some elements (e.g., transportation) and not others (e.g., waste disposal), modeling some relationships (e.g., crime and police presence) and not others (e.g., crime-related death and weapons availability). Players begin to see how this type of system operates and become capable of thinking about appropriate and inappropriate uses of such systems. Only from such beginnings does it become possible to develop a deeper, critical engagement with software operations.

From the perspective of digital media authors, *SimCity* also has another importance. When creating *Raid on Bungeling Bay,* Wright realized that interacting with his terrain editor was more engaging than interacting with its outputs. In a way this is quite similar to the insight offered by the *Tale-Spin* effect: let the audience experience the most interesting parts of the system. *SimCity* illustrates a specific strategy for accomplishing this. Years later, when this strategy was applied to characters, Wright created one of the most culturally and economically successful games of all time.

The Sims

The "Sims" are arguably the most popular human characters ever created in digital media. The game named after them—*The Sims* (Wright, Ryan, London, et al. 2000)—is one of the best-selling games ever released, shifting the broad culture's understanding of computational media and producing chart-topping expansion packs, sequels, and ports to new platforms. Perhaps surprisingly, the game is focused entirely on interaction with and between these characters and their environment. There is no shooting, no platform jumping, no puzzle solving, and not a single test of speed or agility.

Yet the Sims are incredibly simple characters. They don't speak except in iconic cartoon images. They can't be communicated with except by clicking on an object or person, and then directing them to take some action with regard to it. They are represented with such simple graphics—even for the time of the game's release—that they convey almost nothing through facial expression and employ only broad gestures. Most of their actions (whether selected by the player or the Sims themselves in "free will" mode) are determined by eight simple measures of their current state, which must be continually maintained so that they don't fall too low: Hunger, Comfort, Hygiene, Bladder, Energy, Fun, Social, and Room (figure 8.3).

While other media communicate the state of characters through word, gesture, and action, the state of the currently selected Sim is, for much of play, directly visible at the bottom of the screen. A Needs display shows the current reading of each of the eight measures and the direction in which it is moving. A simpler Mood display shows the overall state of the Sim, presented as a set of green or red bars. Other possible displays reveal the iconic topics in which the Sim is most interested (a Sim will gain the most from discussions with those who have similar interests), the current state of the Sim's interpersonal relationships, five measures of the Sim's basic personality (Neat, Outgoing, Active, Playful, and Nice), and so on.

In other words, when one begins playing *The Sims,* the game moves immediately and decisively toward the *SimCity* effect. While audiences may begin playing with their own ideas of what makes a person, *The Sims* works quickly to expose what makes a person in its system—eight meters, continually moving in a negative direction, with certain

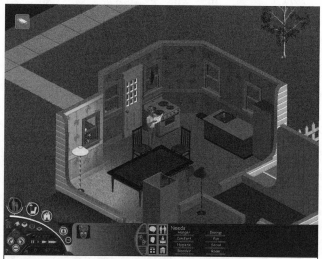

Figure 8.3. A Sim (in *The Sims Party Pack* on a Mac OS system) reads a newspaper standing up. This may help her get a job, but her Needs display shows it's not particularly comfortable (or fun) for her. In the background, a Dialectric range sits beside the door.

activities able to push back the deterioration of one or more measures. Given their personalities and circumstances, some activities work better for some Sims. And that's all. But instead of disappointment with the stark simplicity of its characters, which might have occurred had the simplicity remained hidden beneath the surface, this approach has produced a remarkably successful media experience.

Part of this success has come from the tools made available for playing with the Sims indirectly, through alteration of the environment in which they live. Sims are simple, and the objects that surround them are simple, but the vast number of possible elements and configurations creates an emergent complexity. Further, the differing costs and benefits of particular objects make for a clear progression element and challenge (much like the growth of a *SimCity* urban area) in a game that has no defined "winning" state or point totals.

Many of the objects in *The Sims* are physical possessions, located in the homes of the Sims. Each of these— whether a television set, a toilet, a bed, or an oven—is defined by certain information.[8] It takes up some amount of physical space, which limits where it can be located. It has a graphical appearance, which often falls along an identifiable design direction. It has a textual description, frequently amusing, with the ring of parodic catalog copy. For example:

> Dialectric Free Standing Range $400
>
> Have you ever been shopping in a traditional appliance store and looked at ovens? The similarities are almost incredible. They all look the same. Like the new Dialectric electric range. The Dialectric makes

8. This description is based on lecture notes by Kenneth Forbus and Wright (2001).

cooking a snap! Familiar design. SemiTuph heating elements. Grease waiter. Contradiction of opposite heat currents synthesizes a perfect meal . . . every time.

Hunger: 5

For some players, an important goal in *The Sims* is to produce a household with the appearance they desire (one of the reasons that Celia Pearce calls *The Sims* "the Ikea game" [2004, 148]). But all players must consider the information at the bottom of the description of the Dialectric range. "Hunger: 5" is a description of its impact on the simulation, of the power it has to push back the deterioration of the Hunger need meter (the authoring interface for this is shown in figure 8.4). The oven, like other household objects, will "advertise" its potential impacts to nearby Sims, causing them, in free will mode, to make use of objects that help address their needs. Each object also has a behavior tree that points to the

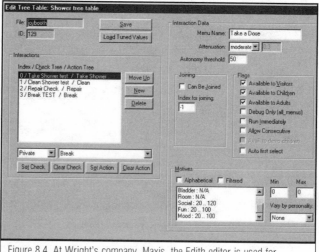

Figure 8.4. At Wright's company, Maxis, the Edith editor is used for creating objects. Here, Kenneth Forbus and Wright (2001, 9) illustrate altering the standard shower from *The Sims* into a "joy booth"—with Social, Fun, and Mood payoffs.

animations necessary for its use, a compartmentalization that simplifies authoring and reduces coherence—as discussed in an earlier chapter.

More expensive objects have stronger positive impacts on the need meters of the Sims. In turn, Sims that leave for work in a better mood perform better in their jobs, leading to promotions, leading to more income, leading to the ability to buy better things, build job skills more effectively, have a bigger house, have more friends over, maintain larger social networks, be happier, perform better at the job, and so forth. Yet there never seems to be enough time. At the start of the game jobs must be found—and then it's a challenge just to get the Sims fed, showered, and urinated before the carpool comes to pick them up. If you don't they'll never get promoted, and if they miss the carpool they'll get fired, but the minutes of the day click by far too quickly. It all starts to feel like a familiar Dialect(r)ic.

Of course, this is what makes the game a challenge to play—and games without challenges don't tend to be best sellers. But Wright also considers the game more reflectively, as a comment on our time-stretched lives and even a parody of consumer culture (Wingfield 2006).[9] Frasca (2001) and others are unconvinced.[10] The very rules of the simulation enforce the roles of commodity capitalism, so what does it matter if the in-game catalog descriptions, or the game's designer, poke gentle fun at its structures?

Taking the discussion somewhat deeper, McKenzie Wark, in *Gamer Theory*, points at what might make an idealized representation of capitalism—a game that boils down to surviving the daily grind—so appealing. Wark's

9. From Wingfield's article: Critics have also charged that the game wrongly equates happiness with consumerism, since much of it revolves around buying clothing, furniture and other goods. Mr. Wright has said the game actually…

10. Frasca writes that he has met people who firmly believe that *The Sims* is a parody and, therefore, it is actually a critique of consumerism. Personally, I disagree. While the game is definitively cartoonish, I am not able to find satire within it.…

Notes continued at end of this chapter.

11. At the time of the blog-based review of this book's manuscript on Grand Text Auto, Richard Evans (already noted as the AI lead for *Black & White*) was working at Maxis on the not-yet-announced title *The Sims 3*. In his comment on this paragraph he wrote…

Notes continued at end of this chapter.

book begins with a question: "Ever get the feeling you're playing some vast and useless game whose goal you don't know and whose rules you can't remember?" After a few related questions the book says to its readers, "Welcome to gamespace." This sets the stage for Wark's discussion of *The Sims*:

> The difference between play and its other may have collapsed, but there is still a difference between play within the bounds of an algorithm that works impersonally, the same for everybody, and a gamespace that appears as nothing but an agon for the will to power. . . . If it is a choice only between *The Sims* as a real game and gamespace as a game of the real, the gamer chooses to stay in The Cave and play games. (2007, paragraph 49)

This can be taken further. It is not simply that the Sims, unlike their players, occupy a predictable, transparent, impersonal version of capitalism. This predictability and transparency also extends to their interior, emotional lives. We don't know what will make us happier. We may think it's a big-screen television, but that's probably wrong. Whereas we know exactly what will make a Sim happier, and exactly how, and also why we can't afford it or have no place to put it, but think maybe if we play for a little more time . . .

Which is to say, again, that the crucial element of *The Sims*—what enables its impact—is the work it does to expose the workings of its simulation. Its design is focused on teaching players to understand and operate within the software system. It succeeds in being an experience about human beings in familiar situations because it communicates on its surface precisely the simplicity of its processes and data. It succeeds through the *SimCity* effect.[11]

The Sims avoids the pitfalls of the *Eliza* effect by not pretending to model more than it does. It avoids the *Tale-Spin* effect by exploiting all that is present in its simulation in the audience experience. In doing this it also raises a question, which Janet Murray gestures toward when she writes, "If there is to be a Charles Dickens or Charlotte Brontë of the digital medium, then Will Wright is surely one of his or her key antecedents" (2004, 4). The question is: Can we find similar success with characters more complex than eight mood meters, and fictions more well formed than *The Sims*'s implied progression through possessions and careers?

Oz

The Oz Project at Carnegie Mellon University—led by Joe Bates from its inception in the late 1980s—has an unusual distinction. While *Tale-Spin* and *Universe* could be considered outliers among software systems for the fact that both are widely credited with outputs they did not produce, the Oz Project may be the only computer science research project most famous for an experiment that did not require computers. This was an experiment in *interactive drama,* carried out with a human director and actors, but aimed at understanding the requirements for software-driven systems (Kelso, Weyhrauch, and Bates 1993).

The dream of interactive drama is often traced back to Brenda Laurel's 1986 dissertation—which in turn draws on a series of memos and articles she wrote, starting in 1981, while working at Atari (first as a software marketing manager and then as a research scientist).[12] After the dramatic rise of Atari's research lab, only to be disbanded after the 1980s crash of the video game market, Laurel's

12. This places her work at Atari and on her dissertation in roughly the same time period as *Universe* and the first phase of *Minstrel.* Some of Laurel's dissertation was later adapted for her book *Computers as Theatre* (1991).

dissertation was positioned as a feasibility study for a particular version of one of the "grand ideas" that motivated the lab's work under the leadership of computer pioneer Alan Kay. Writ large, the idea is of a fantasy amplifier. Laurel's more focused version was cast as a system for first-person interaction (as a "user-character") with system characters and a world model, both under the control of a "playwright" expert system. In Laurel's dissertation she writes: "An 'interactive drama,' then, is a first-person experience within a fantasy world, in which the user may create, enact, and observe a character whose choices and actions affect the course of events just as they might in a play" (1986, 7).

Though the screenwriters of *Star Trek: The Next Generation* would later provide vivid dramatizations of interaction with such a system—in the form of the "holodeck"—the Oz Project experiment is famous because it offers some potential insight into what it might be like to experience unscripted interaction with such a system. The experiment's setting was far from the lush renderings of the holodeck, taking place in a studio theater, with boxes, chairs, and a table as the only set. These were meant to suggest a bus station, which was populated by three characters, each played by trained actors wearing wireless headphones: an unhelpful clerk, a nearly blind passenger, and a larcenous young man (described as a "punk"). The headphones allowed an offstage director, assisted by a "plot graph" of possible events, to give directions to the actors in order to maintain the overall flow of the drama.

In each run of the experiment, an interactor was given the instruction to buy a bus ticket to attend a relative's funeral. But this was a classic misdirection. The ticket buying was delayed by the clerk, and then the interactor was distracted by a request for help from the other passenger, and during this time the young man's requests for money escalated from panhandling to knifepoint robbery. As things came to a climax, the young man cut the clerk's phone line, and the clerk offered the interactor a gun. In the most famous run-through, the interactor fired the gun in the air, from behind the young man, at which point the actor portraying that character—not waiting for a cue from the director—dramatically fell to the ground.

Interactors felt that the experience was incredibly engaging, with one reporting that it "escalate[d] from normal, to annoying, to out of control in a matter of seconds." Those observing the experiment from the outside, on the other hand, felt that the action lagged— and even reported boredom to the point of losing track of events. From this Bates and his colleagues concluded two things. First, most obviously, that engaging pacing for an interactor, immersed in an experience, is quite different from what it would be in a traditional media experience. Second, more theoretically, they took the success at engaging their interactors as a confirmation of their basic design philosophy for interactive drama: placing the audience member as an interacting character within the drama (an interactor), creating expressive and relatively independent non-player characters (NPCs) within the same environment, and guiding the higher-level actions of the NPCs through the interventions of a drama manager tasked with adjusting pacing for the interactor and guiding the story to a successful conclusion.

13. The founding
of Zoesis certainly
wasn't the death
knell for university-
based research in
interactive narrative.
Around the time that
the Oz Project was
winding down, R.
Michael Young's Liquid
Narrative project was
gaining momentum...

Notes continued at end
of this chapter.

Oz Characters

In practice, however, one element of this design philosophy received the lion's share of the attention in the Oz Project's system-building activities: the creation of interactive characters. This was the focus of their early 1990s graphical system (*Edge of Intention,* featuring animated "Woggles" reminiscent of Dr. Seuss; see figure 8.5) and earlier textual system (*Lyotard,* building a relationship with a standoffish simulated house cat). It was also the focus of the Web-based system with which the group's work re-emerged in the year 2000 (*OttoAndIris. com,* playing games with anthropomorphized letters) after most project members left Carnegie Mellon in the later 1990s to found the company Zoesis.[13] Unlike the short-lived, combat-focused characters of *F.E.A.R.*—or the micromanaged, attention-deficit characters of *The Sims*—these characters needed to have both long-term and short-term behaviors, with some behaviors supporting others, multiple behaviors able to take place simultaneously, and

Figure 8.5. The Woggles in *The Edge of Intention.*

320

some reasonable method of choosing what to do at any given time. The Oz Project's language for authoring such character behavior was called Hap.

The Oz work in this area was developed in the context of ongoing computer science work in intelligent agents, a branch of AI encompassing a wide variety of software exhibiting behavior that could be seen as that of a semi-independent entity. More specifically, during the years of the Oz Project a number of research labs were working on "believable" agents—created with the idea of media in mind. Some groups focused more on the internal structure of behaviors and activity (working outward toward animation), while others concentrated first on new animation techniques that would enable more expressive characters (working inward toward higher-level behavior). At the time, I was working at New York University in the lab where Ken Perlin (in collaboration with Athomas Goldberg and others) led an animation-originated interactive character project called Improv (Perlin 1995; Perlin and Goldberg 1996).

Despite their differing directions of movement, the Improv system shared with Hap a focus on the careful hand authoring of each character. Other systems were more invested in various sorts of correctness and generality.[14] Improv's characters felt remarkably alive, compared with other real-time rendered characters of the period. This impression was created by tuning the probabilities and rates of animations, layering animations, and smoothly transitioning between animations for actions such as eye blinking, looking around the room, gesturing, approaching or avoiding moving characters and objects (perhaps controlled by the audience), and speaking (with

14. From the animation direction, work led by researchers such as Norm Badler and Jessica Hodgins focused on biomedically correct animation rather than expressive animation (Badler, Phillips, and Webber 1993; Hodgins et al. 1995). From…

Notes continued at end of this chapter.

each other or the audience). The results were engaging animated experiences when combined with something to move the scenario forward, ranging from a human choreographer directing a graphical dancer's movements in response to improvised music (in the 1994 *Danse Interactif*, see figure 8.6) to a set of probabilities tuned to always produce a slightly different version of a linear set of events (in the browser-based *Sid and the Penguins* from 1998). The technology was spun off into a company in 1999, headed by Goldberg and aimed at taking the expressive animation techniques to a wider audience. The project as a whole created convincing demonstrations of engaging characters performing flexible behavior, but never the more autonomous actors imagined in the dream of interactive drama.

Hap, on the other hand, was designed to let another system handle animation—or have no animation at all, as in the *Lyotard* project. Instead of visual appearance, it was focused on characters that could act appropriately and autonomously in a fictional world, and do this based on

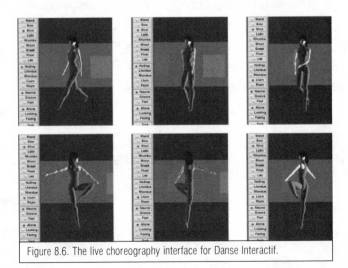

Figure 8.6. The live choreography interface for Danse Interactif.

goals and behaviors crafted by authors for that character. These goals and behaviors may sound similar to the building blocks of *Strips* plans, but the lead designer of Hap, Bryan Loyall, draws a sharp distinction:

> Unlike some notions of goals in artificial intelligence, Hap goals have no meaning in and of themselves. They are not planned for, and there is no grammar or logic in which the system can reason about them. Instead they are given meaning through the agent builder's vision of what they mean, and the behaviors written to express that vision. (1997, 36)

Instead of *Strips*-style reasoning, in a manner similar to the planboxes of *Tale-Spin*, each goal has an author-defined set of possible behaviors that may satisfy it. These behaviors may be made up of sequential steps or steps that can be pursued in any order (including in parallel). For example, the steps in a "wink" behavior are sequential—an exaggerated close of the eye and then a pause, followed by opening the eye. But the steps in a "gather what I need before leaving the house" behavior can be ordered depending on circumstances—the car keys can be picked up before or after the jacket.

As suggested by the differing levels of specificity between winking and item gathering, Hap behaviors can launch subgoals and subbehaviors, finally grounded when they produce a set of primitive mental and physical actions (with the physical actions making the connections to the surface presentation of the Hap character). All of this is organized in a current behavior tree, which at each step either expands something (a behavior or subgoal) or executes something (a mental or physical action).

Goals, actions, and behaviors can succeed, fail,

15. Bates reports on a particular Woggle: Due to a programming error, Shrimp occasionally peppers his ongoing behavior with what seems to be a nervous tick causing him repeatedly to hit his head against the ground. This attracts people's attention…

Notes continued at end of this chapter.

or abort—based on what happens in the world. This propagates up and down the tree, so that a decision to abort going to work would remove subbehaviors such as gathering objects for the trip. Similarly, failing to find the keys might fail the higher goal of going to work or at least of doing so via the character's car, depending on how the behavior is constructed. Loyall also presents further authorial tools in the form of preconditions on situations in which behaviors can be chosen, more specific behaviors for particular circumstances, and "demons" that wait for something in the state of the world to be true before executing behaviors. Finally, an algorithm is used to select which part of the tree to act on for each step, giving precedence to higher-priority actions, and otherwise preferring to continue expanding and executing the same part of the tree.

Oz Limitations

Hap is a powerful tool for defining character behavior. Oz characters such as the Woggles were able to move around, engage in solo behaviors, interact with each other, and interact with the audience. In some ways they were quite successful, widely exhibited and discussed—even if Bates, remarkably candidly, also reports that one of their most memorable behaviors occurred as an outgrowth of system errors.[15]

In this first attempt to use Hap to create a graphical experience, though, a larger problem also presented itself. Phoebe Sengers, an Oz Project PhD student, discusses this in her dissertation's description of building the Woggles:

> Following the Hap design strategy, we first built a set of high-level behaviors such as sleeping,

dancing, playing follow-the-leader, moping, and fighting. Each of these behaviors was reasonably straightforward to implement, including substantial variation, emotional expression, and social interaction. Watching the agents engage in any of these behaviors was a pleasure.

Then came the fatal moment when the behaviors were to be combined into the complete agent. This was a nightmare. Just combining the behaviors in the straightforward way led to all kinds of problems. (1998, 38)

Some of the problems might have arisen from a bug in the way conflicting goals were handled. For example, the Woggles would try to engage in two incompatible behaviors simultaneously, such as "fight" and "sleep." But there is another set of problems that Sengers diagnosed as closer to the core of the Oz approach to characters—a problem that also plagued the agent-based projects of many contemporary groups, such as the simulated dog (Silas) and computer game-playing penguin (Pengi) built by groups at MIT.

The Woggles would jump from behavior to behavior, never settling on one long enough to be comprehended by the audience. They would get stuck in loops, switching back and forth between a pair of behaviors. In this way, the problem of compartmentalized actions—discussed earlier in relationship to FSMs—reared its head in the context of advanced behavior systems. Under deadline pressure, the Oz group sacrificed the key feature of having Woggles that could interleave behaviors from multiple high-level goals. Sengers describes the fieldwide problem this way:

Alternative AI agents generally have a set of black-boxed behaviors. Following the action-selection paradigm, agents continuously redecide which behavior is most appropriate. As a consequence, they tend to jump around from behavior to behavior according to which one is currently the best. What this means is that the overall character of behavior of the agent ends up being somewhat deficient; generally speaking, its behavior consists of short dalliances in individual, shallow high-level behaviors with abrupt changes between behaviors. It is this overall defective nature of agent behavior, caused by under-integration of behavioral units, that I term *schizophrenia*. (40)

Improv animations were able to avoid this problem for a number of reasons. First, the visual presentation of behavior transition and combination was a major area of system research and demonstration, so abrupt transitions were rarely in evidence. Even closer to the heart of the matter, Improv projects were generally either small-scale behavior demonstrations or built with a narrative through-line embedded in their scripts. More autonomous agents required a different solution. Sengers pursued this through a change of perspective.

The Expressivator

For Sengers, the problem with Hap characters grows out of their continuities with traditional AI. The issue is not that a behavior-based architecture is inappropriate. Rather, it is that behaviors tend to be authored from the character's point of view (what should the character be able to do) and selected from the character's point of view (what is the right thing to do in this situation). This may sound like a computer model for what the live human actors provided in the Oz Project's bus stop experiment. But the work of an actor is to take actions that will communicate, not those that are correct. The difference turns out to be crucial.

Responding to her dissatisfaction with standard Hap

characters, Sengers built a set of extensions called the Expressivator. An inspiration for the work was the field of narrative psychology, which instead of seeing patients as sets of disconnected symptoms, attempts a reintegration through narrative. Similarly, the Expressivator attempts "symptom control" for schizophrenic agents by building a system focused on narratively understandable behavior.

This is necessary, in part, because of the differences between characters like Woggles and characters like Sims. A player's Sims are narratively understandable because of elements like the Needs display. Watching a Sim's meter for their Bladder move too low, the player thinks, "She'll need to use the restroom before long." When the Sim abruptly stops an earlier behavior and heads to the restroom, this is understood as a fulfillment of something that has been building over time rather than a mysterious switch. Further, behaviors in *The Sims* are relatively time-consuming, and each is carefully animated as a performance. These lengthy behaviors make it impossible for Sims to appear to "dither" like looping Woggles. Lengthy behaviors also necessitate a visualized queue of current and upcoming behaviors that can be easily canceled, even midexecution, by the player—so that Sims can react quickly to events such as ringing phones or on-fire kitchens.

Sengers sought a way to bring some of the narrative understandability of characters from traditional media—who don't use meters to display the changing state of their needs—to behavior-based digital characters. To accomplish this, the Expressivator organizes character action around authorial intentions for how it will be interpreted. Rather than goals, behaviors, and actions, the system is composed of signifiers and signs. Since character actions take time for the audience to interpret, signifiers and signs are "posted" when the audience is likely to have seen them. Then these are part of the world history, available for use in deciding on the next signifiers and signs. When moving from one behavior to another, each character attempts to communicate why the change is being made, using a set of specifically designed transition behaviors. These, in turn, are a special case of the more general category of metalevel controls, designed to allow authors to express relationships between formerly black-boxed character actions.

In building the Expressivator (and her sample media work, the *Industrial Graveyard*), Sengers demonstrates an interesting middle path. Her focus on audience interpretation in narrative terms, especially in designing transitions aimed at communicating the reasons for behavior changes, begins to create a system with some of the strengths that made Improv's more scripted animations engaging over time. At the same time, the characters have the flexibility and autonomy of behavior-focused designs. What is missing, however, is the reason that the Oz Project needed this flexibility in the first place: for characters to play a role while also following the directions of an offstage drama manager. The first full-scale attempt at this was initiated several years later, by a game industry veteran and the Oz Project's last graduate student.

Façade

I first met Andrew Stern and Michael Mateas at a 1999 Narrative Intelligence symposium sponsored by the Association for the Advancement of Artificial Intelligence. The symposium was organized by Mateas and Sengers, two of the final Oz PhD students. They managed to bring together a number of their mentors, colleagues, and friends with a wide range of people pursuing different facets of the intersection of narrative, character, and AI. The Zoesis team was present, showing off its most advanced demo: *The Penguin Who Wouldn't Swim*. Bringsjord and Ferrucci discussed the active development of *Brutus*. Stern described his company's newest commercial product based on believable agent work: *Babyz*. Mateas and his collaborators premiered *Terminal Time*. It felt like the field was blossoming with new projects, pushing the state of the art to new levels.

But at the same time, Stern and Mateas were pushing each other behind the scenes to take even bigger risks in the project that they had begun to plan. They wanted to create the first real example, as uncompromising as possible, of the dream of interactive drama. As Stern would later say about the resulting project, "When you shoot for the stars, you might hit the moon; with *Façade*, we think we got into orbit. . . . [W]e enjoyed being overly ambitious" (2005).

Façade, released in 2005, begins with the player approaching the apartment door of Grace and Trip—old college friends, now married—who can be heard in a muffled argument as the player decides whether to knock. Over roughly twenty minutes of interaction, the promise of this first moment grows from tense chitchat to full-blown meltdown, and usually the dissolution of Grace and Trip's marriage. The shape of the crisis is determined by the actions of the player, which can also (less commonly) lead Grace and Trip to a new level of mutual understanding, or result in the player's ejection from the room.

All of this takes place in a simulated apartment, with the characters speaking dialogue, and performing actions and emotions. The player can move around freely, picking up items, typing arbitrary text, hugging and kissing, and being generally invited to produce her own performance. Grace and Trip respond dynamically, following up on topics raised by the player, commenting on patterns of player statements and actions, perhaps reestablishing their own interrupted lines of conversation, treating the player differently as she seems to take sides with one or another of them, and so on. It is, in other words, utterly unlike the experience offered by other contemporary digital fictions—nearly as far from a standard dialogue tree as it is from an email novel. *Façade* doesn't always work, but more often than not it does, and with this it demonstrated that the dream of interactive drama could be made a reality.

Façade also does more than provide an existence proof of interactive drama and respond to the problem (one of digital media's "grand challenges") posed by Brenda Laurel two decades before. It illustrates the consequences of a group of choices relative to the issues raised in this book. By doing this it clarifies a future agenda for research, sheds new light on the central concept of "agency," and simultaneously demonstrates that a set of techniques are ready for use in authoring.

Façade Beats

Work on *Façade* sent Stern and Mateas flying straight at a number of unsolved research questions, from natural-language understanding (so that players can type any text they wish) to believable behavior for NPCs. But the key to their approach was the reintroduction of the concept of drama management. Their approach to this problem, in turn, departed from the bus station's plot graph—instead pivoting on a reinterpretation of a concept from dramatic writing: the "beat."

The typical conception of a beat is provided by Robert McKee: "an exchange of behavior in action/reaction. . . . [T]hese changing behaviors shape the turning of a scene" (1997, 37). Mateas and Stern cite a famous beat from *Casablanca*: "*Rick*: 'Why'd you come back? To tell me why you ran out on me at the railway station?' *Ilsa*: 'Yes'" (2007, 191). But as they explain, beats in *Façade* are much larger and more complex, in effect operating as miniature scene structures embedded within the larger drama, built to be intermixed with other elements.

A primary goal of the beats that Stern and Mateas created for *Façade* is to embroil the player in a series of what they call "social games." The first section of the drama has Grace and Trip setting up zero-sum affinity games, in which the player is invited to agree with one of them (and disagree with the other). For example, Grace may initiate a conversation about their redecorating, which she thinks is problematic but Trip likes (figure 8.7). Similarly, Trip may begin a conversation about their recent trip to Italy, which he thought of as a second honeymoon and Grace saw only as a weekend getaway. Even the harmless-seeming activity of choosing drinks has an associated disagreement beat, with Trip urging the player to join him in a fancy mixed drink while Grace pushes for something simple. Simultaneously, throughout these affinity games, Grace and Trip respond to player utterances in a series of hot-button games around topics such as sex, divorce, family background, and emotionally laden objects around the apartment—which also serve to reveal more information about the characters and their stories.

In the second section of the drama the beats are crafted to produce a therapy game, which has the potential to increase character realization. Finally, the drama comes to a dramatic conclusion. Throughout, the drama manager selects beats based on a desired curve (and believed current state) of the tension level, attempting to produce a neo-Aristotelian experience of slowly rising tension leading to catharsis. Producing this experience requires a rather different approach to character behavior than seen in the Sims or Oz agents.

Façade Characters

Like Sengers, Mateas and Stern were strongly influenced by the Hap conception of character behavior. *Façade*'s tool for authoring such behaviors, ABL, is based on Hap. But at the

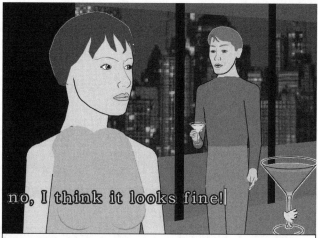

Figure 8.7. In *Façade*, the player disagrees with Grace about the decorating (via typing text) while joining Trip in a fancy drink.

same time, *Façade*'s authors took the autocritique of Hap embodied in the Expressivator further.

Mateas had been convinced of the need for transition behaviors and metalevel controls by his study of Oz work and discussions with Sengers, while Stern had seen it for himself while working on PF Magic's "Petz." The first of the Petz projects, *Dogz* (Frank, Resner, Fulop, et al. 1995), was a computer-based system for building relationships with virtual animals that arrived before Bandai's keychain Tamagotchi (released in 1996) and Tiger's plush Furby (released in 1998)—and long before Nintendo's *Nintendogs* (released in 2005). The original AI, created by Ben Resner, was of a traditional finite-state machine design. When Stern took over the AI direction, starting with building the *Catz* (Frank, Stern, Resner, et al. 1996) system in early 1996, he was working under the direct influence of the Oz Project's technical papers. By *Petz 3* (Harrington, Stern, Frank, et al. 1998) and *Babyz* (Stern, Frank, and Resner 1999) Stern's architecture of goals, behaviors, and emotional states was relatively sophisticated, and included a type of transition behavior with aims similar to those that Sengers pursued simultaneously with the Expressivator. As Stern puts it:

> Well, the concept of transitions between behaviors is an inherent requirement for fluidity and lifelikeness for any character, I think. There were *Petz/Babyz* versions of those transitions—little behaviors like "looking around for what do next" or "looking to the player for reassurance, for a pet/ tickle" after finishing one behavior (e.g. eating) and going on to another behavior (e.g. playing). There were little ad hoc behaviors like that scattered throughout *Petz* and *Babyz*. (Stern and Mateas 2007)

The Expressivator, as a set of extensions to Hap, had

16. Though similar ideas had been pursued in domains such as battlefield simulation (e.g., Tambe 1997).

demonstrated an approach to building an architecture for such transition behaviors—something more principled than an ad hoc collection. In building ABL for *Façade*, Mateas and Stern took this another step, building transition behaviors, and metalevel controls more generally, into the core of the system itself. But *Façade*'s beat-oriented authoring also required a deeper change. While Hap, the Expressivator, and the Petz projects all treated goals and behaviors as aspects of individual, independent characters, *Façade*'s characters can share goals and behaviors.

This was a surprisingly radical notion in the domain of believable characters.[16] Woggles and Petz played together, and the *Industrial Graveyard's* lamp and overseer interacted more grimly, but always by "sensing" and "reacting" to one another. The authors of each system had to work out software solutions to the problems of joint behavior, all hobbled by the AI assumption that they were creating entities that needed to act independently. But in fact, each author was creating a system for performance of behaviors, whether for one character or more—a fact that became inescapable as *Façade*'s design called for fast-paced exchanges of dialogue (rather than looser interactions such

Figure 8.8. PF Magic's *Petz* and *Babyz* used procedural animation (along the lines of Improv) and a behavior-based character architecture (along the lines of the Oz Project) to create digital media entertainment about characters and relationships, rather than physical dexterity or puzzle solving.

as the Woggles' "follow the leader" or Babyz throwing toys at each other). One can see this clearly by looking at *Façade*'s procedural script.[17]

Façade's Procedural Script

Façade's characters perform together based on what Stern and Mateas call "joint dialogue behaviors" (JDBs). Each beat is a structured collection of ten to one hundred JDBs. Each JDB, in turn, is a set of one to five lines of dialogue between Grace and Trip, consisting not simply of recordings of the words but also fifty to two hundred lines of ABL code. This code supports the various ways that the JDB can be performed as well as the ways that JDB alters *Façade*'s internal counters for the affinity game, character self-realization, overall tension, or other elements of story and character state. Part of the reason that beats contain so many JDBs is related to this. Most JDBs are actually authored with three to five alternate versions, with multiple takes of the recordings for each, so that an appropriate one can be selected based on current measures of affinity and tension (and repetitions between playthroughs can be lessened).

Another reason that beats contain a large number of JDBs is in order to support special metalevel controls (called "handlers") that provide appropriate reactions to player statements and actions in the context of the beat. Each beat has a default way it will play out in the absence of interaction, but Mateas and Stern are hoping for another outcome—given that the point of *Façade* is to pursue interactive drama.

So, for example, the JDBs in the beat about fixing drinks include a basic sequence. This sequence is expressed

17. In the initial draft of this chapter I referred to "*Façade*'s script." During the blog-based peer review, Stern objected, saying the term *script* has a strong implied linearity—in both traditional drama and game development. The term is my…

Notes continued at end of this chapter.

as four joint goals, during which both the speaking and nonspeaking characters perform appropriate behaviors. These beat goals are: Trip bringing up the topic of drinks (a transition into the beat), Trip making a drink suggestion (while bragging), Grace making a countersuggestion (and mocking the behavior of Trip, who reacts), and a final response by each of them.

In the basic sequence, the characters wait between each goal for a response from the player. The player can also interrupt. The handlers for responding to the player can alter and rearrange the performance of the next goals, mix in reactions about the topic of the beat, mix in reactions about other topics, or even cause the beat to abort. So, for instance, if the player immediately asks for a beer when the topic of drinks first comes up, Trip will suggest a fancy drink in a different way and Grace's countersuggestion may specifically reference the fact that the player asked for a simple beer. As the player expresses affinity for the positions of the two characters during the beat, their performances can shift to reflect the new landscape of the affinity game.

Of course, the player may also take actions that aren't about drinks. The player may bring up a topic like divorce or therapy, or may refer to one of the objects in the room (by name or by picking it up). This could mix in a JDB about one of the hot-button games at its current level of development. Or for topics on which Grace and Trip have nothing to say (or when the system does not understand the player), *Façade* could mix in a JDB that "deflects" the player action either based on local context or using one of a set of nonresponses that can appear throughout a playthrough. Each beat goal has specially written dialogue used to reestablish context (that is, to make an audience-readable transition) when returning from a mix-in.

Beats are also key to *Façade*'s approach to the incredibly difficult problem of natural-language understanding. No computer system can actually "understand" arbitrary human language—or even, less ambitiously, consistently map human language statements to a logical model. What *Façade* does instead is attempt to map each player statement to a limited set of "discourse acts," such as agreement, thanking, referring to a topic, and so on. Then, each of these discourse acts is handled differently (by a set of "reaction proposers") depending on the current context. For example, after Trip proposes a fancy drink, agreeing with him and thanking him result onto the same reactions in the *Façade* system. Yet when Grace criticizes the decorating, it doesn't make sense to have agreement and thanking produce the same response.

Finally, all of Trip and Grace's joint behavior, in turn, is mixed with individual behaviors. Trip may go on fixing drinks over the boundaries of several beats and mix-ins. Consuming drinks, playing with a magic eight ball, and other individual behaviors take place in parallel with joint beats and mix-ins. Each JDB is written so that it can be performed when the characters are in different physical locations in the room, carrying out other individual behaviors, and so forth. There is a profound result that arises from these individual behaviors, the reactions of handlers, and the prevalence of mix-ins. While character behavior in *Façade* is largely driven by a procedural script, it doesn't feel as though it takes place in a series of scripted segments but rather as a continuity.

Learning from *Façade*

The surface experience produced by *Façade*'s processes and data is shaped by a series of choices that have clear impacts in terms of the *Eliza* and *Tale-Spin* effects. The results are instructive.

Speaking to *Façade*

As with *Eliza/Doctor*, the free-form textual interaction of *Façade* invites play. Unlike *Eliza/Doctor*, the *Façade* system actually models aspects of the current context and ongoing conversation, so there's more potential reward for this play. *Façade*'s audience members may interact in their own styles, whether to influence Trip and Grace, express a particular idea of the player character's identity, or find the edges of the system.

The player aims of individual expression and system edge finding, which sometimes overlap, can produce particularly memorable *Façade* transcripts. For example, one person posting on the *Idle Thumbs* forums decided to play in an unusual way: taking appropriate physical actions (sitting on the couch or answering the phone) but only saying one thing:

> PHONE ** RING **
>
> (GONZALO picks up the phone.)
>
> PHONE ** RING **
>
> PHONE Hello? Hello?
>
> TRIP Gonzalo, no! Don't do that.
>
> GONZALO Brains!!
>
> PHONE Who is this? Travis, is that you? This is your mother.

TRIP Uhh, that's my mother, I can hear her loud voice.

GONZALO Brains!!!!!!

PHONE I don't recognize your voice . . .

PHONE I—I think I have the wrong
number . . . ** click **

GONZALO Brains?

(GONZALO puts down the phone.)

(Mailman 2005)

18. Many make the small selection of available actions visible on the work's surface. Some, however, like text-based interactive fictions, make the search for available actions part of the experience.

As the poster concludes, "Playing as a zombie is fun." Other players on the same forum share transcripts in which they play someone who has just been shot, an alien seeking tissue samples, Darth Vader (who screams "Noooooooooooo!" after being ejected from the apartment), and Grace's secret lover. Of course, there are also many transcripts featuring player characters somewhat closer to *Façade*'s expectations, but those that push the system are especially revealing in terms of the *Eliza* effect. For instance, the aspect of *Façade* that makes the zombie transcript funny is also a clear case of how *Eliza* effect breakdowns reveal something of the shape of the underlying system. In this case, one sees the way that *Façade*'s drama continues executing its beat goals, for the most part, even in the absence of intelligible player behavior.

In using a free-form natural-language interface, *Façade* makes a certain trade-off. Players are invited to perform more richly than in many digital fictions, which often limit interaction to the selection between a set of discrete choices (with everything else producing an error message).[18] On the other hand, the actions of the

19. This is something that Steven Dow and Blair MacIntyre have explored in creating the "wizard" interface for their augmented reality version of *Façade* (Dow 2008).

Façade system actually reduce each player utterance to one of a set of discrete discourse acts—and not always successfully. This creates a serious mismatch. Personally, every time that I have played *Façade* in a manner I considered "according to expectations," a statement that I thought of as perfectly normal produced a reaction so unexpected that I found myself thinking about the shape of the underlying system.

In fact, *Façade*'s authors estimate that natural-language understanding failure takes place about 30 percent of the time. My subjective feeling as a player is that failures are less frequent, but this is due to the clever ways that *Façade* deflects and recovers in many circumstances. And as Mateas and Stern write, "This tradeoff was intentional, since we wanted to better understand the new pleasures that natural language can offer when it *succeeds*" (2007, 206). One can see here that natural-language interaction offers powerful potential to the audience, but also, by digital media authors, must be regarded as an area of active research (rather than a mature technology). It points to other research areas as well, such as interfaces that might allow for players to directly express *Façade*'s discourse acts, removing from the equation any unreliable natural language understanding.[19]

Hearing from *Façade*

Interestingly, *Façade* also presents a similar trade-off in the area of the *Tale-Spin* effect. This is one in which it follows the model of many contemporary games, though, rather than departing from it. This is the choice to use voice acting, so that Grace and Trip's statements are performed by playing a sequence of prerecorded sound files to which their animations are synchronized.

Just as free-form textual input allows players to be expressive, the human expression embodied in *Façade*'s strong voice acting is part of what makes the experience so effective. The nuances of line performance make things by turns funnier and more uncomfortable—and overall, more engaging. On the other hand, *Façade* also required significant authoring effort to appropriately funnel a vast number of possible system states into a much smaller number of possible prerecorded utterances.

If the system had used plain text as output, many more system states could have been experienced meaningfully on the work's surface. This would have been true for two reasons. First, the mixing of prewritten segments could have been more fine grained. *Façade* already sounds strange when it mixes recordings of the player character's name into lines that were specially recorded for the purpose, and going further in this direction would have greatly reduced what the experience gains from its voice acting. Second, plain text output would have opened the door to another interesting research area: the construction of systems like the literary augmented grammars of *Brutus*. These have the potential to adjust the nuance of text, by applying hand-authored rules, depending on the current system state. Yet for performance-oriented systems (such as *Façade* and many modern computer games), this too is best regarded as an area of research. Though speech-generation systems are rapidly improving, for many purposes voice acting will remain the more powerful approach. But for systems such as massively multiplayer online games, in which most NPC dialogue takes place through text, such research could have immediate application.

Agency in *Façade*

Finally, there is also an element of *Façade* that communicates clearly to players and, when natural language understanding is successful, operates much as they expect. This is the combination of drama management, beat goals, joint behaviors, handlers, and mix-ins—what I have called *Façade*'s procedural script. This combination creates a performed story that progresses in a way the audience understands, during which players can direct conversation toward a range of topics, and which can take a variety of shapes that culminate in an appropriate ending.

This experience is not simply that of the *SimCity* effect, because it is not designed to foreground the nature of *Façade* as a system. Rather, as Mateas and Stern indicate, their goal is an experience in interactive media commonly termed "agency" or "intention." *Façade*'s authors point to Janet Murray's formulation of the concept, which has been particularly influential in academic circles: "Agency is the satisfying power to take meaningful action and see the results of our decisions and choices" (1997, 126). In the field of game design the idea is often associated with Doug Church, who writes of "allowing and encouraging players to do things intentionally" (1999)—understanding the game world well enough to make and execute a plan of action, then seeing a clear reaction from the game world. At the same time, it is also worth noting that a version of this concept can be seen from the earliest full-length writing on digital fictions of which I am aware: the PhD dissertation of Mary Ann Buckles. She describes this in relation to the psychological concept of "effectance" as "the desire for competence and feeling effective in dealing with the surrounding environment" (1985, 37). She discusses how the world of the early interactive fiction game *Adventure* works to build this experience in its audience.

The *SimCity* effect is one way to build the experience of agency. *Façade*'s procedural script seeks another. Mateas argues that in general, "a player will experience agency when there is a balance between the material and formal constraints" (2004, 125). The formal constraints are present in the shape of the fictional world, motivating some actions and not others. The material constraints, on the other hand, are the resources available for action. Many contemporary games for children and adults create a sense of agency by presenting a fictional world in which one would want to move across space (e.g., to rescue a princess or find necessary information) and fight enemies (e.g., who are mean animals or are zombies/aliens/robots/Nazis), and providing exactly the tools necessary (well-developed mechanics for spatial movement and combat).

Given this, achieving agency is relatively well understood for game worlds with simple fictional worlds and simple available actions, because it is easy for players to understand and act within the bounds of the system.[20] The *SimCity* effect describes a route to agency for more complex systems and retrospectively clarifies that even simple movement and combat require transitioning from the audience's initial expectation to an understanding of the model implemented by the system (see sidebar: Agency Reconsidered). What *Façade* provides, instead— in its procedural script—is an example of a route to agency that aims to function with less necessity for player understanding of the system. Rather than needing to replace the audience's initial *Eliza* effect notion of drama with one closer to the model of the system, players who

20. Though design failures happen commonly, as when actions that can be used in one context cannot be used in another, for reasons unexplained by the fictional world, reducing the player's ability to formulate and execute intentions.

avoid natural language understanding errors can experience agency in *Façade*'s world while continuing to operate largely based on mental models drawn from theater, media, and human interaction. We might say that this is the true dream of interactive drama.

Unfortunately, this also means that the dream remains somewhat elusive. The *Façade* approach, while powerful, still requires that players learn its mechanics for movement, speaking, and physical action. As discussed earlier, it also suffers from unavoidable errors in natural language

---

Agency Reconsidered

The concept of *agency* or *intention,* discussed in this chapter primarily in connection with *Façade,* is central to thinking about gameplay and interaction in general. In short, agency is a term for the audience's ability to form intentions, take actions, and see satisfying results. It is a widely-used concept, but also one in need of reconsideration along a number of dimensions.

First, discussions of agency can fall into potentially misleading formulations in which player goals and plans appear to determine player actions. As discussed in chapter 5, such formulations have been severely critiqued in cognitive science and artificial intelligence by researchers such as Lucy Suchman and Philip Agre. As outlined in that context, it is important to remember that goals and plans are *resources* for action—which is fundamentally situated and improvisational. Reflecting back on personal experiences of playing a challenging game, in which things rarely go exactly as one plans, is another good reminder. In this vein, perhaps the best antidote to such misleading constructions of agency is *Pilgrim in the Microworld* by David Sudnow (1983), an account of learning to play *Breakout* for the Atari VCS.

On a different front, discussions of agency also commonly bracket a fundamental issue. This is apparent in Murray's primary example of game world navigation as well as in Church's discussion of design strategies that work (e.g., simple and consistent controls, abilities, and physics behavior make planning possible). The fundamental issue is the motivation that players have to move, or plan to move, to particular places. Put another way: What creates the desire that agency satisfies?

The first part of an answer is the fundamental contribution of Mateas's formulation of agency as a balance between material and formal constraints. This moves agency from an amorphous ability to plan and carry out actions, which captures only part of the picture, to a phenomenon in which the actions motivated by a game or other

---

understanding. An alternative, such as players directly expressing discourse acts (rather than typing free-form text), would require teaching the audience to understand the system more deeply, reinforcing the importance of the *SimCity* effect.

Beyond *Façade*

In addition to research in natural language understanding and text generation, *Façade* also points to further work in a number of other areas. For example, in developing the

---

piece of digital media are matched with those it enables. In other words, agency requires evoking the desires a work satisfies.

With the examples discussed in this book, we can now take a further step. Consider *Eliza/Doctor,* which evokes the expectation of a therapy session, motivating the audience to say the things one might say in such a situation, providing the tools necessary for saying them (direct textual input), and responding to each with a further question. While this creates a desire for action and a means of taking that action (and while, as discussed in chapter 4, Murray has called Weizenbaum "perhaps the premier" literary artist in the field [1997, 72]) the result of play with *Eliza* is breakdown. Working with the audience's expectations (e.g., of a therapy session) is a powerful way to evoke desires for action, but the *Eliza* effect is not a route to agency.

SimCity, as discussed in this chapter, also begins with audience expectation—using it to evoke desires to take city planning actions using the tools represented on its surface. This initiates a process designed to transition players, through experimentation and feedback, from their initial assumptions to an understanding of its procedural city. This understanding is what enables agency in *SimCity,* and it accomplishes this at a level much more ambitious than simply moving through virtual space.

This lesson is key because we do not have a holodeck and will not have one in the foreseeable future. We do not have the perfect virtual reality, simulation, and AI technologies that would be necessary to enable the vision of free-form interaction that depends on the same desires and supports available in the everyday world. Even the simpler examples of Murray and Church depend on players coming to games with an expectation of movement and then transitioning to the system's actually implemented model. The *SimCity* effect makes this explicit and takes it further, setting the stage for a more mature understanding of agency.

approach embodied in *Façade*'s procedural script and the large amount of material necessary to support it, Stern and Mateas also developed a set of code templates that they reused repeatedly. As they have speculated, the design elements formalized in these templates could become the primitives in higher-level authoring languages for digital fictions, or even in graphical or AI-assisted authoring tools.

In the meantime, *Façade* has demonstrated the power of the ideas formulated in its procedural script—which should in time find their way into other digital media projects. As authors adopt the techniques pioneered by *Façade,* their strengths and limitations will become yet more apparent. New research will explore new possibilities. As this happens, hopefully, mainstream gaming will abandon the static dialogue tree, thereby increasing the potential richness of existing genres and opening the possibilities for new ones.

Further, while these relatively well-developed techniques—the cumulative result of more than a decade of technology and design research—may be adopted by mainstream digital media, researchers are likely to turn to the next challenge. Experiences like *Façade* will remain limited by the sheer amount of material that must be authored. Future research is likely to consider how to not only produce a wider variety of sentences based on authored rules (as in LAGs) but also automatically assemble structures more akin to *Façade*'s JDBs or even *Façade*'s larger beats, as the current situation dictates. Until this succeeds, *Façade*-like experiences will require large amounts of authoring for every minute of dramatic experience.

More generally, *Façade* provides an important example of how authors can engage the history of AI. It adopts powerful tools that grow from an AI legacy. At the same time, it disposes of limiting concepts that are the baggage of that legacy—especially the insistence on seeing characters as fully "autonomous agents" who sense and react to each other, but should be strongly compartmentalized from one another and the larger system. Of course, like many ideological views, such AI concepts were often compromised in practice, but *Façade* moves away from them as a principled stance, rather than with embarrassment.[21] For those willing to do the conceptual work required by such reconsiderations, the history of AI provides an exciting source of future directions.

Finally, *Façade* manages to create an emotionally engaging, if frequently uncomfortable, interactive experience about the relationships between people. It manages this not simply through the operations of its procedural script and characters but also because it is designed to capitalize on the power of fiction's most powerful tool: language. In this it provides a stark contrast to the history from which it flows, from *Tale-Spin* to the Woggles. But in this way it connects to another, parallel history—a particular branch of which is considered in the next chapter.

21. Principled moves away from such views, and toward architectures oriented to audience experience, were more common in the field of computer graphics. Earlier in this chapter, I discussed the Improv system, which did…

Notes continued at end of this chapter.

Notes

1. Though an expansion focused on crafting the underlying terrain on which the city rests.

2. During the review of this book's draft manuscript on Grand Text Auto, Dennis G. Jerz offered a telling series of observations—including that the graphic user interface (GUI) of *SimCity* is already a much more restricted interaction channel than *Eliza*'s free-form textual input. In his comment he writes:

> On the one hand, you've got the naive user who sits down to *Eliza* with a preconception of the idea of a therapist and a preconception of what it means to communicate through typing—but probably no idea of what a text parser does. On the other hand, you've got the naive user who sits down in front of *SimCity* with preconceptions about cities, and with a pretty good idea of what it means to use a GUI.

> Any GUI interface restricts the meaningful gestures the user can perform, just as the iconic display restricts the possible meanings that the image can convey. So the initial "surface" of the GUI is already a mental model, in a way that I don't think the "surface" of *Eliza* is (at least not until the user has first noticed something fishy about *Eliza*'s responses).

> The resolution of the information that goes into *Eliza* is a lot deeper than the information that goes into *SimCity*. Even if *Eliza* can't actually understand all of that information, the fact that it's there on the screen (or on the fan-fold printout) means that it was available for the user to refer to when interpreting *Eliza*'s responses. But yes, limiting the input to yes/no (or some other finite set of verbs) would replicate the restrictions of *SimCity*'s GUI.

> On the other hand, *SimCity* is a much more complex program. Once you're consciously aware of *Eliza*'s rules, there's not much left to do, unless of course the leading questions guide you to a life-changing self-revelation. In *SimCity* you have to learn how the various resources interact over time.

> The naive users who first played *Eliza* weren't consciously trying to grok the rules of the text parser, but may instead have been very self-conscious about what might have been their first significant encounter with a computer. If we put *SimCity* in historical perspective, we can assume that most players of *SimCity* were familiar with GUIs, and were thus willing to accept restrictions (such as the requirement to zone rectangular areas and not being able to put a railroad, street, and power line in the same space). The GUI has trained us to lower our expectations. But those restrictions break the illusion of being a "real" city planner just as much as *Eliza*'s gaffes break the illusion of talking to a real therapist.

I think Jerz's comments are generally insightful. At the same time, though, I would argue that the experience of *Eliza* or *SimCity* is not fruitfully considered in terms of being a real patient or real mayor. Rather, I think we might employ the conception of interaction as conversation or dialogue, as outlined by authors such as Chris Crawford (2003) and Myron Krueger (1977). For such authors, a successful interactive system has to both "speak" and "listen." When interacting with *SimCity*, the GUI tells us the tools we have available for speaking (acting) and listening (gathering information), while experimentation reveals that the system genuinely has an underlying model of the city that shapes its actions (speaking) and is informed by our actions (listening). Interacting with *Eliza*, on the other hand, reveals that it does not have a model of the conversation—it's not listening in any ongoing way.

3. Though it is technically true that models used by the CBO are open to scrutiny, as are most of those used by nongovernment researchers such as Forrester, Starr tells us that "to most participants in policy debates as well as the public at large, the models are opaque. Only a few can penetrate the black box and understand what is inside" (1994). *SimCity,* on the other hand, shows that carefully designed playability can be an effective tool for helping much larger groups understand how simulations operate. At the same time, as Nick Montfort pointed out in the blog-based review of this manuscript, it is critical to bear in mind the fact that the understanding reached through the *SimCity* effect is limited. In Montfort's comment he writes:

> I get the impression that the lasting impact of Forrester's model from *Urban Dynamics* was largely based on it being open to scrutiny and described in detail in a 300-page book—which led to productive discussion, the development of other models, and so on. Yes, *SimCity* is playable, but it actually isn't as well-documented and modifiable as Forrester's model is, and the assumptions of the model aren't directly expressed.

Since Montfort's remark, the release of the *SimCity* source code (under the name *Micropolis*) has altered how potentially well-documented and modifiable people find *SimCity*'s model. But Montfort's point remains important. While the *SimCity* effect opens system understanding in a manner that is more generally accessible, the understanding gained has crucial limits, and for many purposes must be supplemented by other sources of information.

For this sort of deeper information on the CBO's simulation work, see "Overview of the Congressional Budget Office Long-Term (CBOLT) Policy Simulation Model" (O'Harra, Sabelhaus, and Simpson 2004).

4. The broad learning that takes place around video game playing, rather than the specific learning about the underlying system that is my focus here, is discussed in books such as *What Video Games Have to Teach Us about Learning and Literacy* by James Paul Gee (2004).

5. Something Montfort tells me one's player character might do while experiencing *Dangerous Curves* by Irene Callaci (2000).

6. Interactive fiction (IF) players are often engaged in discovering what words can be employed to take action, rather than how statements can be constructed for parsing, in each fiction's simulated world. While some actions are possible by convention and standard in most IF tool systems (such as compass-point movement), the possibility space for commands is nearly as large as the language used to converse with the fiction. Some authors have implemented verbs such as "remember" or "dare" in their games, as appropriate to the settings and themes involved, which are generally discovered by players through a combination of experimentation and careful attention to descriptions of the game world. Players work to discover not only what commands are accepted by the system but also what their effects are on the underlying simulation. In other words, to what extent and in what ways are the commands simulated? In a particular fictional world, is "remembering" simply a way of bringing up a small snippet of memory text, or does it add new areas of the world for exploration, or does it even expand the set of future actions that the player character may take? This is part of what Douglass (2007) describes as the "implied code" that IF audiences come to understand.

7. Of course, Wright's games are certainly not the only ones for which this is the case. Alex Galloway makes a similar point about the work of Sid Meier, a designer famous for simulation-oriented games such as *Civilization* (Meier and Shelley 1991):

> In the work of Meier, the gamer is not simply playing this or that historical simulation. The gamer is instead learning, internalizing, and becoming intimate with a massive, multipart, global algorithm. To play the game means to play the code of the game. To win means to know the system. And thus to *interpret* a game means to interpret its algorithm (to discover its parallel "allegorithm"). (Galloway 2006, 90–91)

8. This description is based on lecture notes by Kenneth Forbus and Wright (2001).

9. From Wingfield's article:

> Critics have also charged that the game wrongly equates happiness with consumerism, since much of it revolves around buying clothing, furniture and other goods.

> Mr. Wright has said the game actually parodies such habits. The Sims's more conspicuous consumers spend a lot of time fixing broken refrigerators, tending to malfunctioning cars and otherwise being controlled by their property. (2006)

Alex Galloway, in his book *Gaming,* goes further—writing that "*The Sims* is a game that delivers its own political critique up front as part of the gameplay. There is no need for the critic to unpack the game later" (2006).

10. Frasca writes that he has met people who:

> firmly believe that *The Sims* is a parody and, therefore, it is actually a critique of consumerism. Personally, I disagree. While the game is definitively cartoonish, I am not able to find satire within it. Certainly, the game may be making fun of suburban Americans, but since it rewards the player every time she buys new stuff, I do not think this could be considered parody. (2001)

11. At the time of the blog-based review of this book's manuscript on Grand Text Auto, Richard Evans (already noted as the AI lead for *Black & White*) was working at Maxis on the not-yet-announced title *The Sims 3*. In his comment on this paragraph he wrote:

> This is very perceptive. In fact, there is disagreement at the moment amongst the designers on an as yet unannounced product, specifically about this issue. Some want to manifest the agent's interior mental states, for the reasons you give. Others worry that showing everything ruins "player projection"; they argue "the more you show, the less the player will project."

> I disagree—I think that "player projection" (the phenomenon where the player imputes more to the agents than is really going on) is a phenomenon which stands on the shoulders of the player having a clear mental model of how the agents operate. It is only if he understands *most* of why they do what they do that he will impute more to them. If he doesn't have a clear mental model of their interiority, because the designers have hidden the data from him, then he won't be able to project—

you can't stand on the shoulders of nothingness!

Assuming that Evans was talking about *The Sims 3,* I was fascinated to hear that such debates take place even within Maxis. Andrew Stern (2008) took the opportunity of my exchange with Evans to create a new top-level post on Grand Text Auto, continuing an earlier conversation thread about NPCs and transparency. An interesting consensus seemed to emerge in the ensuing conversation: that the pleasure of coming to understand a system's processes through experimentation requires the ongoing availability of system data. The question is which data to expose to the audience, and how.

In some ways this exchange anticipated the discussion, later in this chapter, of interactive drama and *Façade*—as well as harking back to the previous chapter's section on expressive language generation. Each of these seeks ways to expose ongoing system data through the means of the arts: dramatic performance, crafted language, and so on. Of course, the design of *The Sims* is more like *SimCity*. While there are characters, their iconic speech is closer to an animation of a congested roadway than a nuanced dramatic line. For such projects, underlying data must be exposed by other means.

12. This places her work at Atari and on her dissertation in roughly the same time period as *Universe* and the first phase of *Minstrel*. Some of Laurel's dissertation was later adapted for her book *Computers as Theatre* (1991).

13. The founding of Zoesis certainly wasn't the death knell for university-based research in interactive narrative. Around the time that the Oz Project was winding down, R. Michael Young's Liquid Narrative project was gaining momentum at North Carolina State University. As of this writing, their work continues in high gear—and a variety of other groups internationally are engaged in interactive narrative research. Exploring all this work would require a book of its own, so I direct interested readers to the proceedings of the Conference on Artificial Intelligence and Interactive Digital Entertainment, the Joint International Conference on Interactive Digital Storytelling, and the ongoing series of symposia on related topics from the Association for the Advancement of Artificial Intelligence.

14. From the animation direction, work led by researchers such as Norm Badler and Jessica Hodgins focused on biomedically correct animation rather than expressive animation (Badler, Phillips, and Webber 1993; Hodgins et al. 1995). From the behavior side, researchers such as Barbara Hayes-Roth sought to find the right general-purpose "social-psychological model" for interactive characters while Bruce Blumberg was among those building non-human characters based on ethological models (e.g., dog behavior) (Rousseau and Hayes-Roth 1998; Blumberg 1997).

While invested in non-media forms of correctness, much of this work went on to have significant impact on media projects. For example, the C4 architecture developed in Blumberg's group stands in the background of Jeff Orkin's work on *F.E.A.R.* as well as Damian Isla's work on AI for the *Halo* series. In fact, Isla undertook graduate work in Blumberg's group at MIT and his influential "behavior tree" formulation for AI characters (2005) is closely connected to the tradition described in this chapter (e.g., it could be implemented as a programming idiom for a language like ABL).

15. Bates reports on a particular Woggle:

Due to a programming error, Shrimp occasionally peppers his ongoing behavior with what seems to be a nervous tick causing him repeatedly to hit his head against the ground. This attracts people's attention immediately, but to our surprise they build psychological theories, always incorrect, about Shrimp's mental state and seem to find him much more interesting and alive for having this behavior. (1994, 124)

Years later, Zoesis created a new implementation of the agent architecture. Testing *OttoAndIris.com* it found something similar. As Loyall notes:

In an early version of the system, kids testing it drew pictures afterwards of Otto as a "crybaby," and kept talking about the time he refused to sing. The refusal was a bug that caused part of Otto's mind to completely freeze. We thought the bug had ruined the test, but to the kids it showed Otto's strong will and made him seem more alive. (2004, 7)

These behaviors succeed, of course, because they are great opportunities for *Eliza*-style projection. But an entire system composed along these lines would have been a dismal failure. They succeeded by being distinctive within a larger context of behavior that seemed ordinary and appropriate.

16. Though similar ideas had been pursued in domains such as battlefield simulation (e.g., Tambe 1997).

17. In the initial draft of this chapter I referred to "*Façade*'s script." During the blog-based peer review, Stern objected, saying the term *script* has a strong implied linearity—in both traditional drama and game development. The new term is my attempt to capture the fact that *Façade*'s procedural script specifies what characters will say and do (like a traditional script) while actually composing ongoing behavior through a combination of drama management, beat goals, joint behaviors, handlers, and mix-ins.

18. Many make the small selection of available actions visible on the work's surface. Some, however, like text-based interactive fictions, make the search for available actions part of the experience.

19. This is something that Steven Dow and Blair MacIntyre have explored in creating the "wizard" interface for their augmented reality version of *Façade* (Dow 2008).

20. Though design failures happen commonly, as when actions that can be used in one context cannot be used in another, for reasons unexplained by the fictional world, reducing the player's ability to formulate and execute intentions.

21. Principled moves away from such views, and toward architectures oriented to audience experience, were more common in the field of computer graphics. Earlier in this chapter, I discussed the Improv system, which did not commit strongly to agent autonomy and commonly directed characters in coordinated performance. During the blog-based review of this manuscript, Mark J. Nelson commented that the wider field of graphics often finds compromises between autonomous simulation (e.g., of smoke drifting) and directed action (making sure the smoke curls in a particular way at a particular time).

Chapter 9
Playable Language and
Nonsimulative Processes

Opaque Processes

If the thinking for this book has an origin point, I would track it back to my senior year of high school. I was working on my biggest programming project to date: a poetry generator written in Turbo Pascal, which I moved between school and home computers on a 5¼-inch floppy disk. Its main operational logic was simple, but pleasing to me.

I had defined certain words as key connection points in sentences—words as simple as "he," "she," and "it." I had also typed in files of text for the program to employ, with certain indirect connections in their phrasings—such as a description of a whirling witch (from Robert Coover's retelling of *Hansel and Gretel*) and a description of orbiting planetary bodies (from the novel of *2001: A Space Odyssey*). The program dove into a random point in a body of text, initially selecting the beginning of a sentence. It would read until it encountered one of my specially selected words and then it might depart, choosing a random point in another body of text and searching until it encountered the same word. Then it would start reading again, until it encountered either another of my words (in which case it could move to another file again, seeking that word) or the end of a sentence. The connection words made parts of sentences like Lego bricks, able to be recombined at their connection points, and I felt I'd chosen a set of texts with complementary colors and shapes.

Beyond that, the program also had procedures

dedicated to creating poetry-like formatting and so on, but the heart of it was the sentence-building process. I'm afraid it produced poems that (at best) flitted along the boundary of coherence and pretentious nonsense, as adolescent poetry of a certain type tends to do. A friend successfully passed a couple off as her own work, as a sort of unscientific experiment, before she revealed the hoax to her teachers. But the poems weren't really the point.

Personally, I was fascinated with building the system at first and then with a kind of "looking through" the surface output to see the construction process at work, especially when it produced sentences and phrases that were evocative and surprising. I was also frustrated that the results were—for readers outside my little circle of initiates—probably no better than the output of a process I would have considered much less pleasing. In this, though I didn't know it, I was actually experiencing an adolescent version of something with a long history in the arts. While a small circle of experimental writers, artists, or composers (or a larger circle that includes some interested audience members who learn about the context of the work) may understand the clever structures that help produce process-driven work and the reasons those structures are employed, in general the audience only experiences the output. Given this, it should be no surprise that such work is often rejected as opaque (potentially senseless) or uninteresting (bad). People like to be in on the joke—and they judge work by the parts they perceive, not what is hidden—yet the work itself frequently provides no inroad.

In my late teens I couldn't see any way around the opacity problem. But I also felt certain that I wanted to explore the possibilities of computers, and do so as a writer.

So for most of college I shied away from process-driven work, instead using computers to do things like create short fictions as text-and-image collages (using snappy new programs like Aldus PageMaker). At the same time, I was also taking computer science classes, learning more about the construction and power of computational processes. Yet I couldn't see a way to bring the two together.

In the terms of this book, what I experienced with my poetry generator was a small version of the *Tale-Spin* effect. There wasn't much of a model at work, but it was still more interesting than it seemed from the output. What I was missing, of course, was the concept of the *SimCity* effect. I was missing that playing with language might not only be fun for an author, or an interesting thing to design into a system, but also an engaging experience for an audience that (if it bootstrapped from useful assumptions) could help them understand something of the processes at work in the system.

Even if the processes of my high school poetry generator had been immediately visible on the surface, audience members certainly would have understood something quite different from most of the processes described in this book. My sentence-assembly process wasn't an attempt to *simulate* anything. It didn't attempt to determine the events of a fictional world—as with most of the story-generation systems I have discussed—or even do a more poetic version of simulation (e.g., of a string of themes moving through a simulated author's psyche). What it did wasn't as interesting as either of these possibilities, but it did represent another direction for the combination of writing and process. In this it connected with another tradition that I didn't yet know about: Tristan Tzara's poetic cut-up, John Cage's mesostics, and digital poets such as Charles O. Hartman and John Cayley. As I moved further with this work I found myself trying to think through the role of process in digital fictions for which the sequence of events is not variable—when process is not used for the purposes of event simulation.

In this chapter, then, I try to draw some lessons from my own creative work that preceded this book as well as the work of those who inspired me. I consider the possibilities of play with language, "textual instruments," and playable media more generally. I also consider what role process may have in digital fictions beyond simulation.

Legible Data

After college, when I was a visiting artist at New York University in 1994–1995, I found a new interest in combining writing and computation—seeking ways to write fiction specific to the context of the emerging phenomenon of the World Wide Web. I created a "network fiction" called *The Book of Endings,* designed so that readers could drop in at any page, stop at any page, and follow connections to and from the larger Web. (I was quite pleased to be written up in "What's New at NCSA Mosaic.") I later became a research scientist at the same lab. Shortly after starting work, I began collaborating with Michael Crumpton, Chris Spain, and Kirstin Allio to create a complex network of fictions embedded in a body-shaped collage of images from *Gray's Anatomy* called *Gray Matters* (Wardrip-Fruin, Crumpton, Spain, et al. 1995–1997) that could be explored using the lab's newly developed zooming user interface.

When I finally returned to process-oriented work, in

early 1998, my first major project focused on the potential of employing more legible data. I had been able to see what was going on in my high school poetry generator, in part, because I knew the contents of its text files. This helped me identify the connection points between the parts of sentences drawn from different contexts, making it possible to glimpse a process-defined pattern through the text of any given poem. Broadening this experience to the audience was one of the strategies of my next major project: *The Impermanence Agent* (Wardrip-Fruin, Chapman, Moss, et al. 1998–2002).

The Impermanence Agent

The Agent project began as a discussion with Brion Moss over a Vietnamese dinner in San Francisco, and we soon added Adam Chapman and Duane Whitehurst as collaborators. We created something specific to that technohistorical moment, as the Web went through its first years of broad public awareness in the United States. At the time, web sites like Hotwired's Newsbot, the Mining Company (later renamed About.com), and Ask Jeeves used "agent" metaphors to describe their services. These anthropomorphized web sites were presented as solutions to the emerging Web's supposed problems, especially a potentially overwhelming flood of information without the gatekeeping or permanence of large-scale commercial publishing.

Instead of a web site, we created something much more engaged with our audience's ongoing experience across multiple sites: a set of processes that were closer to the computer science conception of an agent. *The Impermanence Agent* monitored all browsing for its audience members, routing their traffic through its proxy. But rather than try to steer people toward specific sites and away from the Web's troubles, the agent used the experience of browsing to provide an opportunity to reflect on the supposed problems of impermanence. It did this in three ways.

First, it would alter web pages as they passed through its proxy server, changing and inserting elements. It was common, say, for the Agent to "decay" advertising images (using the scriptable ImageMagick tool, running on the server). This would make illegible and sometimes aesthetically interesting images out of what most in our audience saw as the junk mail equivalent for the emerging commercial Web.

Second, the Agent had its own small web browser window, containing scrolling text and animating images. (If audience members closed this, but continued to use the Agent's proxy server, we inserted code in regular browser windows to reopen the Agent's window.) One of the uses of this window was to comment on each audience member's ongoing browsing. For example, as browsing (inevitably) resulted in "404 not found" errors, the Agent attempted to lead each audience member through the Kubler-Ross stages of grief, one for each site.

Third, the Agent was also a storyteller. I wrote a story for it of documents and memories preserved and lost, a story of life and death, a family story of impermanence. This story itself was also impermanent. It was "customized" for each reader (following agent logic) by altering the text based on their browsing. For instance, the words from the headings and meta-tags of pages browsed by each audience member were analyzed, using the WordNet database developed by George A. Miller's cognitive linguistics group

at Princeton, in an attempt to determine topics in which
they were interested—and then these topics took the place
of others within the story. Even more dramatic textual
alterations began with *The Impermanence Agent* performing
a simplec analysis of the structures of sentences from
pages browsed by audience members. The Agent would
then collage phrases from them into similarly structured
sentences in the original story (figure 9.1). After about a

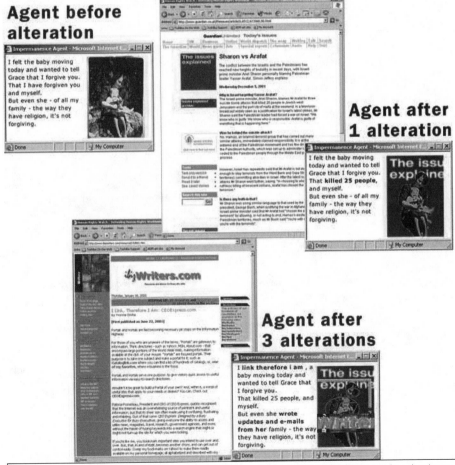

Figure 9.1. *The Impermanence Agent* customizes its text and images for each audience member, drawing on material from the user's individual browsing of the Web.

week of using the Agent by any one audience member, the original story remained in structure, but with its contents unrecognizably transformed by insertions from that reader's browsing.

We didn't create a different version of the Agent's story for each audience member simply to follow agent customization logic. We also hoped that the gradual transformation of the story, using data collected from that audience member's recent browsing, would help make what was going on more recognizable—make our impermanence processes, which were a central element of the work, more legible. Finally, our goal was to imagine a new kind of fiction: one that performed, through its processes, some of the same ideas explored in its text. In the case of the Agent, we were interested in the idea that our stories are impermanent, collaged over by what comes after, and we felt this was a more powerful experience if it was the more recent web pages read by each audience member that covered over the previous reading of our story.

Talking Cure

Unsurprisingly, *The Impermanence Agent* was a great success compared with my high school poetry generator—both in my estimation and that of audiences. It left me wanting to do further projects in which the data came from each audience member individually, making a textual experiment more legible. And that is part of what attracted me to the textual work of Camille Utterback.

Utterback was at New York University's Interactive Telecommunications Program, in the building next door to where I worked (at the Center for Advanced Technology/

Media Research Laboratory). Her *Text Rain* collaboration with Romy Achituv (Utterback and Achituv 1999) was installed in a passageway that connected the two sides of the Interactive Telecommunications Program space, creating an unfolding experience of bodily relationship to text that I had the opportunity to observe repeatedly (both in that context and at venues like the SIGGRAPH 2000 art gallery).

This experience begins with someone walking by the *Text Rain* projection: an image of letters falling. Then, partway through the act of walking past, one experiences a recognition: the walker's own image is now included in the scene, and as he walks the letters with which he collides are "knocked" back upward, partially, only to fall again (figure 9.2). The walker then becomes an audience member, paused to take in the scene; the letters

Figure 9.2. *Text Rain* draws passersby into play with text.

settle on his head and shoulders, and perhaps on an arm experimentally outstretched, before fading away, then being replaced by newly falling letters. Next the audience member becomes player, bouncing the letters, trying to catch particular individuals or groups, perhaps employing objects or recruiting other people. And then the player becomes also a reader, catching enough letters to realize they form words, catching enough words to realize they form phrases, forming lines such as, "At your turning, each part of my body turns to verb." These lines, evoking bodies and language, come from "Talk, You," a poem by Evan Zimroth.

The playful interaction with text made it easy to figure out what was going on in *Text Rain* and encouraged audience engagement, but the textual possibility space was small—basically, the only question was how much text any given audience would decipher. When I saw Utterback's in-development *Written Forms,* on the other hand, it had a rather different look to me. Instead of an image that included text falling from the sky, with simulated physics, inviting and structuring play, *Written Forms* presented an image made entirely out of text. This technique operates by having multiple layers of text, each the size of the projection, with each layer's letters at a different brightness level. Then a video image of the space in front of the projection is used to mix between the three layers. Bright areas of the scene select letters from a bright layer, darker areas of the scene select letters from a darker area, and so on. The result is that it is possible to "read" the projection both as an image of the scene and a mixture of texts.

When I saw this, I immediately thought of the pictures we make with words, and began thinking of situations in which these are particularly powerful. I proposed a collaboration with Utterback, who agreed, and we brought in Clilly Castiglia and Nathan Wardrip-Fruin (my brother). We conceived something rather different from the hallway-style installations of *Text Rain*. Our piece, *Talking Cure* (Wardrip-Fruin, Utterback, Castiglia, et al. 2002; see figure 9.3), includes a table and chair in a darkened room with a large projection screen. An audience member entering the space sees a light shining from the table onto the chair, hears an audio environment made up of mixtures of text, and sees the projection screen filled with one text: excerpts from Joseph Breuer's case study of Anna O. This text—a discussion of the patient who gave the idea of the "talking cure" to Breuer, who then gave it to Sigmund Freud—provides the word pictures of her condition, such as the snake hallucinations she

Figure 9.3. Talking Cure creates an image from text.

described, and her strange fluctuations of language use.

If the visitor sits in the chair, a text image of her upper body fills the screen, created by adding two further layers of text. Her face is largely represented by the brightest layer, an effect created by the room's lighting. This layer is a fiction I wrote, recasting Anna's hallucinations within the story of the Gorgon Medusa, placing the analyst in the position of Perseus—looking, but always indirectly. The middle layer of text, which appears at the borders between dark and light, consists of the words "to torment" repeated (one of the few direct quotations attributed to Anna in the case study). Finally, there is a microphone on the table, and when an audience member speaks aloud her words are (mis)recognized by a speech-to-text engine, replacing the middle layer of the text image, and recorded for addition

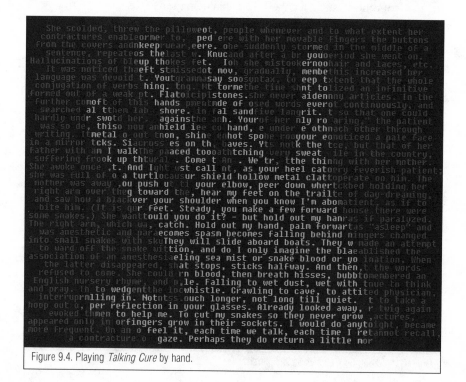

Figure 9.4. Playing *Talking Cure* by hand.

to the mix of the sound environment.

Or this is what we thought would happen. And certainly some people experienced the piece that way. But when we installed the piece at the University of California at Los Angeles (UCLA) for the Electronic Literature Organization's 2002 symposium, I had something of a shock. People interacted with the piece in a manner much more like *Text Rain* than like *The Impermanence Agent*. There was a textual possibility space to explore, immediate feedback, and an audience. So rather than docilely sit in the chair as patient surrogates, most interactors stood over the table, near the camera, using their bodies for performing and *playing* with the text/image. In other words, once they'd figured out the simple model, they wanted to drive it. Some used their hands to catch a consistent amount of light, panning back and forth to read the entire fictional text in a traditional fashion (figure 9.4). Others focused on interesting neologisms and other kinds of mixtures that could be created by controlling the boundaries between textual layers. Others got friends to help them fill the camera's field with wiggling fingers, passing in and out of the cone of light. It was a pleasure to watch people so engaged with our work, and in some ways more of a pleasure than watching people who experienced the installation as we imagined it. Seeing this began a shift in my work—one that drew me toward a conversation beginning in the wider field of electronic literature.

Textual Instruments

Around the time of the UCLA presentation of *Talking Cure,* I was becoming increasingly interested in a discussion within the electronic literature community of texts meant

1. Within this phrase I'm subsuming a discussion, around texts with instrumental qualities, that has used a variety of loose terminology. I'm also abandoning an earlier terminological distinction from my previous writing on this topic between …

Notes continued at end of this chapter.

to be played—what I will refer to here as *textual instruments*.[1] I was particularly influenced by the ideas and work of John Cayley and Stuart Moulthrop. For example, here is Cayley in an interview with Brian Kim Stefans:

> My point is that we are currently writers trying to build relatively simple textual instruments that are intuitive and, hopefully, both affective and significant when they are played. I mean played as musical instruments or sequencers or mixers are played. This is ergodic indeed, but still distinguishable from (hard) work or from the type of play in games which is rewarded by winning, by other forms of "success" or simply by "playability." (2003)

With the term "ergodic" Cayley is referencing the work of Espen Aarseth, whose *Cybertext: Perspectives on Ergodic Literature* I have discussed in earlier chapters. Aarseth defines the term by stating, "In ergodic literature, nontrivial effort is required to allow the reader to traverse the text" (1997, 1). After writing *Cybertext,* Aarseth became one of the leading figures in the emerging field of computer game studies, helping to found the field's first journal as well as the Center for Computer Games Research at the IT University of Copenhagen. In referencing Aarseth's work, Cayley brings to the fore a focus on play as "nontrivial effort" in music, games, and textual instruments. Yet he also specifically distances the textual work he is referencing from the focus on winning (or other "quantifiable outcomes") that has been a persistent feature of computer game studies—as well as from the relatively unstructured play I saw in the *Talking Cure* audience.

I interviewed Moulthrop about these issues at around the same time, and we too discussed some of the potential challenges of the reader/player's nontrivial engagement, but also some of what authors of textual instruments might learn from the designs of folk instruments:

> Maybe some instruments will be hard to play. They may require practice. Or not. As a teacher once said to me about the guitar, "After five or ten minutes you'll make sounds that are almost musical. That's what the frets are for." And that's a great virtue of folk instruments. They do allow you to get in touch with a productive vocabulary very quickly. I think a good instrument would do that. It would stimulate engagement. It should make people want to get in there and interact, and to repeat the experience. (2003a)

But for Moulthrop, perhaps unlike Cayley, musical and literary figures were not the only relevant touchstones. Moulthrop employs musical figures as a vocabulary that can help one imagine projects that occupy a space between two other types of work at play in discussions of instrumental texts. As Moulthrop puts it:

> What I'm particularly taken with is the notion of a middle space between literary texts and ludic texts—between interactive fiction, or hypertext fiction, and games. You have, with instruments, a text with behavior and temporal dimensions that in some ways maps onto the temporal experience and interactive possibilities in game design. (ibid.)

These are intriguing notions, but also somewhat elusive when discussed on a purely theoretical level. How do we conceive of projects that are literary, but played in a somewhat musical manner, and perhaps occupy some ground nearby the established field of games? A deeper inquiry requires looking at specific projects. In particular, Cayley's interview statement about instrumental texts came in the context of an answer to a question about his piece *riverIsland* (2002b). The occasion of my interview with Moulthrop was the release of his piece *Pax* (2003b). I will turn to these next.

riverIsland

Cayley's work often employs a technique he calls "transliteral morphing." This is a letter-by-letter morphing that transitions from one text to another, much as graphical morphing moves points in space so as to transition from one image to another. In transliteral morphing the in-between letters are determined by movement along a loop on which Cayley has arranged Roman characters according to their sounds, as he explains:

> If texts are laid out in a regular grid, as a table of letters, one table for the source and one table for the target, to morph transliterally from one text (one table of letters) to another, is to work out, letter-by-letter, how the source letters will become the target ones. Assume your alphabet (including "space" and apostrophe, 28 letters in all) is arranged in a special loop where letters considered to be similar in sound are clustered together. The aim is to work out the shortest distance round the loop (clockwise or anti-clockwise) from each source to each target. (2002c)

Once the movement for each letter is worked out, the text then moves through fourteen steps (the largest number that might be necessary for any one letter—movement to the opposite side of the twenty-eight-character loop). Some letters go through many more transitions than others. Changes are "reluctant" at the beginning of the process and then "anxious" for completion at the end—so that both the early and final stages are close to readable texts.

A number of Cayley's pieces, such as his well-known *windsound* (1999), employ transliteral morphing in a manner that is performative on the part of the program. Texts morph into other texts under the gaze of the reader/ audience, using the computational capabilities of the computer on which they are displayed. And yet these morphs could be, like most of the graphical morphs we see, prerendered and displayed as moving images (without any computation at the time of reading). The only visible loss would be the small changes in timing from reading to reading on the same computer, and the occasionally larger changes when moving from computer to computer.

Cayley's *riverIsland,* on the other hand, is not only performative on the part of the system but also performative in a manner controlled in part by the reader (figure 9.5). One of the types of performance made available to the reader is relatively straightforward:

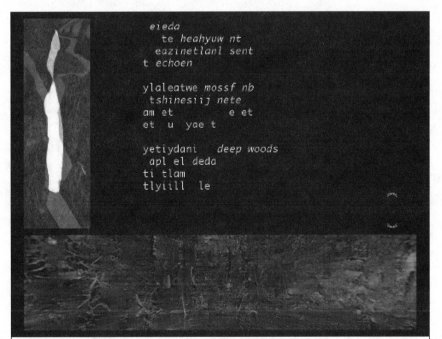

Figure 9.5. *riverIsland* enables traditional, step navigation through its textual morphs via the arrows on the lower-middle right—or for those with knowledge and practice, a more free-form selection of destination texts through the horizontal panorama and/or vertical object movie.

riverIsland is composed of two loops of poems, one horizontal and one vertical, and the reader can use on-screen arrows in order to trigger movement along these loops. When the reader indicates that a move should be made from one poem to another, the appropriate transliteral morph is performed by the computer.

There is another type of reader performance in *riverIsland,* however, that feels quite different to me. And I believe that this is part of what Cayley was getting at in his talk of instruments during his interview with Stefans. In this type of performance, the reader can click and drag on the screen's vertical and horizontal QuickTime movies. The vertical movie is an "object" movie that graphically transitions between images of paths through the woods. The horizontal movie is a panorama of a riverside scene. A reader experienced with *riverIsland* can use these movies to navigate to any point within the work's two loops. A transliteral morph is then performed between the text that was being displayed before the navigation process began (which might itself be an in-process morph) and the destination selected by the manipulation of a movie. This creates an experience for which prerendered morphs could not effectively substitute—like Cayley's figure of the sequencer, it harnesses real-time computational processes to create a performance based on high-level user direction that requires knowledge of its materials and control space.

Pax

The textual instrument of Moulthrop's considered here, *Pax,* presents an experience of reading and performance that differs from *riverIsland.* Its differences in some ways map onto two of the different musical devices that

Cayley and Moulthrop chose for their examples when discussing textual instruments—while Cayley mentioned the sequencer, Moulthrop mentioned the guitar.

A sequencer might play itself for some time after being given instructions, but a guitar demands interaction for each note sounded. Similarly, *Pax* is structured for near-continual interaction. The larger area of the piece, on the left, shows characters floating up (in the first half of the piece's duration) or falling down (in the second). Unless the reader interacts with these characters, almost no text appears. Readers interact by "catching" floating characters with the mouse pointer (figure 9.6). Characters can be released by moving the mouse away, or clicked (either by active clicking or holding them caught for twenty seconds). Clicking elicits text from that character, which appears in the area on the right (this becomes a scrolling text area once there is enough text to scroll). The fourteen characters

Figure 9.6. *Pax* produces texts when the reader catches and clicks on characters that float by—and is otherwise silent. Rather than a narrative "told" to the reader or one "played through" as in, for example, the levels of a narrative first-person shooter, *Pax* is an exploration of character and situation.

float by in different orders, but those recently clicked tend to reappear, making it possible to consistently evoke text from two or three characters as the piece's time passes. Each reading lasts from noon to midnight (the characters' time) and is divided into six thematic movements: "Shaken Out of Time," "American Flyers," "Home Land," "Evil Ones," "Falling," and "Total Information." The text elicited from a character is determined in part by the number of times that the character has been caught and clicked as well as the current movement of the piece. The character texts evoke two situations: being caught in some version of a terminal at the Dallas airport (shut down for security reasons in an even-more-irrational "war on terror" than that which gripped the United States in the wake of the September 11 attacks), and being caught in the space and structure of *Pax* itself (naked, floating, and caught and prodded by the interactor).

While it would be impossible to manipulate the QuickTime movies of *riverIsland* toward particular effects without relatively strong knowledge of the piece, *Pax* provides obvious places to click and quickly understood effects even for the first-time reader. But due to its random elements and the strong impact of time's passage, it would be more difficult to exactly reproduce the same reading (after learning to play) than with *riverIsland*. To put it in terms of the musical analogy, *Pax* may provide frets, but for an instrument with nonlinearities that are perhaps more like a gong's than a guitar's.

And this points to the strength of computer gaming as a figure for understanding textual instruments. In the gaming context there is nothing surprising about behavior that changes over the course of time. There is also nothing surprising about the skills of physical manipulation and memorization that would be required to elicit particular readings from *riverIsland* and *Pax*. And the fact that these "instruments" come packaged with only one composition, from which they cannot be easily decoupled, also makes sense in the context of computer games. And yet these projects are clearly not games in the manner that play is approached. Perhaps what the musical analogy helps with most is the fact that these projects seek a lyric engagement—not easily understood in terms of "contest" or "quantifiable outcome," two of the formula often cited in formal definitions of games. On the other hand, a lack of winning conditions is also present for mainstream games like *The Sims*, as I will discuss further in the next chapter.

Playing Text in Virtual Reality

After my initial engagement with the discussion of textual instruments, my first playable media project was *Screen* (Wardrip-Fruin, McClain, Greenlee, et al. 2003–present). This project combines familiar game mechanics with virtual reality technology to create an experience of bodily interaction with text. At the same time, the language of the text, together with the uncanny experience of touching words, creates an experience that doesn't settle easily into the usual ways of thinking about gameplay or virtual reality.

Screen began in 2002 as one of the initial "finger exercises" performed by an interdisciplinary group—masterminded by novelist and digital media pioneer Robert Coover—that came together to explore the literary possibilities of Brown University's room-size virtual reality display. This display, the "Cave," is similar to the University of Illinois' CAVE: a virtual environment that shows 3-D images while allowing users to continue to see their own bodies, and that does not require users to wear encumbering equipment—unlike head-mounted displays, which are essentially blindfolds with televisions mounted in front of the wearer's eyes (Cruz-Neira, Sandin, and DeFanti 1993). Brown's Cave is an eight-foot cube, missing its top and one side, and its walls and floor are screens. Projectors are pointed at each screen, and they alternately project streams of images meant for the user's left and right eyes. The user wears shutter glasses that alternately occlude the left and right eyes, in synchronization with the projectors. The result is stereo virtual reality—a 3-D vision of computer-generated imagery—combined with the physical presence of the people and objects in the Cave.

Most projects in virtual reality environments of this sort work to make the walls disappear, in favor of a virtual landscape or context-free object(s). The *Traces* project (Penny, Smith, Sengers, et al. 2001)—one of the inspirations for our work at Brown—eschews these

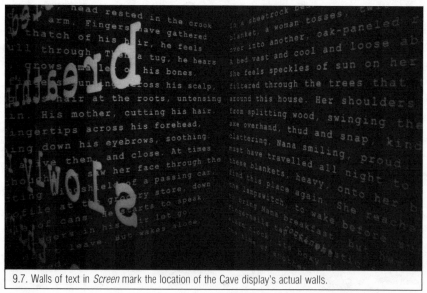

9.7. Walls of text in *Screen* mark the location of the Cave display's actual walls.

conventions in favor of the image of a room, described in some cases as roughly twice as large, and in some cases as the same size, as the room in which the audience is located (the CAVE). One of our first notions at Brown was to take the next logical step: experiment with using the actual Cave walls as one of the locations on which images appear, presenting part of the work at the same time as reinforcing the actual dimensions of the display and actual location of the audience. The finger exercise that led to *Screen* began when Andrew McClain, a member of the group, placed text on the walls in this manner (figure 9.7). But the text didn't stay put—words peeled loose and came toward the audience.

Playing *Screen*

I saw in McClain's experiment an opportunity for play. Joined by sound artist Shawn Greenlee, we created a prototype of the project's design, and I drafted the initial set of texts. McClain stopped working in the Cave shortly afterward, and the project was brought to a completed state with the conceptual, technical, and textual contributions of Josh Carroll and Coover himself. It begins with an introductory text about memory written by Coover that fades in and out on the walls. Then three traditional paragraphs appear, each nearly filling one of the walls. Each of these paragraphs is a short fiction that I wrote, evoking a character's moment of memory that gives rise to the virtual experience of touch. After each wall appears it is read aloud. Once the last has been read there is a pause, and then a word peels from one of the walls, is spoken aloud, and flies toward the reader. If the reader does nothing, the word circles near her. Soon another word peels, and then another, at an increasing pace, flocking around the reader.

The reader can intervene in this process by batting at words with her hand. When a word is hit a sound is heard, and the word flies back toward a wall. If only one word is loose, it will, when hit, return to the space it left empty. But when multiple spaces are empty a word, when hit, may return to any of them. A hit word without a space large enough on the walls will break apart, as may a word hit with a particularly swift motion.

Once the number of words off the walls passes a certain threshold—something that, with the increasing pace of peeling, only active engagement can long delay—all the remaining words come free of the walls, swirl around the reader, and then collapse into the center of the Cave (figure 9.8). A final "closing" text, also written by Coover, is then heard.

In addition to creating a new form of bodily interaction with text, *Screen* creates three reading

9.8. Collapsing words in the SGI (2003–2004) version of *Screen*.

experiences: beginning with the familiar, stable, pagelike text on the walls; followed by the word-by-word reading of peeling and hitting (where attention is focused); and also, simultaneously, a more peripheral awareness of the arrangements of flocking words and the new (often neologistic) text being assembled on the walls. It also takes advantage of audience familiarity with a basic gameplay mechanic: the "collision detection" that is central to many games, starting with early graphical ones.

We might simply discuss *Screen* as a game, rather than with more unusual terms such as *textual instrument*. And in fact, the final moments of *Screen* feature a scattering of knocked-back words (and parts of words) on the walls—which caused one young visitor to the Cave to ask, "Is that my score?" But while the play of *Screen* is reminiscent of classic games, and some players may at moments be driven purely by the gamelike goal of hitting words as quickly as possible, there is no contest or quantifiable outcome (as, again, is required in many academic definitions of games). Even approached purely physically, without any attention to the linguistic nature of the words being played, *Screen* is more like hacky sack than soccer/football. Further, in my observations, players don't approach *Screen* without attention to its words as words. Interactors instead oscillate between reading and playing—with the objects of both coming faster and coming apart—until both experiences can no longer be sustained and the piece ends.

As with *riverIsland* and *Pax,* reader/players can get better at *Screen,* though the fact that interactors do not control the ripping of words alters what is possible via virtuoso performance. Perhaps the most impressive performance of *Screen* I have seen is that of Michelle Higa, who both edited the video documentation of *Screen* and played the role of the interactor within it (Wardrip-Fruin, McClain, Greenlee, et al. 2004). In order to videotape *Screen,* we had to temporarily remove the flickering alternation between the Cave's left- and right-eye images. Higa had become adept enough at the experience of *Screen* that she was able to play it relatively successfully even without stereo cues.

Higa's documentation is of our initial version. Later, after seeing audiences interact with the first completed iteration, and as the Brown Cave moved from SGI Irix machines to IBM Linux machines, I worked with Benjamin ("Sascha") Shine on a major overhaul. This allowed us to improve the animation of words significantly (in the previous version, for example, we were forced to exclude roughly half the words from the final collapse for performance reasons) and also served as the starting point for the development of a writer-friendly set of authoring tools for Cave work.

Finally, in 2007, the project moved to two new forms: the audience-surrounding fifteen-screen StarCave at the University of California at San Diego's branch of Calit2, and a single-screen gallery display at the University of California at Irvine's Beall Center for Art and Technology, made possible by the efforts of Stephen Boyd, Jurgen Schulze, Todd Margolis, and others. Through this work we learned more about projects involving the body and this form of virtual reality. For instance, when creating a version for the gallery (meant to wait for the audience to initiate it rather than run as an application in the Cave), we designed it so that the piece begins only after the audience member whose hand is being tracked touches the title word. We found that with this change, it is not necessary to later provide a visual marker of hand location—as we had in previous versions—and this removes the suggestion that the marker itself is something with which to play (a suggestion that had distracted previous audiences).

This significantly improved the experience of the piece. But it is a change that addresses *Screen* purely as a physical and visual experience. This small piece of instruction would have worked as well if audience members were required to touch a colored box, rather than the text of the piece's title. And this points to a larger issue with the project. While text is central to the experience of *Screen* on one level, both its processes and audience interaction could operate unchanged on groups of colored blocks rather than on various series of letters. In this it is far from alone.

Spatial Logics

Thinking in terms of operational logics has run through the course of this book—at first explicitly developed, and then increasingly taken for granted in later chapters. But it is worth making the notion explicit again here.

Most logics discussed in this book have been considered in terms of what they simulate. Some of the simulations are tellingly odd, as with *Eliza*'s use of a textual-transformation logic to simulate conversational responses and *Tale-Spin*'s use of a planbox-based planning logic to simulate all the behavior of anthropomorphized animals.

Most computer games rely on a different type of simulation: that of space. In fact, a common set of *spatial logics* is central to the operation of many games.[2] Consider the early, iconic game *Pong*. In this game, each player controls a paddle, one on each side of the screen. The top and bottom of the screen are walls. The

2. I originally referred to these spatial logics as graphical logics. As I recall, the change in terminology was suggested by Espen Aarseth.

players move their paddles to intersect with the path of a ball, which bounces back into the playfield—and also bounces off the walls. When a player misses the ball, the other player scores a point.

In terms of the activity being simulated, this has almost nothing to do with another early, influential game: *Spacewar!* (Russell, Samson, Edwards, et al. 1962). Created on a PDP-1 at MIT in the early years of the 1960s, *Spacewar!* is widely considered the first modern video game. Using custom-made controllers, two players control the flight of a virtual spacecraft on the PDP-1's CRT. The spacecraft are pulled toward the star at the center of the screen by simulated gravity, and can fire projectiles at one another. A spacecraft hit by the central star or a projectile is damaged.

Though these simulations of table tennis and space warfare present different fictional worlds, if we look at the operational logics at work we see important points of similarity. One of these is the logic of *collision detection*—noted briefly in this book's introduction. This is the simulation of one virtual object colliding with another. This comes into play when a ball bounces off paddles and walls in *Pong* as well as when spacecraft intersect with projectiles and the central star in *Spacewar!* Both games also offer a logic of navigation—*Pong* along a line, and *Spacewar!* across a plane. Both provide a simulation of basic elements of physics too, though the gravity that is central to *Spacewar!* plays no role in the bouncing trajectory of a *Pong* ball.

This small collection of logics still forms the foundation of much modern computer gaming. From the playful *Mario* games to the gritty *Grand Theft Auto* franchise, collision detection, navigation, simulated physics, and the firing of projectiles are central to the system. Interestingly, these same logics are also at the heart of *Text Rain, Pax,* and *Screen*—though they, like *Pong,* lack projectiles.

Among the examples of textual play I have discussed so far, the exception to the above is Cayley's *riverIsland.* While it is played primarily through the graphical/physical manipulation of QuickTime movies, it does not simulate the movement and collision of virtual objects. Even more significantly, its most salient operational logic—Cayley's transliteral morphing—is based on typographic forms. I view it as a textual logic rather than a spatial one.

Employing Logics

Successful combinations of spatial logics and game rules are repackaged repeatedly. Games such as *Pac-Man* and *Tetris* have had many authorized and unauthorized versions "skinned" with different surface graphics and spatial arrangements, but with the essential logics of spatial movement and gameplay preserved. Such combinations, within a larger range of variation, are also the basis for our identifications of game genres such as "side-scrollers" and "first-person shooters."

On the other hand, while a set of spatial logics often works satisfyingly with many different sets of graphics, the same is not true of textual content. It is for this reason that *Text Rain, Pax,* and *Screen* are each carefully arranged combinations of spatial logic with textual material, creating a connection between the text's themes and the operations of the spatial logics. Certainly, it is technically true that a project such as *Screen* would operate with arbitrary textual material, but only a limited set of texts would resonate with the form created by its spatial logics.[3]

I believe the *Arteroids* project, created by Jim Andrews,

3. This is not to say that all combinations of graphics with spatial logics work equally well. For example, Jesper Juul (2005, 13–15) amusingly demonstrates that the logics of *Space Invaders* work well with both academic theories and …

Notes continued at end of this chapter.

works well to demonstrate this sort of limitation. At first glance *Arteroids* is a version of the well-known arcade game *Asteroids* with many of the graphics replaced by text. But Andrews also created a "Word for Weirdos" to allow others to compose for *Arteroids* and has included texts from others in presentations of the work, such as the texts by Christina McPhee and Helen Thorington included when *Arteroids* was shown in the "page_space" exhibition (Superbunker 2004). To me the results feel arbitrary, though I have enjoyed the work of these writers in other contexts—no different than if the graphics in *Pong* or *Spacewar!* were opened to replacement by arbitrary text.

On the other hand, Cayley has used his transliteral morphing logic in a number of pieces, both interactive and not. The results do not feel arbitrary but rather fitting. As I suggested above, I believe this is because transliteral morphing is a textual logic instead of a spatial one. Just as spatial logics work well with a wide variety of graphics, textual logics work well with a wide variety of texts. Cayley is far from the first to work with textual logics. We encounter textually specific forms of play every day—such as the newspaper crossword puzzle. It is a feature of alphabetic characters that they can simultaneously play roles in two intersecting words. On a different level, a number of writers and artists working before Cayley have invented textual transformation procedures, such as the famous "n + 7" method of dictionary substitution popularized by the writers and mathematicians of the Oulipo.

In other words, while a limited set of texts might be appropriate to match with a set of spatial logics, the same is not necessarily true of a textual logic. This points to an area for further investigation: developing new forms of playful interaction with text that employ operational logics that reflect elements of textual or linguistic, rather than spatial, behavior. This, in turn, would also open the possibility for textual systems that are closer to musical instruments in a particular sense: that of being able to convincingly play multiple compositions (bodies of text) rather than being tied to one. My next project was an initial foray in this direction.

Two N-gram Instruments

This book's discussion of *The Restaurant Game* includes a description of one of the most commonly used statistical models for work with human language: the Markov chain or n-gram. It is a way of predicting (or generating) future behavior, based on patterns in past behavior. For example, a model of this sort could predict that in written English, "q" is more likely to be followed by "u" than "o" (because the two-letter digram "qu" is likely to be found repeatedly in any significant body of English text, whereas the other is unlikely to be found at all).

Models of this type work well for serially ordered data, leading to their application with not only text and spoken language but also areas as diverse as musical performance and human behavior over time. *The Restaurant Game* illuminates some of the potential and pitfalls of the last of these applications—an interesting area of research for computer gaming, but a startling mismatch with real human behavior, and a good illustration of the problems inherent in proposals for massive surveillance on the model of the Total Information Awareness (TIA) program.

The earlier discussion left aside some of the potential in using such models for creative, generative purposes.

For example, n-grams have also been used in assembling language for electronic literature, perhaps most extensively by Cayley. At least seven of his works employ "collocational" word-level digram procedures, including *Book Unbound* (1995, as discussed in Aarseth's *Cybertext*). This approach has also been the primary basis of textual toys such as the DOS program *Babble!*, the emacs "Dissociated Press" command, Hugh Kenner and Joseph P. O'Rourke's *Travesty*, Andrew Plotkin's *chan.c*, and Brion Moss's *prate*—which have themselves at times been used in the generation processes for (nonplayable) literature.

Both the elit and toys based on n-grams, however, have operated entirely in "batch mode." That is to say, the interactor requests a body of text, and then that text is produced—following which the text can be read and another text can be requested, but no interaction with the texts (or interaction during generation) is possible. Given this limited nature of play with n-gram texts, there is also limited context for play—usually a blank text buffer for the program to write text into. After I'd seen how audiences interacted with *Screen,* a conversation with Moss (with whom I'd collaborated on *The Impermanence Agent*) kicked off a consideration of n-grams, and we began to imagine possibilities for linguistic play with this model that was less batch oriented and took place within a textual context.

Moss and I approached Turbulence, an organization that supports digital media art, and it commissioned us to create two pieces. These pieces would be inspired by the idea of textual instruments and operate using the logic of n-grams. After a false start with different collaborators, Moss and I connected with document researcher David Durand (best known for his work in formulating a number of document markup standards, including XML) and designer Elaine Froehlich (principal of Active Surface Design). From there, the project's conceptualization and execution were a team effort, with the initial technical work happening on top of Moss's Java *prate,* and later development built on top of work done by Durand in Tcl/Tk.

Two major design decisions were made early on. The first was that rather than build an n-gram text into an empty text buffer, play would always begin within the context of a precreated document and consist of a progressive alteration of that document. This was motivated in part by the fact that although the text produced by n-gram algorithms has microstructures that are recognizable from its source texts, the larger structures of n-gram texts tend to be similar regardless of the starting material. Some have tried to address this by looking at larger structures in the source texts statistically, but unless the texts in question have been marked up by a human author or editor, this process involves a series of assumptions about the text (e.g., that a period marks that end of a sentence, as it does not in the case of "e.g.") that are both sometimes inaccurate and on some level aesthetically displeasing. These assumptions are displeasing because they depart from the purity of the simple n-gram algorithm, which in its basic form would work with starting texts in Japanese or Braille characters as easily as Roman alphabet ones. There was also another motivation, though. In many n-gram texts, especially those based on short chains, part of the pleasure is based on play between coherence and incoherence—and we found something more interesting and potentially more meaningful in such borderline coherence occurring within the context of traditionally created texts.

The second design decision was the identification of our basic method for making n-gram generation playably interactive rather than oriented toward large batches. We decided that in addition to the starting document (within which play takes place), we would have a body of text used for producing the alterations to the starting document. (We call this second body of text the "alteration text" or "alteration corpus.") When the starting document was displayed, certain words would be highlighted. We chose this as a convention familiar from hyperlinks on web pages, letting interactors know that a click will elicit a response. Nevertheless, these words are not highlighted as the result of author-specified links. They are instead highlighted because a string of n-gram text (of a length specified by the piece's author) appears in both the starting document and the alteration text. We decided that such "bridges" between the two bodies of text would offer interactors the opportunity to open up the starting document and insert text generated from the alteration corpus. More than one generated text would be offered for possible insertion, allowing the interactor to choose one or none (this last leaving the text unaltered). The texts offered would themselves be generated from the alteration text through the use of n-gram techniques. The number of texts offered and the n-gram length used in their production would, again, be determined by the piece's author.

Once these decisions were made, we sketched, mocked up, and eventually tried to make operational a number of interaction designs. Some didn't give the kinds of results we'd hoped for, and others were too computationally expensive to work, but in time we settled on one that—as a first attempt—we found satisfying in terms of the feel of interaction and the shape of the attention to text it creates. For these first compositions (*Regime Change* and *News Reader*) this interaction took place through a simple, Web-style series of windows, which seemed both appropriate and easy to implement. Through creating these first two projects we also learned important lessons about the limitations of this sort of approach.

Regime Change and *News Reader*

Regime Change begins with a news article from April 2003, following the bombardment that began the U.S. invasion of Iraq. George W. Bush cites "eyewitness" intelligence that Saddam Hussein was assassinated by targeted U.S. bombing and clings to the contention that the Iraqi president was hiding "weapons of mass destruction." Playing *Regime Change* brings forth texts generated from a document that records a different U.S. attitude toward presidential assassination and eyewitness intelligence—the report of the Warren Commission.

Once the window with *Regime Change*'s starting text is opened, words in that text, pair by pair, become highlighted (figure 9.9). Clicking on words opens a new window. Interacting with new windows produces new texts that will take the place of the clicked words.

New windows contain texts that begin with the words clicked in the previous window. Each paragraph in the new window is an alternative text—beginning with the same words but potentially (though not necessarily) following many different paths from there. These texts are generated by connecting chains of words (three-grams and four-grams) that may have appeared originally in different parts of the source document.

A new window's texts, once displayed, also begin to have words highlighted within them. Clicking highlighted words will open another new window, containing generated texts that can take the place of the clicked words (figure 9.10). Opening several generations of windows opens wider possibility spaces for the texts that will be created (and that will replace the clicked words in earlier-generation windows). Windows alternate between generation from the Warren Commission text and the original news story.

In any window with generated text, clicking a nonhighlighted word is also a means of interaction. Such a click will close the window and select a text. The selected text will run from the beginning of the clicked paragraph to the clicked word. That selected text will then take the place of the words clicked to open the window (figure 9.11). This creates a kind of stretchtext—the pair of words clicked to open a window are replaced with the words

Figure 9.9. *Regime Change* displaying its starting text.

selected in the open window (usually more than a pair).

After opening several layers of windows, part of play is keeping track of where each window came from—so that it can be collapsed by selecting a word that will make a pleasing segue at the point where it will join the text to which the player intends to connect it. (This may be more than one layer down.) Keeping track of context is made somewhat easier by the title bar of each generated window—which displays the two words that will be replaced by the generated text, followed by the two words that appear after them in the text clicked.

I find that when I'm playing, this cycle of activities— reading, remembering context, selecting a place to click, and reading again—consumes my entire attention. I've found it impossible to "give a reading" of *Regime Change* as I might with other writing projects. My most successful presentations, instead of a traditional reading, are a series of performances in which I played the text and Popahna Brandes read the results aloud.

News Reader operates similarly. Rather than working from a given news article and government report, however, it is software for reading current news and re-forming it. It can be seen as a specialized browser—displaying a selected RSS feed as well as the news stories to which the feed links. Unlike a normal browser, *News Reader* also downloads another set of texts in the background—and uses this material to open each page it displays to textual play. Through this play the concerns and language patterns of the hidden documents, as shaped by the movements and passages selected by the player, are introduced into the original news stories. *News Reader* provides a different way to encounter the daily news, making its patterns of

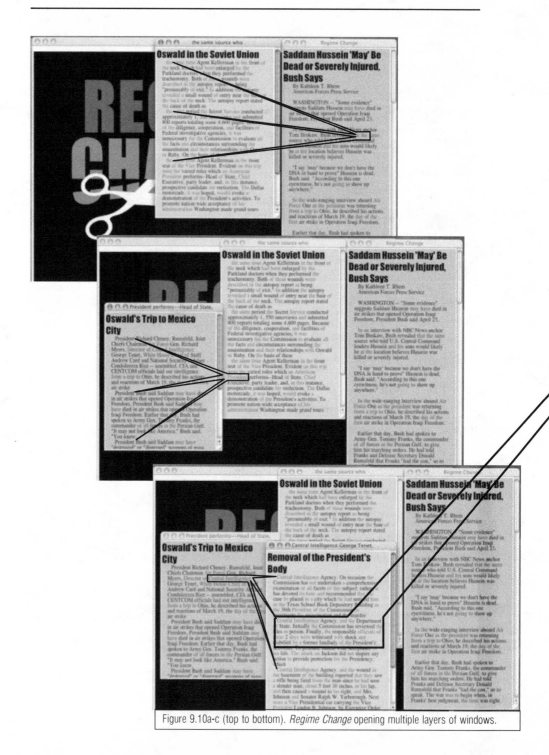

Figure 9.10a-c (top to bottom). *Regime Change* opening multiple layers of windows.

Figure 9.11. Word replacement in *Regime Change*.

repeated phrases into opportunities for disruption and producing results that range from humorous to disturbing.

When *News Reader* launches, it displays a window containing the current headlines from the Yahoo! News RSS feed (figure 9.12). Clicking the headline or preview text opens another *News Reader* window, displaying the story, with links added (figure 9.13a). As with *Regime Change,* these links don't lead to other web pages but rather generate texts out of a statistical text model (in this

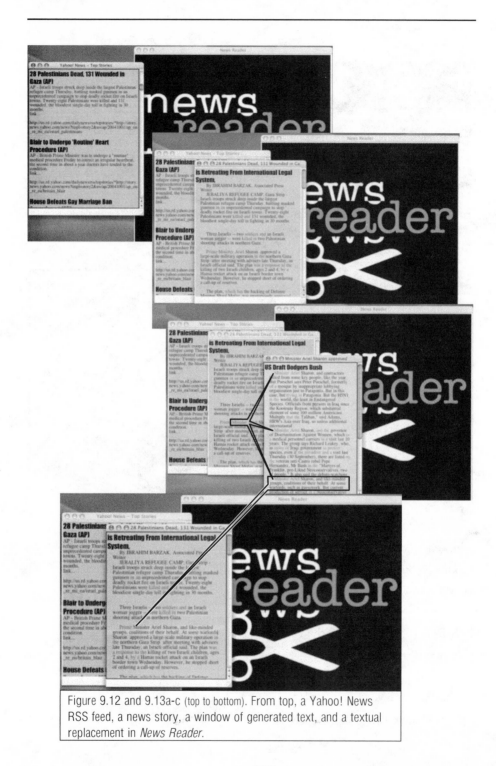

Figure 9.12 and 9.13a-c (top to bottom). From top, a Yahoo! News RSS feed, a news story, a window of generated text, and a textual replacement in *News Reader*.

case, trigrams of the alteration corpus and their relative frequency). These generated texts appear in a new *News Reader* window (figure 9.13b). The alteration corpus is created from the texts of alternative news stories (found at Common Dreams) downloaded in the background when *News Reader* is launched. As with *Regime Change,* windows of generated text contain several paragraphs, each of which is a continuation of an n-gram that begins with the words in the clicked window just prior to that word clicked. And again as with *Regime Change,* clicking a nonhighlighted word will close a window of generated text, replacing the words clicked to open that window (figure 9.13c). The words used to perform this replacement will be those between the clicked word and the opening of the alternate text ("paragraph") it was within.

N-gram Play

These two projects, of course, are quite different from those described earlier in this chapter—particularly *Pax, riverIsland,* and *Screen.* The most obvious difference is that the project authors did not write the text for *Regime Change* and *News Reader,* and for the latter the authors did not even select the text (only the method by which text is gathered at each reading). In part this is connected to the nature of the experiment. A textual instrument meant to play many compositions (make many texts playable) is most convincing if it can work with texts that are not prescreened by their author(s). But there are also other reasons.

When I was living in New York, I remember being asked, "What is the most likely thing to make you angry?" I answered, "The front page of the *New York Times.*" I was something of a news addict at the time—but like many people, I was also left feeling frustrated and angry after many encounters with news. Introducing something playful into the experience of the news was one of my motivations.

It might seem that the playfulness of a project like *News Reader* is purely destructive, leaving nothing but incoherence in its wake—something our group may have unintentionally suggested by characterizing play with our instruments as a way to perform William Burroughs's injunction to "cut word lines." Yet I think Jena Osman (2007) gets at something crucial when she describes *News Reader* as a "poethical" response to the political and linguistic environment of the United States in the early twenty-first century. She compares the project to John Cage's work with mesostics and reaches a revealing conclusion:

> Both *Newsreader* and Cage's mesostics make use of what we now easily recognize as forms of datamining. Both show readership (and authorship) to be an act of sampling, transforming, altering and physically handling text; the act of reading is literally performative.

> But perhaps most importantly, both are functioning on metatextual or metaphorical levels, allegorizing our methods of attention, our methods of processing information, and the ways those forms of processing mirror (or improve) the forms of life we actually live in and with. Rather than the destructive act of cutting word lines that the Textual Instruments home page proclaims as its goal, I would argue that both *Newsreader* and Cage's mesostics actually encourage construction of meaning along new lines.

> But as much as I want to make the case that these procedures are two parts of a continuing project .

. . both seem to be responding specifically to the forms and structures that perform the contents of their times. Cage, in his decision to follow the path of nonintention, was resisting what he saw as the automatic privileging of romantic self-expression and intention. *Newsreader,* built with an architecture of information processing tools, resists the contemporary desire for everything to be knowable, searchable, and analyzable. (ibid.)

To put it another way, my goals with *News Reader* and *Regime Change* are related to those behind this book's discussion of Jeff Orkin's *The Restaurant Game.* I seek to use Orkin's project both to illustrate an approach to digital media and as a legible example that can help us understand the limits of statistical models, informing our decision making about projects such as TIA. Of course, such legible examples are not the only route to what has been called "procedural literacy." Another, which I have discussed as exemplified by *SimCity,* is the kind of understanding that can emerge from play. This is not the sort of understanding that would allow for reimplementation: it is neither sufficiently detailed nor exact. But it can produce a kind of feeling for the algorithm, for the processes at work, for potentials and limits. I hope that *News Reader* and *Regime Change* can help produce such understanding for n-grams.

Of course, these textual instruments are designed to provide something more than an opportunity to develop a feeling for a model used in statistical artificial intelligence (AI). They are a way of playfully exploring a textual possibility space. They are meant, as Osman puts it, to "encourage construction of meaning along new lines." The process creates a new form of reading for oneself or performing texts for others.

These potential outcomes point to a motivation for

doing algorithmic digital media work. It is not simply for the expressive potential of processes, though this is great. It is also because this media, particularly when it is playable, can be a way of developing deeper understandings of the "software society" in which we live today. As Saskia Sassen is credited with saying, "Today, all logics of contemporary society are embedded in software" (Fetveit and Stald 2007). We need to develop understandings of these logics using every tool available.

N-gram Opacity

Unfortunately, now that they have been encountered by audiences, I can see that *Regime Change* and *News Reader* are problematic tools for developing understanding of the operational logic of n-grams—in ways that also make them less successful in terms of all of our goals for the projects. In fact, one critic, Marie-Laure Ryan, explicitly cites them as an example of "anti-WYSIWYG aesthetics" (2005). For Ryan, what is interesting about them cannot be seen on the surface.

The audience members, like Osman, who understand these projects deeply have not generally developed the understanding through play with their surfaces. Rather, they have also read what we've written, perhaps talked with us about them, and maybe even teased out telling differences between our systems and others. I can see in retrospect that the opacity of the project to most audience members arises because we did not go far enough with our two initial design decisions.

First, we chose to have our n-gram play happen in a textual context (that of an existing document) rather than in a blank text buffer. But we sacrificed most of that context in choosing to open a new window with each click. Even I, one of the project designers, have to use much of my attention during play to track the context into which selected words (from a higher-level window) will be inserted (into a window one or more below).

Second, we wanted to make the n-gram text playable rather than produced in batch mode. But our approach was to create "microbatches" from which the player could make partial selections. The n-gram processes that produced these batches remained invisible on a surface that, in the end, was as opaque as that of my high school poetry generator.

In short, *Regime Change* and *News Reader* can create engaging play experiences, with an interplay of intention and improvisation, for people who understand their operations. But the systems themselves do not help develop such understanding for those who do not already know the processes at work, so the most common audience experience is little different from that produced by a random cut-up technique. In the terms of this book, we fell seriously afoul of the *Tale-Spin* effect. Our systems' most interesting processes remain hidden beneath the surface, and play cannot reveal them.

If I were to do another n-gram text project of this sort (and I may) my first thought for an alternative design is one that, simply, delivers more fully on our initial design goals. Play would take place in the textual context where the results of play will reside. Rather than opening several layers of windows, I would begin by splitting a sentence apart at the point of the player's mouse click, with the play area defined by the space between the two sentence sections. Similarly, I would abandon batch mode entirely. Rather than the player choosing between potential multiword continuations from the point of the sentence split, the player would build the text word by word from that point, with individual word options generated by the n-gram model. At each stage, I would highlight the chain of words being used to make the selection (and perhaps use a different area of the screen to display an original context in which they appear).

Of course, as with any speculative digital media system, there is little we can learn from these proposals until they are further developed by authors and encountered by audiences. But my hope is that an approach of this sort could be more successful through its attention to the lessons I have learned in researching and writing this book. In the meantime, these projects are a further step into the area of play through textual logics—which itself is one area of investigation in nonsimulative processes for digital media.

Simulation, Language, and Fiction

I believe that computational processes are our most exciting tool for exploring the future of fiction. One future direction —explored in most of this book—is that of simulating fictional events, characters, and so on, in a manner analogous to the simplified, expressive ways that games (and other forms of playable media) simulate space. But as the electronic literature community has convincingly demonstrated, there are many interesting new fictional forms enabled by digital media that do not involve variability in story events. I believe this is also true for work that is more process intensive than most created by e-lit authors thus far.

I am interested in textual instruments in part because

of the mark they place in this largely unexplored landscape. Playful interaction through textual logics is one possible avenue for future fiction, poetry, and drama that employs computational processes to enable new audience experiences. But again, this is only one possible direction.

Part of what has surprised me in the years since *The Impermanence Agent* is that I have seen so little work along similar lines. The *Agent* is a fiction that uses processes not to model the development of its events but rather some aspect of its theme, which the processes then enact during the audience experience. As with *Regime Change* and *News Reader,* it is only a first, crude attempt. Yet it sets another marker in the ground of the vast possibility space of nonsimulative, process-intensive literary work.

As this chapter outlines, I think one of the major limitations of my projects in these instances is that they do not go far enough to make their processes legible. This is why I hope that others exploring this space will not turn away from games—as those with literary interests unfortunately often do with popular media—but rather closely investigate the possibilities they present for play. Nonsimulative literary processes will offer meaningful new experiences to their audiences only if they are understood on some level, and play is clearly one of the most powerful approaches for making processes legible, along with being a great pleasure for other reasons.

I am certainly not the only one involved in this exploration. A number of noteworthy projects are developing new modes of textual play. Three I have found particularly thought provoking are lead by Warren Sack, Chris Crawford, and Fox Harrell.

4. In *Conversation Map*, the last two of these use the same WordNet tool employed by *The Impermanence Agent*. Yet the similar functions of *Agonistics* steer away from WordNet's synonyms (and other conceptual groupings), instead tracking the exact …

Notes continued at end of this chapter.

Agonistics: A Language Game

Sack has created a number of projects that operate based on computational analysis of language. Perhaps the best known of these is his *Conversation Map* (Sack 1997–2000). This project brings together computational and conceptual tools developed in sociology, linguistics, and information visualization to create software for interacting with very large-scale conversations (VLSCs). Examples of these VLSCs are messages sent to Internet newsgroups and mailing lists. The *Conversation Map* analyzes a VLSC to discover which participants are responding to others, possible themes of the conversation, and "semantic network" mappings of terms that are used similarly.[4]

Just as *Regime Change* and *News Reader* make a first step from batch mode to play, Sack's *Agonistics* (2004) uses techniques much like those of *Conversation Map* but moves in the direction of play. Specifically, rather than focusing on the presentation of batch-processed results that can reveal aspects of the conversation, as *Conversation Map* does, *Agonistics* operates as a turn-based game. To participate, players use an email program or Usenet client to participate in a VLSC being analyzed by *Agonistics*—and also visit a web page in which that VLSC is visualized in terms of the game (figure 9.14). For example, during a show at ZKM in Germany, Sack made it possible to play by posting to alt.politics.bush (in English), fr.soc.politique (in French), or de.soc.politik.misc (in German), providing ZKM-hosted *Agonistics* pages for each of them.

Every participant in the conversation (even those who don't know about the game) is assigned a face. Players who engage in dialogue with others get points and see their face move closer to the center. Players who are seen by *Agonistics* as addressing a theme the group is discussing cause that theme to be shown and a sentence from their message to be highlighted at the top of the screen. As Sack's catalog description states, these rules have certain results:

> Winning players will be those who can (a) build a large coalition by engaging a number of people in dialogue; (b) promote a desired set of themes of discussion that are taken up by others in their posts; and, (c) articulate an influential opinion about the themes of discussion.

For Sack, *Agonistics* is an attempt to make a playable game that operates in a manner inspired by those philosopher linguists (he cites Chantal Mouffe, Gilles Deleuze, Bruno Latour, and others) who imagine democratic debate in gamelike rather than warlike terms. Obviously, such a game can never satisfy demands for a "quantifiable outcome," though it is certainly playable. I am particularly attracted to this project because Sack shows a way to create meaningful multiplayer language play. *Agonistics*

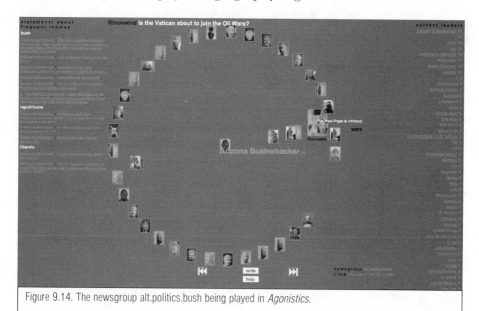

Figure 9.14. The newsgroup alt.politics.bush being played in *Agonistics*.

5. A feature that makes it possible to play *Scrabble* by treating the English language as a set of allowable codes rather than a means of expression.

operates using a model tied to the structure and meaning of language and discussion, rather than, say, using a particular dictionary as a razor for determining legal and illegal moves.[5] It is a far cry from using words as a skin for objects governed by spatial logics.

Deikto: A Language for Interactive Storytelling

Crawford, whose concept of "process intensity" has been a touchstone for this volume, is a towering figure in the field of computer game design. He authored one of the first books on the subject (Crawford 1984) and founded the field's most significant conference. But in the 1990s he abandoned the field of computer games, instead turning his full attention to the pursuit of interactive storytelling. The basis of his current approach is a new language, designed for play.

This language, Deikto, is meant as a response to the limited number of "verbs" presented in most interactive experiences. For example, in many graphical games, the only available verbs are "move" (accomplished by the means of navigation) and "attack" (carried out using the available weapon, toward whatever is in its path). Given that Crawford believes that interactivity is the essence of what computation makes possible for media, and that being able to act as a story's protagonist is the fundamental experience that interactive storytelling should offer, it was necessary for him to find a way for players to express much more complex, nuanced verbs.

The designers of *Façade,* as discussed earlier, sought to address a similar problem by allowing players to type whatever they please. The *Façade* system then attempts to interpret this, based on the current context, as one of a set number of discourse acts, which alter the state of the underlying system in particular ways. This opens up opportunities for a wide variety of player performance, but it also results in two types of failures. First, the system can fail to appropriately map player utterances to discourse acts. Second, the system may not be able to offer any meaningful response to even accurately recognized utterances, with results that are as unsatisfying as those from recognition failure. Crawford was determined to avoid failures of both sorts.

His alternative, Deikto, is a simplified language, with sentences built by players as their way of making moves in the game. Building such sentences creates a much larger possibility space for expression than what is found in standard games, even if the space of what can be said (made to appear on-screen) is smaller than that experienced when playing *Façade* or chatting with *Eliza/Doctor*. More important for Crawford, the options presented to a player building a sentence are those that have meaning in terms of the underlying system. This prevents unsatisfying failures and also provides a way for authors to guide players toward the actions that will produce meaningful system responses—in a much more subtle way than the techniques used in most games (e.g., graphical highlighting of particular objects or hints embedded in quest journal descriptions).

The original design of Deikto was diagrammatic, with lines representing connections between major elements and each utterance capable of expanding into a complex branching structure. This could produce sentences that were quite difficult to read.

As of this writing, Crawford has developed a new "linear Deikto" that intersperses connecting words—not interpreted by the system, and not necessarily grammatically correct—between elements constructed through menu-based interaction with the system, resulting in a more audience-interpretable text. This is critical in part because system-controlled actors also express their storyworld actions in Deikto, so the time needed for audience members to interpret Deikto determines some of the pacing of the story experience. Crawford's team provides an example of linear Deikto, presumably constructed as part of the work on an updated version of his landmark game *Balance of Power* (the new version is being developed using the Storytronics system, for which Deikto is at the heart). I have rendered Deikto elements in brackets:

> USA acts: [You] [start with this approach] to accomplish [Afghanistan hand over bin Laden]
>
> You decide: [I] [offer deal] to: [United Kingdom] in which [I] promises to ask [China] to do this: [China recognizes Taiwan] in return for which [United Kingdom] agrees to ask [Afghanistan] to do this: [Afghanistan hand over bin Laden]

This can be seen as a type of simulation—but it turns a number of common assumptions about the mapping between simulation and language on their heads. It marks a foray into a middle ground, a language designed both for audience interaction and internal operation. In taking this position, it offers the enticing possibility of audience members constructing complex actions without falling into the *Eliza* effect troubles that plague *Façade*—

or indeed, the "search for the verb" problems that have limited the appeal of much textual interactive fiction. It is certainly too early to say how influential Crawford's particular system will be (I write on the verge of its planned release), but I believe the ideas it explores will be crucial as we move forward.

Griot: Call and Response Narrative

Deikto could be seen as one example of a widespread mode of playful linguistic interaction: "call and response." Harrell pursues a different form of call and response in a strand of his digital media work. He relates this work's form of play to turn-taking traditions ranging from signifyin(g) and Capoeira Angola songs to Japanese linked poetry and Oulipian language games. In each of his works in this area, the system and audience co-create short texts—with the audience's contributions brief, and indeed often only a word. Such audience "calls" serve not only as part of the surface experience but also shape the operations of the underlying system, after which the system responds with another text, and frequently another invitation for the audience to make a call in turn.

The underlying system that Harrell uses to support these experiences is called *Griot*. It is designed to make it possible for authors to craft interactive computational narratives and new forms of what he terms "polymorphic discourse" based on the blending of thematically important concepts specified using Joseph Goguen's theory of algebraic semiotics. An author specifies theme domains as sets of axioms, phrase templates as possible output texts with open slots for the results of conceptual blends, and a narrative structure as a sequence for the

6. As discussed below, he is currently exploring alternative interfaces in which alphabetic text is not central. Harrell and his students apply the system not only to texts, but also to user identity representations across media (e.g. avatars, characters …

Notes continued at end of this chapter.

experience defined in terms of the number and types of narrative phrases that can be employed at a given stage. Each audience call is scanned for keywords, which are used to select the theme domains blended in each system response. His early examples focused on textual output, but his framework supports a broader definition of *text* that includes output in multiple modalities—for instance, a type of visual poetry described in this section.[6]

At the heart of the *Griot* system is his Alloy blending algorithm. This algorithm takes as input two algebraically represented concepts to be blended: a base concept that represents the shared structure between those concepts, and mappings between the base concept and other input concepts. It finds all of the possible ways to combine those concepts using a set of principles based on how the concepts are structured, how they map to each other, how much of the input concepts are preserved in the blend, and whether data types change or not as they are blended. *Griot* uses a subset of the full power of the Alloy approach—for example, often just outputting the most optimal blend—and Harrell continues to develop ways to use the generative power of blending to allow texts to create new, thematically constrained meanings on the fly (Goguen and Harrell forthcoming).

We can see specific examples of this in Harrell's variable narrative poem *The Girl with Skin of Haints and Seraphs* (2007). The narrative structure dictates that each poem begins with an abstract phrase and an orientation phrase. Possible opening phrases include "She begins her days (verb-clause)" and "Each morning foes called her (singular-noun)!" The domains include Africa, Europe, angels, demons, skin, and whiteness. The demons keywords include demon, pitchfork, devil, and brimstone. Demons axioms include "Person:demon spawns Emotion:fear" and "Object:fire burns Person:soul."

Harrell, in some cases working with his graduate students, is also extending this work into other types of material. In *Loss, Undersea* he creates a multimedia interactive narrative poem in which a character moving through a standard workday encounters a world submerging into the depths (figure 9.15). In work with Kenny Chow, *Griot* is being employed in a system for "visual renku"—in which the call and response can include some of the imagistic, diagrammatic, and conceptual connections that can be evoked between Chinese characters. In work with Jichen Zhu, *Griot* is part of a storytelling system that invites the audience to call out aspects of how the world is perceived

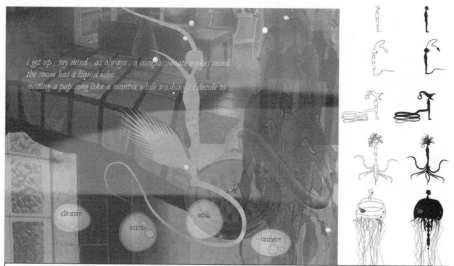

9.15. In *Loss, Undersea*, as a user selects emotion-driven actions for the character to perform, the character dynamically transforms—deep sea creature extensions protrude and calcify around him-and poetic text is generated narrating the loss of humanity and the human world undersea. *Griot* is used to implement blending in several ways. Structural blending (from algebraic semiotics) is the integration of multimedia elements according to diagrammatic and visual meanings, whereas conceptual blending (from cognitive linguistics) is the integration of logical data structures representing concepts.

and engaged by the focalized character, which not only shapes actions in the world but also the extent and tone of stream-of-consciousness character daydreams.

What I find fascinating is Harrell's work to make linguistic play an engagement with underlying conceptual models—while also organizing his system so that both the linguistic and conceptual structures are individually authored for each work. While his conceptual blending methods may require that concepts be represented in similar form in each work, this seems much more promising than assuming the same concepts will be appropriate for every work (an assumption that seems to foreclose one of art's most important possibilities).

Process and Fiction

The research and writing for this book has given me a much greater interest in the possibilities for simulation-oriented approaches to process-intensive fiction. Perhaps because of my training as a fiction writer, I was more inclined to image stories with fixed events, in which computational models opened variability related to language and theme. But the richness of the simulative tradition—much of it little discussed in the books I found on electronic literature and game design, both of which tend to focus on approaches with low process intensity—has convinced me of the potential of this direction. In the meantime, I hope that this chapter has convinced some who have largely seen computational approaches to fiction as synonymous with simulation that a much wider range of possibilities awaits our exploration.

Notes

1. Within this phrase I'm subsuming a discussion, around texts with instrumental qualities, that has used a variety of loose terminology. I'm also abandoning an earlier terminological distinction from my previous writing on this topic between "instrumental texts" and "textual instruments" (2003a, 2005). But the distinction between the ideas is still present here, simply without the confusingly similar terms.

2. I originally referred to these spatial logics as graphical logics. As I recall, the change in terminology was suggested by Espen Aarseth.

3. This is not to say that all combinations of graphics with spatial logics work equally well. For example, Jesper Juul (2005, 13–15) amusingly demonstrates that the logics of *Space Invaders* work well with both academic theories and television personalities—but this assumes that the relationship with both is antagonistic. And of course, the specifics of the fiction depicted by a set of graphics have a great impact on how we interpret spatial logics. Raph Koster (2004, 167–169), for example, demonstrates that the famously abstract game *Tetris* can be turned into a disturbing experience with graphics depicting human bodies being dropped into a gas chamber or mass grave.

4. In *Conversation Map*, the last two of these use the same WordNet tool employed by *The Impermanence Agent*. Yet the similar functions of *Agonistics* steer away from WordNet's synonyms (and other conceptual groupings), instead tracking the exact words and phrases introduced into the conversation.

5. A feature that makes it possible to play *Scrabble* by treating the English language as a set of allowable codes rather than a means of expression.

6. As discussed below, he is currently exploring alternative interfaces in which alphabetic text is not central. Harrell and his students apply the system not only to texts, but also to user identity representations across media (e.g. avatars, characters, and profiles). In other work, he is exploring possibilities for visual iconically-oriented, game-like interfaces that could be used to pass meaningful keywords to the system based on analysis of user behavior, with or without the user's awareness

Chapter 10
Conclusion

This book is certainly about the topics named in the subtitle—digital fictions, computer games, and software studies—but most of all it is about *expressive processing*.

Over the course of this book I have approached this topic from three perspectives. One perspective is oriented toward digital media creation, focused on the potential of understanding computational processes as a powerful tool for authorial expression. Another is oriented toward the critical study of digital media, focused on understanding the aspects of works that aren't apparent on the surface. Finally, I have also taken a political perspective, oriented toward the political stakes in some works and the political lessons to be learned from others. Here, in the conclusion of *Expressive Processing,* I will revisit each of these perspectives, bringing together ideas from throughout the book and suggesting some future directions.

Authors

We have reason to discuss digital media because of the already demonstrated ability of computational processes to define compelling new media forms—from the first-person shooter to the collaborative wiki. The specifics of the processes used to craft such media can shape the audience's experience as fundamentally as the specifics of the images used in a motion picture, if not more so. The harnessing of such specifics for authorial expression is one of the senses in which I mean the term *expressive processing*.

411

I am particularly interested in the potential of expressive processing within the realm of fiction: in creating flexible models of story events, producing a wide variety of language for characters and narration, and also for nonsimulative experiences that make language itself playable or enact procedural transformations that amplify fictional themes. As a fan of computer games, which have greatly developed the expressive simulation of space, I'm particularly interested in the possibilities of flexible models of fiction in this area.

Consider the open world computer role-playing game. In a game like *The Elder Scrolls IV: Oblivion* (Rolston, Howard, Cheng, et al. 2006) the world is simulated spatially, as in many other games. But it is also simulated in other senses. As I move through the world I collect ingredients I can use to make potions. As I make potions my skill in this area improves. As my skill increases I learn more about the possible effects of different ingredients. I can use the resulting potions or sell them into a simulated economy. What I get for selling them is connected to my abilities as a merchant (which get better the more I use them) and the simulated feelings other characters have about me (which can be altered by a conversation-simulation minigame as well as my faction affiliation, whether I'm holding my weapon unsheathed, and so on). And this is only one slice through the types of intersecting activities supported throughout the many spaces of *Oblivion*. In contrast to this vast, explorable world—through which players may move in many ways, with many different goals and paths toward them—the structure of the game's story is rigid. As Ken Rolston, *Oblivion*'s lead designer, writes:

> Exploring has more genuine suspense than following quest stages. There are so many

directions to turn, so many people to talk to, so many holes to crawl into, so many creatures and malefactors to chase after and righteously (or foully) slaughter. By contrast . . . I am forever running up against the boundaries of the plots I'm served, and disappointed in the choices of dialogue lines I'm picking from, and the avenues of inquiry I'm offered. I'm always conscious of the ways the characters and plots limit me—but in the choices of where to go and what to do when I'm exploring, the boundaries are less chafing and frustrating. (2009)

One might address this problem by simply abandoning any hope for fulfilling fictional experiences. Yet in fact, many players of role-playing games turn to this form precisely for an experience of fiction that is more developed and successful than that found in many other game genres. Rather than abandon fiction, it seems a better solution might be to begin to integrate narrative movement into the simulated world, using techniques of the sort explored during decades of research on story generation and interactive drama.

The same might be said of the ways that games like *Grand Theft Auto IV* (Benzies, Garbut, Fowler, et al. 2008) are "incoherent" in Jesper Juul's sense (2005, 123–130): their events make sense only with reference to the game rules, rather being explainable in terms of the fictional world. One can experience such incoherence from the outset of *Grand Theft Auto IV*. For example, in the first major mission the player must deliver his character's cousin to a card game, be on the lookout for loan sharks, and then drive the getaway car after they appear. If the player fails by getting shot by the loan sharks, his character winds up on the sidewalk outside a medical center, having been charged for services. The player needs to demonstrate the

1. The *uncanny valley*—a term coined by Japanese roboticist Masahiro Mori—indicates a phenomenon in representations of human characters. As representations approach reality they appear increasingly familiar up to a …

Notes continued at end of this chapter.

skills required in the mission, so the game encourages the player to try again. If the player tries again, exactly the same conversation leads into exactly the same mission. It's as though one jumped back to an earlier point in the story. But the money for the medical treatment is still gone—which can only be explained by viewing the cost of the treatment as a game-rules punishment for failing the mission, rather than the character's wallet somehow existing in a different time/space continuum. A more coherent world, and a more interesting experience for players redoing missions, would come from abstracting the elements of the mission (driving to, looking out, getting away) and using computational processes to produce a series of missions, coming one after another in fictional time, until the player succeeds in demonstrating a sufficient level of skill.

Both of these would represent steps toward addressing what I call the *unimplemented valley.* I suggest this term as a deliberate reminder of the *uncanny valley*—a phrase that I began to hear more often around the time that Sony was advertising the graphics processor in the PlayStation 2 as an "emotion engine."[1] The most common discussions of the uncanny valley suggest that our ability to identify with human characters is closely tied to their graphical representation. The idea of an emotion engine suggests that greater graphical fidelity is the key to greater emotional involvement. But the non-player characters who seem to actually elicit the greatest emotional engagement don't seem to be the ones with the best graphics, or the best just shy of the uncanny valley.

Consider *The Sims.* As I discussed in an earlier chapter, this game exhibits a remarkable closeness between the surface representation and the underlying simulation. I believe that we can form emotional attachments to Sims in part because they don't speak English. They speak Simlish, made up of symbols representing aspects of the underlying model of interests for Sims. Their graphical representations are actually rather simple, and their animation sequencing can be problematic, but they appear genuinely responsive to changing circumstance—within a limited range that is continually telegraphed to the audience by the design of the system—and this is highly engaging.

The emotion engine view of characters in digital media is the opposite. It is focused on giving characters more expressive faces, body models, and movements.[2] A mildly enlightened cousin of this view also wants to give characters more compelling things to say. But there is little said about the underlying models driving these characters, and the assumption generally seems to be of models simpler than those in *The Sims.* As a result, developing these more expressive faces is just creating a larger and larger gap between the surface and the underlying model, between the appearance of response and the actual ability to respond. Even if this vision succeeded completely at its aims, the eloquent lines expressively performed by these characters would have less meaning in the system of the resulting game than the iconographic Simlish of the Sims.

I propose an alternative. Our research in real-time graphics and natural language generation should be driven by dual aspirations. Not only should we aim for engaging expression but also for expression that communicates the evolving state of the underlying system. We should strive for the closeness of surface and simulation achieved by *The Sims,* but while moving

2. Andrew Stern has called this the "big hair era of games."

415

3. Moving beyond the most basic aspects of life is one of the stated goals of *The Sims 3,* which is not yet released (as of this writing) but is promising, in part because of the involvement of Richard Evans (whose work on *Black & White*'s AI was noted earlier).

both forward and sideways toward elements of human life other than the most basic.[3] Obviously, *Grand Theft Auto* missions that are represented within the simulated world and generated by system processes (rather than hard coded as data) would demonstrate only a small step in this direction—but every step matters.

More generally, just as the simulation of space opened up a wide variety of new game possibilities, so flexible models for story structure, character behavior, and fictional language have the potential to develop experiences that can't be fully imagined (and certainly can't be compellingly executed) using today's common approaches. *Façade* is one example of this—an interactive drama that would fall flat if implemented using quest flags and dialogue trees. As the previous chapter indicates, I am also interested in radically different, nonsimulative directions for expressive processing in the realm of fiction and language.

I believe we are now developing a generation of authors who understand both processes and media, who are ready to begin to seize these possibilities. Given my interest in turning our attention to processes, I find a particularly encouraging sign in the rapid development of the community around the Processing programming language initiated by Casey Reas and Ben Fry (2007). Their book begins with the assumption that computational processes are media-authoring tools—a place I hope more introductions to programming will start in the future.

Critics

Just as authors can seize a great opportunity by grappling with the newly available power of computational processes (an approach much less explored than crafting static words, sounds, or images), so critics of digital media have an opportunity to take their analysis further by turning their attention to the processes that enable such works to operate. The interpretation of processes, however, will require a new set of conceptual frameworks. Most models for digital media do not make a place for processes.

The major exception for digital fictions—Espen Aarseth's traversal function model—takes processes into account, but positions all of them as means of converting strings in the system into text experienced by audiences. This variety of textual transformations could be seen as a family of operational logics. My proposal is that, rather than assume these logics are central to all digital media, critical engagement should begin by identifying the actual logics operating in a particular work and the relationships between them. There are a number of reasons for this, not least what it makes possible for critics to understand about the relationships of a work's particular processes to histories of thought and communities of practice. For example, in this book I demonstrated how such an approach leads to a different interpretation of *Tale-Spin*—based on the connection of its processes and structures with the scruffy tradition of cognitive science and artificial intelligence— than those from critics such as Aarseth and Janet Murray.

I understand such connections as one of the things that processes can "express." At least as important, I am also concerned with the expression of ideas through processes, of which the author may or may not be aware—and which the author may or may not intend. The authors of *Brutus,* for instance, write of the significance of their logical model of betrayal to the system. But a careful examination of the system's operational logics reveals that the model of betrayal is in fact unnecessary in the generation of stories in the actually implemented version of *Brutus*. The concept of story generation that the system's processes express runs directly counter to the authorial account of the system. Not all cases are this dramatic, of course, but being able to interpret what processes express in this sense is another goal I have for the operational logics approach. More generally, I hope an examination of operational logics will become a useful tool in the development of the field of software studies as a whole, joining approaches discussed earlier in this book, ranging from Chris Crawford's process intensity to Ian Bogost's procedural rhetoric.

In addition to outlining and demonstrating the general approach of examining operational logics, this book has also presented three effects that can arise in the relationship between audience, surface, and system processes: the *Eliza, Tale-Spin,* and *SimCity* effects. While I have chosen to largely discuss these effects with reference to the systems for which they are named, they are general effects that one can identify in many types of digital media.

The *Eliza* effect is an initial illusion of system intelligence based on audience expectations. The illusion can be maintained by severely constrained interaction. During less restricted, playful interaction, on the other hand, the illusion breaks down in a manner determined by the shape of the underlying system. While the system for which this effect is named, *Eliza/Doctor,* is not now as ubiquitous as it was in my early days of computing, the experience of the *Eliza* effect is familiar in a variety contemporary forms, which need not be textual. Many game players, for example, are accustomed to NPCs that at first seem to have a general-purpose competence in moving through the game's simulated space. But even in the greatly simplified spaces presented by computer games, this illusion of general competence breaks down regularly—and NPCs end up caught in level geometry, failing at pathfinding when presented with objects as simple as ramps and so on. The specific breakdowns are shaped by the underlying systems of spatial simulation and character navigation. They could be avoided in a game that wanted to simplify space and movement sufficiently (obviously, they couldn't exist in a game like *Myst*), but relatively free-form interaction is also often important to creating the initial illusion. Luckily, in many games the illusion of NPC spatial intelligence is not so central to the experience that breakdown significantly diminishes the enjoyment of play.

The *Tale-Spin* effect, on the other hand, creates a surface illusion of system simplicity, without providing a means for interaction that would allow audiences to come to understand the more complex processes at work within the system. As a result, elegant and thought-provoking systems can appear arbitrary and shallow. This effect is perhaps most familiar to those who work in computer science research and/or digital art. For instance, I have written in a forthcoming book chapter about the intriguing project titled *Amy and Klara* by Marc Böhlen (2006a). This work takes the form of two pink boxes from which large robotic eyelike speakers emerge. Then synthesized speech begins, with one robot commenting on an article from *Salon.com*. This quickly devolves into an uninteresting fight—and audiences can lose interest. But when one begins to look at *Amy and Klara* as a system, with information provided by Böhlen (2006b), further elements become apparent. First, through slots in *Amy and Klara*'s boxes, two cameras look at each other. Second, each robot also houses noise-reducing microphones. The robots of *Amy and Klara,* in other words, not only "speak"; they also "see" and "listen."

In addition, the robots of *Amy and Klara* "read." Each performs a statistical evaluation of the contents of *Salon. com.* This is the starting point for their dialogues, as the Amy robot chooses a topic identified by her reading of *Salon.com* on which to offer a comment. A text-to-speech system turns Amy's comment (assembled by an agent architecture in part based on AIML) into sounds sent through her speaker. Because the robots do not share data, the Klara robot only "hears" Amy's comment through her microphone and must use automatic speech-recognition technology to turn it into text. Given the limitations of software systems for text-to-speech conversion and automatic speech recognition, misunderstandings begin almost immediately, thereby giving rise to disagreements. The "fights" seen by the audience, then, are just epiphenomena emerging from a much more interesting set of interacting processes. The operations of this assemblage of processes express something about recognition and misrecognition, communication and miscommunication, mechanism and emotion. But it is an expression to which the piece's audience experience provides almost no access, displaying the classic elements of the *Tale-Spin* effect.

The *SimCity* effect, in contrast to the other two effects, leads to audience understanding of the operations of an underlying system. It is most interesting for works with a relatively complex set of internal processes—often a procedural representation of what is presented on the surface (such as a fictional world). This begins much as the *Eliza* effect, as an outgrowth of audience expectation. But rather than the breakdown produced by interaction in the *Eliza* effect, in which it is revealed that there is a significant disconnect between initial expectation and system operations, the connection between the elements presented on the surface and those present in the system processes and data allows a different outcome. Through the *SimCity* effect the audience can use observation and experimentation to transition from an understanding based on expectation to one that corresponds more with the underlying system. This not only creates compelling media experiences but also is a powerful way for the public to come to understand complex software systems. Interestingly, relatively complex cases of the *SimCity* effect appear to be on the rise. It can be seen not only in relatively obvious locations (e.g., real-time strategy games) but also, in somewhat different form, in the best cases of the spread of simulation mechanics to new game genres (e.g., the example of *Oblivion,* discussed earlier). As this happens, we are coming to better understand the design challenge of crafting an experience that is both enjoyable and allows an audience to come to understand what Will Wright refers to as an "elaborate system with thousands of variables." This knowledge sets the necessary groundwork for computer games to come into their own, taking the next step away from the expectations of other forms of media and opening a new range of possibilities in genre.

In fact, I believe we come to the point at which the term *game* becomes increasingly problematic for what we wish to describe. This is especially true given the tendency among academics and others to refer to the examples I find most compelling as "not games" or "border cases" (as I have discussed elsewhere; see Wardrip-Fruin 2005). *SimCity* and other simulations are considered toys, not games. Role-playing games, especially of the tabletop and online varieties, are considered borderline because they don't reach a quantifiable end. Experiences like *Façade* are interactive dramas, not games. And so on.

Perhaps the worst thing about such discussions is that it turns attention to a truly boring question: "Is this a game?" This is one of the reasons that I have begun to use a different term when I want to be especially clear that I am speaking broadly, including many "not games" and "border cases": *playable media*. I like it because it turns our attention to more interesting questions—such as, "How is this played?" Also, while it is broader than the word *game*, it is more specific than terms like *interactive*. And while we might debate whether a love letter or *SimCity* is more interactive (believe me, some have), we're unlikely to argue over which is more playable. From there we can move on to the interesting work of interpretation.

Citizens

In our society we are surrounded by software—from everyday Google searches to the high stakes of Diebold voting machines. We need to be prepared to engage software critically, accustomed to interpreting descriptions of processes, able to understand common pitfalls, and aware of what observing software's output reveals and conceals about its inner workings. With this in mind, in *Expressive Processing* I have tried to address the politics of processes in a few ways.

A small part of my discussion has focused on explicitly political systems. Most notably, I looked at a system created by Robert Abelson and his students designed as a simulation of political ideology. While the system processes were intended to be ideologically neutral, with each ideology only represented as data, a close examination revealed specific forms of ideological reasoning encoded into the operational logics as well. Data could make Abelson's system a "Goldwater machine," but not a "Stevenson machine." Learning to understand the ideologies encoded in models and processes, especially when unacknowledged by system authors, is an important future pursuit for software studies.

In this book I have also used fictions and games to provide specific grounding for politically significant software concepts that are often described only in the abstract. In particular, I discussed how the problems of false positives and false negatives make certain forms of government surveillance unworkable, but this can be difficult to grasp in the abstract. The problem is more easily understood (and more amusing to think about) in the context of *The Restaurant Game,* in which similar techniques fail to detect anything unusual as a simulated customer and waitress fill a restaurant with orders for pie and beer.

For the most part, however, I have largely concentrated on the ability to think critically about software and providing specific grounding for particular types of understanding that I view as crucial. For example, while it is a truism that software can initially appear to act with more intelligence than is present in its internal models, it is more vivid and helpful to see the specifics of how *Eliza/ Doctor* plays on our expectations to create its illusion.

Similarly, while we might say, abstractly, that problems of commonsense knowledge limit the possibilities for artificial intelligence systems meant to emulate human thought, it is more memorable to examine the storytelling program *Minstrel* as it portrays a hungry knight eating a princess. In other words, I view the understandings of software important to the critic as also important to the citizen. And perhaps this is one of the main reasons to do critical work on digital media (and train students to do it).

To be better citizens we need to understand software critically. I believe examining digital fictions and computer games is a powerful way to gain that understanding—provided, of course, they are examined with an eye toward expressive processing.

Notes

1. The *uncanny valley*—a term coined by Japanese roboticist Masahiro Mori—indicates a phenomenon in representations of human characters. As representations approach reality they appear increasingly familiar up to a certain point, after which (but before full realism) there is a tendency for humans to find it more difficult to identify with the representations the more realistic they become. They look almost right, but disturbingly wrong.

2. Andrew Stern has called this the "big hair era of games."

3. Moving beyond the most basic aspects of life is one of the stated goals of *The Sims 3*, which is not yet released (as of this writing) but is promising, in part because of the involvement of Richard Evans (whose work on *Black & White*'s AI was noted earlier).

Afterword

An Experiment in Peer Review

When I completed the first draft of this book (in early 2008) things took an unusual turn. I had reached the time in traditional academic publishing when the press sends the manuscript out for peer review: anonymous commentary by a few scholars that guides the final revisions (and decisions). But we decided to do something different with *Expressive Processing*: we asked the community around an academic blog—Grand Text Auto—to participate in an open, blog-based peer review at the same time as the anonymous review.

Blogging had already changed how I worked as a scholar and creator of digital media. Reading blogs started out as a way to keep up with the field between conferences, and I soon realized that blogs also contain raw research, early results, and other useful information that never gets presented at conferences. Of course, that is just the beginning. I cofounded Grand Text Auto, in 2003, for an even more important reason: blogs can foster community. And the communities around blogs can be more open and welcoming than those at conferences and festivals, drawing in people from industry, universities, the arts, and the general public. Interdisciplinary conversations happen on blogs that are more diverse and sustained than any I've seen in person.

Given that digital media is a field in which major expertise is located outside the academy (like many other fields, from noir cinema to Civil War history), the Grand Text Auto community has been invaluable for my work. In fact, while writing the manuscript for *Expressive Processing* I found myself regularly citing blog posts and comments, both from Grand Text Auto and elsewhere.

The blog-based review project started when Doug Sery, my editor at the MIT Press, brought up the question of who would peer-review the *Expressive Processing* manuscript. I immediately realized that the peer review I most wanted was from the community around Grand Text Auto. I said this to Doug, who was already one of the blog's readers, and he was enthusiastic. Next I contacted Ben Vershbow at the Institute for the Future of the Book to see if we could adapt their CommentPress tool for use in an ongoing blog conversation (figure 11.1). Ben not only agreed but also became a partner in conceptualizing, planning, and producing the project. With the ball rolling, I asked the Committee on Research of the University

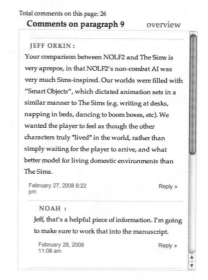

9 In *The Sims* the problem comes from something other than the logic of FSMs. Rather than animations driven by FSMs that are segregated according to character goals, in *The Sims* actions and their animations are compartmentalized via smart objects (e.g., a "shower object" contains information about its impact on the Sim and how it is used, including a pointer to the animation involved). This is another approach to managing complexity using a simple structure with limited points of interconnection — one which I will discuss further in a later chapter. This form of compartmentalization made it possible to manage the complexity created by the massive number of expansion packs for *The Sims* (each of which introduced many new objects) but also, as Perlin observed, resulted in breakdowns similar to those seen in NOLF2.

10 Avoiding these compartmentalization-driven breakdowns requires an approach to managing complexity that doesn't isolate each action from the rest of the world. As it happens, I have already outlined such an approach: *Tale-Spin*'s. Each planbox in *Tale-Spin* is able to access a shared memory space — and a character only attempts to alter the world to suit planbox preconditions if those conditions aren't already met. So, for example, a *Tale-Spin* planbox for playing with a baby might have a precondition of holding the baby. If the *Tale-Spin* character is already feeding the baby, rather than returning to a neutral state

Total comments on this page: 26
Comments on paragraph 9   overview

JEFF ORKIN :
Your comparison between NOLF2 and The Sims is very apropos, in that NOLF2's non-combat AI was very much Sims-inspired. Our worlds were filled with "Smart Objects", which dictated animation sets in a similar manner to The Sims (e.g. writing at desks, napping in beds, dancing to boom boxes, etc). We wanted the player to feel as though the other characters truly "lived" in the world, rather than simply waiting for the player to arrive, and what better model for living domestic environments than The Sims.

February 27, 2008 8:22 pm   Reply »

NOAH :
Jeff, that's a helpful piece of information. I'm going to make sure to work that into the manuscript.

February 28, 2008 11:08 am   Reply »

Figure 11.1. Screenshot detail of CommentPress in use during the blog-based peer review of *Expressive Processing*. The review took place on Grand Text Auto (http://grandtextauto.org), a blog I coauthor with Mary Flanagan, Michael Mateas, Nick Montfort, Andrew Stern, and Scott Rettberg.

of California at San Diego's Academic Senate for some support (which it generously provided) and approached Jeremy Douglass (of that same university's newly formed Software Studies initiative), who also became a core collaborator—especially (and appropriately) for the software-related aspects.

Our project started with some lessons learned from examining two earlier, highly influential projects involving the Institute for the Future of the Book. These projects both explore innovative models for online peer review and community participation in scholarly work. The first, *Gamer Theory*, was a collaboration with author McKenzie Wark. This placed the entire initial manuscript of Wark's book online, attracting a community that undertook distributed peer review and section-specific discussion with the author. The second project, *The Googlization of Everything*, is (as of this writing) an ongoing collaboration with author Siva Vaidhyanathan. While Wark's project was successful, it lacked the high-level flow of conversation through time that has been found a particularly powerful way to engage the public in ideas. In response, Vaidhyanathan is going to the other extreme: researching and writing the book "in public" via a blog sponsored by the institute, so that the entire project is based in conversation through time. As with Wark's project, attention from the public, media, and scholarly communities has been swift to arrive as well as largely positive.

Nevertheless, I felt there was a feature of these projects that made them both problematic as models for the future of peer review and scholarly publishing. Both of them sought to build new communities from scratch, via widespread publicity, for their projects. But this cannot be done for every scholarly publication—and a number of fields already have existing online communities that function well, connecting thinkers from universities, industry, nonprofits, and the general public. I thought a more successful and sustainable model would bring together:

- the paragraph-level commenting and discussion approach of *Gamer Theory*

- the emphasis on conversation through time of *The Googlization of Everything*

- the context of an already-existing, publicly accessible community discussing ideas in that field.

This is precisely what we attempted with the blog-based peer review for this book. Further, because we also undertook this project in collaboration with a scholarly press, carrying out a traditional peer review in parallel with the blog-based peer review, we were also able to compare the two forms. I found the results enlightening.

Four Surprises

The review was structured as part of the ongoing flow of conversation on the Grand Text Auto blog. Because the book's draft manuscript was already structured around chapters and sections, we decided to post a new section each weekday morning. Comments were left open on all the sections—not just the most recent—so while commenting was often most active on *Expressive Processing* posts from that day and one or two prior, there was also frequently comment activity taking place in several other areas of the draft manuscript. These posts and comments were interspersed, both in time and spatial arrangement on the page, with Grand Text Auto posts and comments on other topics.

There were, of course, a number of outcomes that I expected from the project—the ones that motivated me to undertake it in the first place. I anticipated a good quality of comments, along the lines of those regularly left by Grand Text Auto readers responding to posts that weren't part of the peer review. I expected those comments would not only be interesting but also in many cases flow directly into possible manuscript revisions. And at a different level, I thought the process was likely to provide another useful data point as people inquire about and experiment with new models of peer review.

All of this took place as planned, but the project held a number of surprises as well.

Review as Conversation

My first surprise came during the review's initial week. In particular, it was during discussion of a section that was, in that draft, located in the introduction (it has since moved to the fourth chapter). Perhaps it shouldn't have been unexpected, given my previous experience with blog comments—and my stated goals for the review project— but my assumptions about the structure of a "review" may have been in the way.

I wrote about this in one of my "meta" posts during the course of the review:

> In most cases, when I get back the traditional, blind peer review comments on my papers and book proposals and conference submissions, I don't know who to believe. Most issues are only raised by one reviewer. I find myself wondering, "Is this a general issue that I need to fix, or just something

that rubbed one particular person the wrong way?" I try to look back at the piece with fresh eyes, using myself as a check on the review, or sometimes seek the advice of someone else involved in the process (e.g., the papers chair of the conference).

But with this blog-based review it's been a quite different experience. This is most clear to me around the discussion of "process intensity" in section 1.2. If I recall correctly, this began with Nick [Montfort]'s comment on paragraph 14. Nick would be a perfect candidate for traditional peer review of my manuscript—well-versed in the subject, articulate, and active in many of the same communities I hope will enjoy the book. But faced with just his comment, in anonymous form, I might have made only a small change. The same is true of Barry [Atkins]'s comment on the same paragraph, left later the same day. However, once they started the conversation rolling, others agreed with their points and expanded beyond a focus on *The Sims*—and people also engaged me as I started thinking aloud about how to fix things—and the results made it clear that the larger discussion of process intensity was problematic, not just my treatment of one example. In other words, the blog-based review form not only brings in more voices (which may identify more potential issues), and not only provides some "review of the reviews" (with reviewers weighing in on the issues raised by others), but is also, crucially, a *conversation* (my proposals for a quick fix to the discussion of one example helped unearth the breadth and seriousness of the larger issues with the section).

On some level, all this might be seen as implied with the initial proposal of bringing together manuscript review and blog commenting (or already clear in the discussions, by Kathleen Fitzpatrick and others, of "peer to peer review"). But, personally, I didn't foresee it. I expected to compare the recommendation[s] of commenters on the blog and the anonymous, press-solicited reviewers—treating the two basically the same way.

> But it turns out that the blog commentaries will
> have been through a social process that, in some
> ways, will probably make me trust them more.
> (Wardrip-Fruin 2008)

In the end, as I will discuss below, I did not have to decide whether to trust the blog-based or anonymous comments more. But this does not lessen the importance of the conversational nature of blog-based peer review. I'm convinced that the ability to engage with one's reviewers conversationally, and have them engage with each other in this way, is one of the key strengths of this approach. It should be noted, however, that the conversational nature of the blog-based review process also had a less-positive side, which produced my second surprise.

Time Inflexibility

Like many people, the demands on my time fluctuate over the course of weeks and months. I hit periods during the *Expressive Processing* review when I barely had time to read the incoming comments—and certainly couldn't respond to them in a timely manner. For anonymous reviews this generally isn't an issue. When one is required to respond to such reviews, and one isn't always, it is generally possible to ask for some additional time. It isn't a problem if a busy period takes one's attention away from the review process entirely.

But the flow of blog conversation is mercilessly driven by time. While it is possible to try to pick up threads of conversation after they have been quiet for a few days, the results are generally much less successful than when one responds within a day or, better yet, an hour. I hadn't anticipated or planned for this.

I remember speaking to Wark about his project

when we were both at a gathering for the University of Southern California's *Vectors* journal—itself a fascinating set of online publishing experiments. He mentioned a number of aspects of his project that I chose to emulate, but at the time I didn't consider one that I now wish I had pursued: carrying out the participatory review during a period of reduced teaching (a sabbatical, in his case, if I recall correctly).

While I learned much from the *Expressive Processing* review on Grand Text Auto, I am certain I could have learned more if I had been able to fully engage in discussion throughout the review period, rather than waxing and waning in my available time. Of course, generally pursuing blog-based review with time for full conversational engagement would require a shift in thinking around universities. It isn't uncommon for authors to request release time for book writing and revisions, yet it has almost never been requested in order to participate more fully in community peer review. I hope that will change in the future.

Comparison with Press-Solicited Reviews

One concern expressed repeatedly about the blog-based review form—by blog commenters, outside observers, and myself—is that its organization around individual sections might contribute to a "forest for the trees" phenomenon. While individual sections and their topics are important to a book, it is really by the wider argument and project that most books are judged. I worried the blog-based review form might be worse than useless if its impact was to turn authors (myself included) away from major, systemic issues with manuscripts and toward the section-specific comments of blog visitors with little sense of the book's project.

My concerns in this area became particularly acute as the review went on. A growing body of comments seemed to be written without an understanding of how particular elements fit into the book's wider frame. As I read these comments I found myself thinking, "Should I remind this person of the way this connection was drawn, at length, in the introduction?" Yet I largely restrained myself, in no small part because I wanted to encourage engagement from those who had expertise to offer particular sections, but not time to participate in the entire, extended review process. At the same time, I worried that even those who had been loyal participants all along were becoming less able to offer big-picture feedback (especially after a month had passed since the review of the book's introduction, where I laid out the overall argument at length). The commenters feared they were losing the thread as well. Ian Bogost, for example, wrote a post on his own blog that reads, in part:

> The peer review part of the project seems to be going splendidly. But here's a problem, at least for me: I'm having considerable trouble reading the book online. A book, unlike a blog, is a lengthy, sustained argument with examples and supporting materials. A book is textual, of course, and it can thus be serialized easily into a set of blog posts. But that doesn't make the blog posts *legible* as a book. For my part, I am finding it hard to follow the argument all the way through. (2008)

When the press-solicited anonymous reviews came in, however, they turned this concern on its head. This is because the blog-based and anonymous reviews both pointed to the same primary revision for the manuscript:

distributing the main argument more broadly through the different chapters and sections, rather than concentrating it largely in a dense opening chapter. What had seemed like a confirmation of one of our early fears about this form of review—the possibility of losing the argument's thread— was actually a successful identification, by the blog-based reviewers, of a problem with the manuscript also seen by the anonymous reviewers.

That said, the anonymous reviewers solicited by the press also did seem to gain certain insights by reading the draft manuscript all at once, rather than spread over months. All of them, for instance, commented that the tone of the introduction was out of character with the rest of the book. The blog-based reviewers offered almost no remarks comparing chapters to one another— perhaps because they experienced the manuscript more as sections than chapters. Still, as I will discuss below, they also offered much more detailed section-specific commentary, much of it quite useful, than it would be possible to expect from press-solicited anonymous reviews.

And even though it is an approach to books that the academy views less seriously (you get tenure for a book with an important overall argument), the fact is that many book readers approach texts the same way occasional visitors to Grand Text Auto approached my draft manuscript: in relatively isolated pieces. Especially among academic readers, amusingly enough, there is a tendency to seek all the relevant writing about a particular topic— and then strategically read the sections that relate to one's own project. I believe it is critical for books to hold up to both kinds of reading (I hope this book manages it) and I see the dual-peer-review process as a good way of getting responses from both kinds of readers.

Generosity with Expertise

It may sound strange to say, but my final surprise is that I find myself with so many people to thank—and so much indebted to a number of them. Undertaking the anonymous, press-solicited review of a book manuscript is already a generous act. (My press-solicited reviewers were particularly generous, offering thoughtful and helpful comments it must have been time-consuming to produce.) But at least the system is designed to provide some acknowledgment for such reviewers: perhaps free books or an honorarium, a curriculum vitae line indicating that one reviews for the press (a recognition of expertise), and the completion of some widely understood service to the field (which is an expectation of most academic jobs).

Participants in the blog-based review of *Expressive Processing,* on the other hand, received no such acknowledgment. And yet their comments contributed a huge amount to improving the manuscript and my understanding of the field. Further, they contributed things that it would have been nearly impossible to get from press-solicited reviews.

This isn't because presses choose poor reviewers or because the reviewers don't work hard. Rather, it is because the number of manuscripts that require review dictates that only a few reviewers should consider each manuscript. Otherwise, the burden of manuscript review would impede the completion of other work.

When only a few reviewers look at each manuscript, each will have some areas of relevant expertise. But for many manuscripts, especially interdisciplinary ones, there will be many topics discussed for which none of the reviewers possess particular expertise. There's no real way around this.

Blog-based review, for me, created a different experience. Early in the review when I posted a section about *Prince of Persia: The Sands of Time,* a topic on which none of my press-solicited reviewers commented, commentary and conversation quickly developed involving three scholars who had written about it (Barry Atkins, Drew Davidson, and Jason Rhody) as well as other blog readers who had played and thought about the game. This happened repeatedly, with humanities and social science scholars, digital media designers, computer science researchers, game players, and others offering helpful thoughts and information about everything from dialogue system interface specifics to statistical artificial intelligence models.

As the review progressed, deep expertise also showed itself on another level, as the manuscript began to get comments and host conversation involving people who rarely review academic manuscripts: the creators of the projects being discussed. This led to some of the best exchanges in the review process, including people like Scott Turner (*Minstrel*), Jeff Orkin (*F.E.A.R.* and *The Restaurant Game*), and Andrew Stern (*Façade*). The last person mentioned in the previous sentence, as some readers of this afterword may realize, is also a Grand Text Auto blogger. The mix between blog reader and blog coauthor comments was also present for the creators of examples I touched on more briefly, as with reader Richard Evans (*Black & White*) and coauthor Nick Montfort (*nn*).

Some have asked me if the involvement of project

authors in the review is likely idiosyncratic, possible only for someone writing on a topic like mine. Certainly on this front, I feel that digital media is a lucky area in which to work because so many of the authors of field-defining projects are still alive (and online). Yet I think the same sort of blog-based review involving project creators could happen for authors in many other areas. For example during the 2007 Writers Guild of America strike, a light was shown on the involvement of many movie and television writers in blog communities. I would not be at all surprised if such writers, already engaged in reading and writing on blogs, took an interest in academic writing that discusses their work—especially as part of a blog-based peer review that might generate revisions before the text is put into print. But only further experimentation will reveal if I am correct in this.

Another question, posed in response to the same "meta" post mentioned earlier, is whether this form of review only works because I have already developed some reputation in my field (e.g., from editing other books). My belief is that my personal reputation is not the primary issue. Rather, it is Grand Text Auto's reputation that matters. It makes sense to do a blog-based review because we have, in blogs, already-existing online communities that attract university-based experts, industry-based experts, and interested members of the public. The way we use blogs also already encourages discussion and questioning.[1] Of course, widely read blogs won't want to be completely taken over by manuscript review, but I can imagine them hosting two or three a year, selected for their level of interest or because they are written by one of the blog's authors.

It is possible that the interest of blog readers would flag

1. This connects to my main critique of the Gamer Theory project: starting a new site for each manuscript reviewed, and gathering a new community to that site, is not a sustainable model for review, and not likely to result in the best possible …

Notes continued at end of this chapter.

under such circumstances. But nothing in my experience points to that. I think there is a hunger, on both sides, to connect the kinds of inquiry and expertise that exist inside universities and outside of them. Blogs are one of our most promising connection points—and blog-based peer review offers one simple way for the two groups to contribute to common work. If my experience is any guide, this can elicit remarkably generous responses. Especially given that I am a public employee (I work for the University of California at Santa Cruz), I look forward to pursuing this type of public connection further in the future.

Note

1. This connects to my main critique of the Gamer Theory project: starting a new site for each manuscript reviewed, and gathering a new community to that site, is not a sustainable model for review, and not likely to result in the best possible signal-to-noise ratio. Inserting a new form of review into the ongoing flow of conversation on an existing blog can address these issues.

References

Aarseth, Espen J. 1997. *Cybertext: Perspectives on ergodic literature*. Baltimore: Johns Hopkins University Press.

———. 2004. Beyond the frontier: Quest games as post-narrative discourse. In *Narrative across media: The languages of storytelling (frontiers of narrative series)*, ed. Marie-Laure Ryan. Lincoln: University of Nebraska Press.

Abelson, Robert P. 1963. Computer simulation of "hot" cognition. In *Computer simulation of personality: Frontier of psychological theory*, ed. Silvan S. Tomkins and Samuel Messick, 277–298. Somerset, NJ: John Wiley and Sons.

———. 1973. The structure of belief systems. In *Computer models of thought and language*, ed. Roger C. Schank and Kenneth Colby, 287–339. San Francisco: W. H. Freeman Co.

———. 1975. The reasoner and the inferencer don't talk much to each other. In *TINLAP '75: Proceedings of the 1975 workshop on theoretical issues in natural language processing*, 3–7. Morristown, NJ: Association for Computational Linguistics.

Abelson, Robert P., and J. Douglass Carroll. 1965. Computer simulation of individual belief systems. *American Behavioral Scientist* 8 (9): 24–30.

Agre, Philip E. 1997. *Computation and human experience*. Cambridge: Cambridge University Press.

Akst, Daniel. 2004. Computers as authors? Literary luddites unite! *New York Times*, November 22, E1. American Civil Liberties Union. 2008. ACLU watch list counter. <http://www.aclu.org/privacy/spying/watchlistcounter.html>.

Anderson, Timothy, Marc Blank, Bruce Daniels, and Dave Lebling. 1980. *Zork: The great underground empire*. Z-machine file. Infocom.

Atkins, Barry. 2003. *More than a game: The computer game as fictional form*. Manchester: Manchester University Press.

———. 2007. Killing time: Time past, time present, and time future in *Prince of Persia: The Sands of Time*. In *Videogame, player, text*, ed. Barry Atkins and Tanya Krzywinska, 237-253. Manchester: Manchester University Press.

Badler, Norman I., Cary B. Phillips, and Bonnie Lynn Webber. 1993. *Simulating humans: Computer graphics animation and control*. New York: Oxford University Press.

Barton, Matt. 2008. *Dungeons & desktops: The history of computer role-playing games*. Wellesley, MA: A K Peters, Ltd.

Bass, Len, and Bonnie E. John. 2001. Supporting usability through software architecture. *Computer* 34 (10): 113–115.

Bateman, Chris. 2006. *Game writing: Narrative skills for videogames*. Rockland, MA: Charles River Media, Inc. Bateman, Chris, Richard Boon, Bob Buckley, Richard Dansky, Wendy Despain, Raphael van Lierop, and James Swallow. 2003. IGDA's guide to writing for games. Tech. Rep., International Game Developers Association.

Bates, Joseph. 1994. The role of emotion in believable agents. *Communications of the ACM* 37 (7): 122–125.

Benzies, Leslie, Aaron Garbut, Adam Fowler, Alexander Roger, Obbe Vermeij, Imran Sarwar, William Mills, Dan Houser, and Rupert Humphries. 2008. *Grand Theft Auto IV*. Xbox 360 and PlayStation 3. Edinburgh: Rockstar North, Rockstar Games.

Black, Maurice J. 2002. The art of code. PhD diss., University of Pennsylvania.

Blakely, John, Andrew Sites, Bruce A. Ferguson, Rich Waters, Scott Hartsman, Joe Shoopack, Stuart Compton, Daniel Lewis, Heather Sowards, Steve Danuser, Chris Cao, and Joseph Russo. 2004. *EverQuest II*. Windows client, massively multiplayer servers. Sony Online Entertainment.

Blumberg, Bruce M. 1997. Old tricks, new dogs: Ethology and interactive creatures. PhD diss., Massachusetts Institute of Technology.

Bogost, Ian. 2006. *Unit operations: An approach to videogame criticism*. Cambridge, MA: MIT Press.

———. 2007. *Persuasive games: The expressive power of videogames*. Cambridge, MA: MIT Press.

———. 2008. Reading online sucks: Reflections on scholarly writing on the web. <http://www.bogost.com/blog/reading_online_sucks.shtml>.

Böhlen, Marc. 2006a. Amy and Klara. In *Procedings of ISEA 2006*, ed. Steve Deitz. <http://01sj.org/content/view/261/49/>.

———. 2006b. Amy and Klara: Towards machinic male-dicta and synthetic hissy fits. <http://www.realtechsupport.org/new_works/male-dicta.html>.

Bolter, Jay D., and Diane Gromala. 2003. *Windows and mirrors: Interaction design, digital art, and the myth of transparency*. Cambridge, MA: MIT Press.

Bootz, Philippe. 2006. *Les basiques: La littérature numérique*. Leonardo/Olats. http://www.olats.org/livresetudes/basiques/litteraturenumerique/basiquesLN.php . .

Bringsjord, Selmer, and David A. Ferrucci. 2000. *Artificial intelligence and literary creativity: Inside the mind of Brutus, a storytelling machine*. Hillsdale, NJ: Lawrence Erlbaum Associates.

Brooks, Rodney A. 1990. Elephants don't play chess. *Robotics and Autonomous Systems* 6 (1–2): 3–15.

Buckles, Mary Ann. 1985. Interactive fiction: The computer storygame *Adventure*. PhD diss., University of California at San Diego.

Cage, David, Guillaume de Fondaumière, Christophe Vivet, Damien Castelltort, Christophe Brusseaux, Josselin Authelet, and Sophie Buhl. 2005. *Indigo prophecy*. Multiple platforms. Quantic Dream, Atari Europe.

Callaci, Irene. 2000. *Dangerous curves*. Z-machine file.

Calvino, Italo, and William Weaver. 1974. *Invisible cities*. Orlando, FL: Harcourt.

Cayley, John. 1995. *Book unbound: Indra's net VI*. Wellsweep Press. <http://homepage.mac.com/shadoof/net/in/incat>.html.

———. 1999. *windsound*. <http://www.shadoof.net/in/windsound.html>.

———. 2002a. The code is not the text (unless it is the text). *Electronic Book Review*. <http://www.electronicbookreview.com/thread/electropoetics/literal>.

———. 2002b. *riverIsland*. <http://www.shadoof.net/in/riverisland.html>.

———. 2002c. riverIsland. Text accompanying download of *riverIsland*.

Champandard, Alex J. 2007. Memento, temporal coherence, and debugging planners. <http://aigamedev.com/essays/memento-debugging-planner>.

Church, Doug. 1999. Formal abstract design tools. *Game Developer* 3 (28).

Colley, Steve, and Greg Thompson. 1973–1974. *Maze war*. Imlacs terminals at NASA Ames Research Center and MIT.

Costikyan, Greg. 1984. *Toon: The cartoon roleplaying game*. Austin: Steve Jackson Games.

———. 1993. *Bestial acts: A roleplaying game / a drama*. Los Angeles: Alarums and Excursions.

———. 2006. Process intensity. <http://www.manifestogames.com/node/2348>.

Crawford, Chris. 1984. *The art of computer game design*. Berkeley, CA, USA: Osborne/McGraw-Hill.

———. 1987. Process intensity. *Journal of Computer Game Design* 1(5).

———. 2003. *The art of interactive design: A euphonious and illuminating guide to building successful software.* San Francisco: No Starch Press.

———. 2004. *Chris Crawford on interactive storytelling.* Berkeley: New Riders Games.

Crowther, William, and Donald Woods. 1976. *Adventure.*

Cruz-Neira, Carolina, Daniel J. Sandin, and Thomas A. DeFanti. 1993. Surround-screen projection-based virtual reality: The design and implementation of the CAVE. In *Siggraph '93: Proceedings of the 20th annual conference on computer graphics and interactive techniques*, 135–142. New York: ACM Press.

Davidson, Drew. 2008. Well played: Interpreting *Prince of Persia: The Sands of Time. Games and Culture* 3 (3–4): 356–386.

Dehn, Natalie. 1981a. Memory in story invention. In *Proceedings of the third annual conference of the cognitive science society*, 213–215. Berkeley: Cognitive Science Society.

———. 1981b. Story generation after *Tale-Spin.* In *Proceedings of the 7th International Joint Conference on Artificial Intelligence*, 16–18. Vancouver: International Joint Conference on Artificial Intelligence.

Domike, Steffi, Michael Mateas, and Paul Vanouse. 2003. The recombinant history apparatus presents: *Terminal Time.* In *Narrative intelligence*, ed. Michael Mateas and Phoebe Sengers. Amsterdam: John Benjamins Publishing Co.

Douglass, Jeremy. 2007. Command lines: Aesthetics and technique in interactive fiction and new media. PhD diss., University of California at Santa Barbara.

Dow, Steven. 2008. Understanding user engagement in immersive and interactive stories. PhD diss., Georgia Institute of Technology.

Eco, Umberto. 1994. *The name of the rose: Including postscript to the name of the rose.* Fort Washington, PA: Harvest Books.

Edwards, Paul N. 1997. *The closed world: Computers and the politics of discourse in cold war America.* Cambridge, MA: MIT Press.

Ellison, Brent. 2008. Defining dialogue systems. *Gamasutra.* <http://www.gamasutra.com/view/feature/3719/defining_dialogue_systems.php>.

Engelbart, Douglas C., and William K. English. 1968. A research center for augmenting human intellect. *AFIPS conference proceedings, fall joint computer conference* 33:395–410.

Evans, Richard. 2002. Varieties of learning. In *AI game programming wisdom*, ed. Steve Rabin, 567–578. Boston: Charles River Media, Inc.

Evans, Richard, and Thomas Barnet Lamb. 2002. Social activities: Implementing Wittgenstein. *Gamasutra.* <http://www.gamasutra.com/features/20020424/evans_01.htm>.

Falkner, David, Steven Gilmour, Casey Hudson, Drew Karpyshyn, James Ohlen, Preston Watamaniuk, and Derek Watts. 2003. *Star wars: Knights of the old republic.* Multiple platforms. BioWare, LucasArts.

Fetveit, Arild, and Gitte Stald. 2007. Online debate on digital aesthetics and communication. *Northern Lights* 5 (1): 141–158.

Fikes, Richard E. 1971. Monitored execution of robot plans produced by STRIPS. Technical Note 55, Stanford Research Institute Project 8973. Menlo Park, CA: Stanford Research Institute. Also in *Proceedings of IFIP congress '71, Ljubljana, Yugoslavia.*

Forbus, Kenneth D., and Will Wright. 2001. Some notes on programming objects in *The Sims.* Lecture notes, Northwestern University.

Forrester, Jay. 1989. The beginning of system dynamics. Banquet talk at the international meeting of the System

Dynamics Society, Stuttgart.

Frank, Adam, Ben Resner, Rob Fulop, and Ted Barnett. 1995. *Dogz: Your computer pet*. Windows 3.x. PF Magic, Virgin Interactive Entertainment.

Frank, Adam, Andrew Stern, Ben Resner, Jeremy Cantor, and Jonathan Shambroom. 1996. *Catz: Your computer petz*. Windows and Windows 3.x. PF Magic, Virgin Interactive Entertainment.

Frasca, Gonzalo. 2001. *The Sims*: Grandmothers are cooler than trolls. *Game Studies* 1 (1).

———. 2003. Simulation versus narrative: Introduction to ludology. In *The video game theory reader*, ed. Mark J. P. Wolf and Bernard Perron. London: Routledge.

Frasca, Gonzalo, Sofía Battegazzore, Nicolás Olhaberry, Pepe Infantozzi, Fabián Rodriguez, and Federico Balbi. 2003. *September 12th: A toy world*. Newsgaming.com. <http://www.newsgaming.com/games/index12.htm>.

Fuller, Matthew, ed. 2008. *Software studies: A lexicon*. Cambridge, MA: MIT Press.

Galloway, Alexander R. 2006. *Gaming: Essays on algorithmic culture*. Minneapolis: University of Minnesota Press.

Galloway, Alexander R., and Eugene Thacker. 2007. *The exploit: A theory of networks*. Minneapolis: University of Minnesota Press.

Gardner, Howard. 1985. *The mind's new science: A history of the cognitive revolution*. New York: Basic Books, Inc.

Gee, James Paul. 2004. *What video games have to teach us about learning and literacy*. Basingstoke, UK: Palgrave Macmillan.

Gillespie, William, Scott Rettberg, Dirk Stratton, and Frank Marquardt. 1999. *The unknown*. <http://www.unknownhypertext.com>.

Goguen, Joseph, and D. Fox Harrell. Forthcoming. Style, computation, and conceptual blending. In *The structure of style: Algorithmic approaches to understanding manner and meaning*, ed. Shlomo Argamon and Shlomo Dubnov. Berlin: Springer-Verlag.

Goldman, Neil M. 1975. Conceptual generation. In *Conceptual information processing*, ed. Roger C. Schank, 289–371. New York: Elsevier Science Inc.

Goldwater, Barry M. 2007. *The conscience of a conservative*. Princeton, NJ: James Madison Library in American Politics, Princeton University Press. (Orig. pub. 1960.)

Google. n.d. Our search: Google technology. <http://www.google.com/technology/>.

Greenberg, David. 2000. Adlai Stevenson: The last of the beautiful losers. <http://www.slate.com/id/85306/>.

Gygax, Gary, and Dave Arneson. 1974. *Dungeons & dragons*. Lake Geneva, Wisconsin: Tactical Studies Rules.

Harrell, D. Fox. 2007. Griot's tales of haints and seraphs: A computational narrative generation system. In *Second person: Role-playing and story in games and playable media*, ed. Pat Harrigan and Noah Wardrip-Fruin, 177–182. Cambridge, MA: MIT Press.

Harrington, Alan, Andrew Stern, Adam Frank, and Jonathan Shambroom. 1998. *Petz 3*. PF Magic, Mindscape.

Hart, Peter, Nils Nilsson, and Michael Wilber. 1972. *Shakey: An experiment in robot planning and learning*. Film. Menlo Park, CA: Stanford Research Institute.

Hayes-Roth, Barbara, and Frederick Hayes-Roth. 1979. A cognitive model of planning. *Cognitive Science* 3 (4): 275–310.

Hayles, N. Katherine. 2005. *My mother was a computer: Digital subjects and literary texts*. Chicago: University of Chicago Press.

———. 2008. *Electronic literature: New horizons for the literary*. Notre Dame, IN: University of Notre Dame Press.

Hodgins, Jessica K., Wayne L. Wooten, David C. Brogan, and James F. O'Brien. 1995. Animating human athletics. In *Siggraph '95: Proceedings of the 22nd annual conference on computer graphics and interactive techniques*, 71–78. New York: ACM Press.

Hovy, Eduard. 1987. Generating natural language under pragmatic constraints. *Journal of Pragmatics* 11 (6): 689–719.

Howard, Jeffrey. 2008. *Quests: Design, theory, and history in games and narratives*. Wellesley, MA: A K Peters, Ltd.

Hubbard, Craig, Chris Hewett, Jonathan Gramlich, Brad Pendleton, John Mulkey, C. Wes Saulsberry III, Jeff Orkin, Kevin Francis, Doug McDiarmid, and John O'Rorke. 2005. *F.E.A.R.: First encounter assault recon.* Windows. Monolith Productions, Vivendi Universal Games.

Hubbard, Craig, Chris Hewett, Jonathan Gramlich, Brad Pendleton, John Mulkey, C. Wes Saulsberry III, Jeff Orkin, Kevin Francis, Doug McDiarmid, John O'Rorke, and T. J. Wagner. 2006. *F.E.A.R.: First encounter assault recon.* Xbox 360. Monolith Productions, Day 1 Studios, Vivendi Universal Games.

Hubbard, Craig, Samantha Ryan, Brad Pendleton, Kevin Francis, Jeff Orkin, John Mulkey, and David Longo. 2002. *No one lives forever 2: A spy in H.A.R.M.'s way.* Windows and Macintosh. Monolith Productions, Fox Interactive, Sierra Entertainment.

Huber, William H. 2009. Epic spatialities: The production of space in *Final Fantasy* games. In *Third person: Authoring and exploring vast narratives*, ed. Pat Harrigan and Noah Wardrip-Fruin. Cambridge, MA: MIT Press.

Hudson, Casey, Preston Watamaniuk, Drew Karpyshyn, Derek Watts, David Falkner, Jonathan K. Cooper, Shane Welbourn, Mike Spalding, Michael Trottier, Adrien Cho, Shareef Shanawany, Ken Thain, Dusty Everman, Yanick Roy, and Darren Wong. 2007. *Mass effect.* Xbox 360. BioWare, Microsoft Game Studios.

Hunicke, Robin, Marc LeBlanc, and Robert Zubek. 2004. MDA: A formal approach to game design and game research. In *Proceedings of the challenges in game AI workshop, nineteenth national conference on artificial intelligence*.

Isla, Damian. 2005. Handling complexity in the Halo 2 AI. In *Proceedings of the 2005 Game Developers Conference.* New York: CMP Media.

Jackson, Steve. 1986. *GURPS basic set.* Austin: Steve Jackson Games.

John, Bonnie E., and Len Bass. 2002–2004. Avoiding "We can't change THAT!" Software architecture and usability. Tutorial, ACM Conference on Computer-Human Interaction.

Juul, Jesper. 2005. *Half-real: Video games between real rules and fictional worlds.* Cambridge, MA: MIT Press.

Kelso, Margaret Thomas, Peter Weyhrauch, and Joseph Bates. 1993. Dramatic presence. *Presence* 2 (1): 1–15.

Kirschenbaum, Matthew G. 2003. Virtuality and VRML: Software studies after Manovich. *Electronic Book Review.* <http://www.electronicbookreview.com/thread/technocapitalism/morememory>.

———. 2008. *Mechanisms: New media and the forensic imagination.* Cambridge, MA: MIT Press.

Klein, Sheldon, John D. Oakley, David I. Suurballe, and Robert A. Ziesemer. 1971. A program for generating reports on the status and history of stochastically modifiable semantic models of arbitrary universes. Technical report TR142, University of Wisconsin at Madison. <http://www.cs.wisc.edu/techreports/1971/TR142.pdf>.

Knuth, D. E. 1968. *The art of computer programming. Vol. 1 of fundamental algorithms.* Reading, MA: Addison-Wesley.

Koster, Raph. 2004. *Theory of fun for game design.* Phoenix: Paraglyph.

Krueger, Myron. 1977. Responsive Environments. In *AFIPS 46 National Computer Conference Proceedings,*

423–33. Montvale, N.J.: AFIPS Press

Landow, George P. 2005. *Hypertext 3.0: Critical theory and new media in an era of globalization.* Baltimore: Johns Hopkins University Press.

Langkilde, Irene, and Kevin Knight. 1998. The practical value of n-grams in generation. In *Proceedings of the ninth international workshop on natural language generation,* ed. Eduard Hovy, 248–255. New Brunswick, NJ: Association for Computational Linguistics.

Laurel, Brenda. 1986. Toward the design of a computer-based interactive fantasy system. PhD diss., Ohio State University.

———. 1991. *Computers as theatre.* Reading, MA: Addison-Wesley Publishing.

Lebling, P. David, Marc S. Blank, and Timothy A. Anderson. 1979. Zork: A computerized fantasy simulation game. *Computer* 12 (4): 51–59.

Lebowitz, Michael. 1984. Creating characters in a story-telling universe. *Poetics* 13:171–194.

———. 1985. Story-telling as planning and learning. *Poetics* 14:483–502.

———. 1987. Planning stories. In *Proceedings of the ninth annual conference of the cognitive science society, Seattle, Wa,* 234–242.

Lee, Elan, Sean Stewart, Jim Stewartson, and Jane McGonigal. 2004. *I love bees.* Network media, live performance. 42 Entertainment, Microsoft.

Leonard, Andrew. 1997. *Bots: The origin of the new species.* Wired Books, Incorporated.

Linden, Greg, Brent Smith, and Jeremy York. 2003. Amazon.com recommendations: Item-to-item collaborative filtering. *IEEE Internet Computing* 7 (1): 76–80.

Loyall, Bryan. 1997. Believable agents: Building interactive personalities. PhD diss., Carnegie Mellon University.

———. 2004. Response to Janet Murray. In *First person: New media as story, performance, and game,* ed. Noah Wardrip-Fruin and Pat Harrigan, 2–9. Cambridge, MA: MIT Press.

Mailman. 2005. Review: Façade forum post. <http://www.idlethumbs.net/forums/showthread.php?p=43359 # post43359>.

Manovich, Lev. 2001. *The language of new media.* Cambridge, MA: Leonardo Books, MIT Press.

Marino, Mark C. 2006a. Critical code studies. *Electronic Book Review.* <http://www.electronicbookreview.com/thread/electropoetics/codology>.

———. 2006b. I, chatbot: The gender and race performativity of conversational agents. PhD diss., University of California at Riverside.

Mateas, Michael. 2002. Interactive drama, art, and artificial intelligence. PhD diss., Carnegie Mellon University.

———. 2004. A preliminary poetics for interactive drama and games. In *First person: New media as story, performance, and game,* ed. Noah Wardrip-Fruin and Pat Harrigan, 19–33. Cambridge, MA: MIT Press.

———. 2007. Re: backpack, terminal time. Email correspondence.

Mateas, Michael, and Nick Montfort. 2005. A box, darkly: Obfuscation, weird languages, and code aesthetics. In *Proceedings of digital arts and culture 2005.* Copenhagen.

Mateas, Michael, and Andrew Stern. 2005. *Façade.* Windows and Macintosh. Portland, OR: Procedural Arts.

———. 2007. Writing *Façade:* A case study in procedural authorship. In *Second person: Role-playing and story in games and playable media,* ed. Pat Harrigan and Noah Wardrip-Fruin, 183–207. Cambridge, MA: MIT Press.

Mateas, Michael, Paul Vanouse, and Steffi Domike. 2000. Generation of ideologically-biased historical documentaries. In *Proceedings of the seventeenth national conference on artificial intelligence and twelfth conference on innovative applications of artificial intelligence,* 236–242. Cambridge, MA: MIT Press.

References

McKee, Robert. 1997. *Story: Substance, structure, style, and the principles of screenwriting*. New York: HarperEntertainment.

Mechner, Jordan. 2007. *The sands of time:* Crafting a video game story. In *Second person: Role-playing and story in games and playable media*, ed. Pat Harrigan and Noah Wardrip-Fruin, 111–120. Cambridge, MA: MIT Press.

Mechner, Jordan, Yannis Mallat, Patrice Désilets, Claude Langlais, David Châteauneuf, and Raphaël Lacoste. 2003. *Prince of persia: The sands of time*. Multiple platforms. Ubisoft.

Meehan, James Richard. 1976. The metanovel: Writing stories by computer. PhD diss., Yale University.

———. 1980. *Tale-Spin* program listing. Fanfold printout, 112 pages. Listing identified with User TALE-SPIN [300,2005] Job TSPIN Seq. 4733 Date 13-Apr-80 21:50:13 Monitor U C Irvine SY45(4) DL033.

———. 1981. Tale-spin. In *Inside computer understanding: Five programs plus miniatures (artificial intelligence series)*, ed. Roger C. Schank and Christopher K. Riesbeck, 259–307. Hillsdale, NJ: Lawrence Erlbaum Associates.

———. 2006. The story of meehan's tale-spin. <http://grandtextauto.org/2006/09/13/the-story-of-meehans-tale-spin>/.

———. 2008. Re: Alive and well and living in Sunnyvale. Email correspondence.

Meehan, James Richard, and Warren Sack. 1992. Common Lisp version of *Micro Tale-Spin*. Internet-released source code.

Meier, Sid, and Bruce Shelley. 1991. *Sid Meier's civilization*. Hunt Valley, MD: MicroProse Software.

Mirapaul, Matthew. 1999. Fiction-writing software takes on humans. *New York Times*, November 11.

MIT Humanoid Robotics Group. 2003. Cog: Overview. <http://www.ai.mit.edu/projects/humanoid-robotics-group/cog/overview.html>.

Molyneux, Peter, Mark Webley, Jonty Barnes, Giles Jermy, Jean-Claude Cottier, Alex Evans, Richard Evans, Paul McLaughlin, Mark Healey, Eric Bailey, James Leach, and Russell Shaw. 2001. *Black & white*. Windows. Surrey, UK: Lionhead Studios, Electronic Arts.

Mona, Erik. 2007. From the basement to the basic set: The early years of *Dungeons & Dragons*. In *Second person: Role-playing and story in games and playable media*, ed. Pat Harrigan and Noah Wardrip-Fruin, 25–30. Cambridge, MA: MIT Press.

Montfort, Nick. 1999. *Winchester's nightmare: A novel machine*. Z-machine file and dedicated-laptop "hardback."

———. 2003. *Twisty little passages: An approach to interactive fiction*. Cambridge, MA: MIT Press.

———. 2007. Generating narrative variation in interactive fiction. PhD diss., University of Pennsylvania.

Montfort, Nick, and Scott Rettberg. 2004. *Implementation*. Sticker novel. <http://nickm.com/implementation/>.

Montfort, Nick, and Andrew Stern. 2008. Provocation by program: Imagining a next-revolution Eliza. Presentation at Visionary Landscapes: Electronic Literature Organization 2008 conference, Washington State University, Vancouver, May 31.Montfort, Nick, and Noah Wardrip-Fruin. 2004. *Acid-free bits: Recommendations for long-lasting electronic literature*. Electronic Literature Organization. <http://www.eliterature.org/pad/afb.html>.

Moulthrop, Stuart. 2003a. Interview with Noah Wardrip-Fruin. *The Iowa Review Web*. <http://www.uiowa.edu/~iareview/tirweb/feature/moulthrop>

———. 2003b. *Pax*. <http://iat.ubalt.edu/moulthrop/hypertexts/pax>.

Mueller, Erik T. 2006. *Commonsense reasoning*. San Francisco: Morgan Kaufmann Publishers Inc.

Murray, Janet H. 1997. *Hamlet on the holodeck: The future of narrative in cyberspace*. New York: Free Press.

———. 2004. From game-story to cyberdrama. In *First person: New media as story, performance, and game*, ed. Noah Wardrip-Fruin and Pat Harrigan, 2–11. Cambridge, MA: MIT Press.

Nelson, Theodor Holm. 1974. *Computer lib/dream machines.* Self-published.

——. 1987. *Computer lib/dream machines.* Microsoft Press.

Norman, Donald A. 1988. *The psychology of everyday things.* New York: Basic Books.

O'Harra, Josh, John Sabelhaus, and Michael Simpson. 2004. Overview of the congressional budget office long-term (CBOLT) policy simulation model. Tech. Rep. 2004-1, Congressional Budget Office, Washington, DC.

Orkin, Jeff. 2005. Agent architecture considerations for real-time planning in games. In *AIIDE*, ed. R. Michael Young and John E. Laird, 105–110. Menlo Park, CA: AAAI Press.

——. 2006. 3 states & a plan: The AI of F.E.A.R. In *Game developers conference proceedings.*

——. 2007. Learning plan networks in conversational video games. Master's thesis, Massachusetts Institute of Technology.

Orkin, Jeff, and Deb Roy. 2007. The restaurant game: Learning social behavior and language from thousands of players online. *Journal of Game Development* 3 (1): 39–60.

Osman, Jena. 2007. Playing the world: Poetry and the newsreader. Talk at "Documentary Poetics" panel, *Modern Language Association annual convention, Chicago.*

Oster, Trent, Marc Holmes, Scott Greig, Don Moar, Mark Brockington, Brent Knowles, James Ohlen, Rob Bartel, and Tobyn Manthorpe. 2002. *Neverwinter nights.* Multiple platforms. BioWare, Infogrames.

Pavel, Thomas G. 1986. *Fictional worlds.* Cambridge, MA: Harvard University Press.

PC Gamer Staff. 2002. *No one lives forever 2* interview. *PC Gamer.*

Pearce, Celia. 2002. Sims, battlebots, cellular automata, God, and go: A conversation with Will Wright. *Game Studies* 2 (1). <http://www.gamestudies.org/0102/pearce/>.

——. 2004. Towards a game theory of game. In *First person: New media as story, performance, and game*, ed. Noah Wardrip-Fruin and Pat Harrigan, 141–151. Cambridge, MA: MIT Press.

Penny, Simon. 2004. Representation, enaction, and the ethics of simulation. In *First person: New media as story, performance, and game*, ed. Noah Wardrip-Fruin and Pat Harrigan, 71–82. Cambridge, MA: MIT Press.

Penny, Simon, Jeffrey Smith, Phoebe Sengers, Andre Bernhardt, and Jamieson Schulte. 2001. Traces: Embodied immersive interaction with semi-autonomous avatars. *Convergence: The journal of research into new media technologies* 7 (2).

Pérez y Pérez, Rafael, and Mike Sharples. 2004. Three computer-based models of storytelling: BRUTUS, MINSTREL and MEXICA. *Knowledge-Based Systems* 17 (1): 15–29.

Perlin, Ken. 1995. Real time responsive animation with personality. *IEEE Transactions on Visualization and Computer Graphics* 1 (1): 5–15.

——. 2004. Can there be a form between a game and a story? In *First person: New media as story, performance, and game*, ed. Noah Wardrip-Fruin and Pat Harrigan, 12–18. Cambridge, MA: MIT Press.

Perlin, Ken, and Athomas Goldberg. 1996. Improv: A system for scripting interactive actors in virtual worlds. In *Siggraph '96: Proceedings of the 23rd annual conference on computer graphics and interactive techniques*, 205–216. New York: ACM Press.

Petersen, Sandy. 1981. *Call of Cthulhu.* Hayward, CA: Chaosium.

Pontius, Andrew. 2000. *Rematch.* TADS file.

Propp, Vladimir A. 1968. *Morphology of the folktale.* Austin: University of Texas Press.

Purcell, Steve, Sean Clark, Collette Michaud, Michael Stemmle, Jonathan Ackley, and Livia Knight. 1993. *Sam & Max hit the road.* DOS. LucasArts Entertainment.

Raley, Rita. 2002. Interferences: [net.writing] and the practice of codework. *Electronic Book Review.*

<http://www.electronicbookreview.com/thread/electropoetics/net.writing>.

Rattermann, Mary Jo, Lee Spector, Jordan Grafman, Harvey Levin, and Harriet Harward. 2001. Partial and total-order planning: Evidence from normal and prefrontally damaged populations. *Cognitive Science* 25 (6): 941–975.

Reas, Casey, and Ben Fry. 2007. *Processing: A programming handbook for visual designers and artists.* Cambridge, MA: MIT Press.

Reiter, Ehud, and Robert Dale. 1997. Building applied natural language generation systems. *Natural Language Engineering* 3 (1): 57–87.

Rettberg, Jill Walker. 2003. Fiction and interaction: How clicking a mouse can make you part of a fictional world. DA diss., University of Bergen.

———. 2007. A network of quests in *World of Warcraft.* In *Second person: Role-playing and story in games and playable media*, ed. Pat Harrigan and Noah Wardrip-Fruin, 307–310. Cambridge, MA: MIT Press.

Rhody, Jason. 2005. Game fiction: Playing the interface in *Prince of Persia: The Sands of Time* and *Asheron's Call. Digital Games Research Association conference, Vancouver, Canada.*

———. 2008. Error, interface, and the myth of immersion: A riposte to Jordan Mechner. *Electronic Book Review.* <http://www.electronicbookreview.com/thread/firstperson/poprip>.

———. Forthcoming. Game fiction: Narrative in new media contexts. PhD diss., University of Maryland.

Riesbeck, Christopher K., and Roger C. Schank. 1989. Case-based reasoning: An introduction. In *Inside case-based reasoning*, ed. Christopher K. Riesbeck and Roger C. Schank. Hillsdale, NJ: Lawrence Erlbaum Associates.

Rolston, Ken. 2009. My story never ends. In *Third person: Authoring and exploring vast narratives.* Cambridge, MA: MIT Press.

Rolston, Ken, Todd Howard, Ashley Cheng, Guy Carver, Craig Walton, and Matthew Carofano. 2006. *The elder scrolls IV: Oblivion.* Multiple platforms. Bethesda Game Studios, 2K Games, Bethesda Softworks.

Rousseau, Daniel, and Barbara Hayes-Roth. 1998. A social-psychological model for synthetic actors. In *Agents '98: Proceedings of the second international conference on autonomous agents*, 165–172. New York: ACM.

Russell, Stephen, Peter Samson, Dan Edwards, Martin Graetz, Alan Kotok, Steve Piner, and Robert A Saunders. 1962. *Spacewar!* PDP-1, CRT display, custom controllers.

Ryan, Marie-Laure. 1992. *Possible worlds, artificial intelligence, and narrative theory.* Bloomington: Indiana University Press.

———. 2005. Narrative and the split condition of digital textuality. *Dichtung Digital* (1). <http://www.dichtung-digital.com/2005/1/Ryan>.

———. 2006. *Avatars of story.* Minneapolis: University of Minnesota Press.

Sack, Warren. 1997–2000. *Conversation map.* Newsgroup browser.

———. 2004. *Agonistics: A language game.* Web presentation of online conversation analysis.

———. 2005. Agonistics: A language game. In *Making Things Public: Atmospheres of Democracy,* ed. Bruno Latour and Peter Weibel, 966-969. Cambridge, MA: MIT Press.

Saini, Angela. 2008. Solving the Web's image problem. *BBC News.* <http://news.bbc.co.uk/1/hi/technology/7395751.stm>.

Schank, Roger C. 1975a. Conceptual dependency theory. In *Conceptual information processing*, ed. Roger C. Schank, 22–82. New York: Elsevier Science Inc.

———. 1975b. Using knowledge to understand. In *TINLAP '75: Proceedings of the 1975 workshop on theoretical issues in natural language processing*, 117–121. Morristown, NJ: Association for Computational Linguistics.

———. 2006. Comment on Lebowitz's *Universe,* part 2. <http://grandtextauto.org/2006/03/06/lebowitzs-universe-part-2/ # comment-82580>.

Schank, Roger C., and Christopher K. Riesbeck. 1981. The theory behind the programs: A theory of context. In *Inside computer understanding: Five programs plus miniatures*, ed. Roger C. Schank and Christopher K. Riesbeck, 27–40. Hillsdale, NJ: Lawrence Erlbaum Associates.

Schneier, Bruce. 2006. Why data mining won't stop terror. *Wired News.* <http://www.wired.com/politics/security/commentary/securitymatters/2006/03/70357>.

Scott, Jason. 2005. *BBS: The documentary*. Eight episodes on DVD. Bovine Ignition Systems.

Sengers, Phoebe. 1998. Antiboxology: Agent design in cultural context. PhD diss., Carnegie Mellon University.

Shannon, Claude E. 1948. A mathematical theory of communication. *Bell System Technical Journal* 27:379–423, 623–656.

Sheldon, Lee. 2004. *Character development and storytelling for games*. Boston: Thomson Course Technology PTR.

Simons, Barbara, and Eugene H. Spafford. 2003. Letter to chairman Warner and senator Levin, Senate Committee on Armed Services. <http://usacm.acm.org/usacm/Letters/tia_final.html>.

Slade, Stephen. 1987. The Yale artificial intelligence project: A brief history. *AI Magazine* 8 (4): 67–76.

Sommers, Carl. 1999. By the way; Inspiration or computation? *New York Times*, November 28.

Starr, P. 1994. Seductions of sim, policy as a simulation game. *American Prospect* 5 (17). <http://www.prospect.org/print-friendly/print/V5/17/starr-p.html>.

Steele, Guy L., Jr., and Richard P. Gabriel. 1993. The evolution of Lisp. *ACM SIGPLAN Notices* 28 (3): 231–270.

Stefans, Brian Kim. 2003. From byte to inscription: An interview with John Cayley. *Iowa Review Web.* <http://www.uiowa.edu/ iareview/tirweb/feature/cayley/>.

Stern, Andrew. 2005. A few *Façade* post-release comments. <http://grandtextauto.org/2005/08/09/a-few-facade-post-release-comments/>.

———. 2008. Transparency, or not? It remains unclear. <http://grandtextauto.org/2008/03/14/transparency-or-not-it-remains-unclear/>.

Stern, Andrew, Adam Frank, and Ben Resner. 1999. *Babyz*. Windows.

Stern, Andrew, and Michael Mateas. 2007. Façade, petz, and the expressivator. <http://grandtextauto.org/2007/12/16/facade-petz-and-the-expressivator>.

Suchman, Lucy A. 1987. *Plans and situated actions: The problem of human-machine communication*. Cambridge: Cambridge University Press.

Sudnow, David. 1983. *Pilgrim in the microworld*. Clayton, Victoria, BC: Warner Books.

Superbunker, Machine Poetics Research Unit. 2004. page_space at machine. Online catalog, exhibition curated by Braxton Soderman and Jason Brown. <http://www.superbunker.com/machinepoetics/page_space/show_machine.html>.

Tambe, M. 1997. Towards flexible teamwork. *Journal of Artificial Intelligence Research* 7:83–124.

Thompson, Rodney, Sterling Hershey, John Jackson Miller, and Abel G. Pena. 2008. *Knights of the old republic campaign guide*. Renton, CA: Wizards of the Coast.

Tosca, Susana. 2003. The quest problem in computer games. In *Proceedings TIDSE 2003, Darmstadt, Germany*, 69–82. Stuttgart: Fraunhofer IRB Verlag.

Turing, Alan M. 1950. Computing machinery and intelligence. *Mind: A Quarterly Review of Psychology and*

Philosophy 59 (236): 433–460.

——. 2004. *The essential Turing: Seminal writings in computing, logic, philosophy, artificial intelligence, and artificial life plus the secrets of enigma*. New York: Oxford University Press.

Turkle, Sherry. 1984. *The second self: computers and the human spirit*. New York: Simon and Schuster.

——. 1995. *Life on the screen: Identity in the age of the Internet*. New York: Simon and Schuster Trade.

Turner, Scott R. 1994. *The creative process: A computer model of storytelling and creativity*. Hillsdale, NJ: Lawrence Erlbaum Associates.

——. 2007. Scott Turner on Minstrel. <http://grandtextauto.org/2007/10/30/scott-turner-on-minstrel/>.

Turner, Scott R., and Michael G. Dyer. 1985. Thematic knowledge, episodic memory, and analogy in MINSTREL, a story invention system. In *Proceedings of seventh annual conference of the cognitive science society*. Hillsdale, NJ: Lawrence Erlbaum Associates.

Tweet, Jonathan. 1992. *Over the edge*. Saint Paul: Atlas Games.

Utterback, Camille, and Romy Achituv. 1999. *Text rain*. Interactive installation.

von Ahn, Luis, Laura Dabbish, Jared Silver, Ian Graham, and David Kitchin. 2005. *The ESP game*. Carnegie Mellon University. <http://www.espgame.org/>.

Walton, Kendall L. 1993. *Mimesis as make-believe: On the foundations of representational arts*. Cambridge, MA: Harvard University Press.

Wardrip-Fruin, Noah. 2003. From instrumental texts to textual instruments. In *Proceedings of digital arts and culture 2003*. Melbourne, Australia.

——. 2005. Playable media and textual instruments. *Dichtung Digital*. <http://www.dichtung-digital.com/2005/1/Wardrip-Fruin>.

——. 2008. *EP* meta: Chapter four. <http://grandtextauto.org/2008/02/16/ep-meta-chapter-four/>.

Wardrip-Fruin, Noah, Adam Chapman, Brion Moss, and Duane Whitehurst. 1998–2002. *The impermanence agent*. <http://www.impermanenceagent.com/>.

Wardrip-Fruin, Noah, Michael Crumpton, Chris Spain, and Kirstin Allio. 1995–1997. *Gray matters*. Pad++ Zooming Interface.

Wardrip-Fruin, Noah, David Durand, Brion Moss, and Elaine Froehlich. 2004. Regime Change. Turbulence.org. 7 September. <http://turbulence.org/Works/twotxt/rc-index.htm>.

—— News Reader. 2004. Turbulence.org. 4 October. <http://turbulence.org/Works/twotxt/nr-index.htm>

Wardrip-Fruin, Noah, Andrew McClain, Shawn Greenlee, Robert Coover, and Joshua J. Carroll. 2004. *Screen* video documentation. *Aspect: The Chronicle of New Media Art* 4. Video by Michelle Higa.

——. 2003–present. *Screen*. Virtual reality, motion tracking, audio environment.

Wardrip-Fruin, Noah, and Nick Montfort, eds. 2003. *The new media reader*. Cambridge, MA: MIT Press.

Wardrip-Fruin, Noah, Camille Utterback, Clilly Castiglia, and Nathan Wardrip-Fruin. 2002. *Talking cure*. Installation.

Wark, McKenzie. 2007. *Gamer theory*. Cambridge, MA: Harvard University Press.

Weizenbaum, Joseph. 1966. Eliza: A computer program for the study of natural language communication between man and machine. *Communications of the ACM* 9 (1): 36–45.

——. 1974. Automating psychotherapy. ACM Forum, *Communications of the ACM* 17 (7): 543.

——. 1976. *Computer power and human reason: From judgment to calculation*. New York: W. H. Freeman.

Williams, Mark. 2006. The total information awareness project lives on. *Technology Review*. <http://www.technologyreview.com/read_article.aspx?id=16741>.

Wilson, Robert A., and Frank C. Keil, eds. 1999. *The MIT encyclopedia of the cognitive sciences*. Cambridge, MA: MIT Press.

Wingfield, Nick. 2006. Master of the universe. *Wall Street Journal*, May 27, A1.

Wittig, Rob. 2001. *Blue company*. Tank 20. <http://www.robwit.net/bluecompany2002/>.

Wizards of the Coast. 2005. The living greyhawk campaign, part of the RPGA network. <http://www.wizards.com/default.asp?x=lg/welcome>.

Wright, Will. 1984. *Raid on bungeling bay*. Multiple platforms. Brøoderbund Software.

———. 1989. *SimCity*. Multiple platforms. Maxis Software, Brøoderbund Software.

———. 2004. Will Wright chat transcript. <http://simcity.ea.com/community/events/will_wright_01_08_04.php>.

Wright, Will, Kana Ryan, Charles London, Jamie Doornbos, and Eric Bowman. 2000. *The sims*. Multiple platforms. Emeryville, CA: Maxis Software, Electronic Arts.

Wright, Will, Lucy Bradshaw, Alex Hutchinson, Brodie Andersen, Andrew Willmott, Michael A. Khoury, Dan Moskowitz, Chris Hecker, and Caryl D. Shaw. 2008. *Spore*. Multiple platforms. Maxis Software, Electronic Arts.

Yob, Gregory. 1973. *Hunt the wumpus*. Basic program.

Index